The High Performance Fortran Handbook

Scientific and Engineering Computation
Janusz Kowalik, Editor

Data-Parallel Programming on MIMD Computers
by Philip J. Hatcher and Michael J. Quinn, 1991

Unstructured Scientific Computation on Scalable Multiprocessors
edited by Piyush Mehrotra, Joel Saltz, and Robert Voigt, 1991

Parallel Computational Fluid Dynamics: Implementations and Results
edited by Horst D. Simon, 1992

Enterprise Integration Modeling: Proceedings of the First International Conference
edited by Charles J. Petrie, Jr., 1992

The High Performance Fortran Handbook
by Charles H. Koelbel, David B. Loveman, Robert S. Schreiber, Guy L. Steele Jr. and Mary E. Zosel, 1994

The High Performance Fortran Handbook

Charles H. Koelbel
David B. Loveman
Robert S. Schreiber
Guy L. Steele Jr.
Mary E. Zosel

The MIT Press
Cambridge, Massachusetts
London, England

Second printing, 1997

© 1994 Massachusetts Institute of Technology

All rights reserved. No part of this book may be reproduced in any form by any electronic or mechanical means (including photocopying, recording, or information storage and retrieval) without permission in writing from the publisher.

This book was set in LaTeX by the authors and was printed and bound in the United States of America.

Library of Congress Cataloging-in-Publication Data

The High performance Fortran handbook / Charles H. Koelbel . . . [et al.].
    p.   cm. — (Scientific and engineering computation)
  Includes bibliographical references and index.
  ISBN 0-262-11185-3. — ISBN 0-262-61094-9 (pbk.)
  1. FORTRAN (Computer program language) I. Koelbel, Charles H. II. Series.
QA76.73.F25H53   1994
005.13'3—dc20   93-6204
                                                          CIP

Contents

	Series Foreword	xi
	Acknowledgments	xiii
0	**Sneak Preview**	1
0.1	Basics of High Performance Fortran	1
0.2	Programming Model	1
0.3	Fortran 90	2
0.4	Data Mapping	2
0.5	Data Mapping for Procedure Arguments	4
0.6	Data Parallelism	4
0.7	Intrinsics and Library Procedures	5
0.8	Extrinsic Procedures	6
0.9	Subset High Performance Fortran	7
0.10	Appendices	7
1	**Basics of High Performance Fortran**	9
1.1	Fortran Development	9
1.2	Goals of HPF	12
1.3	Fortran 90 Binding	14
1.4	Notation	15
1.5	Conformance	16
1.6	HPF Directives and Their Syntax	17
1.7	For Further Reading	21
2	**Programming Model**	23
2.1	Parallel Machines	23
2.2	Parallel Computation	26
	2.2.1 Data Parallel Operations	27
	2.2.2 Extrinsic Procedures	29
2.3	Communication	30
2.4	Putting It All Together	38

3	**Fortran 90**		**51**
3.1	Fortran 90 Features		51
3.2	Ease-of-Use Improvements		52
	3.2.1	Ease of Writing	52
	3.2.2	Ease of Program Control	52
	3.2.3	Enhanced Input and Output	53
3.3	Data Facilities		54
	3.3.1	Intrinsic Data Types	54
	3.3.2	Structured Data Types	54
	3.3.3	Entity-Oriented Declarations and Allocatable Arrays	55
3.4	Array Features		56
	3.4.1	Array Overview	56
	3.4.2	Array Concepts and Terminology	57
	3.4.3	Whole Array Operations and Assignment	58
	3.4.4	Array Subsections	58
	3.4.5	Expressions	59
	3.4.6	Vector-Valued Subscripts	61
	3.4.7	Array Constructors	61
	3.4.8	Masked Array Assignments	62
	3.4.9	Array-Valued Functions with Array-Valued Arguments	63
	3.4.10	Array Objects and Their Specifications	64
3.5	User-Defined Data Types		65
3.6	Pointers		67
3.7	Modularization		70
	3.7.1	The Structure of a Fortran Program	70
	3.7.2	Procedures	71
	3.7.3	Modules and Abstraction	73
3.8	Intrinsic Procedures		75
3.9	Language Evolution		76
	3.9.1	Avoiding Assumptions of Linear Memory	83
3.10	Fortran Coding Style		85
	3.10.1	Upper-Case and Lower-Case Conventions	85

		3.10.2	Spacing Conventions	87
		3.10.3	Indentation, Alignment and Blank Line Conventions	87
		3.10.4	Free Source Form	88

4 Data Mapping — 91

4.1	Overview of Data Mapping	91
4.2	The Data Mapping Model	98
4.3	Syntax of Data Alignment and Distribution Directives	102
4.4	DISTRIBUTE and REDISTRIBUTE Directives	103
4.5	ALIGN and REALIGN Directives	112
4.6	DYNAMIC Directive	120
4.7	Allocatable Arrays and Pointers	121
4.8	PROCESSORS Directive	124
4.9	TEMPLATE Directive	127
4.10	Fortran Storage Association and HPF	129
	4.10.1 Informal Introduction to Storage Association	129
	4.10.2 Storage Association in More Detail	131

5 Data Mapping for Procedure Arguments — 139

5.1	Data Mapping for Dummy Variables	139
5.2	DISTRIBUTE Directives and Dummy Arguments	147
5.3	ALIGN Directives and Dummy Arguments	148
5.4	INHERIT Directive	149
5.5	Rules for Explicit Interfaces	150
5.6	Descriptive DISTRIBUTE Directives	151
5.7	Examples of DISTRIBUTE Directives for Dummy Arguments	157
5.8	Explicit Dynamic Remapping of Dummy Arguments	160
5.9	Argument Passing and Sequence Association	161
	5.9.1 Argument Requirements	162
	5.9.2 Sequence Association Examples	163
	5.9.3 Formal Sequence Association Rules	166

6	**Data Parallelism**		167
6.1	Overview of Data Parallelism		167
6.2	The FORALL Statement		170
	6.2.1	Form of the FORALL Statement	170
	6.2.2	Meaning of the FORALL Statement	172
	6.2.3	Discussion of the FORALL Statement	175
6.3	The PURE Attribute		184
	6.3.1	Form of the PURE Attribute	185
	6.3.2	Meaning of the PURE Attribute	188
	6.3.3	Discussion of the PURE Attribute	188
6.4	The INDEPENDENT Directive		192
	6.4.1	Form of the INDEPENDENT Directive	192
	6.4.2	Meaning of the INDEPENDENT Directive	192
	6.4.3	Discussion of the INDEPENDENT Directive	195
7	**Intrinsic and Library Procedures**		203
7.1	System Inquiry Functions		203
7.2	Mapping Inquiry Subroutines		204
7.3	Computational Functions		206
	7.3.1	Array Location Functions	206
	7.3.2	Bit Manipulation Functions	206
	7.3.3	Array Reduction Functions	207
	7.3.4	Array Combining Scatter Functions	208
	7.3.5	Array Prefix and Suffix Functions	210
	7.3.6	Array Sorting Functions	215
7.4	Alphabetical List of Intrinsic and Library Procedures		218
8	**Extrinsic Procedures**		223
8.1	Definition and Invocation of Extrinsic Procedures		226
	8.1.1	EXTRINSIC Prefix Syntax	227
	8.1.2	Requirements on the Called Extrinsic Procedure	229
8.2	Coding Local Procedures		230

8.3		Conventions for Local Subprograms	231
	8.3.1	Conventions for Calling Local Subprograms	232
	8.3.2	Calling Sequence	232
	8.3.3	Information Available to the Local Procedure	233
8.4		Local Routines Written in HPF	234
	8.4.1	Restrictions	234
	8.4.2	Argument Association	235
	8.4.3	HPF Local Routine Library	238
8.5		Local Routines Written in Fortran 90	241
	8.5.1	Argument Association	242
8.6		Example HPF Extrinsic Procedures	242
9		**Subset High Performance Fortran**	**245**
9.1		HPF Extensions and Subset High Performance Fortran	245
	9.1.1	HPF Features in the Subset	245
	9.1.2	HPF Features Not in the Subset	245
9.2		Fortran 90 and Subset High Performance Fortran	246
	9.2.1	Fortran 90 Features in the Subset	246
	9.2.2	Fortran 90 Features Not in the Subset	248
A		**Definition of Terms**	**249**
B		**Description of HPF Library and Intrinsic Procedures**	**255**
C		**Formal Syntax Rules**	**305**
D		**Formal Syntax Cross-reference**	**317**
		Bibliography	323
		Index	325

Series Foreword

The world of modern computing potentially offers many helpful methods and tools to scientists and engineers, but the fast pace of change in computer hardware, software, and algorithms often makes practical use of the newest computing technology difficult. The Scientific and Engineering Computation series focuses on rapid advances in computing technologies and attempts to facilitate transferring these technologies to applications in science and engineering. It will include books on theories, methods, and original applications in such areas as parallelism, large-scale simulations, time-critical computing, computer-aided design and engineering, use of computers in manufacturing, visualization of scientific data, and human-machine interface technology.

The series will help scientists and engineers to understand the current world of advanced computation and to anticipate future developments that will impact their computing environments and open up new capabilities and modes of computation.

This book in the series describes High Performance Fortran (HPF), a language that combines the full Fortran 90 language with special user annotations dealing with data distribution. It is expected that HPF will be a standard programming language for computationally intensive applications on many types of machines, such as traditional vector processors and newer massively parallel MIMD and SIMD multiprocessors. If successful, the HPF language with its modern features and powerful capabilities will become the new revitalized version of Fortran for scientists and engineers solving complex large-scale problems.

Janusz S. Kowalik

Acknowledgments

Our thanks first go to the High Performance Fortran Forum (HPFF), the developers of HPF, without whom our book really would not exist. More than 60 people attended one or more of the HPFF working group meetings and well over 500 participated through the mailing lists. As much as we would like to, it is impossible to thank all of them individually. We do want to mention some of the most visible contributors, however.

Many people served in positions of responsibility in the HPFF meetings. HPFF would not have been possible if Ken Kennedy and Geoffrey Fox had not volunteered to convene the first meeting. Ken Kennedy chaired all the working group meetings with remarkable patience, diplomacy, and vision; he also encouraged us in writing this book. The authors of this book served as heads of subgroups where technical discussions took place, and as the overall language specification document editors. Other subgroups were led by Marina Chen, Bob Knighten, Marc Snir, and Joel Williamson.

A number of other people contributed sections to either the HPF Language Specification or the HPF Journal of Development, including Alok Choudhary, Tom Haupt, Maureen Hoffert, Piyush Mehrotra, John Merlin, Tin-Fook Ngai, Rex Page, Sanjay Ranka, Richard Shapiro, Matt Snyder, Richard Swift, and Min-You Wu. Other regular attendees at the meetings, all of whom contributed ideas if not actual wording, included Alan Adamson, Robert Babb II, Ralph Brickner, Barbara Chapman, James Cownie, Andy Meltzer, Jean-Laurent Philippe, David Presberg, J. Ramanujam, P. Sadayappan, Randy Scarborough, Vince Schuster, Henk Sips, and Hans Zima. Clemens-August Thole also attended every meeting and furthermore organized a complementary group in Europe that was instrumental in making HPFF an international effort. Comments from Michael Metcalf, J. L. Schoenfelder, the ANSI X3J3 committee, and groups at Cray Research and MasPar Computer were influential in completing the language specification. To all these people, and to the employers who supported their involvement in HPFF, go our sincere thanks.

The following organizations made the language draft available by anonymous FTP access and/or mail servers: AT&T Bell Laboratories, Cornell Theory Center, GMD-I1.T (Sankt Augustin), Oak Ridge National Laboratory, Rice University, Syracuse University, and Thinking Machines Corporation. These outlets were instrumental in distributing the HPF documents.

Finances for the HPFF meetings came from several sources. In the United States, the National Science Foundation and the Defense Advanced Research Projects Agency (now the Advanced Research Projects Agency) supported HPFF itself and many of the academic participants. In Europe, ESPRIT supplied travel money for several participants. Finally, Rice University kept HPFF running financially while the organizers searched for steady funding.

The HPF Language Specification is copyrighted by Rice University and appeared as a special issue of *Scientific Programming*, published by John Wiley & Sons. Both organizations have dedicated the language definition to the public domain. We thank them for making it available and for permission to use portions of it in this book.

The authors specifically want to thank their employers: Rice University, Digital Equipment Corporation, the Research Institute for Advanced Computer Science, Thinking Machines Corporation, and Lawrence Livermore National Laboratory, for the time and resources to participate in the HPF process and produce this book. Dr. Koelbel's efforts were also supported by research grants from the Advanced Research Projects Agency and from the State of Texas.

Thanks to Jill Diewald of Digital Equipment Corporation for her contributions to Section 3.4.8.

The High Performance Fortran Handbook

0 Sneak Preview

Welcome to the *High Performance Fortran Handbook*! This book describes High Performance Fortran (HPF), a set of extensions to Fortran expressing parallel execution at a relatively high level. The "official" definition of these extensions is the *High Performance Fortran Language Specification, version 1.0* [14]; this book is an adjunct to that work, presenting the same information in a more tutorial manner. To make a long story short, HPF was designed to provide a portable extension to Fortran 90 for writing data parallel applications. It includes features for mapping data to parallel processors, specifying data parallel operations, and methods for interfacing HPF programs to othe programming paradigms.

This chapter is a road map to *The High Performance Fortran Handbook*. It gives a quick introduction to each of the other chapters, and a few simple examples of what you will find there. In short, it serves the same purposes as Chapter 0 of the *Fortran 90 Handbook* [1] (which is, of course, where we got this idea). All the material here is meant to be illustrative, rather than definitive. The chapters are relatively independent of each other, and may be read in any order.

0.1 Basics of High Performance Fortran

Chapter 1 contains some basic facts about HPF, including a short history of Fortran, the goals of HPF, notation conventions used in this book, and references for related material.

0.2 Programming Model

Chapter 2 describes HPF's programming model. A programming language is not much good if you don't know what a program in the language means; Chapter 2 gives a framework for understanding HPF programs. Our model is divided into two parts: parallelism and communication.

The parallelism in a program, expressed by constructs like array assignment, **FORALL** statements, **DO INDEPENDENT** loops, intrinsic and standard library procedures, and **EXTRINSIC** procedures, determines how many operations a computer could possibly do at one time. Many of today's fastest machines are capable of performing tens, hundreds, or even thousands of operations simultaneously (or *in parallel*). HPF's parallel constructs make it easy for the programmer to indicate potentially parallel operations. It is then the compiler's responsibility to schedule those operations on the physical machine so that the program runs as fast as possible.

Communication in a program is an overhead that opposes parallelism. Another feature of today's parallel machines is that sharing data (through memory, or by explicit messages) is slower than pure computation. Moreover, languages prior to HPF forced the programmer to handle nearly all the details of communication, leading to complex code, bugs, and general frustration. HPF puts more of this burden on the compiler; the user supplies a very high-level data mapping strategy and the system generates the details of the communication it implies.

Unfortunately, the parallelism and communication of an HPF program are often intertwined in complex ways. The final portion of Chapter 2 is devoted to illustrating some of these relationships.

0.3 Fortran 90

Chapter 3 describes Fortran 90. HPF is based on Fortran 90, which is the latest in a long line of Fortran standards. In a perfect world, we would not need to describe Fortran 90 separately, since all practicing Fortran programmers would already be familiar with it. However, a number of factors (both technical and sociological) have slowed Fortran 90's entrance into the world of scientific computing. In light of this, we thought it would be a good idea to give a short introduction to Fortran 90, with emphasis on its new features (as compared with the older FORTRAN 77 standard). We cannot give a full account of Fortran 90 in a book of this size—the already-mentioned *Fortran 90 Handbook* is over 700 pages long. Instead, we provide just enough background for Fortran 90 by means of suggestive examples so the reader can see how it relates to HPF. We hope that our explanation also whets your appetite to find out more about Fortran 90.

0.4 Data Mapping

Chapter 4 describes the data mapping features in HPF. These are probably the most publicized features in HPF, although they are certainly not the only important ones. In short, HPF can describe how data is to be divided up among the processors in a parallel machine. The presumption is that the processor responsible for some data (also called the processor that owns the data) can read or write it much faster than another processor. This reflects the way that many current parallel machines operate. HPF describes the data-to-processor mapping in two stages: the **DISTRIBUTE** and **ALIGN** operations.

DISTRIBUTE is an HPF directive that describes how an array is divided into even-sized pieces and distributed to processors in a regular way. For example, given the array declaration

```
REAL A(100,100)
```

and four processors, the **DISTRIBUTE** directive can express any of the following patterns:

- Each processor receives a 50 × 50 block of **A** (i.e., one processor gets `A(1:50,1:50)`, another gets `A(51:100,1:50)`, etc.). The directive to say this is

  `!HPF$ DISTRIBUTE A(BLOCK,BLOCK)`

- Each processor receives every 4th row of **A** (i.e., one processor gets `A(1,1:100)`, `A(5,1:100)`, `A(9,1:100)`, etc.; another gets `A(4,1:100)`, `A(8,1:100)`, `A(12,1:100)`, etc.). The directive to say this is

  `!HPF$ DISTRIBUTE A(CYCLIC,*)`

There are many other patterns that can be generated with **DISTRIBUTE** alone.

ALIGN is an HPF directive that describes how two arrays "line up" together. Basically, this describes one array's mapping in terms of another. For example, the **ALIGN** directive can express any of the following relations:

- Two arrays **X** and **Y** are always distributed the same. The directive to say this is

  `!HPF$ ALIGN X(I) WITH Y(I)`

- Elements of **X** correspond to the odd elements of **Y** (in this case, **X** can have at most half as many elements as **Y**). The directive to say this is

  `!HPF$ ALIGN X(I) WITH Y(2*I-1)`

- Each element of **X** is aligned with the entire corresponding column of **A** (in this case, elements of **X** may be replicated). The directive to say this is

  `!HPF$ ALIGN X(I) WITH A(*,I)`

As with **DISTRIBUTE**, this list is not exhaustive. Some of these patterns could be achieved using the **DISTRIBUTE** directive only; some require **ALIGN**.

There are also several other data mapping features. **REDISTRIBUTE** and **REALIGN** perform the same tasks as **DISTRIBUTE** and **ALIGN**, but work dynamically (as executable statements) rather than statically (as declarations). The **TEMPLATE** directive declares a phantom array that can be used in **DISTRIBUTE** and **ALIGN** directives; this is useful when no array is quite the right size to describe some mapping. Similarly, **PROCESSORS** defines a set of abstract processors that is useful for precisely defining some mappings. The rules relating this mapping to ordinary Fortran storage association (**COMMON** block reshaping and **EQUIVALENCE**) are also in this chapter. Although full support of storage association is not compatible with the data mapping features of HPF, some important special cases are allowed.

0.5 Data Mapping for Procedure Arguments

Chapter 5 expands Chapter 4 to cover dummy procedure arguments. Procedure arguments are different from local variables because they sometimes need information about the corresponding actual argument. In particular, all of the following are reasonable things to say about a dummy argument:

- "I don't care how the actual is mapped—move the data to this distribution before starting this subroutine." Directives to do this look the same as directives for local variables, as shown above.
- "I don't care how the actual is mapped—keep the data there for the duration of this subroutine." One way to say this is

    `!HPF$ INHERIT X`

- "I know the actual has a certain distribution before coming into this subroutine—don't move it." One way to say this (when the actual's distribution is `BLOCK`) is

    `!HPF$ DISTRIBUTE X *(BLOCK)`

More complex cases are also possible, such as relating two actual arguments to each other.

Equally important for converting older codes to HPF is handling Fortran's sequence association. (This is the old method of passing arrays, in which the shape of the actual and the dummy argument do not have to match.) Full support for this feature is not compatible with HPF's data mapping directives; instead, special directives must be inserted to warn the compiler that trickiness is going on.

0.6 Data Parallelism

Chapter 6 describes HPF's constructs for data parallelism. These constructs describe operations (typically, large numbers of operations) that can be performed in parallel if the computer has the resources. The presumption is that doing many operations at once will be faster than doing the same operations one at a time. Even when there are many more parallel operations than there are processors on the target machine, HPF allows the extra parallelism to be specified. This way, when the program is ported to a more parallel machine it can immediately take advantage of the extra speed available. Chapter 6 discusses two data parallel constructs: the `FORALL` statement and the `INDEPENDENT` directive.

The `FORALL` is a new statement that extends Fortran 90 array operations. For example,

```
FORALL (I = 2:N-1)
   A(I,I) = A(I-1,I-1) + A(I,I) + A(I+1,I+1)
END FORALL
```

does a vector addition along the main diagonal of array `A` (something you can't do directly with normal array assignments). HPF also introduces `PURE` functions, which are guaranteed to have no side effects, to allow `FORALL` statements to perform complex elementwise computations.

The `INDEPENDENT` directive gives the compiler more information about a `DO` loop or `FORALL` statement. For example, it tells the compiler that a `DO` loop does not make any "bad" data accesses that force the loop to be run sequentially. The first line of this code:

```
!HPF$ INDEPENDENT
      DO I = 1, N
         X(INDX(I)) = Y(I)
      END DO
```

amounts to an assertion that `INDX` does not contain any repeated values. With this information, a compiler knows it is safe to produce parallel code. Note that `INDEPENDENT` is a promise by the programmer that a program, as coded, already behaves a certain way; it is not correct to try to use `INDEPENDENT` to change the results of a program.

0.7 Intrinsics and Library Procedures

Chapter 7 describes HPF's intrinsic and library procedures (both functions and subroutines). All these procedures are available to any programmer writing in HPF. Many of them are data parallel operations, including some new reduction operations, prefix and suffix operations, combining-scatter operations, and sorting. For example, the following statement computes the powers of `S` in increasing order

```
X(1:N) = S
X(1:N) = PRODUCT_PREFIX(X(1:N))
```

Users have found these functions useful in writing data parallel programs. In addition, HPF has a number of inquiry subroutines to give a programmer information about the state of the machine or an array's distribution. For example,

```
        CALL HPF_DISTRIBUTION(A, AXIS_TYPE=DISTS)
```

uses the array **DISTS** to return information about the distribution of array **A**. HPF also has a few new standard functions that were somehow left out of Fortran 90 but which certain user communities need in their work. Most of these operate on the bits of an integer. For example,

```
        I = POPCNT(J)
```

counts the number of bits set to 1 in **J**. Chapter 7 gives a brief introduction to all the standard HPF functions.

0.8 Extrinsic Procedures

Chapter 8 describes **EXTRINSIC** procedures in HPF. **EXTRINSIC** is a means to invoke other programming paradigms from HPF. For example, parallel branch-and-bound searches are at best difficult to write in HPF, because their very purpose is to exploit indeterminacy and HPF strives for determinacy. Using **EXTRINSIC** allows a programmer to escape from HPF's constraints to write such a program. The normal HPF facilities are available outside of the **EXTRINSIC** procedure for data parallel tasks; for example, the initial setup or final analysis of the branch-and-bound search could be coded this way. Chapter 8 describes two aspects of such procedures: a general interface mechanism for invoking a variety of programming models, and a specific SPMD programming model that is efficient on many (but not all) current parallel machines.

The interface mechanism consists of the **EXTRINSIC** attribute, which is applied to functions in much the same way as the **RECURSIVE** attribute. For example,

```
        INTERFACE
          EXTRINSIC(PROPRIETARY) SUBROUTINE MY_SORT(A)
            INTEGER, DIMENSION(:), INTENT(INOUT) :: A
          END SUBROUTINE MY_SORT
        END INTERFACE
```

is an interface for a subroutine named **MY_SORT** written in the **PROPRIETARY** programming model (presumably a model proprietary to the computer vendor's machine). **EXTRINSIC** interfaces do two things: they alert the compiler that the program is entering a different model (which may in turn require the compiler to change the procedure calling sequence), and they constrain the behavior of the called routine. In essence, the overall behavior of an **EXTRINSIC** routine as observed by the caller must be consistent with an HPF routine with the same interface. For example, an **EXTRINSIC** routine may not take data that is consistently replicated in HPF and make it inconsistent.

HPF also defines the **HPF_LOCAL** programming model, which essentially consists of the same program executed on every processor of a parallel machine. This model is useful for two things. First, it is a model supported by many parallel machines and is therefore directly useful for many programmers. In situations where execution speed is more important than portability, **EXTRINSIC(HPF_LOCAL)** allows tuning of some operations that do not appear explicitly in HPF, such as low-level synchronization operations. Second, it serves as an example of how a particular programming model can be defined for use as an HPF **EXTRINSIC**. Vendors may define their own system-specific models, either as extensions to **HPF_LOCAL** or as entirely new models.

0.9 Subset High Performance Fortran

Chapter 9 describes Subset HPF, a minimal starting language defined to encourage early releases of compilers with HPF features. HPF is a rather large and complex language to implement. This subset contains features that are high on users' priority lists yet considered implementable relatively quickly by compiler writers. Compiler vendors are always encouraged to implement the full HPF language; however, if resource constraints make this impossible, Subset HPF is a suitable language for early implementation.

0.10 Appendices

Appendix A contains definitions of the technical terms defined in HPF, as well as relevant technical terms defined in Fortran 90.

Appendix B contains detailed specifications of the intrinsic and library routines introduced in Chapter 7.

Appendix C provides the formal syntax definitions for HPF. It is taken verbatim from the *High Performance Fortran Language Specification, version 1.0* [14].

Appendix D provides a cross-reference of syntax symbols used in the formal syntax rules. It is taken verbatim from the *High Performance Fortran Language Specification, version 1.0* [14].

The bibliography includes further references to HPF and Fortran 90.

The index contains entries for all technical terms defined in this document, keywords in HPF and Fortran 90, and syntax symbols used in the grammars.

1 Basics of High Performance Fortran

This chapter describes conventions of terminology and notation used throughout the rest of this book. It also discusses the goals of the High Performance Fortran Forum in defining HPF, and some sources of additional information.

1.1 Fortran Development

Although the [Fortran] group broke new ground ... they never lost sight of their main objective, namely, to produce a product that would be acceptable to practical users with real problems to solve.

Fortran ... is still by far the most popular language for numerical computation ...
　　　　　　　　　　　　　　　　　　　　　　　　Maurice V. Wilkes [30]

Since its introduction almost four decades ago, Fortran[1] has been the language of choice for scientific and engineering programming. HPF is the latest set of extensions to this venerable language. However, it is *not* a standard recognized by the formal national and international standards committees. The current ANSI and ISO programming language standard in this area is Fortran 90.

The first programming language to be called Fortran was developed by IBM in the early 1950's [7]. It became quite popular after the first compiler was delivered to a customer in 1957, in large part because it was both efficient and much easier to write and maintain than the assembly languages that had come before. The language gained increasing acceptance as it was ported to more and more machines. In 1966, the American Standards Association (ASA, later to become the American National Standards Institute (ANSI)) published the first formal standard for Fortran [28]. This standard included many of the core features of Fortran, including:

- The familiar **INTEGER**, **REAL**, and **DOUBLE PRECISION** data types.
- A notation for array references and arithmetic computations.
- **DO** loops for iteration (but not the **END DO** statement).
- **IF** conditionals (but not the block **IF** statement).
- Subroutines, functions, and the independent compilation of program units.
- Global variables (through the mechanism of **COMMON** blocks).

---
[1] Note that the spelling of the name of the language is case-sensitive, a change made by the Fortran standards committee: "FORTRAN" refers to the FORTRAN 77 and earlier standards and, typically, products based on them; "Fortran" refers to the Fortran 90 standard and, typically, newer products. Except for references to particular standards or products, we will consistently use the term "Fortran" to identify the language.

It also included the Hollerith data type, which was later replaced with the **CHARACTER** type. The standard was later dubbed FORTRAN 66, to differentiate it from later versions.

The Fortran language continued to evolve, and in 1978 ANSI and the International Standards Organization (ISO) published a new standard [3]. FORTRAN 77 provided a number of additional language features now well known to engineering and scientific programmers, including:

- **IF...THEN...ELSE IF ...END IF** conditional statements.
- The **COMPLEX** data type, **COMPLEX** constants, and operations on **COMPLEX** numbers.
- The **CHARACTER** data type, **CHARACTER** constants, and operations on strings.
- Formatted, unformatted, and direct-access file input and output.

In 1978 the US Department of Defense published an addendum to the FORTRAN 77 standard, designated MIL-STD-1753, with language features required by all compilers to be sold to the US government [29]. Virtually every Fortran compiler supports these features:

- The **END DO** statement.
- The **DO WHILE** statement.
- **INCLUDE** lines.
- The **IMPLICIT NONE** statement.
- Syntax for octal and hexadecimal constants.
- Eleven bit manipulation procedures.

Soon after publication of the FORTRAN 77 standard, work began on a revision to the standard, with the working title of Fortran 8x [6]. By the time the new standard was accepted by ISO in 1991 (and by ANSI the following year), it had been renamed Fortran 90 [17]. In the words of that standard, its goal was to "modernize Fortran, so that it may continue its long history as a scientific and engineering programming language." A secondary goal was to use the modern language features to allow programmers to discontinue use of obsolescent and no longer desirable forms in FORTRAN 77. These forms include nine features identified as obsolescent and a (now empty) category of removed features listed in Appendix B of the standard. Although Fortran 90 provides significant new capabilities, it did not ignore the requirements of "legacy" codes; Fortran 90 includes as a subset all of FORTRAN 77 and MIL-STD-1753.

Even before the Fortran 90 standard had been formally approved, calls were heard for more extensions. In particular, standard features were needed to enable portable, efficient programming on the new generation of parallel machines. (Section 1.2 details more of these concerns.) The first group to discuss standardization of parallel Fortran features was the Parallel Computing Forum (PCF). Their original goals were to standardize language features for task oriented parallelism on shared memory machines [24]. This effort continues as the ANSI X3H5 committee. The X3H5 Fortran language extensions [5] for parallelism are first-class language extensions (not directives) and make control of the parallelism very visible to the programmer with explicit constucts for synchonization, worksharing, etc.[2] These extensions were, however, closely tied to the shared-memory paradigm for parallel computation, making them difficult to implement on newer distributed-memory machines.

In November, 1991 Digital Equipment Corporation organized a birds-of-a-feather meeting at the Supercomputing '91 conference in Albuquerque, New Mexico, to discuss their proposed language (already named "High Performance Fortran"). Along with original material, this proposal synthesized ideas from Connection Machine Fortran (from Thinking Machines), Fortran 77D and Fortran 90D (from Rice and Syracuse Universities), Vienna Fortran (from the University of Vienna), several compiler projects undertaken by COMPASS Inc., and other sources. The session was followed in January, 1992 by the kickoff meeting for the High Performance Fortran Forum (HPFF) in Houston, Texas, hosted by the Center for Research on Parallel Computation (CRPC) at Rice University. Over 130 people attended to hear presentations from Convex Computer, Cray Research, Digital, IBM, Rice University, Thinking Machines, the University of Vienna, and others on various aspects of the proposed language. There was a strong consensus that a common set of Fortran extensions for data parallel programming would be valuable and that this was a good time to define such a set of extensions. However, it was clear that a meeting of this size was too large to draft a technical proposal. A series of smaller "working group" meetings was scheduled to create the language draft.

The HPFF working group, consisting of about 40 people, met for the first time in Dallas, Texas, in March, 1992. Eight further meetings were held, drawing attendees from industry, academia, and government; from Austria, England, France, Germany, Japan and the United States; and from the ranks of computer vendors, Fortran users, and general computer scientists. Through electronic mail, every effort was made to keep the HPFF process open to the public, and requests for comments on the draft produced voluminous responses. Although the effort was not sponsored by national and international standards organizations such as ANSI and ISO, the working group received several helpful communications from the ANSI X3J3 committee. The working group produced the *High Performance Fortran Language Specification, version 1.0* in May,

---

[2] In contrast, HPF chooses to use directives where possible and leaves control of parallelism to the compiler.

History of Fortran	
1954	"Preliminary Report, Specifications for the IBM Mathematical FORmula TRANslating System, FORTRAN" (J. W. Backus, et al.)
1957	FORTRAN for the IBM 704
1958	FORTRAN II for the IBM 704
1962	FORTRAN IV for the IBM 7030 STRETCH
1966	X3.9-1966, American Standard (ASA) FORTRAN (FORTRAN 66)
1969	Federal Information Processing Institute standard FIPS 69-1
1978	ANSI X3.9 -1978 American National Standard Programming Language FORTRAN (FORTRAN 77)
1978	MIL-STD-1753: FORTRAN, DoD Supplement to American National Standard X3.9-1978
1980	ISO 1539-1980 (E), international Fortran standard; same as ANSI
1987	S8.104 — Draft Standard, Fortran 8x for public review
1991	Parallel Extensions for FORTRAN 77, X3H5 Language Binding, [X3H5/91-0040-C]
1991	S8.118 accepted as ISO/IEC 1539:1991 (E), Fortran 90
1992	ANSI X3.198-1992; same Fortran 90 standard as ISO
1993	High Performance Fortran Language Specification

Table 1.1
A brief history of Fortran

1993 [14]. This book is based on that document. Recognizing that some important issues, such as parallel input/output facilities, could not be resolved within the time that HPFF allowed itself, the working group recommended that another series of meetings be held during 1994. These meetings will consider both new extensions and experience gained with the first version of HPF.

Major milestones in the history of Fortran are presented in Table 1.1.

1.2 Goals of HPF

Given the history outlined above, it is fair to ask, "Why do we need yet another Fortran extension?" It might seem that Fortran is serving its role quite nicely.

Despite its past success, Fortran is reaching its limitations on the latest generation of high-performance machines. Fortran was originally developed for serial machines with linear memory architectures. In the past several years it has become increasingly apparent that a language design relying on these architectural features creates difficulties when executing on parallel machines. One symptom of this is the proliferation of parallel Fortran dialects, each specialized to the machine where it was first implemented. As the number of competing parallel machines on the market increases, the lack of a standard parallel Fortran is becoming increasingly serious. Without a standard programming interface, writing a parallel program ties a scientist to one machine for all his or her work. Perhaps worse, the difficulty of programming in almost any of the available languages creates a high barrier to entry; scientists are unwilling to make the substantial effort to move to the new parallel machines.

As these difficulties became apparent, new research is also suggesting an answer: data parallel programming. The essence of the idea is that many scientific programs have a "natural" parallelism at a fine-grain level, such as performing the same (conceptual) operation on all the elements of an array. Moreover, other research suggests that many of the complex details of communication and synchronization could be generated by the compiler automatically, if only a little high-level data partitioning information were provided. HPF builds on these approaches.

The overriding goal of HPF was therefore to produce a dialect of Fortran that could be used on a variety of parallel machines. At the first meeting, the HPFF working group refined this goal, saying its mission was to define language extensions and feature selection for Fortran supporting:

- Data parallel programming (defined as single-threaded control structure, global name space, and loosely synchronous parallel execution).
- Top performance on MIMD and SIMD computers with non-uniform memory access costs (while not impeding performance on other machines).
- Code tuning for various architectures.

It also established a number of secondary goals, including:

- Portability (existing code): Allow relatively easy conversion from existing sequential code to parallel code.
- Portability (new code): Allow efficient code on one parallel machine to be reasonably efficient on other machines.
- Compatibility: Deviate minimally from other standards, particularly FORTRAN 77 and Fortran 90.
- Simplicity: Keep the resulting language simple.
- Interoperability: Define open interfaces to other languages and programming styles.
- Availability: Make compiler availability feasible in the near term.
- Promptness: Present a near-final proposal in November, 1992 and accept the final draft in January, 1993. (Note that this schedule was set in March, 1992.)

The HPFF working group made a number of compromises due to try to reach these goals. Much discussion was spent trying to balance portability between machines with ability to tune programs for a specific architecture. Some features were not accepted into HPF because they caused severe hardships for certain classes of machines, even though they were efficient on other machines. Finally, the *HPF Journal of Development* [15] chronicles some proposals that did not achieve consensus, although they may have had technical merits.

HPF does not solve all the problems of parallel programming. Its purpose is to provide a portable, high-level expression for data parallel algorithms. For algorithms that fall into this rather large class, HPF promises to provide some measure of efficient portability. We also hope that the new constructs are intuitive, thus lowering the entrance barrier to parallel machines. In short, HPF is a step toward bringing the convenience of sequential Fortran to the complex parallel machines of today. (It will not be the last such step—see Section 1.7 below.) It should be noted that, although HPF was motivated by parallel architectures, the constructs can be used on any computer, in much the same way that Fortran 90 vector assignments can also be used on scalar processors.

1.3 Fortran 90 Binding

HPF is an extension of Fortran 90. The array calculation and dynamic storage allocation features of Fortran 90 make it a natural base for HPF. The new HPF language features fall into four categories with respect to Fortran 90:

- New directives.
- New language syntax.
- Library routines.
- Language restrictions.

The HPF *directives* are special comments that suggest implementation strategies or assert facts about a program to the compiler. They may affect the efficiency of the computation performed, but do not change the value computed by the program. Section 1.6 describes the general form of these directives in more detail.

HPF adds a few new language features, including the **FORALL** statement, the **PURE** and **EXTRINSIC** attributes for procedures, and some intrinsic functions. These features had to be first-class language constructs rather than comments because they can affect the interpretation of a program. For example, the new intrinsics return values used in expressions.

The *HPF library* defines a standard interface to routines that have proven valuable for high performance computing including additional reduction functions, combining scatter functions, prefix and suffix functions, and sorting functions. It is a Fortran 90 **MODULE**.

Full support of Fortran sequence and storage association is not compatible with the data distribution features of HPF. Some restrictions on the use of sequence and storage association are imposed. These restrictions may require insertion of HPF directives into standard Fortran 90 programs in order to preserve correct semantics under HPF.

1.4 Notation

This book uses most of the same notation as the *Fortran 90 Handbook* [1] by Adams et al. In particular, nearly the same conventions are used for syntax rules. (Typesetting buffs will notice that we have changed fonts; otherwise the conventions are identical.) We define the syntax of a construct by giving its name and a schematic of its form; for example, a *combined-directive* (H301) has the form:

combined-attribute-list :: *entity-decl-list*

The number following the name refers to the *rule number*, as explained below.

When a construct may take several forms, they are listed one per line following the words "one of:"; for example, *combined-attribute* (H302) is one of:

```
ALIGN align-attribute-stuff
DISTRIBUTE dist-attribute-stuff
DYNAMIC
INHERIT
TEMPLATE
PROCESSORS
DIMENSION ( explicit-shape-spec-list )
```

Any characters in **TYPEWRITER FONT** in these forms should be interpreted literally. Words in *italic font* are names of syntax elements defined separately. Material in [square brackets] is an optional part of the syntax. Three dots ... indicate that the preceding word or bracketed expression may be repeated.

Some names are implicitly defined. An *xyz-list* has the form:

xyz [, *xyz*] ...

That is, an *xyz-list* is a comma-separated list of *xyz* items. An *int-xyz* is an *xyz* that is constrained to be of type integer. An *xyz-name* is a *name* (R304) that is associated with an *xyz*.

All references to syntax rule numbers refer to either the HPF language specification or the Fortran 90 standard. HPF syntax rules have identifying numbers of the form H*snn* where *s* is a one-digit section number (in the HPF language specification) and *nn* is a one- or two-digit sequence number. Fortran 90 rules are numbered in the form R*ssnn*, where the one- or two-digit section number *ss* refers to a section in the Fortran 90 standard.

A BNF description of HPF in the style used in the Fortran 90 standard appears in Appendix C of this book, indexed by rule number. Appendix D contains a cross-reference of both HPF symbols and the Fortran 90 symbols that they reference.

The first time that we use or define a *technical term* it appears in italics. Appendix A collects the definitions of these terms. Subsequent references to technical terms normally are not italicized.

HPF and Fortran 90 keywords such as `FORALL` and `IF` appear in typewriter font in the text, as do variables and other elements taken from program examples.

1.5 Conformance

The Fortran 90 standard defines *standard-conforming* to mean that a program uses only the syntax and semantics (including obeying restrictions on use) that are defined by the standard. Similarly, the HPF language specification defines *HPF-conforming* to mean that a program obeys the syntax and semantics defined by the specification. Finally, a program is *Subset-conforming* if it obeys the syntax and rules of Subset HPF. Program units, such as individual subroutines, conform to a standard or specification if they can be incorporated into a program that then conforms to the same standard or specification.

All this has the following practical effect: Fortran 90 and HPF explicitly leave undefined what happens if you break any of their rules. Some compilers will detect such rule-breaking and report an error. In fact, Fortran 90 requires that compilers be able to detect and report non-standard-conforming syntax. Some compilers will impose their own interpretations on non-conforming programs. For example, the restriction that two iterations of an `INDEPENDENT DO` loop cannot both assign to the same location is very difficult to check, either in the compiler or while the program is running. Two executions of the same program, when processed by two different compilers, might assign different values to the location in this case, making the result machine-dependent. Indeed, two executions of the same program as processed by the same compiler might assign different values to the location, making the result unpredictable even on a single machine; HPF simply does not specify what happens when the restriction is violated. When we say in the text that a program may not do something, we mean that the resulting construct would not be HPF-conforming. We strongly recommend that programmers not use non-

HPF-conforming features, even if they happen to work on their current compiler; the cost of finding and fixing these features when the compiler changes will be very large.

Some features are HPF-conforming, but their precise definition varies from system to system. For example, the mapping for an array with no explicit **ALIGN** or **DISTRIBUTE** directives can be anything that HPF can express. The Fortran 90 standard labels these features *processor-dependent*, where the "processor" is the language processor that prepares the Fortran program for running. We use the terminology *compiler-* or *system-dependent* to mean the same thing. It should be understood that we mean "compiler" in a rather broad sense in this book; it includes interactive interpreters, translators to other dialects of Fortran, and runtime libraries in addition to traditional compilers. Standard-conforming programs can use compiler-dependent features, but the results of the program may change from system to system (or even from run to run on the same system). This, of course, hurts portability. We recommend not relying on these features if they can be avoided, and documenting assumptions about them when they must be used. Frequently the careful programmer can compensate for system dependencies through the careful use of inquiry procedures such as **NUMBER_OF_PROCESSORS** and **HPF_ALIGNMENT**.

1.6 HPF Directives and Their Syntax

Compiler directives form the heart of the HPF language. As directives, they are technically just Fortran comments. Their presence may be ignored by a standard Fortran compiler. But to an HPF compiler they supply the information needed to optimize performance. The form of an *hpf-directive-line* (H201) is:

directive-origin hpf-directive

where a *directive-origin* (H202) is one of:

```
!HPF$
CHPF$
*HPF$
```

HPF directives are consistent with Fortran 90 syntax in the following sense: if any HPF directive were to be adopted as part of a future Fortran standard, the only change necessary to convert an HPF program would be to remove the directive origin from each such directive. This has further implications. The directives must conform to the Fortran rules for the source form of the surrounding text. The first thing to notice is that Fortran 90 allows comments to begin with "C" and "*" as well as "!" in the fixed source form, but allows only "!" to begin a comment in free source form. We recommend that programmers always use the "!HPF$" form of the *directive-origin* so that it will work in either form.

HPF directives follow the free source form rule about spaces within the directive line. Spaces are significant. At least one space is required anywhere two keywords or a keyword and a variable name are adjacent. Furthermore, a space may not occur in the middle of a keyword or variable name. This rule applies even in directives using the fixed source form. (If HPF directives are converted to true statements in some future Fortran standard, this rule will undoubtedly be changed. HPF directives have been designed to be syntactically unambiguous if this happens.)

The directives also follow the Fortran convention regarding their location. There are two forms of directive:

specification-directive
executable-directive

A *specification-directive* (H204) must appear in the specification part of the program unit containing the other declarations relating to the data described. These directives include the following kinds (all defined in later sections of this book):

align-directive
combined-directive
distribute-directive
dynamic-directive
inherit-directive
processors-directive
sequence-directive
template-directive

An *executable-directive* (H205) appears with the other Fortran 90 *executable-constructs* in the program unit. There are three executable directives:

realign-directive
redistribute-directive
independent-directive

Even though the directives are "comments" there are additional rules about how they may be intermixed with other Fortran statements and comments. There are also rules for how to continue the directives in the case that they do not fit on a single line of the source. The basic rule of thumb is to think of the HPF directive as a regular Fortran statement, with one important exception. The Fortran free source form allows multiple statements on a single source line. This is not allowed for HPF directives; they must start at the beginning of the source line (possibly preceded by blanks). Non-directive comments may follow an HPF directive on the same source line.

Example 1.1 The following directive is HPF-conforming:

```
!HPF$ DISTRIBUTE (CYCLIC) :: PERIODIC_TABLE  !one element at a time
```

Note that there is a trailing comment on the same source line. □

Example 1.2 This code is not HPF-conforming:

```
! *** The following line is not HPF-conforming! ***
REAL PERIODIC_TABLE(103); !HPF$ DISTRIBUTE PERIODIC_TABLE(CYCLIC)
```

The HPF directive should not have any non-blank characters preceding it on the same source line. The code may be corrected by splitting it onto two source lines:

```
REAL PERIODIC_TABLE(103)
!HPF$ DISTRIBUTE PERIODIC_TABLE(CYCLIC)
```

Now the HPF directive is on its own source line. □

Example 1.3 This code is not HPF-conforming:

```
! *** The following line is not HPF-conforming
!HPF$ DISTRIBUTE PERIODIC_TABLE(CYCLIC); DISTRIBUTE LOG_TABLE(BLOCK)
```

HPF currently does not allow more than one directive to appear in a single source line. The code may be corrected by splitting it onto two source lines:

```
!HPF$ DISTRIBUTE PERIODIC_TABLE(CYCLIC)
!HPF$ DISTRIBUTE LOG_TABLE(BLOCK)
```

Now each HPF directive is on its own source line. □

HPF directive lines must not appear within a continued Fortran statement. This would violate the idea that the directive might later become a regular Fortran statement. HPF directives can be continued. Other comments may be mixed within the continued HPF directive, but other Fortran statements may not appear between the lines of a continued directive. To continue an HPF directive, the rules of the surrounding source form are applied, but the HPF directive-origin must appear on each line of the continued directive.

Example 1.4 An HPF directive continuation in free source form:

```
!HPF$ ALIGN ANTIDISESTABLISHMENTARIANISM(I,J,K) &
!HPF$         WITH ORNITHORHYNCHUS_ANATINUS(J,K,I)
```

The directive origin must appear on *each* source line. □

Example 1.5 An HPF directive continuation in fixed source form:

```
!HPF$ ALIGN ANTIDISESTABLISHMENTARIANISM(I,J,K)
!HPF$*WITH ORNITHORHYNCHUS_ANATINUS(J,K,I)
```

Observe that column 6 must be blank or zero on the first source line of the directive and not blank or zero on continuation lines. □

Example 1.6 This HPF directive continuation is "universal"; it works properly both in fixed source form and in free source form (see Section 3.10.4.

```
!HPF$ ALIGN ANTIDISESTABLISHMENTARIANISM(I,J,K)                                &
!HPF$&WITH ORNITHORHYNCHUS_ANATINUS(J,K,I)
```

Note that the "&" in the first line is in column 73. □

Example 1.7 This HPF directive has an embedded ordinary comment line, which is acceptable to HPF.

```
!HPF$ ALIGN ANTIDISESTABLISHMENTARIANISM(I,J,K)                                &
! The duckbill platypus is not usually so political.
!HPF$&WITH ORNITHORHYNCHUS_ANATINUS(J,K,I)
```

However, it would not be acceptable to put another directive or an ordinary Fortran statement between the lines of a directive:

```
      ! *** This code is not HPF-conforming! ***
!HPF$ ALIGN ANTIDISESTABLISHMENTARIANISM(I,J,K)                                &
      LOGICAL PLATYPUS
!HPF$&WITH ORNITHORHYNCHUS_ANATINUS(J,K,I)
```

Such code is Fortran-conforming, but not HPF-conforming. □

1.7 For Further Reading

Although we have tried to be thorough, there are some topics relevant to HPF that are outside the scope of this book. This includes the HPF base documents, the definitions of precursors to HPF, and deeper discussions of Fortran 90. The purpose of this chapter is to give the interested reader some entry points into that literature.

The "official" definition of HPF can be found in the *High Performance Fortran Language Specification, version 1.0 final* [14]. The document is available in an issue of *Scientific Programming*, and as a technical report from Rice University. Our book is derived from this material, explaining it in a more tutorial manner, adding examples, and giving advice on the use of features. The *High Performance Fortran Journal of Development* [15], also available from the same sources, contains a number of proposals that were not adopted into HPF, version 1.0. Some of these may be considered in future revisions of HPF. We have not used any material from the *Journal of Development* in this book.

Although we have included some material on Fortran 90, we have not covered it in depth, due in part to the size of the language. The official definition of the language is *Fortran 90* [17], a standard available from ISO and ANSI. Several other reference and text books covering Fortran 90 are also available. We particularly recommend *Fortran 90 Explained* by Michael Metcalf and John Reid [23], the *Fortran 90 Handbook* by Jeanne Adams, *et al.* [1], and *Programmer's Guide to Fortran 90* by Walter Brainerd, Charles Goldberg and Jeanne Adams [9] for these purposes.

It is probably impossible to trace all the influences on the development of HPF. Any list of major technical influences would have to include:

- Parallelizing compilers [31, 33].
- Compiler techniques for array operations [2, 12, 18].
- Data distribution languages, including Adapt [22], Fortran D [16], Fortran 90D [32], Kali [21], and Vienna Fortran [10].
- Computer vendor implementations, including Connection Machine Fortran [27] and the Cray MPP programming model [25].

This list does not begin to suggest the general work on parallel computation that fed into HPF and these languages. *Solving Problems on Concurrent Processors* [13] by Fox *et al.* contains a wealth of material on this subject, although presented in a very different framework than this book.

Several papers on HPF have appeared in various journals and conferences, ranging from progress reports while the language was being defined to detailed critiques of the final result. Koelbel [19], Loveman [20], and Steele [26] surveyed the language at various times during its development. Chapman, Mehrotra, and Zima [11] were more critical. This list is by no means complete.

HPFF is an ongoing activity. In particular, this book is appearing just as a new series of working group meetings is being organized. If you would like to observe or participate in these discussions, send electronic mail with the line

add hpff

to **hpff-request@cs.rice.edu**. This will put you on the main mailing list. There are also a number of more specialized lists for detailed discussions.

Documents related to HPF are available for anonymous FTP from **titan.cs.rice.edu** in the directory **/public/HPFF**. The latest language specification is stored in several formats in the subdirectory **draft**. See the **README** file in the main directory for the current list of available files.

2 Programming Model

Every programming language assumes an underlying *programming model* that explains how a program will be executed. The purpose of the model is to provide a framework for designing and analyzing programs; in particular, a model usually tells what programs mean and gives a rough idea of the execution speed of a program. FORTRAN 77, for example, assumes that statements are executed in the order they were written and that memory is arranged in a linear array. Therefore, a programmer knows that the loop

```
X = 0.0
DO I = 1, 10000
  X = X + A(I)
END DO
```

will add up the first 10,000 elements of array A and take about 10,000 times the time of a floating point addition. This chapter gives the basic programming model for High Performance Fortran. Mostly, we will concentrate on the performance aspects of the programming model here, leaving the details of the meaning of constructs to be defined in other chapters. First, however, we make a short digression to describe modern parallel architectures.

2.1 Parallel Machines

Figure 2.1 shows a block diagram of a modern parallel computer that serves as the basis for the HPF programming model. The major features of this machine are:

- *Processors* that can operate in parallel, that is, at the same time.
- *Memory modules* that are associated with the processors.
- An *interconnection network* that allows processors to cooperate and share data.

This is obviously not a complete model—for one thing, it does not represent any input or output devices—but it does cover the machine features that HPF tries to describe.

The distinguishing feature of a parallel machine is that it can have many processors active at once. This is called *parallel computation*, and is how the machine gets its speed. If one processor can perform a million computations per second, then 100 processors can (theoretically) execute a hundred million computations in the same time. The machine's manufacturer will usually report this number as the machine's peak performance. (Users often call it the machine's "speed of light," since the computer will never go faster than the peak performance.) In practice, various overheads will usually prevent the machine from achieving such perfect speedup. The actual performance considering these overheads is often called the machine's sustained performance.

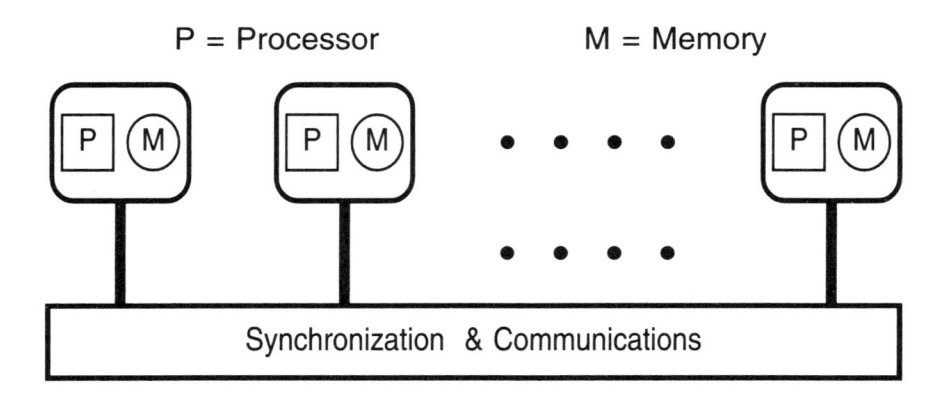

Figure 2.1
A parallel machine

In most parallel machines, each processor has an area of memory that it can access faster than other memory on the machine. We call this the processor's *local memory*, and other memory areas its *remote memory*. Because the local memory can be accessed faster than remote memory, an efficient program on the machine will use local memory as much as possible. Some machines have several levels of local memory, forming a memory hierarchy. HPF considers only one level of this hierarchy directly.

A parallel machine must provide a way for the processors to coordinate their activities. There has to be a way for one processor to get data from another; doing this is called *communication*. Similarly, if a processor cannot proceed without a result from another processor it must wait, an operation called *synchronization*. Both communication and synchronization are overheads that can keep a parallel machine from reaching its peak performance. Efficient parallel programs avoid them when it is possible.

Some examples may help to explain the HPF model.

Example 2.1 One common class of parallel machines is the *MIMD message-passing* architecture. MIMD stands for "Multiple Instruction stream, Multiple Data stream," meaning that the processors can all be executing different instructions at the same time. Every processor in a message-passing machine is connected to a local memory, which no other processor can access directly. To share data (and to synchronize with each other) processors must send and receive messages. These messages travel through an interconnection network which ensures, either in hardware or software, that all the data arrives intact. Machines in this class include the Intel, Meiko, and nCUBE product lines. In addition, the Thinking Machines CM-5 belongs to this class, and some workstation vendors such as Digital, Hewlett Packard, and IBM provide products that allow a network of workstations to be used as a single machine in this way. For this class of machines, the correspondence to the model in Figure 2.1 is very clear. Communication through the network in these machines is much more expensive than computation on a processor (often by two or three orders of magnitude); thus, programs must minimize the volume of communication. Also, a message may have a large start-up cost; therefore, it often pays to combine two short messages into one large one. □

Example 2.2 Another common type of parallel machine is the *MIMD shared-memory* class. Like the MIMD message-passing machines, processors on these machines can execute different instructions in parallel. Unlike those machines, at least part of the memory is shared between processors; thus, data can be shared without explicit messages. Engineering constraints, however, make it difficult to sustain enough memory bandwidth to keep all the processors busy. One solution to this problem is to add caches to the processors. When a processor references a location, the hardware delivers the data to the processor's cache if it is not already there; if it is there, then access is faster because it is local. In terms of the HPF model, we consider the processor caches to correspond to the memory modules of Figure 2.1. The hardware connections used to route the data correspond to the communication and synchronization network there. Machines made by Kendall Square Research fall into this category, as did Alliant and BBN machines before those companies left the market. Machines made by Cray Research and Tera Computer also fall into the shared-memory category, although they use other mechanisms for avoiding the memory bandwidth problem. In these machines the communications time is much less than in message-passing machines (although the local access time is typically higher). Still, efficient programs here will tend to make local accesses as much as possible. □

Example 2.3 A final class of parallel machine is the *SIMD* architecture. SIMD stands for "Single Instruction stream, Multiple Data stream," meaning that all processors must execute exactly the same instruction at the same time. (Processors may be turned off temporarily, if not all are required for a computation.) Each processor has its own memory, and can communicate with other processors using special instructions. Typically, this provides finer-grain communication than in the MIMD message-passing machine. SIMD machines are often, however, sensitive to the pattern of data movement, since routing must be resolved at a low level. As with MIMD message-passing machines, the correspondence with Figure 2.1 is clear. Machines made by MasPar are good examples of this class, as is the Thinking Machines CM-2. In SIMD machines, much of the program complexity comes from ensuring that all processors execute precisely the same instructions. Also, because the performance is tied to the communications patterns it is important to optimize the methods for sharing data. □

The conclusion to draw from these examples is that many current parallel machines reward programmers for keeping many processors busy working on local data. HPF provides ways to express both the parallelism in a program and the locality of data at a relatively high level. The next two sections give more detail regarding HPF's parallel and locality features.

2.2 Parallel Computation

If HPF tied itself closely to any one style of parallelism, then programs would not be easily portable to other machines. Instead, HPF expresses parallelism at a more abstract level that can be efficiently implemented on many machines. Besides portability, this abstraction mechanism has the advantage that it is a natural framework for many programs.

Several varieties of parallelism appear in scientific and engineering applications:

- *Data parallelism*, in which operations are applied to many elements of an array (or other data structure). An example of this would be adding the corresponding elements of two arrays to produce a third array.
- *Functional parallelism* (sometimes called *task parallelism*), in which conceptually different operations are performed at the same time. An example of this would be a series of filters used in image processing.
- *Master-slave parallelism*, in which one process assigns subtasks to other processes. An example of this would be a numerical integration program that decomposed the problem domain in a master process, leaving the work of integrating the resulting subdomains to a set of slave processes.

All these types of parallelism, and others as well, are useful in certain applications. It is difficult, however, to support all of them in the same language. HPF concentrates primarily on data parallel computations, which is a widely useful class. To provide some access to other types of parallelism, HPF also defines extrinsic procedures as an "escape hatch" into other programming paradigms. Section 2.2.1 below introduces HPF's data parallel constructs, while Section 2.2.2 describes the extrinsic procedure interface.

Operation type	Example	Parallel Time	Number of Processors
Elemental	SIN(A(1:N))	$O(1)$	$O(N)$
Array Manipulation	CSHIFT(A(1:N),K)	$O(1)$	$O(N)$
Array Construction	SPREAD(X,NCOPIES=N)	$O(1)$	$O(N)$
Array Reduction	SUM(A(1:N))	$O(\log N)$	$O(N)$
Prefix or Suffix	SUM_PREFIX(A(1:N))	$O(\log N)$	$O(N)$
Sorting	GRADE_UP(A(1:N))	$O(\log N)$	$O(N)$

Table 2.1
Theoretical performance of array intrinsic and HPF library operations

2.2.1 Data Parallel Operations

HPF can express data parallelism in several ways:

1. Fortran 90 array expressions and assignment (including masked assignment in the **WHERE** statement).
2. Array intrinsics defined in Fortran 90.
3. The **FORALL** statement.
4. The **INDEPENDENT** assertion on **DO** and **FORALL**.
5. Array library functions defined in the HPF library.

Fortran 90 features are discussed in detail in Chapter 3; **FORALL** and **INDEPENDENT** are discussed in Chapter 6; the HPF library is discussed in Chapter 7.

The *granularity* of parallelism in a construct is the amount of work that may be performed in each parallel unit. Data parallel constructs generally have rather fine granularity. For example, array expressions define an independent computation for each element of the result; the same can be said for every index value in a **FORALL** statement. Similarly, the iterations of an **INDEPENDENT** loop can also be thought of as *potentially parallel*. Array intrinsics and HPF library operations have degrees of parallelism that vary by the type of intrinsic. Table 2.1 shows the best performance for these operations on a Concurrent-Read, Exclusive-Write Parallel Random Access Memory (CREW PRAM) machine (one of several popular theoretical models). It should be noted that the constant factors hidden in the "big O" notation are quite large for sorting; it may be more realistic to consider sorting to be $O(\log^2 N)$ on $O(N)$ processors.

Regardless of how the data parallelism is expressed, the easiest way for a user to understand what is happening is to think of a single stream of control. Operations are executed in order, as defined by the usual **DO** and **IF** statements. When the program

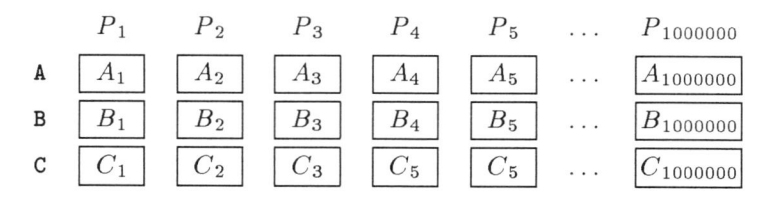

$$
\begin{array}{cccccccc}
 & P_1 & P_2 & P_3 & P_4 & P_5 & \ldots & P_{1000000} \\
A & \boxed{A_1} & \boxed{A_2} & \boxed{A_3} & \boxed{A_4} & \boxed{A_5} & \ldots & \boxed{A_{1000000}} \\
B & \boxed{B_1} & \boxed{B_2} & \boxed{B_3} & \boxed{B_4} & \boxed{B_5} & \ldots & \boxed{B_{1000000}} \\
C & \boxed{C_1} & \boxed{C_2} & \boxed{C_3} & \boxed{C_5} & \boxed{C_5} & \ldots & \boxed{C_{1000000}} \\
\end{array}
$$

Figure 2.2
Distribution of three length-1,000,000 arrays onto 1,000,000 processors in a manner ideal for elementwise computation

reaches a data parallel construct, many operations can be executed at once. The program temporarily forks into many fine-grain tasks, each of which performs one parallel operation. When all the operations are complete, the tasks rejoin and the program continues its execution. When parallel constructs are nested, the fork-and-join process happens recursively. Because all processors are executing the same program during this process, it is sometimes referred to as the *SPMD* ("Single Program Multiple Data") model.[1] Note that this is a conceptual model for how the program behaves and may not reflect how HPF is actually implemented on a particular machine. In particular, much of the fine-grain synchronization implied above can be eliminated in typical programs by using compiler analysis.

Example 2.4 Suppose that the arrays A, B, and C each have one million elements. The array assignment

```
C = A + B
```

represents one million individual, independent assignments that could be carried out simultaneously if only one had a million processors, assuming that processor P_j were to contain array elements A(J), B(J), and C(J) in its memory (see Figure 2.2).

The same computation might also be expressed using a **FORALL** statement:

```
FORALL (J = 1:1000000)   C(J) = A(J) + B(J)
```

The **FORALL** statement has the same semantics as an array assignment and is parallel for the same reason.

Yet another way to express the computation is a **DO** loop with an **INDEPENDENT** directive:

---

[1] Chapter 8 discusses a somewhat different "SPMD" model, in which communication is explicit and there are exactly as many tasks as processors. Unfortunately, the terminology of this field is still in flux, creating confusion even among co-authors.

```
!HPF$ INDEPENDENT
      DO J = 1, 1000000
        C(J) = A(J) + B(J)
      END DO
```

Here, **INDEPENDENT** is an assertion that it is safe to execute all iterations of the loop in parallel. (Some compilers would detect the potential parallelism of this loop without the **INDEPENDENT** directive.)

All three of these program fragments express the same computation: one million independent and potentially concurrent assignments. □

For many programs and parallel machines, the extent of data parallelism is much larger than the machine size. In Example 2.4, for example, no current machine has one million processors. When this happens, the compiler must assign some (perhaps many) conceptually parallel operations onto the same processor. Considering parallelism only, the optimal assignment of tasks to processors is any pattern that puts the same amount of work on each processor. Assigning tasks in this way is called *load balancing*. For example, if the computations in Example 2.4 were executed on 100 processors, one load-balanced scheme would be to assign each processor a contiguous block of 10,000 elements; another would be to assign each processor every 100th element. Section 2.4 examines some of the complications that arise when communication must also be taken into account. For now, it is enough to observe that perfect load balancing is not always possible. For example, one million is not evenly divisible by 128, so executing the computations in Example 2.4 would give some processors at least 7813 elements to compute and some 7812 elements (or less). This effect is more important on smaller problems; for example, 500 computations on 128 processors leaves 4 elements on some processors and 3 on others, a 25% difference.

2.2.2 Extrinsic Procedures

Although data parallelism is important for many problems, it is not the only type of parallel execution. Moreover, even data parallel programs may benefit from tuning in the target machine's "native language." The **EXTRINSIC** mechanism of Chapter 8 handles just such cases by providing an "escape hatch" to other programming paradigms. In particular, **EXTRINSIC(HPF_LOCAL)** lets the programmer write a subroutine as a "node program." That is, the **EXTRINSIC(HPF_LOCAL)** routine consists of code that will be executed essentially without change on every processor, in much the same way that many task parallel systems are programmed. This allows the programmer great control over what will happen on the physical machine, which in turn allows highly efficient machine-specific code to be written. On the other hand, it also means that the programmer must specify the details of data movement and synchronization, making the program harder to read and write.

The execution model for **EXTRINSIC(HPF_LOCAL)** is closer to the physical machine than the data parallel model. Essentially, all processors call the **EXTRINSIC** routine together. Once inside the routine, however, each processor is totally independent of the others. There is no coordination between processors unless the programmer explicitly puts it in. Similarly, each processor has direct access only to its own data, rather than access to all of memory. The **EXTRINSIC** call returns when all the processors have finished their executions.

EXTRINSIC routines are not properly part of HPF—they are routines written in a different programming paradigm, and possibly in a completely different language. Therefore, we will not discuss them further in this chapter. However, these routines are very important to have in practice, and their interface forms a vital part of HPF.

2.3 Communication

While parallelism speeds programs up, moving data between processors slows them down. The exact cost of this communication is machine-dependent, as is its most natural expression on a particular machine. HPF takes an abstract view of this sort of communication.

The basic HPF data model is simple. All data is stored in a *global name space*, which means that all processors "see" the same set of variables. In particular, there are no "private" variables visible to only a subset of the processors. Array declarations declare the entire size of an array, not the portion on a single processor as in many task parallel languages. The *data mapping* part of HPF (defined in Chapter 4) describes how a variable can be divided among processors according to regular patterns.

Communication must occur when two data items are referenced together but are not stored on the same processor. The basic idea is to apply the definitions of the HPF data mapping directives to compute the home processor of each array element involved. Since we have not given those definitions yet, we will present this through examples rather than through formal definitions; we leave adding rigor to these examples as an exercise for the reader.

The communication requirement for an operation with two inputs is clear from the above; communication occurs if the inputs are mapped to different processors, and not otherwise. Larger operations build their communication requirements up from their parts. For the moment, we will present a simple model of this. Section 2.4 discuss some more complex cases.

We assume that the total communication for a program fragment is the sum of the communications that are needed for its parts. Moreover, in this section we will assume that every scalar expression and assignment to a scalar location (i.e., an assignment to one array element, rather than to an array section) is executed on only one processor. If one statement references several distributed array elements, then one element (such as the left-hand side in an assignment) will be local, and the communications can be computed relative to that reference. Iterative constructs like DO loops generate the sum of the inherent communication for nested statements. The same is true of data parallel statements like FORALL and array assignment; the communication is the sum of the communications requirements for the individual elements. Perhaps less obviously, conditional statements like the IF and CASE constructs require at least the communication needed by the branch that is taken.

We will start with a series of examples involving FORALL statements and then generalize. The importance of the FORALL is not its parallelism (see Example 2.16 for an explanation of why); rather, the FORALL is an easy way to specify operations on many array elements at once. Our purpose here is to illustrate the effect of data distribution specifications on communication requirements, not to suggest that this is the precise compiler implementation. The examples in this section use the declarations in Figure 2.3. The lines starting with "!HPF$" are the HPF directives for mapping the arrays to processors. In this case, there are four processors named PROCS(1), PROCS(2), PROCS(3), and PROCS(4). Figure 2.4 shows how the arrays are mapped among the processors. The DISTRIBUTE directives completely define the mappings for arrays A, B, C, D, and INDX. The ALIGN directive does not specify the complete mapping of arrays X and Y, but does indicate their relative alignment. It causes X(I) and Y(I+1) to be stored on the same processor for all values of I, regardless of the actual distribution chosen by the compiler for the arrays. Figure 2.4 shows this as pairs of elements grouped in imaginary processors PROCS?. Elements Y(0) and Y(1) are not aligned with any element of X and therefore occupy processors alone.

Example 2.5 Consider the following code:

```
FORALL (I = 1:16) A(I) = B(I)
```

The identical distribution of A and B ensures that for all values of I, A(I) and B(I) are mapped to the same processor. Therefore, this statement requires not communication.
□

Example 2.6 Consider the following code:

```
FORALL (I = 1:16) A(I) = C(I)
```

```
      REAL, DIMENSION(16)     :: A, B, C
      REAL, DIMENSION(32)     :: D
      REAL, DIMENSION(8)      :: X
      REAL, DIMENSION(0:9)    :: Y
      INTEGER, DIMENSION(16)  :: INX
!HPF$ PROCESSORS, DIMENSION(4) :: PROC
!HPF$ DISTRIBUTE (BLOCK) ONTO PROCS  :: A, B, D, INX
!HPF$ DISTRIBUTE (CYCLIC) ONTO PROCS :: C
!HPF$ ALIGN (I) WITH Y(I+1)          :: X
```

Figure 2.3
HPF data mapping declarations

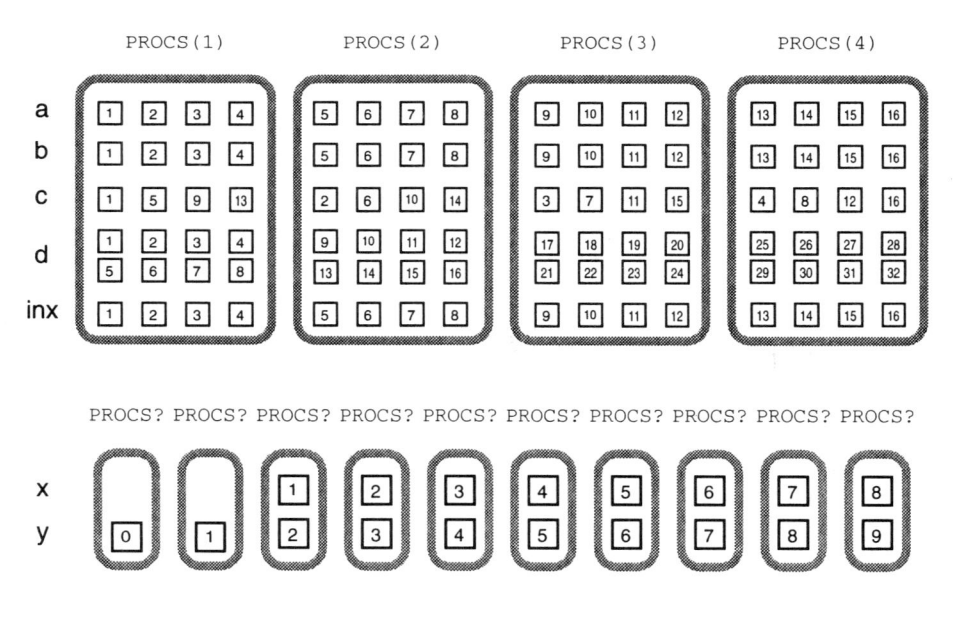

Figure 2.4
Data mappings from Figure 2.3

The communication requirements here are very different from Example 2.5 due to the different distributions of A and C. The first row of boxes in Figure 2.5 shows the data movement needed for all values of I. Small squares represent array elements; larger gray boxes represent the processors. Each arrow represents the assignment for one I value; if the arrow crosses from one gray box into another, then communication is needed for that value. The figure is difficult to read because of all the communicated elements; three-fourths of the elements are not aligned with their "partners." The total communication is 12 elements; moreover, every processor must receive data from every other processor. □

Example 2.7 Consider the following code:

```
FORALL (I = 1:15) A(I) = B(I+1)
```

The A(I) and B(I) references are on the same processor for all but three of the possible values of I. The exceptions to this are I=4*K for K=1, 2, or 3 (when A(I) is on PROCS(K) and A(I+1) is on PROCS(K+1)). The second row of Figure 2.5 shows the resulting shift communication pattern. Only one boundary element on each processor (except the end processor) needs to be communicated, giving a total of 3 communicated elements. Each processor receives data from at most one other processor. □

Example 2.8 Consider the following code:

```
A(I) = B(2*I-1)
```

As the third row of Figure 2.5 shows, the strided access to B means that each active processor potentially receives data from two others. The total communications load is 12 elements. □

Example 2.9 Consider the following code:

```
FORALL (I = 1:16) A(I) = D(I)
```

The array sizes of A and D are different. This size difference in turn makes the data mappings different, although both are described as BLOCK. The effect on communication is shown in the fourth row of boxes in Figure 2.5. The total communications requirement is 12 elements, with each processor receiving data from at most one other processor. A processor must send values to at most two other processors. □

Example 2.10 Consider the following code:

```
FORALL (I = 1:16) A(I) = D(2*I-1)
```

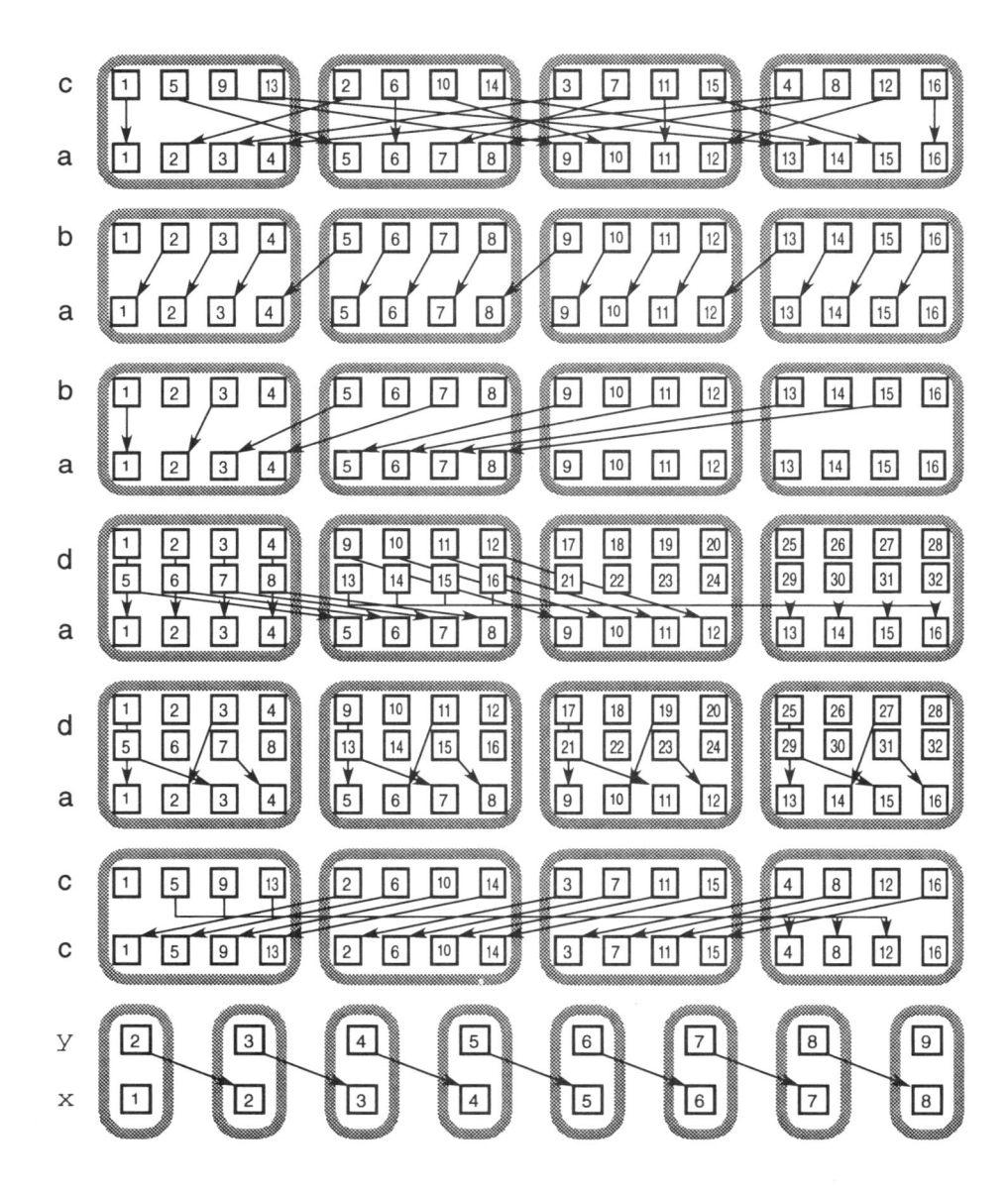

Figure 2.5
Communications patterns for some example assignments

This assignment shows how different distributions may be used together without causing communication: The fifth row of Figure 2.5 shows the reference pattern for the assignment; note that no arrow crosses from one processor to another. It is easy to see why—the strided entry "cancels out" the difference in array sizes. □

Example 2.11 Consider the following code:

```
FORALL (I = 1:15) C(I) = C(I+1)
```

While superficially similar to Example 2.7, this code has very different communication behavior because the distribution of C is CYCLIC rather than BLOCK. This distribution maps the references to C(I) and C(I+1) to different processors for any value of I. The sixth row of Figure 2.5 shows that the resulting communications pattern moves 15 array elements. Each processor receives data from one other processor in a shift pattern (with wraparound on the ends). □

Example 2.12 The following code requires no communication:

```
FORALL (I = 1:8) X(I) = Y(I+1)
```

In this case, the relative alignment of the two arrays matches the assignment statement for any actual distribution of the arrays. □

Example 2.13 The following code *may* require communication:

```
FORALL (I = 1:8) X(I) = Y(I)
```

The only information available in this example is that X(I) and Y(I+1) are on the same processor; this has no logical consequences for the relationship between X(I) and Y(I). The seventh row of Figure 2.5 shows this as communication between abstract processors. Since there are more abstract processors than physical processors, some of these communications may actually be local references. Whether this actually happens is very machine- and compiler-dependent. □

Example 2.14 The following code also has very limited information regarding its communication requirements.

```
FORALL (I = 1:16) A(I) = B(INX(I))
```

Clearly, A(I) and INX(I) are mapped together. Without knowledge of the values stored in INX, however, the relation between A(I) and B(INX(I)) is unknown. Therefore, it is impossible to say what the communications requirements are (except that a most 16 elements are sent and received). □

A few generalizations are worth making.

Accessing arrays with different mappings will generally require communication even for apparently simple operations. We saw this in Examples 2.6 and 2.9. In a simple assignment between a `BLOCK`-distributed and a `CYCLIC`-distributed array, if each array has n elements on p processors, then corresponding the elements are located on the same processor if and only if $\lfloor (i-1)/(n/p) \rfloor = (i-1) \bmod p$. (This can be seen by inspecting the definitions of `BLOCK` and `CYCLIC` in Chapter 4.) Such a coincidence happens $1/p$ of the time, which is not often on large machines. Similar effects can occur for other combinations of distributions if the block sizes of the mappings are different. It is sometimes possible to construct expressions to avoid this communication, as in Example 2.10, but this is rather difficult for the programmer to write (and for the compiler to unravel).

Shift operations like Examples 2.7 and 2.11 are common in practice. Communicating boundary elements as in Example 2.7 is the general case for `BLOCK` distributions and small shift distances. (Shifting by a large distance—more than the number of elements on a processor—requires communication for every element, however.) Similarly, communicating every element in a `CYCLIC`-distributed array is also the common case. (The exception to this is shifting by a multiple of the number of processors, which avoids all communication.) These characteristics make `BLOCK` a good choice for algorithms that perform many operations involving neighboring array elements. `CYCLIC` distribution, however, may provide better load balance in some situations—see Example 2.19.

Strided references as in Examples 2.8 and 2.10 produce more complications for the general case. For `BLOCK` distributions, if the reference stride is k then a processor may require data from $k+1$ others. (The number is $k+1$ rather than k because boundaries may not match evenly.) On most machines, this is more expensive than communicating with one other processor as in Example 2.7. The compiler can, however, schedule this data movement at compile-time. The situation with a `CYCLIC` distribution is similar, but the communications pattern is quite different.

It is difficult or impossible to make general statements about arbitrary references like Examples 2.12 through 2.14. This will tend to produce slower code, since the techniques for handling such cases must be more general. We advise giving the compiler as much information as possible using the HPF directives; this tends to make the programs more efficient and portable.

Example 2.15 The above `FORALL` statements could be converted to array assignments without changing the communications requirements. For example,

```
A(1:15) = B(2:16)
```

is equivalent to Example 2.7. □

Example 2.16 Similarly, the communication needs of Examples 2.5 through 2.14 would not change if the `FORALL` statements were changed to `DO` loops. For example,

```
DO I = 1, 15
  A(I) = B(I+1)
END DO
```

has the same communications requirements as Example 2.7. In general, converting a `FORALL` statement to a `DO` loop changes its meaning and inherent parallelism, however. This is an important point—the communication requirements of a program may be completely independent of its parallelism. □

Example 2.17 This loop must communicate between 0 and 12 elements, depending on the original values in `A`.

```
!HPF$ INDEPENDENT
   DO I = 1, 16
     IF (A(I) < 0.0) THEN
       A(I) = B(I)
     ELSE IF (A(I) > 0.0) THEN
       A(I) = C(I)
     END IF
   END DO
```

(Compare with Examples 2.5 and 2.6.) Negative elements of `A` do not require communication; most positive elements do. □

A few other complex features deserve mention. Some array intrinsics have inherent communication costs as well. For example, consider the statements:

```
X       = SUM(A(1:16))               ! Intrinsic 1
A(1:16) = SPREAD(B(1), NCOPIES=16)   ! Intrinsic 2
A(1:16) = CSHIFT(A(1:16), 1)         ! Intrinsic 3
```

In general, the inherent communication derives from the mathematical definition of the function. For example, the inherent communication for computing `SUM` is one element for each processor storing part of the operand, minus one. (Further communication may be needed to store the result.) The optimal communication pattern is machine-specific. Similar remarks apply to any accumulation operation. Prefix and suffix operations may require a larger volume based on the distribution. The `SPREAD` intrinsic above requires a broadcast from `PROCS(1)` to all processors, which may take advantage of available hardware. The `CSHIFT` operations produce a shift communication pattern (with wraparound). This list of examples illustrating array intrinsics is not meant to be exhaustive.

A `REALIGN` directive (see Chapter 4) may change the location of every element of the array. This will cause communication of all elements that change their home processor; in some compilation schemes, data will also be moved to new locations on the same processor. The communication volume is the same as an array assignment from an array with the original alignment to another array with the new alignment. The `REDISTRIBUTE` directive changes the distribution for every array aligned to the operand of the `REDISTRIBUTE`. Therefore, its cost is similar to the cost of a `REALIGN` on many arrays simultaneously. Compiler analysis may sometimes detect that data movement is not needed because an array has no values that could be accessed; such analysis and the resulting optimizations are beyond the scope of this book.

2.4 Putting It All Together

The purpose of this section is to show how parallelism and communication combine to determine the total performance of an HPF program. As we move from simple examples to more complex ones, it will become clear that our model does not describe all relevant characteristics of HPF execution. The performance of an HPF program will depend on the programming model, compiler design, target machine characteristics, and other factors. This does not mean that HPF is not a useful language; it simply means that programmers have to remember their computing environment.

A simple model for the total computation time of a parallel program is

$$T_{total} \;=\; T_{par}/P_{active} + T_{serial} + T_{comm} \qquad (2.4.1)$$

where:

- T_{total} is the total execution time.
- T_{par} is the total work that can be executed in parallel.
- P_{active} is the number of (physical) processors that are active, that is, actually executing the work in T_{par}.
- T_{serial} is the total work that is done serially.
- T_{comm} is the cost of communications.

This formula assumes that all parallel parts of the program have the same number of active processors; this is true of our examples, but not for most large programs. When a program has several parallel phases, then a better model would define several T_{par_i}

and P_{active_i}, and the total parallel time would be their sum. If a computation cannot be load balanced, then the term T_{par}/P_{active} should be replaced with the largest time on any processor. One can think of this as rounding the division result upwards (although the real reason for the load imbalance may be more complex).

Example 2.18 Consider this bit of prototypical "stencil code":

```
REAL, ARRAY(16,16) :: X, Y
...
FORALL (J=2:15, K=2:15)
   Y(J,K) = (X(J,K)+X(J-1,K)+X(J+1,K)+X(J,K-1)+X(J,K+1))/5.0
END FORALL
```

Note that this code accesses all elements of X but updates only the interior elements of Y.

If we have four processors P_1, P_2, P_3, and P_4, there are a number of ways we might assign the elements of X to processors; some of these are illustrated in Figure 2.6, along with the HPF directives that produce them. We will assume that the Y array is assigned in the same way as X, and that each element of Y is computed on the processor to which it is assigned.

One obvious approach might be to take the elements of X in the usual Fortran column-major array element order, divide them into four equal groups, and assign one group to each processor. The result is that each processor holds four adjacent columns of X—see Figure 2.6(a)). With this organization, processors P_2 and P_3 each must compute 56 elements of Y (a 14×4 subarray of Y), while processors P_1 and P_4 need compute only 42 elements of Y (a 14×3 subarray of Y). We can see already that while this distribution of array elements equalizes the memory requirements of the four processors, it does not equalize the computational load. Moreover, processor P_2 must exchange 14 elements of X with processor P_1 and another 14 elements with processor P_3. Processor P_3 has the same computation and communication load as P_2. Processors P_1 and P_4 have less work to do, so the overall completion time will be dictated by the time required by processors P_2 and P_3. So the computational load (T_{par}/P_{active}) is 56 element-computations and the communications overhead (T_{comm}) is 28 element-exchanges.

Alternatively, the processors might be organized in a 2×2 square, with each processor holding an 8×8 subarray of X—see Figure 2.6(b). With this organization, each processor must compute 49 elements of Y, that is, a 7×7 subarray of Y. For example, P_1 must compute Y(2:8,2:8). Each processor can compute 36 elements of Y (the 6×6 interior of the 8×8 subarray) without requiring elements of X from another processor; but to compute the other 13 elements of Y it must obtain 7 elements of X from each of two other

(a) DISTRIBUTE X(*, BLOCK)

(b) DISTRIBUTE X(BLOCK, BLOCK)

(c) DISTRIBUTE X(*, CYCLIC)

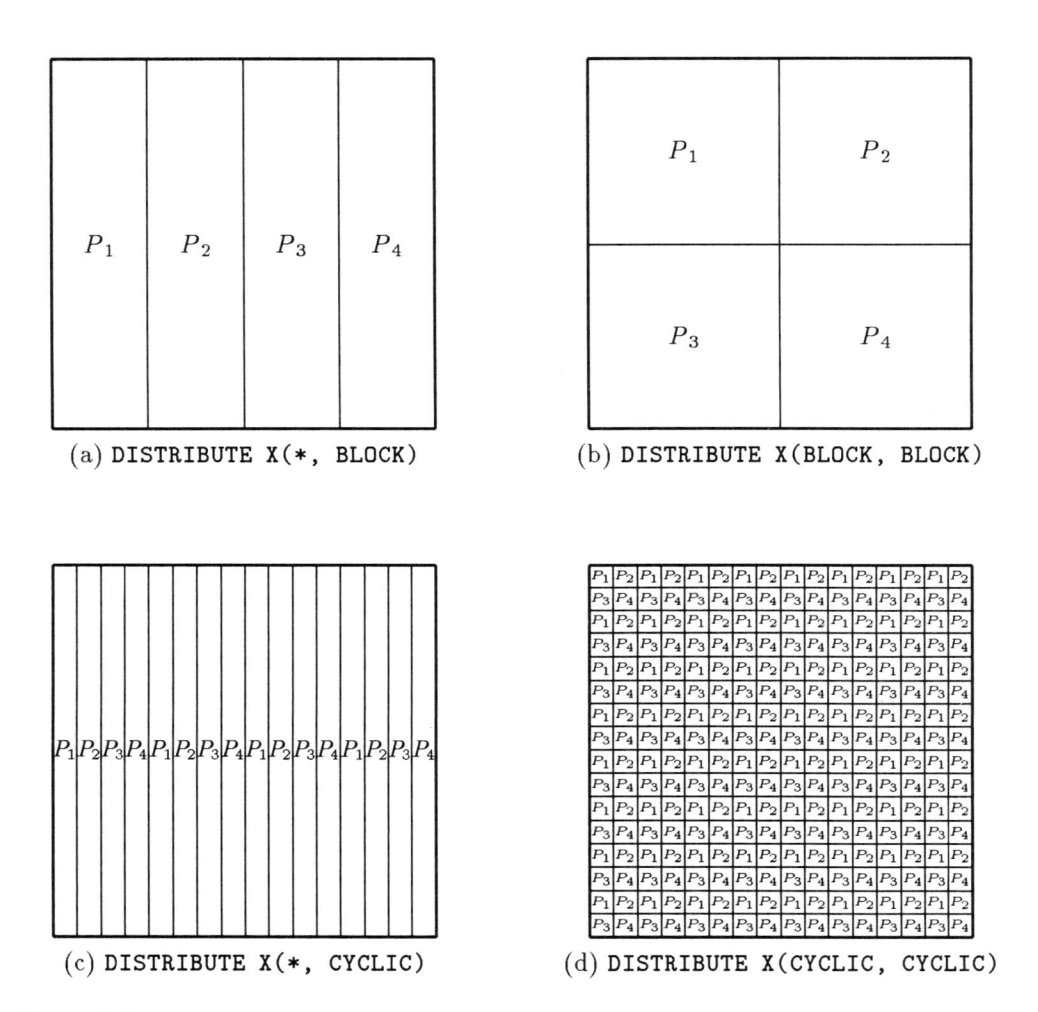

(d) DISTRIBUTE X(CYCLIC, CYCLIC)

Figure 2.6
Various distributions of a 16 × 16 array onto four processors

processors. So the computational requirement per processor (T_{par}/P_{active}) is 49 element-computations and the communications overhead (T_{comm}) is 14 element-exchanges. This distribution of data onto processors is a notable improvement because it balances the computational load *and* reduces the communications overhead.

The distributions shown in Figures 2.6(a) and 2.6(b) are examples of *block* distributions: each processor contains a contiguous subarray of the specified array. Figure 2.6(c) illustrates a *cyclic* distribution in which columns of an array are distributed onto four processors so that each processor, starting from a different offset, contains every fourth column. Unfortunately, this happens to produce the same computational imbalance as the block distribution of Figure 2.6(a) and furthermore has a higher communications overhead.

Figure 2.6(d) shows a distribution that is cyclic in both dimensions onto four processors arranged in a 2 × 2 square. This distribution, like the two-dimensional block distribution shown in Figure 2.6(b), would balance the computational load evenly for our stencil example. Unfortunately, the communications overhead would be far greater: for *every* array element, all four nearest neighbors reside in other processors! □

Example 2.19 Lest the last example suggest that cyclic distributions are inefficient, we present a different algorithm where they are useful. Consider this simple code for LU decomposition by Gaussian elimination:

```
REAL X(16,16)
...
DO I = 1,15
  FORALL (J = I+1:16)
    X(J,I) = X(J,I) / X(I,I)
    FORALL (K = I+1:16)
      X(J,K) = X(J,K) - X(J,I)*X(I,K)
    END FORALL
  END FORALL
END DO
```

Incrementing the outer `DO` loop's index must be done sequentially, creating a small T_{serial} overhead. Also, all the elements assigned in the `X(J,I) = ...` statement are located on the same processor in the one-dimensional mappings (Figures 2.6(a) and 2.6(c)); for the purposes of this example, we will assume these are also serial overhead. The parallel computation estimates below do not include this overhead.

For each value of `I`, the inner `FORALL` construct carries out `(16-I)**2` assignments, potentially in parallel. Successive iterations of the `DO` loop update smaller and smaller

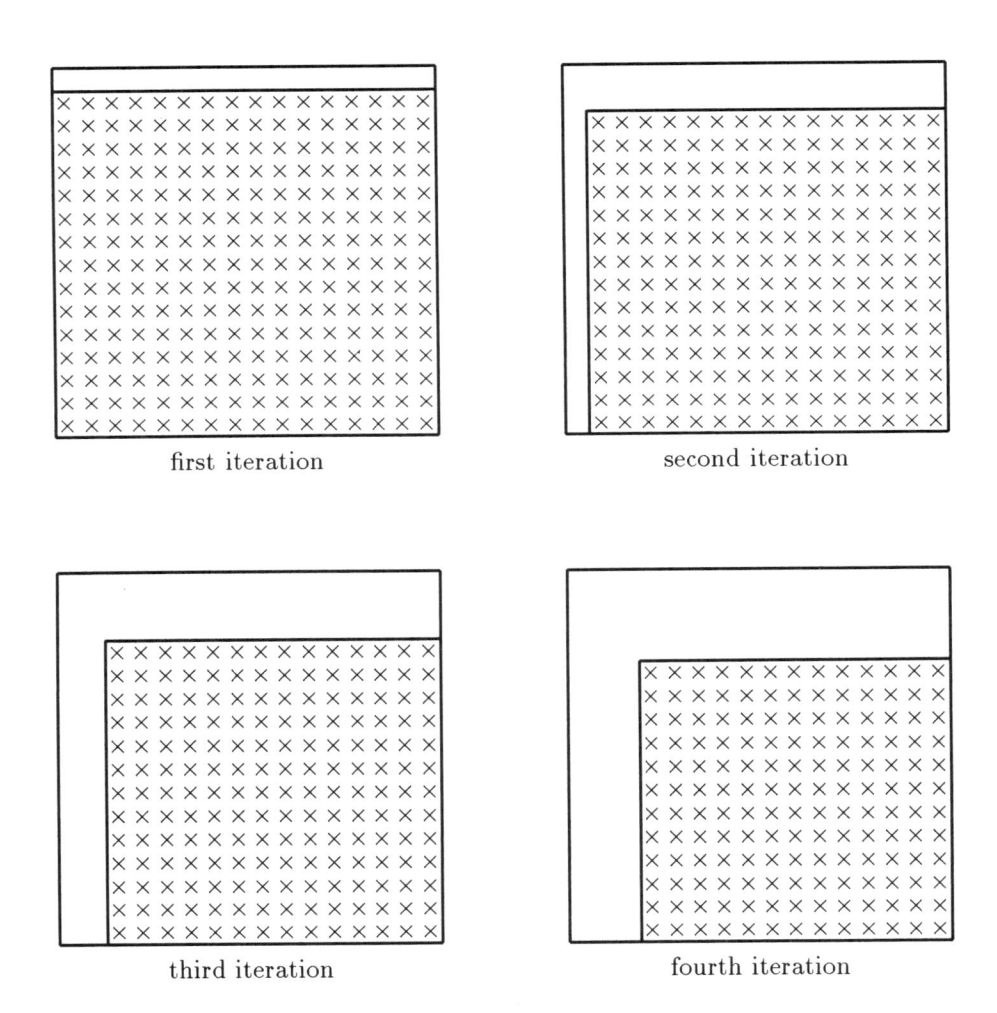

Figure 2.7
Regions of an array updated during successive iterations of LU-decomposition

regions of the array X, as illustrated in Figure 2.7. With the assignment shown in Figure 2.6(a), after the first eight iterations none of the elements assigned to processors P_1 and P_2 will be updated again. Considering the load imbalance, the parallel computation time (T_{par}/P_{active}) for all the inner FORALL index values is 470 element updates. The situation is even worse for the two-dimensional block mapping (Figure 2.6(b)): after the first eight iterations the elements of X to be updated *all* reside in one processor, giving $T_{par}/P_{active} = 652$. The cyclic distributions keep the computational load approximately balanced across all the processors over the entire course of the computation; at every stage, the busiest processor has at most one more column to compute than the most idle. Figure 2.6(c) has a computation load of 356 element updates, taking these small load imbalances into account; Figure 2.6(d) improves this to 344 element updates.

The communications overheads for the different mappings do not depend on whether a block or cyclic mapping is used; instead, they only depend on the number of dimensions that are partitioned. In Figures 2.6(a) and (c), the references to X(I,I) and X(J,K) will cause communication. The total number of elements sent is 120, with most of those elements received by more than one processor. For the two-dimensional mappings (Figures 2.6(b) and (d)), the reference X(J,I) also causes communication, leading to a T_{comm} of 225. Because there are so few processors, each element is received only once; in general, the elements would be sent to all processors in a row, or all processors in a column. □

We now turn to some complications that real programs (and compilers) may bring to the model on page 2.4.1. The assumptions in Section 2.3 may overestimate the communication, particularly for good compilers. A major optimization on parallel machines is to reduce the communication cost. This can be done in several ways. One way is to avoid redundant communication—if a data value has been communicated once and has not changed, then it can be reused without another trip through the communications network. Reuse like this is common in sequences of statements. Another optimization is to carefully choose the location for a computation, possibly splitting the computation of one statement among several processors. Such optimizations are particularly useful for array expressions. There are far too many other optimizations to discuss here. Instead, we show two simple examples to give a flavor of how these work.

Example 2.20 To illustrate removing redundant communication, consider the following statements.

```
      REAL, DIMENSION(1000)     :: R, S, T
!HPF$ PROCESSORS, DIMENSION(10) :: PROCS
!HPF$ DISTRIBUTE (CYCLIC) ONTO PROCS :: R, S, T
```

```
      ...
      R(I)   = S(I+2)                       ! Statement 1
      S(I)   = T(I+3)                       ! Statement 2
      S(I+2) = 2 * R(I+2)                   ! Statement 3
      T(I)   = R(I+1) + S(I+2) + T(I+3)     ! Statement 4
```

To simplify the discussion, assume that all four statements are executed on the processor storing the array element on the left-hand side. (This is an optimal strategy for this example, although not for all programs.) Statements 1 and 2 each require one array element to be communicated for any value of I. Statement 3 requires no communication. All the references in Statement 4 are on different processors. There is no redundancy to be exploited in the first three statements. However, for Statement 4:

- Element R(I+1) needs communication, since it is not local and was not used earlier.
- Element S(I+2) needs communication, since Statement 3 overwrote the value communicated for Statement 1.
- Element T(I+3) *does not* need new communication, since it was used in Statement 2 and not changed since.

Thus, the minimum total communication in this program fragment is four array elements, rather than five as Section 2.3 suggests. □

Example 2.21 The reader may think that Example 2.20 was a lot of work for little gain. However, the same reasoning can be applied to aggregate operations with greater effect. Consider the following FORALL statement.

```
      REAL, DIMENSION(1000)         :: U, V, W
!HPF$ PROCESSORS, DIMENSION(10) :: PROCS(10)
!HPF$ DISTRIBUTE (BLOCK) ONTO PROCS :: U, V, W
      ...
      FORALL (K = 3:998)
         U(K) = (U(K-1)*W(K-1) + U(K)*W(K) + U(K+1)*W(K+1)) / 3.0
         V(K) = (W(K-2) + W(K-1) + W(K) + W(K+1) + W(K+2)) / 5.0
         W(K) = (U(K-1)+U(K)+U(K+1)) * (W(K-1)+W(K)+W(K+1)) / 9.0
      END FORALL
```

Here, the total communication per processor (except for PROCS(1) and PROCS(10)) is 8 elements:

- Two elements for W(K-1) and W(K+1), used in all the assignments.
- Two elements for U(K-1) and U(K+1), used in the assignment to U.

- Two elements for W(K-2) and U(K+2), used in the assignment to V.
- Two elements for U(K-1) and U(K+1), used in the assignment to W. (These cannot be reused from the assignment to U, because they were overwritten there.)

Values of W are not overwritten due to the definition of the **FORALL** statement. If each statement and each index value were treated separately, as in Section 2.5, then two values of the **FORALL** indices (the first and last on each processor) would produce 6 communicated elements each, and two other index values (next to the ends) would need 1 communicated element. The grand total would therefore be 14 elements; optimization has gained almost a factor of 2 in communication volume in this case. □

Example 2.22 To illustrate computation placement (or scheduling, as it is sometimes called), consider the following code.

```
      REAL, DIMENSION(100,100) :: X, Y, Z
!HPF$ DISTRIBUTE (BLOCK,*)     :: X, Y, Z
      ...
      X = TRANSPOSE(Y) + TRANSPOSE(Z) + X
```

A straightforward implementation would require two transposition (communication) operations, one for each of Y and Z. The communication pattern is similar to the **CYCLIC** to **BLOCK** conversion in Example 2.6. An optimizing compiler might algebraically rewrite this as:

```
      REAL, DIMENSION(100,100) :: X, Y, Z, T1
!HPF$ DISTRIBUTE (BLOCK,*)     :: X, Y, Z, T1
      ...
      T1 = Y + Z
      X = TRANSPOSE(T1) + X
```

with only one use of transposition, thus cutting the communication volume in half. □

Example 2.23 After all that minimization, it is almost embarrassing to note that sometimes it is better to send more data than is really needed. In Example 2.17, the cost of checking which data needed to be communicated might be more than the communication itself. In this case, a good compiler would communicate the entire contents of array C even though some of that data was not used due to the **IF**. □

Equation 2.4.1 also allows some tradeoffs to be made. An extreme example is completely eliminating communication by putting all the data on a single processor and executing the entire computation there. Of course, this eliminates all parallelism (not to mention that there may not be enough local memory on one processor). Unless the communication cost T_{comm} is very high, this is unlikely to be an advantage. There are, however, several more interesting tradeoffs that an implementation can make:

- Add communication to distribute parallel work among more processors. T_{comm} increases, but T_{par}/P_{active} decreases.
- Perform some parallel operations redundantly to avoid communication. T_{par}/P_{active} increases, but T_{comm} decreases.
- Partially parallelize the serial work, perhaps reducing the number of active processors. T_{serial} decreases, T_{par}/P_{active} increases.
- In practice, parallelizing serial work often means adding communication. The tradeoff may actually be T_{serial} decreases, T_{par}/P_{active} and T_{comm} increase.

Note that all of these tradeoffs can also be run in reverse—for example, restricting parallelism (creating coarser-grain parallelism) decreases T_{comm} and increases T_{par}/P_{active}. There are other tradeoffs one can attempt to make; we leave listing them as an exercise for the reader. When faced with options like this, the correct choice is always to think about the system(s) the code will be running on. All of the parameters in our equation are system-dependent, and whether some of the tradeoffs are legal depends on the algorithm.

Example 2.24 Choosing an intermediate storage location is sometimes more complex than Example 2.22 showed. Consider the following array assignment.

```
      REAL, DIMENSION(1000)     :: Q, R, S, T
      INTEGER, DIMENSION(1000)  :: IX
!HPF$ PROCESSORS, DIMENSION(10) :: PROCS
!HPF$ DISTRIBUTE (CYCLIC) ONTO PROCS :: Q, R, S, T, IX
      ...
      Q = R(IX) + S(IX) + T(IX)
```

and the following implementation strategies:

- Evaluate each element of the right-hand side on the processor where it will be stored. This strategy potentially requires fetching three values (the elements of R, S, and T) for each element computed. It always uses the maximum parallelism of the machine.
- Evaluate each element of the right-hand side on the processor where the corresponding elements of R(IX), S(IX), and T(IX) are stored. This potentially communicates one result for each element computed. If the values of IX are evenly distributed, then it also uses the maximum machine parallelism. But if IX(I)=1 for all I, then all the computation

is done on one processor. (Similarly, if `IX(I)=10*((I+9)/10)`, then `PROCS(10)` does all the work, even though `IX` contains many different values.)

On the basis of communication only, the second strategy is 3 times better. Considering parallelism as well, the picture is much cloudier. Minimizing the total cost is a very machine- and input-dependent problem. □

Example 2.25 Some algorithms have inherent, input-independent conflicts between computation and communication. For example, consider the code below.

```
      REAL, DIMENSION(6,6)     :: X, Y
!HPF$ PROCESSORS, DIMENSION(3) :: PROCS
!HPF$ DISTRIBUTE (*,BLOCK) ONTO PROCS :: X, Y
      ...
      DO I = 2, 6
         X(I, :) = X(I, :) - X(I-1, :)*Y(I, :)
      END DO
      DO J = 2, 6
         X(:, J) = X(:, J) - X(:, J-1)*Y(:, J)
      END DO
```

Figure 2.8 shows how data flows in this problem.

In the `DO I` loop, there is no conflict; the array assignments are perfectly parallel and there is no communication. The `DO J` loop also has a potential parallelism of `N` on each iteration. However, all elements of `X(:,J)` and `Y(:,J)` are located on the same processor. Therefore, exploitation of any of the potential parallelism will require scattering the data to other processors. (This is independent of the communication required for the reference to `X(:,J-1)`.) There are several implementation strategies available for the `DO J` loop:

1. Execute the vector operations in the `DO J` loop sequentially. Since each processor must wait for a vector of values from its neighbor, the entire loop runs serially. In terms of Equation 2.4.1, $T_{par} = T_{serial}$. This is the simplest possible strategy, but it means that the program will spend most of its time in sequential computation.

2. Transpose `X` and `Y` before the `DO J` loop, and transpose them again at the end. The `DO J` loop can then be executed exactly as the `DO I` loop—that is, in parallel without communication. This allows parallel updates of both the rows and columns of `X`, at the cost of two all-to-all communication operations. It corresponds to increasing T_{comm} and T_{par} in order to eliminate T_{serial}. This strategy works well if the target system has a fast transpose operation and enough memory to store the transposed arrays.

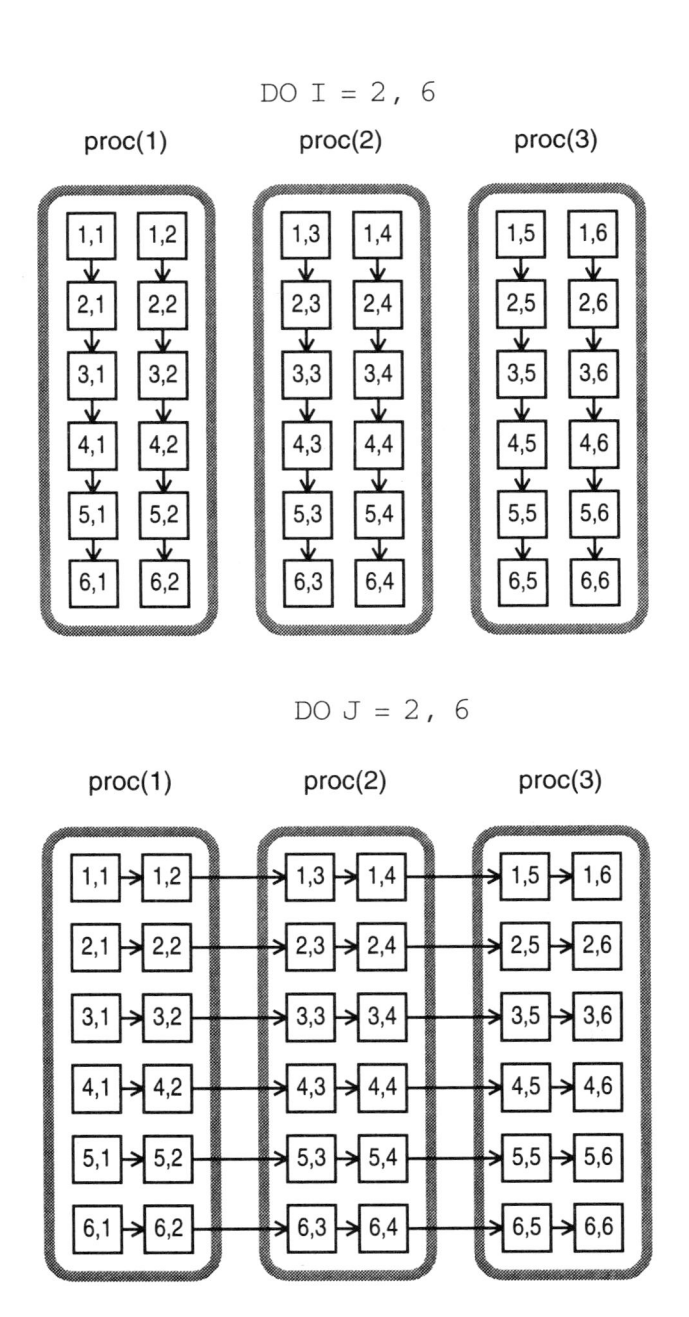

Figure 2.8
Data flow in Example 2.25

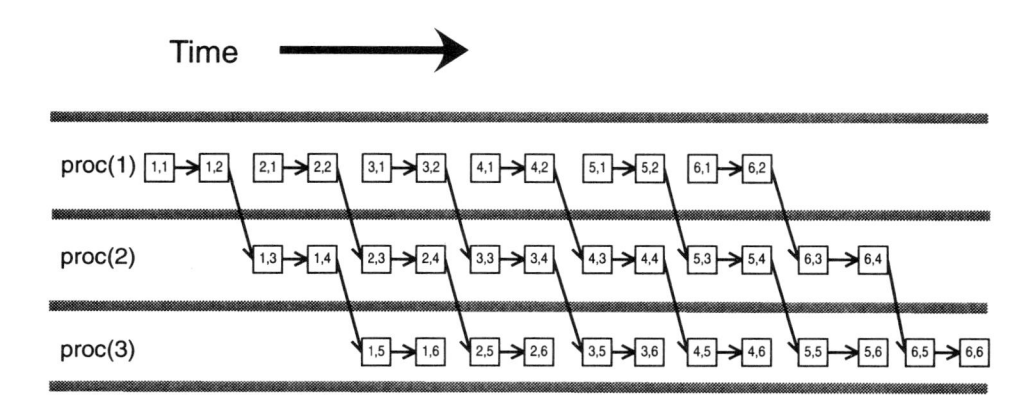

Figure 2.9
Pipelined execution for Example 2.25

3. Compute the results in row order on each processor, sending the last value to the next processor as soon as it is ready. This strategy can produce a pipelined effect, as shown in Figure 2.9. The communications volume is the same as method 1, but the data is sent in smaller packets. This allows some parallelism, but parts of the algorithm execute serially. In terms of our model, work has been moved from T_{serial} to T_{par}. This strategy works best if the target system can sustain fine-grain communication and synchronization.

4. A variant of the last method is for each processor to compute a few rows before communicating the results. The effect is much the same as in Figure 2.9, except that the pipeline startup is longer. However, on machines with a large communications startup time (for example, MIMD message-passing machines) this reduces the number of communication events, thus reducing overhead. In terms of our model, this reduces T_{comm} while increasing T_{par}/P_{active}. This is the strategy of choice for machines which cannot handle fine-grain communication.

This list is not exhaustive. It should be obvious that the optimal implementation of this algorithm depends very much on the target machine. It is also true that any of the above strategies could be implemented directly in HPF or could be incorporated into the compiler. □

In light of the tradeoffs described above, the reader may wonder what the "best" way to write HPF programs is. There is no single answer. In some situations, programmers are willing to invest extreme effort in tuning an application for a particular architecture; in other situations, the ability to run on a variety of different machines is paramount. The advice to the programmer for these environments would have to be quite different. We can, however, make some general observations:

- Programs will execute operations fastest if the dimension encapsulating the parallelism is distributed among processors.
- Programs will execute operations fastest if the work is evenly divided among processors; typically, this also implies that data should be evenly distributed.
- Programs will execute operations fastest if there are few (or no) elements communicated.

Many data parallel algorithms fit these criteria for a number of data distributions; Fox et al. [13] is full of such examples. Using such algorithms is highly recommended—they will be reasonably efficient everywhere. This efficiency can be enhanced by carefully matching the data mapping to a particular target machine. The particular mapping that produces the highest performance will sometimes vary from system to machine (although all machines should execute correctly with all distributions), so this process may be considered machine-dependent optimization. In cases where conflicts cannot be avoided, such as Example 2.25 (as written), the user may have to consider the characteristics of his or her target machine(s) in detail to decide the best strategy. We hope that vendors will eventually provide tools for such tasks, but as of this writing such tools are still immature.

3 Fortran 90

This Chapter summarizes the new features of Fortran 90, particularly those that have an impact on High Performance Fortran.

3.1 Fortran 90 Features

> *I don't know what the technical characteristics of the standard language for scientific and engineering computation in the year 2000 will be ... but I know it will be called Fortran.*
>
> remark attributed to John Backus

In addition to all of the FORTRAN 77 and Department of Defense standard language features, Fortran 90 provides significant new facilities some of which, such as array syntax, make it easier for a compiler to determine that operations may be carried out concurrently.

Ease-of use improvements provide capabilities to ease the writing of programs, enhance control over program execution, and facilitate data input and output.

Data facilities include an entity-oriented declaration syntax, user specification of numerical precision of data and additional numeric data types, user-defined arbitrary data structures, dynamically allocatable data, and pointer-based linked data structures.

Array features include array subsection notation, vector-valued subscripts, expressions, assignment, and masked assignment; array constructors; elemental, transformational, and inquiry array intrinsic functions; and array-valued user functions.

Modularization facilities allow the packaging of data and procedures; the definition and packaging of data abstractions including the definition of operators and assignment for defined types; procedure improvements such as optional and keyword arguments, recursion, and internal procedures; and compiler checking across compilation units.

A large number of *intrinsic procedures* provide built-in support for mathematical operations, especially the construction of, computation on, and transformation of arrays. In addition, there are procedures to inquire about numerical accuracy and bit manipulation procedures.

The concept of *language evolution*, under which old language features are identified as obsolescent and subject to possible removal in future standards, highlights the requirement for the use of modern programming practices and the choice of a modern coding style.

3.2 Ease-of-Use Improvements

Ease-of use improvements provide capabilities to ease the writing of programs, enhance control over program execution, and facilitate data input and output.

3.2.1 Ease of Writing

Fortran 90 provides three capabilities to ease the writing of programs:

- Names can be up to 31 characters long, a significant improvement over the old limit of 6.
- An expanded character set includes lower-case letters and the underscore character for use in names, and the forms ==, /=, <, >, <=, and >= for the relational operators .EQ., .NE., .LT., .GT., .GE., and .LE.
- A new free source form removes the column dependences of the old fixed source form and adds conveniences such as the use of significant blanks, "!"-delimited comments which may end a line, and ";"-separated statements on a single line.

3.2.2 Ease of Program Control

Control of program execution is enhanced by several new constructs:

- Named **IF**, **CASE**, and **DO** constructs allowing named matching of construct parts and eliminating requirements for statement numbers. An example is:

```
CHECK_IT: IF (.NOT. DONE) THEN
             ...
          ELSE IF (.NOT. HOME) THEN CHECK_IT
             ...
          ELSE CHECK_IT
             ...
          END IF CHECK_IT
```

- New **DO** statement capabilities including **DO** for infinite loops (with loop termination programmed in the loop body); **END DO** to match **DO** without statement numbers; **DO WHILE** some condition is true; **CYCLE** to the next iteration of a loop; and **EXIT** from a nest of loops. For example:

```
FOREVER: DO
            DO WHILE (I .NE. 10)
INNER:         DO I = 1, N
                  IF ( ... ) THEN CYCLE INNER
```

Fortran 90

```
            ...
            IF ( ... ) THEN EXIT FOREVER
            ...
          END DO INNER
        END DO
      END DO FOREVER
```

- A **CASE** construct that allows selection from a number of alternatives based on the value of an expression. (You can almost think of an **IF** construct as merely a two-way logical case construct.) Case alternatives may be selected for a single value or for a range of values, as in:

```
      SELECT CASE (I)
        CASE (:-1)            ! For values of I < 0
          J = -1
        CASE (0)              ! For I = 0
          J = 0
        CASE (1:5)            ! For values of I = 1, 2, 3, 4, or 5
          J = 2 * I - 1
        CASE DEFAULT          ! Or CASE (6:) for values of I > 5
          J = 10
      END SELECT
```

3.2.3 Enhanced Input and Output

Input/output capabilities are enhanced in four areas:

- *Non-advancing input/output*, sometimes called *partial record* or *stream I/O*, allows character-oriented I/O in addition to the traditional Fortran record-oriented I/O.
- *Namelist input/output*, the ability to do I/O on a named group of data objects, has been a *de facto* standard facility in Fortran implementations and now has been officially standardized.
- New I/O *edit descriptors* support binary, octal, hexadecimal, engineering, and scientific notations.
- Several new specifiers extend the operations of the **INQUIRE**, **OPEN**, **READ**, and **WRITE** statements.

3.3 Data Facilities

3.3.1 Intrinsic Data Types

Fortran 90, like its predecessors, provides six *intrinsic data types*: `INTEGER`, `REAL`, `DOUBLE PRECISION`, `COMPLEX`, `CHARACTER`, and `LOGICAL`. It gives the programmer greater choice in the characteristics of these data types, however.

Processors may provide more than one representation for a data type. (For example, Digital Equipment Corporation's Fortran compilers for the Alpha microprocessor directly support 1, 2, 4, and 8 byte integers and 2, 4, and 8 byte floating point numbers.) The `KIND` facility provides for the parameterization of the intrinsic types, except for `DOUBLE PRECISION`, providing data types with user-specified precision and range[1]. This allows specification of, for example, short and long integers, more than two precisions for real and complex, additional large character sets (as used in some foreign languages), and both packed and unpacked logicals. Some examples are:

```
REAL(SELECTED_REAL_KIND(8,70)) :: A    ! Precision of 8 digits,
                                       ! range of -10**70 to 10**70
INTEGER, PARAMETER   :: SHORT = SELECTED_INT_KIND (4)
INTEGER(KIND=SHORT)  :: K = 2345_SHORT ! Must allow -9999 to 9999
REAL(KIND(0.0D0))    :: R              ! Same as DOUBLE PRECISION
COMPLEX(KIND(0.0D0)) :: C              ! Same as DOUBLE COMPLEX,
                                       ! which is not in Fortran 90
                                       ! (or FORTRAN 77)
CHARACTER(KIND=KANJI), PARAMETER :: ORIENTAL = KANJI_'...'
```

Numeric inquiry intrinsic functions such as `MAXEXPONENT` return information about the actual representations of types and kinds of numbers while a program is running.

3.3.2 Structured Data Types

In addition to the capabilities of intrinsic data types, some programs need to define and use arbitrary structures of data. Fortran 90 provides two extension mechanisms to do this: *arrays* (described in Section 3.4) and *derived types*, sometimes called *user-defined types* (described in Section 3.5). An *array* is a collection of objects of the same type which are identified by their position within the array. Arrays have been a mainstay

---

[1] Most FORTRAN 77 compilers provide a similar capability through a *de facto* industry-standard extension, the * notation for data typing as in `INTEGER*1`, `INTEGER*2`, `INTEGER*4`, `INTEGER*8`, `REAL*2`, `REAL*4`, `REAL*8`, and `DOUBLE COMPLEX`. The "*" notation, however, specifies the number of bytes in the representation rather than the precision and range desired. Some processors support multiple floating point representations of the same size.

of Fortran since its earliest implementations, but Fortran 90 significantly expands their set of supporting operations. A derived type, or *structure*,[2] is a collection of objects of (possibly) different types which are identified by their name within the structure. Derived types provide the ability to use structured data and, together with modules, the ability to define abstract data types (see Section 3.7.3).

3.3.3 Entity-Oriented Declarations and Allocatable Arrays

Fortran 90 allows declarations organized either by attribute, as in FORTRAN 77, or by entity, as in the declarations of **SHORT** and **K** above. The entity form allows the programmer to group the type, attributes, and optional initialization value of an entity into a single statement. As the example showed, one of the attributes may be **PARAMETER**, meaning that the entity is a named constant of the specified type and value. Other attributes, such as **DIMENSION** and **SAVE** can be specified similarly.

Often an array serves as a kind of working storage, and should take up space only when required. Three ways of accomplishing this are *automatic arrays*, *allocatable arrays*, and *pointers* to arrays.

Within a procedure, the extents in each dimension of an array are determined when control enters the procedure. Storage for the array is then allocated, and freed when control leaves the procedure. As a consequence, an array can be declared to be the same size as a dummy argument, as in:

```
SUBROUTINE ARRAY_SWAP(X, Y)
  REAL, DIMENSION (:), INTENT(INOUT) :: X, Y
  REAL, DIMENSION (SIZE(X))          :: Z
  Z = X
  X = Y
  Y = Z
END SUBROUTINE ARRAY_SWAP
```

Dynamic storage allocation of arrays is available via the mechanism of **ALLOCATABLE** arrays. The declaration:

```
REAL, DIMENSION(:,:), ALLOCATABLE :: A
```

declares **A** to be a two-dimensional array for which storage has not yet been allocated. Given this, the executable statement

```
ALLOCATE (A(2*N, 2*N+1))
```

---

[2] Some programming languages use the term "record" to refer to what Fortran 90 means by "structure." In Fortran 90, a *record* is one of the elements of a file subject to input/output operations.

calculates the values 2*N and 2*N+1 and allocates appropriate storage for A. This storage continues to exist until a DEALLOCATE A statement is reached (or until flow of control leaves the scope of the declaration of A). The ALLOCATED intrinsic can test whether or not A is *currently allocated*.

Pointers are discussed in Section 3.6.

3.4 Array Features

Fortran 90 contains features to allow operations on entire arrays without explicit DO loops: a programmer can now say A = B + C to add two arrays together and store them into a third array. These features were introduced because many scientists have found them to be a natural and readable way of expressing algorithms. In addition, they have proven to have efficient implementations on a variety of computer architectures. We expect that these facilities will make Fortran 90 the programming language of choice for scientific and engineering numerical calculations on high performance computers. Their value has already been proven in a number of compiler products. The introductory overview in the Fortran 90 standard [17] states:

> *Operations for processing whole arrays and subarrays (array sections) are included in Fortran 90 for two principal reasons: (1) these features provide a more concise and higher level language that will allow programmers more quickly and reliably to develop and maintain scientific/engineering applications, and (2) these features can significantly facilitate optimization of array operations on many computer architectures.*

3.4.1 Array Overview

Although the semantics of Fortran 90 are defined without reference to a particular underlying machine model, efficient execution can be realized on a variety of parallel machines. This is true despite the fact that Fortran 90 programs can be viewed as providing a global name space and a single thread of control Consider the following Fortran 90 declarations:

```
REAL :: S                    ! A scalar floating point variable
REAL, DIMENSION (N) :: A, B  ! Two N element arrays
INTEGER :: I, J              ! Two scalar integer variables
INTEGER, DIMENSION (N) :: P  ! An integer index array
```

Fortran 90 provides for element-by-element operations on entire arrays, where the particular order of evaluation is not specified by the language. The semantics of Fortran 90 allows these statements to be executed in parallel. The following *array assignment* statement multiplies each element of B by itself, adds that value to the square root of the corresponding element of A, and replaces the corresponding element of A with the new value:

```
A = SQRT(A) + B**2
```

The following statement performs a *masked array assignment* in which each value of A is replaced by that value divided by the corresponding value of B except in those cases where the value of B is 0:

```
WHERE (B /= 0) A = A/B
```

A number of Fortran 90 statements imply communication in a distributed memory implementation. Examples include broadcast, when a scalar is assigned to an array:

```
A = S/2
```

permutation, when array section notation, index vectors, or some array intrinsics are used:

```
A(I:J) = B(J:I:-1)
A(P) = B                 ! A(P(i)) = B(i), forall i = 1:N
A = CSHIFT(A, 1)         ! Circular shift left of A
```

and reduction, such as summing all of the elements of an array:

```
S = SUM(B)
```

As the last two examples hint, there are also a number of intrinsic functions for dealing with arrays; these are listed in Tables 3.1 through 3.6.

3.4.2 Array Concepts and Terminology

Consider the following declarations:

```
REAL, DIMENSION(10, 5:24, -5:M) :: A
REAL, DIMENSION(0:9, 20, M+6)   :: B
```

The *rank* of A is 3, the *shape* of A is (/10, 20, (M+6)/), the *extent* of dimension 2 of A is 20, and the *size* of A is 10 * 20 * (M+6). Arrays can be zero-sized if the extent of any dimension is zero. The rank must be fixed when the program is written, but the extents in any dimension, the lower bounds, upper bounds, and strides, do not have to be fixed until the array comes into existence. We saw examples of this in the previous section. Two arrays are *conformable* if they have the same shape, that is, the same rank and the same extents in corresponding dimensions; A and B are conformable. An arbitrary array and a scalar are said to conform; the scalar is treated as if it were a conforming array each of whose elements had the scalar as its value. An *elemental operation elemental intrinsic* is an operation defined on scalars producing a scalar result, that has the property that, when it is applied to conformable arrays, it operates on corresponding elements of the arrays and produces a conformable array result.

3.4.3 Whole Array Operations and Assignment

An array, strictly speaking, is not a type; rather DIMENSION is an attribute that may be applied in the declaration of objects of any type, intrinsic or user-defined. Thus, Fortran 90 has no concept of "arrays of arrays," although, of course, it does have multi-dimensional arrays. The usual intrinsic arithmetic, comparison, and logical operations for scalars of that type, as well as assignment, are elemental, and may be applied element-by-element to arrays. Thus:

```
A = 2.5*A + B + 2.0
```

replaces each element of A by its value multiplied by 2.5 and added to the corresponding element of B, plus 2. Thus, this particular assignment statement is equivalent to the triply nested set of loops (assuming the array bounds in Section 3.4.2):

```
DO i = 1, 10
  DO J = 5, 24
    DO K = -5, M
      A(I,J,K) = 2.5*A(I,J,K) + B(I-1,J-4,K+6) + 2.0
    END DO
  END DO
END DO
```

except that the program does not restrict the order in which the elements as updated.

3.4.4 Array Subsections

Fortran 90 provides the ability to access *elements* of an array and parts, or *sections*, of arrays using *subscript triplet notation*. If an array is declared:

```
REAL, DIMENSION(100, 100) :: A
```

the array element references A(1,1), A(100,1), A(1,100), and A(100,100) reference the four corners of A while the array sections A(1,:), A(100,:), A(:,1), and A(:,100) reference the first and last rows and the first and last columns of A. The array section

A(2:99, 2:99) references the interior of A. Elements of an array section need not be contiguous. For example, A(1,1:100:2) references the odd elements of the first row of A and A(1:100:99,1:100:99) is a 2 by 2 array section that references all four corners.

Array element references behave just the same in expressions as do scalar references, while array sections behave as do arrays. For example, A(1,:) is a rank-one array with 100 elements while A(2:99, 2:99) is a rank-two 98 by 98 element array. Syntactically, however, the only references allowed are to an element or a section of a named array. To reference an element of a section, for example, the section must first be assigned to an array temporary.

A program can pass an array element or an array section (including a whole array) as an actual argument to a procedure. In general, the dummy argument must have the same type, kind, and rank as the actual argument. To use certain features the programmer must provide an *explicit interface* to the caller so the compiler can check for correctness and provide appropriate linkage conventions. Fortran 90 also supports an old style of argument passage by sequence association in which an array element is passed by reference to the procedure and can be used as either a scalar or the first element of a sequence, such as a column, to the procedure. This form of argument passage puts significant limits on both what can be expressed[3] and the execution performance of the program on more advanced computers with distributed rather than linear memories. We strongly recommend using the modern form of argument passing in all cases.

3.4.5 Expressions

Fortran 90 interpretation rules for expressions and assignment require freedom from side effects, allow short-circuit evaluation, require the entire right-hand side of an assignment to be evaluated before the left-hand side is modified, and prohibit attempts to do multiple updates to a left-hand side. The following are some statements from the standard [17]:

- *The evaluation of a function reference must neither affect nor be affected by the evaluation of any other entity within the statement.* [7.1.7]

- *It is not necessary for the processor to evaluate all the operands of an expression if the value of the expression can be determined otherwise.* [7.1.7.1]

- *Execution of an intrinsic assignment causes, in effect, the evaluation of the expression [on the right-hand side] and all expressions within [the left-hand side], the possible conversion of [the right-hand side] to the type and type parameters of [the left-hand side] and the definition of [the left-hand side] with the resulting value.* [7.5.1.5]

---

[3] A program can pass a column this way, but not a row or more complex section.

> • *When [the left-hand side] in an intrinsic assignment is an array, the assignment is performed element-by-element ... The processor may perform the element-by-element assignment in any order. [7.5.1.5] A many-one array section is an array section with a vector subscript having two or more elements with the same value. A many-one array section must not appear on the left of the equals in an assignment statement or as an input item in a READ statement. [6.2.2.3.2]*

(We note in passing that similar restrictions also appeared in older Fortran standards, but many programmers are unaware of them.)

For example, since the entire right hand side is evaluated before the left hand side is updated, the assignment statement:

```
V(LB:UB) = V(LB-1:UB-1)
```

has a meaning equivalent to

```
DO I = LB, UB
  temp(I) = V(I-1)
END DO
DO I = LB, UB
  V(I) = temp(I)
END DO
```

This, of course, is inefficient in both space and time. The "obvious" naive scalarization:

```
! *** WRONG!!!  Produces incorrect answer!!! ****
DO I = LB, UB
  V(I) = V(I-1)
END DO
```

is incorrect. It takes a rather sophisticated compiler analysis to determine a correct, efficient scalarization, running the loop backwards:

```
DO I = UB, LB, -1
  V(I) = V(I-1)
END DO
```

Other array expressions require even more complex translations to scalar code.

3.4.6 Vector-Valued Subscripts

Vector-valued subscripts provide a more general way to form an array section that does the subscript triplet notation. An index vector can index an array along a particular dimension; the elements of this index vector select the elements of the indexed array to be in the subsection. In an expression, these selected elements may be arbitrary and involve duplication. If a vector-valued subscript is used on the left-hand side of an assignment, however, it may not have duplicate values. Since Fortran 90 does not specify an order for update in an assignment, if duplicates were allowed the resulting value would depend on the order chosen. Be careful; in general a compiler will probably not check for duplicates because of the performance cost in doing so. For example:

```
INTEGER, DIMENSION(6) :: A = (/ 10, 20, 30, 40, 50, 60 /)
INTEGER, DIMENSION(3) :: B
INTEGER, DIMENSION(3) :: ODD_LOCATIONS = (/ (I, I=1:6:2) /)
INTEGER, DIMENSION(3) :: GENERAL_LOCATIONS = (/ 4, 2, 4 /)
...
B = A(ODD_LOCATIONS)       ! B == (/ 10, 30, 50 /)
A(ODD_LOCATIONS) = 15      ! A == (/ 15, 20, 15, 40, 15, 60 /)
B = A(GENERAL_LOCATIONS)   ! B == (/ 40, 20, 40 /)
A(GENERAL_LOCATIONS) = 25  ! *** Not Fortran 90-conforming!!!
                           ! Trying to update A(4) twice
```

3.4.7 Array Constructors

An *array constructor* provides a way to write a sequence of scalar values of the same type to be interpreted as a rank-one array. A component of an array constructor may be either an expression or an *implied DO*. If an expression has an array value, it is treated as a sequence of elements in *array sequence order*, with the first subscript position varying the fastest. An implied DO allows generation of a set of values by iteration. Since an array constructor is of rank one, the **RESHAPE** intrinsic can be used function to construct arrays of higher rank. If an array constructor is "simple enough"[4] it can be an initial value for an array in a declaration.

```
... (/ 1, 2, 3, M, N+2, F(X) /) ! Size is 6
... (/ B /)                     ! Elements of B in element order
... (/ Q, A(I:J:K), 3.0/)       ! Size is ((J-I)/K + 1) + 2
... (/ (I, I = 1, N, 2) /)      ! Odd numbers <= N
```

---

[4] In general, an *initialization expression* must have every subexpression be a constant, reference only certain intrinsic functions that can be evaluated at compile-time, and obey a few other restrictions.

```
... RESHAPE(SOURCE=(/ (1, (0, I=1, N), J=1, N-1), 1 /),    &
    SHAPE =(/ N, N /))   ! Identity matrix
... (/ ((FUN(I), I = 1, F()), J, J = 1, UB) /)
            ! Size can only be computed by calling F() UB times.
            ! Values of FUN(I) must computed at the same time.
```

3.4.8 Masked Array Assignments

A *masked array assignment* is an array assignment occurring in a **WHERE** statement or construct in which assignment occurs only to elements selected by the true elements of a logical array expression. In each such masked assignment statement, the mask expression, the variable being assigned to, and the right-hand-side expression must be conformable, and the assignment must be intrinsic and not defined. For example, in

```
INTEGER, DIMENSION(5) :: A = (/ 0, 1, 1, 1, 0 /)
INTEGER, DIMENSION(5) :: B = (/ 10, 11, 12, 13, 14 /)
INTEGER, DIMENSION(5) :: C = -1

WHERE (A .NE. 0) C = B / A
```

the resulting value of C will be (/ -1, 11, 12, 13, -1 /).

In a **WHERE** construct the mask expression is evaluated once and, effectively, its values are saved. Every assignment statement following the **WHERE** is executed as if it were

WHERE (*mask-expression-values*)   *assignment-statement*

and every assignment statement following the **ELSEWHERE** is executed as if it were

WHERE (.NOT. *mask-expression-values*)   *assignment-statement*

This is important to remember if the statements have side effects or modify each other or the mask expression. In this example of the **WHERE** construct:

```
REAL, DIMENSION(1000) :: PRESSURE, TEMP, PRECIPITATION
WHERE (PRESSURE .GE. 1.0)
  PRESSURE = PRESSURE + 1.0
  TEMP = TEMP - 10.0
ELSEWHERE
  PRECIPITATION = .TRUE.
END WHERE
```

the assignment to **PRESSURE** does not change the value of the mask as used in the other assignment statements in the **WHERE** construct.

The mask is applied to the actual arguments of a function reference on the right-hand-side of the masked array assignment only if the function is an elemental intrinsic function. Otherwise the function's actual arguments are not masked by the mask expression. For example, since **LOG** is an elemental intrinsic function, in:

```
WHERE (A .GT. 0)  B = LOG(A)
```

the mask is applied to **A** and **LOG** is executed only for the positive values of **A**. The result is assigned to those elements of **B** for which the mask is true.

In the following example, since **SUM** is a transformational intrinsic and not an elemental, it is evaluated fully for all values of **A**. The assignment only happens for those elements of **B** that are greater than 0:

```
REAL, DIMENSION(10,10) :: A
REAL, DIMENSION(10)    :: B
WHERE (B > 0.0)  B = SUM(A, DIM=1)
```

In this example:

```
REAL, DIMENSION(10,10) :: A
REAL, DIMENSION(10)    :: B, C
WHERE (C .GT. 0.0) B = SUM(LOG(A), DIM=1) / C
```

since **SUM** is not elemental, all of its arguments are evaluated fully regardless of whether they are elemental or not. Thus **LOG(A)** is fully evaluated for all elements of **A** even though **LOG** is elemental. Notice that the mask is applied to the result of the **SUM** and to **C** to determine the right-hand-side. One way of thinking about this is that everything inside the argument list of a non-elemental function does not use the mask, everything outside does.

3.4.9 Array-Valued Functions with Array-Valued Arguments

Section 3.8 describes Fortran 90's large set of intrinsic functions, most of which can take array arguments and return array results. In addition to these, user-defined subroutines and functions can take array arguments where appropriate and, in the case of functions, return array results. A program can only select an element or take a section of a named array, so to select an element or take a section of a function result it must first be stored in a temporary variable.

3.4.10 Array Objects and Their Specifications

Arrays may be specified in four different ways:

• An *explicit-shape array* is an array that is declared with explicit values for the bounds in each array dimension. An *automatic array* is an explicit-shape array declared in a procedure; its bounds do not have to be constant and their values are determined at procedure entry. An explicit-shape array dummy whose size is determined by arguments passed into the procedure is referred to as an *adjustable array*. Adjustable arrays depend on the linear memory assumptions of sequence association; their function is better performed by assumed-shape arrays.

• An *assumed-shape array* is a non-pointer dummy array whose shape is taken from its associated actual array. The array inquiry intrinsic functions apply to an assumed-shape array; this frees the programmer from the old-style Fortran practice of having to pass array bounds information as extra arguments along with the array itself.

• A *deferred-shape array* must be specified with its rank, and has two forms: an *allocatable array* and an *array pointer*. A deferred-shape array assumes its shape when space is allocated for it in an **ALLOCATE** statement or, in the case of an array pointer, when it is associated with a target by pointer assignment.

• An *assumed-size array* is a dummy array argument whose size is assumed from its associated actual. Its rank and extents may differ, from its actual, only its size is assumed, and only in the last dimension. This is an old form that depends on the linear memory assumptions of sequence association.

Some annotated examples follow:

```
REAL FUNCTION F(M, N, W, X, Y, Z)

    INTEGER                      :: M, N
    REAL, DIMENSION(10, 10)      :: W ! Explicit shape
    REAL, DIMENSION(M, N)        :: X ! Explicit shape adjustable
    REAL, DIMENSION(:, 2:)       :: Y ! Assumed shape
    REAL, DIMENSION(N, *)        :: Z ! Assumed size

    REAL, DIMENSION(10, 10)      :: A ! Explicit shape
    REAL, DIMENSION(M, N)        :: B ! Explicit shape, automatic
    REAL, DIMENSION(SIZE(W, 1))  :: C ! Explicit shape, automatic
    REAL, DIMENSION(:), ALLOCATABLE :: D
                                 ! Deferred-shape allocatable
    REAL, DIMENSION(:, :), POINTER :: P ! Deferred-shape pointer
```

3.5 User-Defined Data Types

A *derived type* is defined in a *derived type definition* in which the named components may themselves be of any type, including other derived types or arrays. A variable (structure) of that type is declared in a *type declaration statement*. Of course, a variable can be an array of objects of derived type; indeed, a variable of derived type can have any attribute (such as **PARAMETER** or **INTENT**) that a variable of intrinsic type can have. The following example defines a derived type **PERSON** consisting of three components **NAME**, **AGE**, and **IS_FEMALE**, each of different type, declares a parameter **ANN** of type **PERSON** with an initial value given by a *structure constructor*, and an array called **EMPLOYEE** of 10 elements, each of type **PERSON**:

```
TYPE PERSON
  CHARACTER(LEN = 10) :: NAME
  INTEGER             :: AGE
  LOGICAL             :: IS_FEMALE
END TYPE PERSON

TYPE(PERSON), PARAMETER    :: ANN = PERSON("ANN", 35, .TRUE.)
TYPE(PERSON), DIMENSION(10) :: EMPLOYEE
```

Objects of derived types act like "ordinary" variables with "ordinary" values; they are first-class citizens of Fortran 90. Assignment for objects of the same derived type is defined intrinsically to be an order unspecified, component-by-component assignment. No other operations are defined intrinsically for objects of derived type. The *user-defined operator* and *user-defined assignment* mechanisms may be used, especially in conjunction with modules, to provide abstract data types. Structure constructors may be used to create structures, and a component of a structure may be accessed by use of the % notation, as in the following continuation of the above example:

```
INTERFACE OPERATOR (==)
  LOGICAL FUNCTION EMPLOYEE_EQUAL_TEST(E1, E2)
    TYPE(PERSON), INTENT(IN) :: E1
    TYPE(PERSON), INTENT(IN) :: E2
  END FUNCTION EMPLOYEE_EQUAL_TEST
END INTERFACE

INTEGER                      :: SUM, N
```

```
      EMPLOYEE(1) = PERSON ("EUNICE", 25, .TRUE.)
      EMPLOYEE(2) = PERSON ("OSCAR", 42, .FALSE.)
      EMPLOYEE(3) = ANN
      ...
      SUM = 0
      N = 0
      DO I = 1, 10
        IF (.NOT. (EMPLOYEE(I) == ANN) THEN
          PRINT *, I, EMPLOYEE(I)
          N = N + 1
          SUM = SUM + EMPLOYEE(I)%AGE
        END IF
      END DO
      PRINT *, "AVERAGE AGE OF ", N, "EMPLOYEES IS ", SUM/N
```

With an appropriate definition of **EMPLOYEE_EQUAL_TEST** to compare two objects of type **PERSON** for equality, this example would calculate the average age of all employees who are not equivalent to **ANN**.

In general, there is no order in memory implied by the order of the components in a derived type definition. Thus, a compiler is free to reorder the components (consistently of course) in order to achieve a better packing of data. If the program must have the components in a structure allocated according to the Fortran rules for sequence association, for example to be able to pass a structure consistently to a non-Fortran 90 procedure, it must specify the **SEQUENCE** property in the derived type definition. This allows use of the old-style Fortran memory tricks such as array reshaping and **EQUIVALENCE** on the new derived types. We recommend that you avoid the use of the **SEQUENCE** property by using a module to make the derived type definition visible to caller and callee. The resulting code will be easier to maintain, and may even be faster on some machines.

As we have seen, the Fortran 90 array facilities allow a number of array section references. These extend to arrays of structures, and subarrays of structure components. For example:

```
      TYPE STRUCT
        REAL                :: SCALAR_COMPONENT
        REAL, DIMENSION(20) :: ARRAY_COMPONENT
      END TYPE STRUCT
      TYPE (STRUCT), DIMENSION(10) :: ARRAY_OF_STRUCTS
      ...
      ARRAY_OF_STRUCTS(I)%ARRAY_COMPONENT(J:K) = ...
```

assigns to "elements J through K of the **ARRAY_COMPONENT** of the Ith element of **ARRAY_-OF_STRUCTS**." A program can also access "the **SCALAR_COMPONENT** parts of the J through K elements of **ARRAY_OF_STRUCTS**" or even "the Ith elements of the **ARRAY_COMPONENT** parts of the J through K elements of **ARRAY_OF_STRUCTS**:"

```
... ARRAY_OF_STRUCTS(J:K)%SCALAR_COMPONENT
... ARRAY_OF_STRUCTS(J:K)%ARRAY_COMPONENT(I)
```

Both may be used in any context that any other array section can be used. The limitation on such sectioning is that in a reference of the form **A%B%C**... only one of the components may have a rank greater than 0. Thus, the following is *not* Fortran 90 conforming:

```
ARRAY_OF_STRUCTS(I:J)%ARRAY_COMPONENT(K:L)  ! *** Nonconforming!!!
```

3.6 Pointers

Fortran 90 provides a concept of pointers but **be careful**, your intuition about pointers, derived from vendor-specific extensions to FORTRAN 77[5] or from other languages, is liable to be incorrect. In Fortran 90 a *pointer* is an *alias*, or another name which can refer to an object and is not a unique type of object itself. Thus, **POINTER** does not indicate a data type, but rather is an attribute of an object such as an array, an arbitrary scalar variable, or a structure. In addition, a pointer may alias a row, column, or more complex slice of an array, or a component of a structure.

No storage is allocated for an object declared with the attribute **POINTER**. Thus, the program may not reference it until some object is *pointer associated* with it by use of an **ALLOCATE** statement or *pointer assignment*. The **ASSOCIATED** intrinsic function checks whether a pointer is associated with a particular target, or with any target.

Anything that can be done with allocatable arrays can be done with pointers. The earlier example of an allocatable array could have been done as:

```
REAL, DIMENSION(:,:), POINTER :: A
...
ALLOCATE (A(2*N, 2*N+1))
```

---

[5] Many vendors such as Cray, Digital, Sun Microsystems, and others provide an extension to their FORTRAN 77 implementations known as *Cray pointers*. The meaning of Cray pointers is dependent on the FORTRAN 77 concepts of sequence and storage association and the implementation assumption of a linear memory address space. In effect, a Cray pointer is a memory address, on which address arithmetic may be performed. This feature, with its implementation assumptions, is difficult to optimize and difficult to implement on distributed memory hardware architectures. The Fortran 90 pointer concept provides many of the capabilities of Cray pointers, but with a different syntax and an architecture-independent semantics.

Allocatable arrays are most appropriate in the simple situation where all that is really required is control over storage allocation. An allocatable array has only one "name" or alias, aiding compiler optimization, whereas an array that is pointed to can have multiple aliases at the same time. This situation can occur by means of pointer assignment. Continuing the previous example, suppose the program also declared:

```
REAL, DIMENSION(:,:), POINTER :: B
```

and, after the **ALLOCATE** statement, contained:

```
B => A
```

This pointer assignment statement (notice the use of "=>" instead of "=") causes B to be an alias for (point to) A. As a result, an assignment to B(I,J) will change the value referenced by A(I, J) and vice versa. Pointer assignment can be used to have the effect of assignment without the copying of data.

When a pointer is used outside of pointer assignment, it refers to the object that it points to. Continuing the last example:

```
ALLOCATE (B(2*N, 2*N+1))
B = A
```

makes B an alias for an anonymous array and copies the values of the array A into it. Since A and B are now aliases for two different arrays, an assignment to B(I,J) will not change the value referenced by A(I,J).

The allocated storage stays associated with B until either execution control leaves the scope of the declaration of B or until it is explicitly deallocated through the use of a **DEALLOCATE** statement. Storage that is not accessible by some name in the program is said to be *inaccessible*. Since Fortran 90 does not require a compiler to reclaim inaccessible storage, the programmer must ensure that all allocated storage is explicitly deallocated, or risk running out of memory.

A declared data object that will be the *target* of a pointer must have the **TARGET** attribute in its declaration. The **TARGET** attribute allows the compiler to know what may be and what cannot be aliased, helping optimization. You should only give a data object the **TARGET** attribute if you are going to alias it with a pointer.

Consider the following example (derived from examples in the *Fortran 90 Handbook*):

```
REAL, DIMENSION(100, 100), TARGET :: A
REAL, DIMENSION(:, :), POINTER    :: CORNERS
REAL, DIMENSION(:, :), POINTER    :: INTERIOR
REAL, DIMENSION(:, :), POINTER    :: ODD_COLUMNS
```

```
REAL, DIMENSION(:), POINTER      :: ARBITRARY_ROW
REAL, POINTER                    :: ELEMENT_POINTER
...
CORNERS => A(1:100:99, 1:100:99)
INTERIOR => A(2:99, 2:99)
ODD_COLUMNS => A(:, 1:100:2)
ARBITRARY_ROW => A(I, :)
ELEMENT_POINTER => ARBITRARY_ROW(J)
```

The variable names accurately describe the sections of **A** that the pointers alias. The pointers can now be used to operate on the targeted elements. For example, the following doubles the elements in the row aliased by **ARBITRARY_ROW**:

```
ARBITRARY_ROW = 2 * ARBITRARY_ROW
```

Pointers can also alias any other array section described by array section notation. They can dynamically change their targets at runtime, but unfortunately cannot be initialized when they are declared.

The previous examples showed the use of pointers to alias parts of existing arrays. A more typical use is to control storage allocation and to construct dynamic data structures such as trees or linked lists, as in the following example:

```
TYPE NODE
   INTEGER              :: VALUE
   TYPE(NODE), POINTER  :: NEXT
END TYPE NODE

TYPE(NODE), POINTER :: P, LIST
TYPE(NODE), TARGET  :: FIRSTNODE

!Start with empty list
NULLIFY (FIRSTNODE%NEXT)
LIST => FIRSTNODE
...
! Prepend (append) to list
ALLOCATE (P)
P%VALUE = N
P%NEXT => LIST    ! If append:  LIST%NEXT => P
LIST => P
```

```
! List walk
P => FIRSTNODE
DO WHILE (ASSOCIATED(P))
  PRINT *, P%VALUE
  P => P%NEXT
END DO
```

Note the use of the **NULLIFY** statement to make a pointer point to nothing. Since pointers are not data types, there is no "value" to "assign" to a pointer to do this. Since functions can return pointers, the types and operations above could be packaged in a module for use as an abstract data type.

3.7 Modularization

3.7.1 The Structure of a Fortran Program

Fortran allows the top-down functional decomposition of a program by partitioning it into *program units*: a *main program* and some number of *external, independently compiled* functions and subroutines. An *explicit interface* to a procedure, which may be provided by an *interface block* for an external procedure, allows a high quality compiler to provide better checking and optimization of procedure calls.

Module program units can be used to structure the bottom-up development of a program as libraries of commonly used procedures, encapsulated derived data types and their defined operators and assignment, and packages of related global data definitions:

• Using a module containing multiple module procedures provides a Fortran 90 library mechanism.

• Using a module containing multiple interface blocks provides an interface to a pre-existing library, possibly coded in a language other than Fortran.

• Using a module to provide a set of procedures accessing private data (data global to them but invisible to others) eliminates the need to use procedures with *multiple entry points* for the same purpose.

• Using a module to define a collection of optionally initialized data entities eliminates the need to use *common blocks*, include lines, and *block data program units* for the same purpose. It also avoids the need to maintain consistency of declarations across multiple files, a well-known source of bugs using the older techniques.

Modules provide an effective method for defining in one place and controlling access to global data, global procedures, and encapsulated data abstractions.

3.7.2 Procedures

There are two forms of procedures, *subroutines* and *functions*. These are quite similar except that a subroutine is invoked in a `CALL` statement and does not return a value while a function is invoked in an expression and does return a value. Both forms of procedures accept arguments that may pass data into, out of, or both into and out of the procedure. This intention may be declared as an attribute of a dummy, either `INTENT(IN)`, `INTENT(OUT)`, or `INTENT(INOUT)`. Such a declaration allows a compiler to check for incorrect usage, such as a procedure in which an assignment to an `INTENT(IN)` dummy occurs. It also may allow the generation of more efficient code. For example, the value of an actual argument corresponding to an `INTENT(IN)` dummy argument is known not to be changed by the call; this may allow the optimization of constant propagation to occur across the procedure call.

When a procedure is called, the actual arguments are "linked" to the dummy arguments by means of *argument association*. The dummy must have the same type and kind as the actual to which it is associated. The most straightforward way to pass an array actual is to pass it to an assumed-shape dummy. Fortran does have other, older, ways to pass arrays, such as assumed-size and explicit-shape*explicit-shape array*, but these mechanisms depend on the use of sequence association and the assumption that the hardware architecture provides a linear memory. Since the use of sequence association and the assumption of a linear memory is not always efficient on modern machines, we strongly recommend against its use.

Fortran allows for the use of argument *keywords* and for arguments to be *optional*. By default, the list of actual arguments is matched one-for-one in order with the list of dummy arguments. Alternatively, some of the arguments (possibly none) may be matched in order and the remainder matched by expressions of the form `D=A` where `D` is the name of a dummy argument and `A` is the actual argument. These *keyword arguments* may occur in any order. In addition, if a dummy argument is given the attribute `OPTIONAL`, it may be omitted from the argument list completely. In the procedure the intrinsic function `PRESENT` can test whether, on a particular call, an `OPTIONAL` dummy argument has a corresponding actual argument. These two facilities are very useful for invoking procedures, such as graphics routines, with a large number of arguments many of which optionally set various modes of usage. As a result, the old usage of the `ENTRY` statement to provide an alternate entry to a procedure is now obsolescent.

Fortran allows a function to be called recursively, either directly or indirectly, if the function is declared to be `RECURSIVE`. Ordinarily, the name of a function can be used within the function as the value being returned by the function. The function `RESULT` allows an unambiguous distinction between the value being calculated in the function and a recursive call of the function from within the function. The following example uses an inefficient approach to summing an array as an illustration (the SUM intrinsic function is much more efficient):

```
RECURSIVE REAL FUNCTION ARRAY_SUM(ARRAY) RESULT(A_SUM)
  REAL, INTENT(IN), DIMENSION(:) :: ARRAY
  REAL :: A_SUM
  IF (SIZE(ARRAY) = 0) THEN
    A_SUM = 0
  ELSE
    A_SUM = ARRAY(1) + ARRAY_SUM(ARRAY(2:))
  END IF
END FUNCTION ARRAY_SUM
```

A main program, external function, or external subroutine may be a host for contained internal procedures that have access to data in the host environment by means of *host association*. In the following example A, B, C, D, and E are all accessible in INNER. However, the X in SAM is not accessible because there is an overriding definition of X in INNER. Note that INNER allocates E, which may be used in SAM after a call on INNER.

```
SUBROUTINE SAM(A)
  USE LIB, ONLY: B ! Only B is available from LIB
  TYPE Q
    INTEGER D
  END TYPE
  TYPE(Q) :: C
  INTEGER, ALLOCATABLE, DIMENSION(:) :: E
  REAL X
   ...
  CONTAINS
    SUBROUTINE INNER (C)
      INTEGER X
      C%D = 3
      X = B  ! Assigns B in LIB to integer X in INNER
      ALLOCATE (E(1000))
       ...
    END SUBROUTINE INNER
END SUBROUTINE SAM
```

Using any of the following features requires an *explicit interface*:

- Keyword arguments.
- User-defined operator or assignment.
- Generic name references.
- Optional and intent-specified arguments.
- Array-valued and pointer-valued function results.
- Assumed-shape, pointer, and target dummies.

An explicit interface provides information about the attributes of a procedure and its dummy arguments so that a compiler can check a reference of that procedure for correctness and can generate a correct and efficient invocation. Explicit interfaces are provided "automatically" for internal procedures, module procedures, and intrinsic procedures. If an external separately compiled procedure uses any of the features that requires an explicit interface, the programmer must provide one, in the form of an interface block, to each program unit that calls the procedure. Although this seems like a lot of effort, the rewards include the use of the more advanced Fortran capabilities, better compile-time checking of programs, and a better structured, easier to read, and easier to maintain program. For multiple usage, an interface block can always be packaged in a module, as the example in the next section shows.

3.7.3 Modules and Abstraction

A module can define new derived types and specify that the details of the structure of entities of these types should be **PRIVATE** and not accessible to users of the module. Those details are still accessible to procedures defined in the module, allowing the creation of abstract data types and their operations. FORTRAN 77 provided *generic intrinsic procedures* where the same generic name refers to multiple specific procedures. Fortran 90 extends this concept to allow user-defined generic procedures. It further allows overloading operators and assignment, to give them procedural definitions for user-defined data types.

For example, consider an application that requires the concept of rational numbers. (This example is derived from an example found in the Ada programming language standard [4].) The module **RATIONAL_NUMBERS** provides a definition for the derived type **RATIONAL**, the subroutine **MAKE_RATIONAL**, and overloadings for the ==, and + operators. Notice that in the module procedures an entity of type **RATIONAL** can be created by means of the standard mechanism of using the name of the type as a structure constructor. A user of the module, however, can not do this since the structure of the type **RATIONAL** is **PRIVATE**. Thus, the module includes a subroutine **MAKE_RATIONAL** to serve that purpose. A production implementation of the concept of rational numbers would, of course, be more complex. (In particular, this version never reduces rationals to lowest terms, so cascaded arithmetic operations are likely to overflow.)

```
MODULE RATIONAL_NUMBERS
  TYPE (RATIONAL)
    PRIVATE
    INTEGER :: NUMERATOR
    INTEGER :: DENOMINATOR     ! Must be kept positive
  END TYPE (RATIONAL)

  INTERFACE OPERATOR(==)
    LOGICAL FUNCTION EQUAL(X, Y)
      TYPE (RATIONAL), INTENT(IN) :: X, Y
    END FUNCTION EQUAL
  END INTERFACE

  INTERFACE OPERATOR(+)
    TYPE (RATIONAL) FUNCTION ADD_RATIONALS(X, Y)
      TYPE (RATIONAL), INTENT(IN) :: X, Y
    END FUNCTION ADD_RATIONALS
  END INTERFACE

  ! Et cetera, et cetera, et cetera...

CONTAINS

  LOGICAL FUNCTION EQUAL(X, Y)
    TYPE (RATIONAL), INTENT(IN) :: X, Y
    EQUAL = X%NUMERATOR*Y%DENOMINATOR==Y%NUMERATOR*X%DENOMINATOR
  END FUNCTION EQUAL

  TYPE (RATIONAL) FUNCTION MAKE_RATIONAL(X, Y)
    INTEGER, INTENT(IN) :: X, Y
    IF (Y > 0) THEN
      MAKE_RATIONAL = RATIONAL(X, Y)
    ELSE
      MAKE_RATIONAL = RATIONAL(-X, -Y)
    END IF
  END FUNCTION MAKE_RATIONAL
```

```
      TYPE (RATIONAL) FUNCTION ADD_RATIONALS(X, Y)
        TYPE (RATIONAL), INTENT(IN) :: X, Y
        ADD_RATIONALS = RATIONAL(                                   &
          X%NUMERATOR*Y%DENOMINATOR + Y%NUMERATOR*X%DENOMINATOR,    &
                   X%DENOMINATOR*Y%DENOMINATOR)
      END FUNCTION ADD_RATIONALS

      ! Et cetera, et cetera, et cetera...

    END MODULE RATIONAL_NUMBERS

    PROGRAM TEST_RATIONALS
      USE RATIONAL_NUMBERS
      TYPE(RATIONAL) :: X, Y
      X = MAKE_RATIONAL(1, 2)
      Y = X + MAKE_RATIONAL(3, -6)
      IF (Y == MAKE_RATIONAL(0,1)) THEN
        PRINT *, "Passes Test"
      ELSE
        PRINT *, "Fails Test"
      END IF
    END PROGRAM TEST_RATIONALS
```

3.8 Intrinsic Procedures

Fortran 90 defines 108 *intrinsic functions* and 5 *intrinsic subroutines*. *Intrinsic procedures* are provided in Fortran 90 because they satisfy three major requirements:

- They provide functionality that is frequently required in applications.
- They can be implemented efficiently on a variety of computer architectures, including pipelined RISC and parallel as well as conventional.
- As part of a Fortran 90 implementation they are well tested, documented, and reliable.

The names of the intrinsic procedures, being pre-defined by Fortran, are always available unless the program creates its own procedure with the same name. All of the intrinsic procedures have explicit interfaces. The names of the arguments of the intrinsic procedures are used consistently. For example, DIM is used as the name of the argument specifying the dimension of an array to be used and **MASK** is used to select values of interest from an array in a way similar to the **WHERE** statement. Intrinsic procedures behave like "ordinary" procedures and follow all of the ordinary rules for procedures. Arguments may be passed by name and optional arguments may be omitted. For example, **SUM(ARRAY=A, DIM=2)** sums all values of the array **A** in the second dimension.

There are four categories of intrinsic procedures. *Elemental functions* operate on a single element, and return a single value. Given an array as an argument, they return an array of the same shape, the result of applying the function to each of the elements of the array in an unspecified order. For example, **SQRT(4.0)** returns 2.0 while **SQRT((/4.0, 9.0, 16.0/))** returns [2.0, 3.0, 4.0]. *Inquiry functions* return properties of their arguments. For example, **SIZE((/4.0, 9.0, 16.0/))** returns 3. *Transformational functions* usually have array arguments and return values that depend on many or all of the elements of its arguments. For example, **SUM((/4.0, 9.0, 16.0/))** returns 29.0. *Intrinsic subroutines* perform a variety of tasks. For example, **CALL DATE_AND_TIME(DATE=D)** where **D** is a scalar default character variable of length 8 will set **D** to a string of the form *ccyymmdd*, corresponding to century, year, month, and day respectively.

Fortran 90 defines three *representational models*: the *bit model*, the *integer number system model*, and the *real number system model*. The intrinsic functions that return values related to these models allow applications to be both numerically accurate and portable. For details of the models, we refer you to the Fortran 90 Standard.

Most of the intrinsic procedures are *generic* in that they may be called with arguments of different types. The correct *specific procedure* will be determined by the types of the arguments. In some cases a specific procedure may have the same name as the generic. For example, the generic reference to **SIN(X)** refers to the specific function **DSIN(X)** if **X** is double precision real, to **CSIN(X)** if **X** is default **COMPLEX**, or to **SIN(X)** if **X** is default real. If an intrinsic function itself, as opposed to the result of a call, is used as an actual argument to a procedure, only specific names can be used and the corresponding dummy argument in the procedure can have only scalar arguments.

A brief summary of the Fortran 90 intrinsic procedures is presented in Tables 3.1 through 3.6 in which italics are used to indicate optional arguments.

3.9 Language Evolution

> *Users who change over to Fortran 90 will ... [want] to adapt their own style of programming, dropping FORTRAN 77 features now regarded as outmoded and embrace the newer facilities.*
>
> Maurice V. Wilkes [30]

Function	Value Returned
Argument Presence Inquiry Function	
PRESENT(A)	True if an actual argument has been supplied for the optional dummy argument A
Numeric Functions	
ABS(A)	Absolute value of A
AIMAG(Z)	Imaginary part of complex number Z
AINT(A, *KIND*)	A truncated to a whole number
ANINT(A, *KIND*)	A rounded to the nearest whole number
CEILING(A)	Least integer greater than or equal to A
CMPLX(X, Y, *KIND*)	Complex number (X, Y)
CONJG(Z)	Complex conjugate of Z
DBLE(A)	A converted to double precision
DIM(X, Y)	X-Y if positive, otherwise 0
DPROD(X, Y)	Double precision product of reals X and Y
FLOOR(A)	Greatest integer less than or equal to A
INT(A, *KIND*)	Truncated integer value of A
MAX(A1, A2, *A3*, ...)	Maximum value of A1, A2, A3, ...
MIN(A1, A2, *A3*, ...)	Minimum value of A1, A2, A3, ...
MOD(A, P)	Remainder function of A and P, value has sign of A
MODULO(A, P)	Modulo function of A and P, value has sign of P
NINT(A, *KIND*)	A rounded to the nearest integer
REAL(A, *KIND*)	A converted to real type
SIGN(A, B)	Absolute value of A times the sign of B
Mathematical Functions	
ACOS(X)	Arc cosine of X
ASIN(X)	Arc sine of X
ATAN(X)	Arc tangent of X
ATAN2(Y, X)	Arc tangent of complex number (X, Y)
COS(X)	Cosine of X
COSH(X)	Hyperbolic cosine of X
EXP(X)	Exponential of X

Table 3.1
Fortran 90 intrinsic procedures —argument presence, numeric, and mathematical

Function	Value Returned
Mathematical Functions —continued	
LOG(X)	Natural logarithm of X
LOG10(X)	Common logarithm of X
SIN(X)	Sine of X
SINH(X)	Hyperbolic sine of X
SQRT(X)	Square root of X
TAN(X)	Tangent of X
TANH(X)	Hyperbolic tangent of X
Character Functions	
ACHAR(I)	Character in position I in ASCII collating sequence
ADJUSTL(STRING)	Adjust STRING to the left by removing leading blanks and padding on the right with blanks
ADJUSTR(STRING)	Adjust STRING to the right by removing trailing blanks and padding on the left with blanks
CHAR(I, *KIND*)	Character in position I in processor collating sequence
IACHAR(C)	Position of character C in ASCII collating sequence
ICHAR(C)	Position of character C in processor collating sequence
INDEX(STRING, SUBSTRING, *BACK*)	Starting position of SUBSTRING in STRING
LEN_TRIM(STRING)	Length of STRING excluding trailing blank characters
LGE(STRING_A, STRING_B)	True if STRING_A is lexically greater than or equal to STRING_B
LGT(STRING_A, STRING_B)	True if STRING_A is lexically greater than STRING_B
LLE(STRING_A, STRING_B)	True if STRING_A is lexically less than or equal to STRING_B
LLT(STRING_A, STRING_B)	True if STRING_A is lexically less than STRING_B
REPEAT(STRING, NCOPIES)	Repeated concatenation of copies of STRING
SCAN(STRING, SET, *BACK*)	Scan STRING for a character in SET
TRIM(STRING)	Remove trailing blank characters from STRING
VERIFY(STRING, SET, *BACK*)	True if all characters of STRING are in SET

Table 3.2
Fortran 90 intrinsic procedures — mathematical and character

Function	Value Returned
Character Inquiry Function	
`LEN(STRING)`	Number of characters in `STRING`
Kind Functions	
`KIND(X)`	Value of kind type parameter of `X`
`SELECTED_INT_KIND (R)`	Integer kind type parameter value for range `R`
`SELECTED_REAL_KIND (P, R)`	Real kind type parameter value for precision `P` and range `R`
Logical Function	
`LOGICAL(L, KIND)`	Convert logical `L` to logical kind `KIND`
Numeric Inquiry Functions	
`DIGITS(X)`	Number of significant digits for type and kind of `X`
`EPSILON(X)`	A very small number of type and kind of `X` that is almost negligible compared to one
`HUGE(X)`	The largest number of the type and kind of `X`
`MAXEXPONENT(X)`	Maximum exponent for type and kind of `X`
`MINEXPONENT(X)`	Minimum(most negative) exponent for type and kind of `X`
`PRECISION(X)`	Decimal precision for type and kind of `X`
`RADIX(X)`	Base for type and kind of `X`
`RANGE(X)`	Decimal exponent range for type and kind of `X`
`TINY(X)`	Smallest positive number for type and kind of `X`
Bit Inquiry Functions	
`BIT_SIZE(I)`	Number of bits for type and kind of integer `I`
Bit Manipulation Functions	
`BTEST(I, POS)`	True if bit position `POS` of `I` is 1
`IAND(I, J)`	Logical and of `I` and `J`
`IBCLR(I, POS)`	Clear bit position `POS` of `I` to 0
`IBITS(I, POS, LEN)`	Bit sequence of `I` starting at position `POS` of length `LEN`

Table 3.3
Fortran 90 intrinsic procedures — character inquiry, kind, logical, numeric inquiry, and bit inquiry

Function	Value Returned

Bit Inquiry Functions —continued

IBSET(I, POS)	Set bit POS in I to 1
IEOR(I, J)	Exclusive or of I and J
IOR(I, J)	Inclusive or of I and J
ISHFT(I, SHIFT)	Logical end-off shift of SHIFT bits of I
ISHFTC(I, SHIFT, SIZE)	Circular shift of SHIFT bits of I
NOT(I)	Logical complement of I

Transfer Function

TRANSFER(SOURCE, MOLD, SIZE)	Treat physical representation of SOURCE as if it were of the type and kind of MOLD

Floating-point Manipulation Functions

EXPONENT(X)	Exponent part of X
FRACTION(X)	Fractional part of X
NEAREST(X, S)	Nearest different machine representable number to X in the direction indicated by the sign of S
RRSPACING(X)	Reciprocal of the relative spacing of model numbers near X
SCALE(X, I)	Multiply a real X by its base to an integer power I
SET_EXPONENT(X, I)	Set exponent part of X to I
SPACING(X)	Absolute spacing of model numbers near X

Vector and Matrix Multiply Functions

DOT_PRODUCT (VECT_A, VECT_B)	Dot product of two rank-one arrays VECT_A and VECT_B
MATMUL(MATRIX_A, MATRIX_B)	Matrix multiplication of MATRIX_A and MATRIX_B

Array Reduction Functions

ALL(MASK, DIM)	True if all values of MASK are true
ANY(MASK, DIM)	True if any value of MASK is true

Table 3.4
Fortran 90 intrinsic procedures —bit inquiry, transfer, floating-point manipulation, vector and matrix multiply, and array reduction

Function	Value Returned
Array Reduction Functions — continued	
COUNT(MASK, *DIM*)	Number of true elements in MASK
MAXVAL(ARRAY, *DIM*, *MASK*)	Maximum value in ARRAY
MINVAL(ARRAY, *DIM*, *MASK*)	Minimum value in ARRAY
PRODUCT(ARRAY, *DIM*, *MASK*)	Product of elements in ARRAY
SUM(ARRAY, *DIM*, *MASK*)	Sum of elements in ARRAY
Array Inquiry Functions	
ALLOCATED(ARRAY)	True if ARRAY is allocated
LBOUND(ARRAY, *DIM*)	Lower dimension bounds of ARRAY
SHAPE(SOURCE)	Shape of an array or scalar SOURCE
SIZE(ARRAY, *DIM*)	Total number of elements in ARRAY
UBOUND(ARRAY, *DIM*)	Upper dimension bounds of ARRAY
Array Construction Functions	
MERGE(TSOURCE, FSOURCE, MASK)	Choose value from TSOURCE or FSOURCE according to value of MASK
PACK(ARRAY, MASK, *VECTOR*)	Pack ARRAY into a rank one array under a mask MASK
SPREAD(SOURCE, DIM, NCOPIES)	Replicate array SOURCE NCOPIES times in dimension DIM
UNPACK(VECTOR, MASK, FIELD)	Unpack VECTOR into array of shape MASK, FIELD replacing 0's from MASK
Array Reshape Function	
RESHAPE(SOURCE, SHAPE, *PAD*, *ORDER*)	Reshape SOURCE into shape of SHAPE

Table 3.5
Fortran 90 intrinsic procedures — array reduction, array inquiry, array construction, and array reshape

Function	Value Returned

Array Manipulation Functions

CSHIFT(ARRAY, SHIFT, *DIM*)	Circular shift of **ARRAY SHIFT** positions
EOSHIFT(ARRAY, SHIFT, *DIM*, *BOUNDARY*)	End-off shift of **ARRAY SHIFT** positions
TRANSPOSE(MATRIX)	Transpose of **MATRIX**

Array Location Functions

MAXLOC(ARRAY, *MASK*)	Location of a maximum value in **ARRAY**
MINLOC(ARRAY, *MASK*)	Location of a minimum value in **ARRAY**

Pointer Association Status Inquiry

ASSOCIATED (POINTER, *TARGET*)	True if **POINTER** is associated

Intrinsic Subroutines

DATE_AND_TIME(*DATE*, *TIME*, *ZONE*, *VALUES*)	Returns date and time information
MVBITS(FROM, FROMPOS, LEN, TO, TOPOS)	Elemental subroutine to copy a sequence of **LEN** bits from **FROMPOS** in integer **FROM** to **TOPOS** in integer **TO**
RANDOM_NUMBER (HARVEST)	Returns a pseudo-random number or an array of pseudo-random numbers
RANDOM_SEED(*SIZE*, *PUT*, *GET*)	Initializes or queries the random number generator seed
SYSTEM_CLOCK(*COUNT*, *COUNT_RATE*, *COUNT_MAX*)	Returns data from processor's real time clock

Table 3.6
Fortran 90 intrinsic procedures — array manipulation, array location, pointer association status, and intrinsic subroutines

Removed and Obsolete Features Identified in Annex B of the Standard	
For	Use
No removed features at this time.	
Arithmetic IF statements	IF statements or IF constructs
Real and double precision DO control variables and DO loop control expressions	Integer control variables and expressions
Shared DO termination and termination on a statement other than END DO or CONTINUE	An END DO for each DO
Branch to an END IF from outside its IF block	Branch to the statement directly following the END IF
Procedure alternate return	Return code and a CASE construct on return
PAUSE statement	An appropriate READ statement
ASSIGN and assigned GO TO	The internal procedures they are often used to simulate
Assigned FORMAT specifiers	Character variables and constants
cH edit descriptor	Character constant edit descriptor

Table 3.7
Removed and Obsolete Features Identified in Annex B of the Standard

The Fortran 90 standard, for the first time, introduces a concept of *language evolution* in which the addition of new features is understood to cause old features to become redundant and, eventually to be phased out. The Standard sites some examples and identifies (in Annex B) *removed features* and obsolescent or *redundant features* for which there are better methods. In addition to these features, a number of authors have identified antiquated features to be avoided by the use of more modern Fortran 90 features. Some of these features, and their suggested replacements, are shown in Table 3.7 and Table 3.8.

3.9.1 Avoiding Assumptions of Linear Memory

Whenever a computer architecture is directly visible in a programming language, one should expect two consequences: good performance on that architecture and difficulty in porting applications to other computer architectures. Not surprisingly, traditional Fortran implementations have tended to provide excellent execution performance on traditional linear memory computer architectures. To achieve good performance on distributed memory computer architectures, however, it is necessary to avoid those older features of Fortran that depend on linear memory concepts. These features were avail-

Antiquated Fortran Features and Their Replacements	
For	**Use**
`DOUBLE PRECISION`	Numeric kind facility
Sequence association of array element actual arguments with dummy arrays	Array section actual arguments associated with assumed shape array dummies
`BLOCK DATA` and `COMMON`	Modules
`DO` loop old forms and `CONTINUE`	The `DO` ... `END DO` form.
Statement labels and the `GO TO` statement	Are still considered harmful and should be avoided
Computed `GO TO` statement	`CASE` construct
`DO WHILE` statement	`IF` ... `EXIT` in a `DO` ... `END DO`
The `RETURN` statement effect	Happens at procedure `END`
The `STOP` statement effect	Happens at `END` of main program
`IMPLICIT` statements	`IMPLICIT NONE` and explicit typing of all variables
Attribute specification statements	"::" form of type declaration statement grouping all of the attributes of an entity in one place
`DATA` statement	Initialization expression in type declaration statements (except for `BOZ` data)
Hollerith data	Character data type and constants
`COMMON` blocks	Modules
`EQUIVALENCE` statements	Modules, storage allocation, structures, pointers, and `TRANSFER` intrinsic function
Block data program units	Modules
Fixed source form	Free source form
Specific intrinsic functions	Generic intrinsic functions
`FORMAT` statements	Character variables
Arithmetic statement functions	Internal functions
Assumed size arrays	Assumed shape arrays
`INCLUDE` lines	Modules
`ENTRY` statements	Modules with `PRIVATE` procedures

Table 3.8
New features in Fortran 90 and what they replace

able to provide such necessary capabilities as the ability to pass a column of an array as an argument to a procedure and to reuse data storage no longer required. Fortunately, Fortran 90 provides modern features to meet these requirements that are efficient and do not depend on a model of memory.

A linear memory model is visible in Fortran in two ways:

- *Sequence association* is the definition of the mapping of multi-dimensional arrays to a linear sequence ordering, the so-called column-major order. Sequence association is particularly visible when an array expression or array element is associated with an assumed size or explicit size dummy array argument. Sequence association may be avoided in Fortran 90 through the use of assumed shape dummy array arguments and the use of intrinsic functions to reshape arrays.
- *Storage association* is the definition of the mapping of data objects to underlying storage units, and was typically used to reshape **COMMON** and **EQUIVALENCE** data and to simulate allocatable storage. Storage association may be avoided in Fortran 90 through the use of allocatable data and the use of intrinsic functions.

3.10 Fortran Coding Style

Fortran 90 is a large language with a number of alternative ways of expressing the same intention, in part resulting from Fortran 90's backwards compatibility with previous Fortran standards. We *strongly* recommend that you choose a reasonable coding style and stick with it. While conforming to a style may add a few minutes to your typing time, it will be rewarded over and over as others, and you in the future, try to figure out the meaning of a section of code. The following sections present a number of code style guidelines that have proven to be useful. Figure 3.1 shows a number of these guidelines in a single example.

3.10.1 Upper-Case and Lower-Case Conventions

Fortran 90 treats upper-case and lower-case letters in programs equivalently except, of course, in character constants and **H** format specifiers. This allows a variety of coding styles. For example, the following **CALL** statements are all equivalent:

```
CALL MY_SUB(MAX(A,3), LEN=12)   ! all upper case
call my_sub(max(a,3), len=12)   ! all lower case
CALL my_sub(MAX(a,3), LEN=12)   ! Fortran 90 names in upper case
call MY_SUB(max(A,3), len=12)   ! user names in upper case
Call My_Sub(Max(A,3), Len=12)   ! initial letters in upper case
```

```
        PROGRAM PI_EXAMPLE
          ! Compute the value of pi by numerical integration

          INTEGER, PARAMETER   :: N = 1000       ! Number of rectangles
          REAL, PARAMETER      :: H = 1.0 / N    ! Width of a rectangle

          REAL                 :: PI
          REAL, DIMENSION(N)   :: RECT_AREA
!HPF$     DISTRIBUTE (CYCLIC) :: RECT_AREA

          INTERFACE
            SUBROUTINE PRINT_RESULT(X)
              REAL :: X
            END SUBROUTINE PRINT_RESULT
          END INTERFACE

          FORALL (I=1:N)
            RECT_AREA(I) = H * F(H*(I-0.5))
          END FORALL
          PI = SUM(RECT_AREA)

          CALL PRINT_RESULT(PI)

        CONTAINS

          REAL FUNCTION F(X)
            REAL :: X
            F = 4 / (1.0 + X*X)
          END FUNCTION F

        END PROGRAM PI_EXAMPLE
```

Figure 3.1
A complete Fortran 90 program

There are advantages and disadvantages to all of these, and other conventions. We recommend that you choose a style that you are comfortable with and use it consistently. Our examples use the "all upper-case" convention for the simple reason that it tends to make keywords and user names self-quoting when they appear in explanatory text.

3.10.2 Spacing Conventions

In choosing a horizontal spacing convention, there is a tradeoff between the improved readability resulting from the addition of white space and the decreased readability if the extra space forces continuation lines. We recommend using white space to improve readability within reason.

We recommend following the free source form rules for blank characters even when using fixed source form:

- Blank characters must not appear in lexical tokens, except within a character context. For example, there can be no blanks between the two characters of the exponentiation operator **.
- Blank characters must be used to separate names, constants, or labels from adjacent keywords, names constants, or labels. For example, a blank is required between the DO and its index variable.

In addition, we recommend that blank characters be used at natural breaks in the program text, including around the = in assignments and following semicolons and most commas.

3.10.3 Indentation, Alignment and Blank Line Conventions

As a result of its fixed source form and its origins in the days of punched cards, Fortran programs have traditionally not used an indentation convention; programs have been written as lists of statements all beginning in "column 7," even though nothing in the definition of Fortran required non-indentation. We believe that modern style calls for appropriate indentation to show the nesting structure of a program unit. (As with blank space, we temper this advice if the indentation causes continuation lines.) We have used a two-space indentation style throughout this book; other programmers may prefer more or less.

The following Fortran 90 constructs are candidates for nesting:

- The statements in the *specification-part*, *execution-part*, and *internal-subprogram* of any of the forms of *program-unit*: *main-program*, *function-subprogram*, *subroutine-subprogram*, *module*, or *block-data*.

- The statements in the *case-construct, forall-construct, if-construct, do-construct,* and *where-construct.*
- The components of a derived type definition or an interface block.
- In general, long assignment statements should break at a logical place in the right hand side expression and continue aligned with the beginning of the right hand side expression, unless deeper indentation (and perhaps more white space) makes the code more readable. For example:

```
NEW_VAL(I,J) = .25 * (   OLD_VAL(I-1,J) + OLD_VAL(I,J-1)    &
                       + OLD_VAL(I+1,J) + OLD_VAL(I,J+1)   )
```

In addition to nesting, we recommend that, in general, the :: symbols in multiple succeeding declarations and the exclamation points in multiple succeeding trailing comments should be lined up. Blank lines can also improve readability by, for example, separating parameter declarations, variable declarations, interface-blocks, and sections of executable code.

The HPF directives were designed so that if HPF ever becomes part of the Fortran language, the !HPF$ could be edited out to leave a correct program. In this book, we have arranged things so that the directive bodies are aligned with the Fortran 90 statements in the surrounding program. This allows the reader to skip over the !HPF$ in the left margin.

3.10.4 Free Source Form

We strongly recommend the use of Fortran 90 free source form to improve readability and have used free source form exclusively, except when we need to illustrate specific fixed source form features. Source code can be written to be interpreted correctly in either free or fixed source form by following these rules:

- Limit statement labels, if they are absolutely necessary, to positions 1 through 5 and statements to positions 7 through 72.
- Treat blanks as being significant.
- Use the exclamation point (!) for a comment, but don't place it in position 6.
- To continue statements, use the ampersand (&) in position 73 of the line being continued, and position 6 of the continuation line. Following the ampersand in the line being continued, there can be only blanks or a comment. Positions 1 to 5 in the continuation line must be blank.

Figure 3.2 shows an example that is valid in both source forms. The "&" at the end of line 4 appears in column 73, while the "&" beginning line 5 appears in column 6.

```
      ! Define the user function MY_SIN

      DOUBLE PRECISION FUNCTION MY_SIN(X)
        MY_SIN = X - X**3/FACTORIAL(3) + X**5/FACTORIAL(5)          &
   &               - X**7/FACTORIAL(7) + X**9/FACTORIAL(9)
      CONTAINS
        INTEGER FUNCTION FACTORIAL(N)
          FACTOR = 1
          DO I = 2, N
            FACTORIAL = FACTORIAL * I
          END DO
        END FUNCTION FACTORIAL
      END FUNCTION MY_SIN
```

Figure 3.2
A Fortran 90 function that can be interpreted as either free source form or fixed source form

4 Data Mapping

HPF data alignment and distribution directives allow the programmer to advise the compiler about how data objects (especially array elements) should be assigned to processor memories.

4.1 Overview of Data Mapping

The goal of data mapping directives in HPF is to allow the programmer to control the distribution of data to processors. Chapter 2 showed how this distribution could be used to improve the performance of programs (or could cause them to run slowly, if the data mapping was misused).

Often, the most convenient way to specify a data mapping is to give a simple pattern using the DISTRIBUTE directive. There are two major types of patterns that can be specified this way: *block* and *cyclic* distributions. In a block distribution, each processor contains a block—a contiguous subarray—of the specified array. For example,

```
      REAL, DIMENSION(100,100)   :: X, Y
!HPF$ DISTRIBUTE (*, BLOCK)      :: X
!HPF$ DISTRIBUTE (BLOCK, BLOCK)  :: Y
```

breaks the arrays X and Y into groups of columns and into rectangular blocks, respectively. In the form shown here, the block sizes are chosen to be as nearly equal as possible; it is also possible to pick a specific block size, if one wants an unequal distribution. Cyclic mappings distribute the elements of a dimension onto P processors so that each processor, starting from a different offset, contains every P^{th} column. For example,

```
      REAL, DIMENSION(100,100)   :: X, Y
!HPF$ PROCESSORS PROC1(10), PROC2(2,5)
!HPF$ DISTRIBUTE (CYCLIC,*) ONTO PROC1      :: X
!HPF$ DISTRIBUTE (BLOCK,CYCLIC) ONTO PROC2 :: Y
```

places every 10th row of X on the same processor. Combining the block and cyclic distributions as shown effectively places half of every fifth column on one processor; a given processor will always have either all "top" halves, or all "bottom" halves. Examples 2.18 and 2.19 in Chapter 2 contain several similar examples.

Sometimes it more convenient to specify the desired distribution of an array by describing its relationship to another array. For example, one might have a 16×16 array X and a 14×14 array Y, where elements of Y are intended to interact computationally with the interior of X. Of course, one could simply declare Y to be the same size as X,

(a) a 14 × 14 array aligned with the interior of a 16 × 16 array

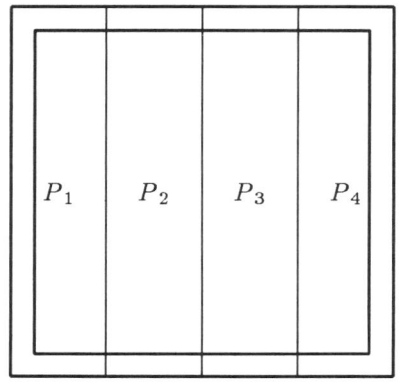

(b) distribution (*,BLOCK)

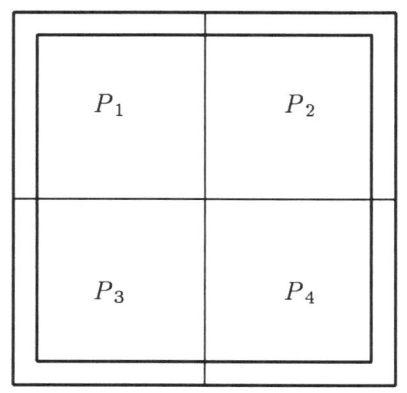

(c) distribution (BLOCK, BLOCK)

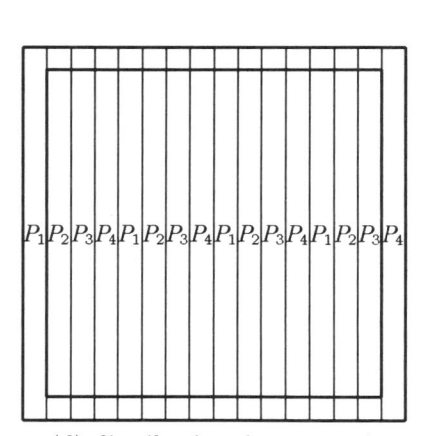

(d) distribution (*,CYCLIC)

Figure 4.1
Alignment of a 14 × 14 array with a 16 × 16 array

distribute it in the same way as X, and then use only the interior of Y in the computation, but this could result in a clumsier coding style throughout the program. The desired relationship between X and Y can be expressed by an HPF alignment directive:

```
      REAL X(16,16), Y(14,14)
!HPF$ ALIGN Y(I,J) WITH X(I+1,J+1)
```

See Figure 4.1, which assumes four processors storing the arrays. Here I and J are dummy variables that range over the valid subscript values for Y. For every element of Y, a corresponding element of X is indicated; whatever processor memory contains that element of X should also contain that element of Y. If X is distributed (*,BLOCK), whether by an explicit directive or by the compiler's discretion, Y will be distributed accordingly, as illustrated in Figure 4.1(b). Note that while X is distributed evenly across the four processors, Y is not, so as to assure that Y(I,J) is always in the same processor as X(I+1,J+1). If X were to be distributed (BLOCK, BLOCK), the result would be as shown in Figure 4.1(c); this distribution does coincidentally cut Y as well as X into four equal pieces. The result of a (*,CYCLIC) distribution for X is shown in Figure 4.1(d).

It might be desirable to align several elements of one array to the same single element of another array; this is called a *collapsing alignment*. Figure 4.2(a) illustrates an alignment of a matrix M to a vector V, specified by the directive

```
!HPF$ ALIGN M(I,*) WITH V(I)
```

Wherever a given element of V is distributed, the entire corresponding row of M should also be distributed. (The directive could also be written

```
!HPF$ ALIGN M(I,J) WITH V(I)
```

but the use of an asterisk provides a stronger visual cue that collapsing is intended.)

With this alignment established, the distribution of M is dictated by the distribution of V. If V is given a BLOCK distribution:

```
!HPF$ DISTRIBUTE V(BLOCK)
```

then the rows of M are given a matching distribution, resulting in an assignment to processors such as shown in Figure 4.2(b). If instead V were given a CYCLIC distribution:

```
!HPF$ DISTRIBUTE V(CYCLIC)
```

then the rows of M would be given a matching distribution, resulting in an assignment to processors such as shown in Figure 4.2(c).

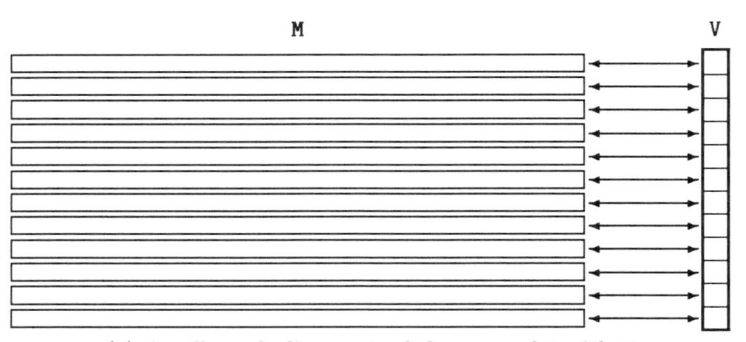

(a) A collapsed alignment of the rows of M with V

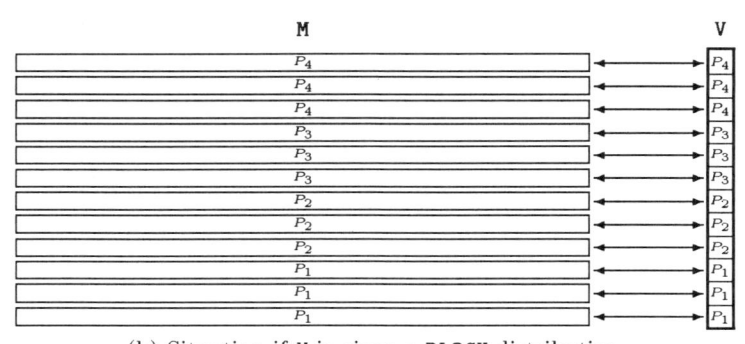

(b) Situation if V is given a BLOCK distribution

(c) Situation if V is given a CYCLIC distribution

Figure 4.2
Collapsed alignment of rows of a matrix with elements of a vector

Data Mapping

(a) an array and a lookup table

(b) replicating the lookup table to align with each array element

(c) actual implementation effect, replicating once per processor with a (BLOCK, BLOCK) distribution

(d) actual implementation effect, replicating once per processor with a (*,BLOCK) distribution

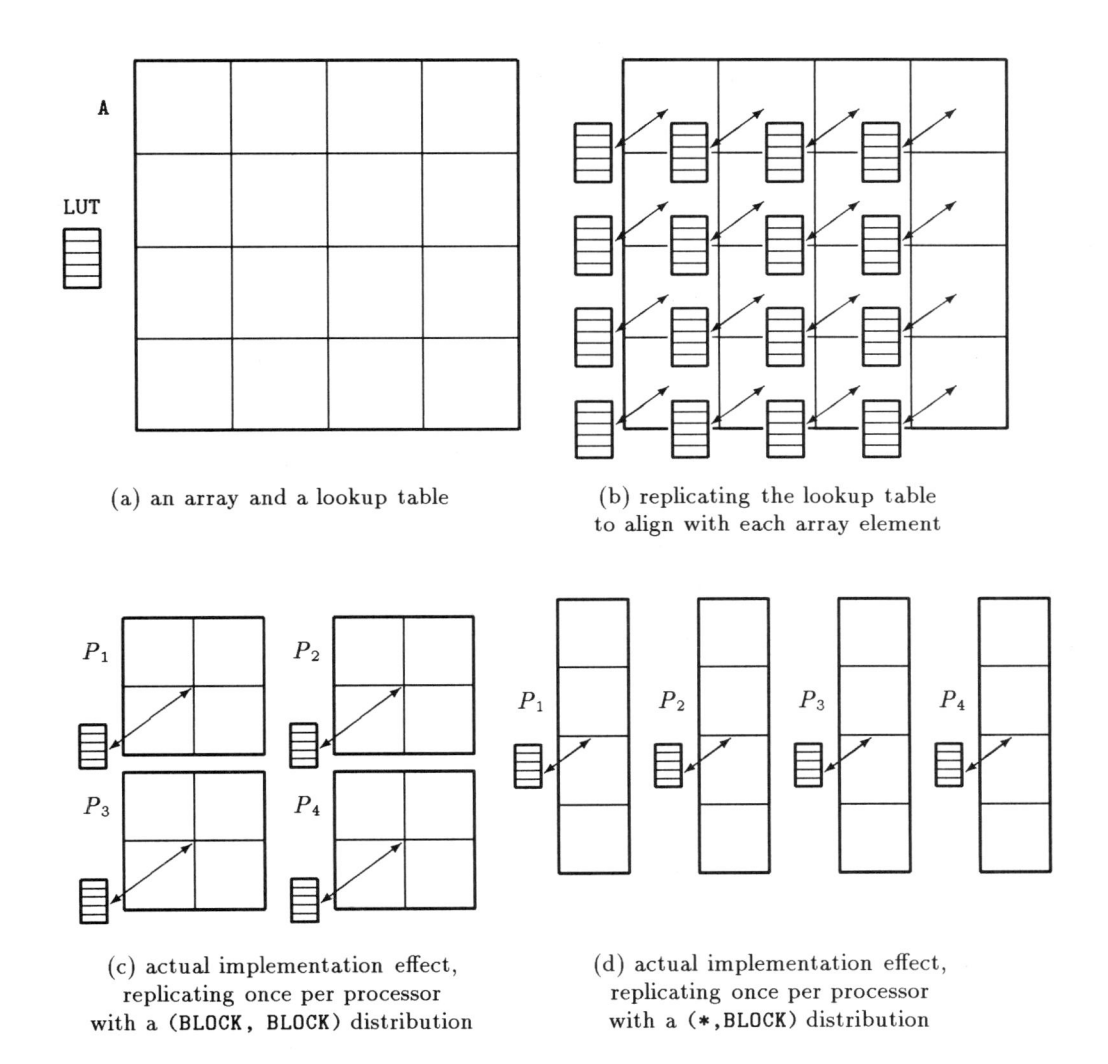

Figure 4.3
Replicated alignment of a lookup table with elements of an array

The converse of collapsing is *replication*; HPF provides a form of *replicating alignment*. Suppose that one must repeatedly evaluate a simple function from small integers to arbitrary values not easily represented as a formula. An efficient solution is to construct a lookup table and use the small integers as subscripts.

```
REAL LUT(1:147)
...
code to initialize lookup table
...
```

Now suppose that the function must be evaluated for every position of an array that may be distributed over many processors:

```
FORALL (I=1:4, J=1:4)   A(I,J) = A(I,J) * LUT(INT(B(I,J)))
```

See Figure 4.3(a). Whether the lookup table resides in one processor or is split across many processors, there can be a great deal of communications overhead when processors need values from the lookup table that reside in the memories of other processors. In this situation it is often advantageous to trade space for time by making many copies of the lookup table so that each processor can have its own copy.

Now, the programmer could code such a replicated lookup table explicitly by making it two-dimensional, with the extra dimension equal to the number of processors, and then carefully distributing the table:

```
REAL LUT(147,4)
!HPF$ DISTRIBUTE LUT(*, BLOCK(1))
```

However, this requires some care; in particular, whenever the lookup table is updated, all the copies must be updated. It is much easier to let the HPF compiler take care of the details by specifying a replicating alignment:

```
      REAL LUT(147)
      REAL A(4,4),B(4,4)
!HPF$ ALIGN LUT(*) WITH A(*,*)          !Replicating
!HPF$ ALIGN B(I,J) WITH A(I,J)
```

The alignment of LUT is actually both replicated and collapsed: a copy of the *entire* (collapsed) array LUT is to be aligned with *every* element of A. This situation is illustrated in Figure 4.3(b). Wherever an element of A might reside, there will be a copy of LUT in the same processor memory. The program is then written as if there were only a single copy of LUT; whenever LUT is updated, the HPF compiler arranges to update all copies consistently. (In practice, a good HPF compiler will not make a copy of **LUT** for every element of **A**, but only one copy in each processor that might contain elements of **A**. For a (**BLOCK, BLOCK**) distribution of **A** onto four processors, this would produce the situation shown in Figure 4.3(c). A (*,**BLOCK**) distribution for **A** would produce the situation shown in Figure 4.3(d).)

The data mapping directives illustrated so far are all *static*. They are like declarations; they take effect on entry to a scoping unit and describe how a data object is to be created. HPF also provides the *dynamic* data mapping directives **REDISTRIBUTE** and —**REALIGN**. They are just like **DISTRIBUTE** and and **ALIGN** with three differences:

- **REDISTRIBUTE** and **REALIGN** are like executable statements, not declarations, and so must appear in the *execution-part* (R208) of a scoping unit.
- Because **REDISTRIBUTE** and **REALIGN** are not declarations, they may not be combined with declaration-type directives using :: syntax.
- **REDISTRIBUTE** and **REALIGN** may not be applied to just any data object, but only to an object having the **DYNAMIC** attribute, specified by an HPF **DYNAMIC** directive. (This is similar in spirit to the Fortran 90 restriction that a pointer variable may not point to just any data object, but only to an object having the **TARGET** attribute.)

Consider an elaboration of a previous example:

```
      REAL, ARRAY(16,16) :: X, Y
!HPF$ PROCESSORS SQUARE(2,2), LINE(4)
!HPF$ ALIGN WITH X :: Y
!HPF$ DISTRIBUTE (BLOCK, BLOCK) ONTO SQUARE :: X
!HPF$ DYNAMIC X
```

Here the arrays **X** and **Y** are initially aligned and distributed as shown in Figure 4.1(c). However, we have declared an additional processor arrangement **LINE** and have specified the **DYNAMIC** attribute for **X**. (By the way, we could have combined the last two directives thus:

```
!HPF$ DYNAMIC, DISTRIBUTE (BLOCK, BLOCK) ONTO SQUARE :: X
```

in exactly the same manner that attributes may be combined in a Fortran 90 type declaration. HPF generalizes this syntax in not requiring a type declaration to be part of a combined directive.)

Because **X** is **DYNAMIC**, it is permitted to change the mapping of **X** on the fly. Therefore in the executable code we might insert this directive:

```
!HPF$ REDISTRIBUTE (*,BLOCK) ONTO LINE :: X
```

This advises the compiler that **X** should be remapped at that point in the program execution. Redistribution is required to maintain alignment relationships; because **Y** is aligned with **X**, **Y** will also be redistributed when **X** is. After execution passes the **REDISTRIBUTE** directive, the situation is roughly as shown in Figure 4.1(b).

We had to say "roughly" in the last remark because there is a subtle point about what HPF does and does not guarantee about distributions onto processors. In our example there are two declared processors arrangements, **SQUARE** and **LINE**. Each arrangement has four processors. It is likely, *but not guaranteed*, that the physical processors used to implement **SQUARE** will be the same physical processors used to implement **LINE**; that is an implementation-dependent detail. Moreover, even if the same physical processors are used, it is *not guaranteeed* that **LINE(1)** represents the same physical processor as **SQUARE(1,1)**; that is an implementation-dependent detail. So when **X** is remapped from **SQUARE** to **LINE**, it is likely that there will be a great deal of interprocessor communication, but the details of what must be communicated are implementation-dependent. One might, for example, conclude from inspection of Figures 4.1(c) and 4.1(b) that processor P_1 needs to export only half its data to perform the redistribution, but that conclusion is not guaranteed by HPF. The processor numberings in the figures are only illustrative and not definitive.

Another subtle point is that **Y** can be remapped even though it was not declared **DYNAMIC**, because it is (statically) aligned to $\hat{X}$, which is **DYNAMIC**. The absence of a **DYNAMIC** attribute for **Y** does mean, however, that one may not use **REALIGN** to change the alignment of **Y**. So while **Y** can be remapped *implicitly* whenever **X** is, the alignment relationship between **Y** ands **X** is always maintained and cannot be changed.

4.2 The Data Mapping Model

HPF directives allow the user to advise the compiler on the allocation of data objects to processor memories. The model is that there is a two-level mapping of data objects to the memories of *abstract processors*. Data objects (typically array elements) are first *aligned* relative to one another; a group of arrays is then *distributed* onto a rectilinear arrangement of abstract processors. (The implementation then uses the same number, or perhaps some smaller number, of physical processors to implement these abstract processors. This mapping of abstract processors to physical processors is system-dependent.) This model is illustrated in Figure 4.4.

The basic concept is that every array (indeed, every object) is created with *some* alignment to an entity, which in turn has *some* distribution onto *some* arrangement of abstract processors. There are three cases of interest:

Data Mapping

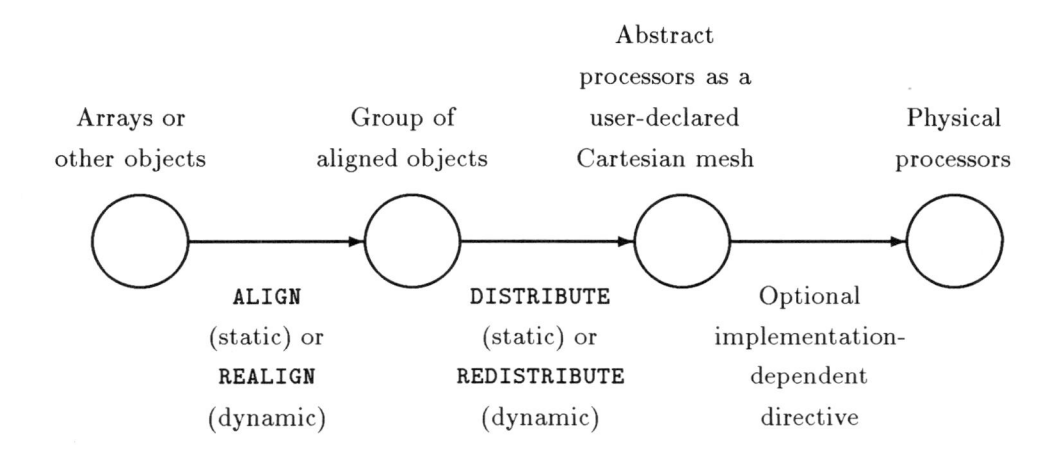

```
Arrays or          Group of         Abstract          Physical
other objects      aligned          processors as a   processors
                   objects          user-declared
                                    Cartesian mesh

     O ──────────────► O ──────────────► O ──────────────► O
          ALIGN             DISTRIBUTE        Optional
          (static) or       (static) or       implementation-
          REALIGN           REDISTRIBUTE      dependent
          (dynamic)         (dynamic)         directive
```

Figure 4.4
The HPF data mapping model

- If the specification statements contain explicit specification directives specifying the alignment of an array **A** with respect to another array **B**, then the distribution of **A** will be dictated by the distribution of **B**.
- Otherwise, the distribution of **A** itself may be specified explicitly (and it may be that other arrays are aligned with **A**).
- If the user does not provide explicit directives for mapping a data object, then the compiler must choose a data mapping.

In any case, data mapping specifications are conceptually used *as a data object is created* rather than as a separate step.

This model gives a better picture of the actual amount of work that needs to be done than a model that says "the array is created in some default location, and then realigned and/or redistributed if there is an explicit directive." Using **ALIGN** and **DISTRIBUTE** specification directives doesn't have to cause any more work at run time than using the implementation defaults.

There is a clear separation between directives that serve as specification statements and directives that serve as executable statements. Specification statements are carried out on entry to a program unit, as if all at once; only then are executable statements carried out. (While it is often convenient to think of specification statements as being handled at compile time, some of them contain specification expressions, which are permitted to depend on run-time quantities such as dummy arguments, and so the values of these expressions may not be available until run time, specifically the very moment that program control enters the scoping unit.)

In the case of an allocatable object, we say that the object is created whenever it is allocated. Specification directives for allocatable objects (and allocated pointer targets) may appear in the *specification-part* of a program unit, but take effect each time the array is created, rather than on entry to the scoping unit.

Alignment is considered an *attribute* of a data object (in the Fortran 90 sense). If an object **A** is aligned (statically or dynamically) with an object **B**, which in turn is already aligned to an object **C**, this is regarded as an alignment of **A** with **C** directly, with **B** serving only as an intermediary at the time of specification. (This matters only in the case where **B** is subsequently realigned; the result is that **A** remains aligned with **C**.) We say that **A** is *immediately aligned* with **B** but *ultimately aligned* with **C**. If an object is not explicitly aligned with another object, we say that it is ultimately aligned with itself. The alignment relationships form a tree with everything ultimately aligned to the object at the root of the tree; however, the tree is always immediately "collapsed" so that every object is related directly to the root. Any object that is not a root can be explicitly realigned but not explicitly redistributed. Any object that is a root can be explicitly redistributed but then cannot be explicitly realigned.

Every object that is the root of an alignment tree has an associated *template* or index space. Typically, this template has the same rank and size in each dimension as the object associated with it. (The most important exception to this rule is dummy arguments with the **INHERIT** attribute, described in Section 5.4.) We often refer to "the template for an array," which means the template of the object to which the array is ultimately aligned. (When an explicit **TEMPLATE** (see Section 4.9) is used, this may be simply the template to which the array is explicitly aligned.)

The *distribution* step of the HPF model technically applies to the template of an array, although because of the close relationship noted above we often speak loosely of the distribution of an array rather than of its template. Distribution partitions the template among a set of abstract processors according to a given pattern. The combination of alignment (from arrays to templates) and distribution (from templates to processors) thus determines the relationship of an array to the processors; we refer to this relationship as the *mapping* of the array. These remarks also apply to a scalar, which may be regarded as having an index space whose sole position is indicated by an empty list of subscripts. So every atomic data object is ultimately aligned to some data object, possibly itself, which is in turn distributed onto some specific abstract processor. (An *atomic data object* is a data object that has no subobjects.)

Data Mapping

Every object is created as if according to some complete set of specification directives; if the program does not include complete specifications for the mapping of some object, the compiler provides defaults. HPF imposes certain constraints on default mappings but also allows an HPF language processor certain specific freedoms.

- By default an object is not aligned with any other object; it is ultimately aligned with itself.
- The default distribution is system dependent, but must be expressible as explicit directives for that implementation. (The distribution of a sequential object has to be expressible as explicit directives only if it is an aggregate cover (see Section 4.10.2).)
- Identically declared objects need not be provided with identical default distribution specifications. The compiler may, for example, take into account the contexts in which objects are used in executable code. (The programmer can, if necessary, force identically declared objects to have identical distributions by specifying such distributions explicitly.)
- Unlike objects, identically declared processor arrangements *are* guaranteed to represent "the same processors arranged the same way." This is discussed in more detail in Section 4.8.

Once an object has been created, it can be remapped in one of two ways:

- by realigning the object itself; or
- by redistributing the object to which it is ultimately aligned.

Such remapping will typically carry some cost in interprocessor communication. Realignment causes remapping of only the object to be realigned, but redistributing an object causes *all* objects then ultimately aligned with it also to be redistributed so as to maintain the alignment relationships.

By analogy with the Fortran 90 **ALLOCATABLE** attribute, HPF includes the attribute **DYNAMIC**. It is not permitted to **REALIGN** an object that has not been declared **DYNAMIC**. Similarly, it is not permitted to **REDISTRIBUTE** an object or template that has not been declared **DYNAMIC**. (A subtle point: it is possible to remap an object **A** that has not been declared **DYNAMIC** if it has been aligned to another object **B** that is declared **DYNAMIC**. Redistributing **B** will then cause **A** to be redistributed as well, so as to maintain the statically declared alignment relationship.)

Sometimes it is desirable to consider a large index space with which several smaller arrays are to be aligned, but not to declare any array that spans the entire index space. HPF allows one to declare a **TEMPLATE**, which is like an array whose elements have no content and therefore occupy no storage; it is merely an abstract index space that can be distributed and with which arrays may be aligned.

It should be noted that HPF directives are technically regarded as *advice* to an HPF compiler rather than as *commands*. Alignment and distribution directives merely *recommend* to the compiler that certain data objects should reside in the same processor: if two data objects are mapped (via the two-level mapping of alignment and distribution) to the same abstract processor, it is a strong recommendation to the implementation that they ought to reside in the same physical processor. The converse is not true; mapping two data objects to different abstract processors is not necessarily a strong recommendation that the objects reside in different physical processors. HPF takes this stance for two reasons:

- To provide flexibility for compiler implementors. In particular, as the technology of automatic data layout improves, compilers may judiciously override user directives in order to improve performance. (This is similar to the situation in the C programming language, which provides explicit **register** directives. When algorithms for automatic register allocation became sufficiently powerful, the best C compilers would ignore or override programmer directives when appropriate.)
- To provide for maximum portability of HPF codes. In particular, it is always legitimate to compile an HPF program for a single-processor target machine.

While directives are technically merely advisory, all the directives in a complete HPF program must be consistent. An HPF compiler is permitted to rely on the consistency of directives across separately compiled program units.

4.3 Syntax of Data Alignment and Distribution Directives

Specification directives in HPF have two forms: specification statements, analogous to the **DIMENSION** and **ALLOCATABLE** statements of Fortran 90; and an attribute form analogous to type declaration statements in Fortran 90 using the "::" punctuation.

The attribute form allows more than one attribute to be described in a single directive. HPF goes beyond Fortran 90 in not requiring that the first attribute, or indeed any of them, be a type specifier.

For syntactic convenience, the executable directives **REALIGN** and **REDISTRIBUTE** also come in two forms (statement form and attribute form) but may not be combined with other attributes in a single directive.

The form of a *combined-directive* (H301) is:

combined-attribute-list :: *entity-decl-list*

where a *combined-attribute* (H302) is one of:

```
ALIGN  align-attribute-stuff
DISTRIBUTE  dist-attribute-stuff
DYNAMIC
INHERIT
TEMPLATE
PROCESSORS
DIMENSION ( explicit-shape-spec-list )
```

Rules and restrictions:
1. The same *combined-attribute* must not appear more than once in a given *combined-directive*.
2. If the DIMENSION attribute appears in a *combined-directive*, any entity to which it applies must be declared with the HPF TEMPLATE or PROCESSORS type specifier.
3. The HPF keywords PROCESSORS and TEMPLATE play the role of type specifiers in declaring processor arrangements and templates. The HPF keywords ALIGN, DISTRIBUTE, DYNAMIC, and INHERIT play the role of attributes. Attributes referring to processor arrangements, to templates, or to entities with other types (such as REAL) may be combined in an HPF directive without having the type specifier appear.
4. Dimension information may be specified after an *object-name* or in a DIMENSION attribute. If both are present, the one after the *object-name* overrides the DIMENSION attribute (this is consistent with the Fortran 90 standard).

Example 4.1 The directive

```
!HPF$ TEMPLATE, DIMENSION(64,64) :: A, B, C(32,32), D
```

specifies that A, B, and D are 64×64 templates; C is 32×32. □

4.4 DISTRIBUTE and REDISTRIBUTE Directives

The DISTRIBUTE directive specifies a mapping of data objects to abstract processors in a processor arrangement. For example,

```
      REAL SALAMI(10000)
!HPF$ DISTRIBUTE SALAMI(BLOCK)
```

specifies that the array SALAMI should be distributed across some set of abstract processors by slicing it uniformly into blocks of contiguous elements. If there are 50 processors, the directive implies that the array should be divided into groups of 200 elements, with

	P_1	P_2	P_3	P_4
	1	2	3	4
	5	6	7	8
	9	10	11	12
	13	14	15	16
	17	18	19	20
	21	22	23	24
	25	26	27	28
	29	30	31	32
	33	34	35	36
	37	38	39	40
	41	42	43	44
	45	46	47	48
	49	50	51	52

(a) the 52 elements of DECK_OF_CARDS with distribution CYCLIC

P_1	P_2	P_3	P_4
1	6	11	16
2	7	12	17
3	8	13	18
4	9	14	19
5	10	15	20
21	26	31	36
22	27	32	37
23	28	33	38
24	29	34	39
25	30	35	40
41	46	51	—
42	47	52	—
43	48	—	—
44	49	—	—
45	50	—	—

(b) the 52 elements of DECK_OF_CARDS with distribution CYCLIC(5)

Figure 4.5
Cyclic and block-cyclic distributions of a deck of cards

SALAMI(1:200) mapped to the first processor, SALAMI(201:400) mapped to the second processor, and so on. If there is only one processor, the entire array is mapped to that processor as a single block of 10000 elements.

The block size may be specified explicitly:

```
REAL WEISSWURST(10000)
!HPF$ DISTRIBUTE WEISSWURST(BLOCK(256))
```

This specifies that groups of exactly 256 elements should be mapped to successive abstract processors. (There must be at least $\lceil 10000/256 \rceil = 40$ abstract processors if the directive is to be satisfied. The fortieth processor will contain a partial block of only 16 elements, namely WEISSWURST(9985:10000).)

HPF also provides a cyclic distribution format:

```
REAL DECK_OF_CARDS(52)
!HPF$ DISTRIBUTE DECK_OF_CARDS(CYCLIC)
```

If there are 4 abstract processors, the first processor will contain DECK_OF_CARDS(1:49:4), the second processor will contain DECK_OF_CARDS(2:50:4), the third processor will have

DECK_OF_CARDS(3:51:4), and the fourth processor will have DECK_OF_CARDS(4:52:4). Successive array elements are dealt out to successive abstract processors in round-robin fashion—see Figure 4.5(a). If the array elements were instead dealt out five at a time:

!HPF$ DISTRIBUTE DECK_OF_CARDS(CYCLIC(5))

the result would be a *block-cyclic* distribution that assigned the first processor DECK_OF_CARDS(1:5), DECK_OF_CARDS(21:25), and DECK_OF_CARDS(41:45)—see Figure 4.5(b).

Distributions may be specified independently for each dimension of a multidimensional array:

```
      INTEGER CHESS_BOARD(8,8), GO_BOARD(19,19)
!HPF$ DISTRIBUTE CHESS_BOARD(BLOCK, BLOCK)
!HPF$ DISTRIBUTE GO_BOARD(CYCLIC,*)
```

The CHESS_BOARD array will be carved up into contiguous rectangular patches, which will be distributed onto a two-dimensional arrangement of abstract processors. The GO_BOARD array will have its rows distributed cyclically over a one-dimensional arrangement of abstract processors. (The "*" specifies that GO_BOARD is not to be distributed along its second axis; thus an entire row is to be distributed as one object. This is sometimes called "on-processor" distribution.)

The REDISTRIBUTE directive is similar to the DISTRIBUTE directive but is considered executable. An array (or template) may be redistributed at any time, provided it has been declared DYNAMIC (see Section 4.6). Any other arrays currently ultimately aligned with an array (or template) when it is redistributed are also remapped to reflect the new distribution, in such a way as to preserve alignment relationships (see Section 4.5). (This can require a lot of computational and communication effort at run time; the programmer must take care when using this feature.)

The form of a *distribute-directive* (H303) is:

DISTRIBUTE *distributee dist-directive-stuff*
DISTRIBUTE *dist-attribute-stuff* :: *distributee-list*

(Note that the second form is a special case of a *combined-directive* (H301).)

The form of a *redistribute-directive* (H304) is one of:

REDISTRIBUTE *distributee dist-directive-stuff*
REDISTRIBUTE *dist-attribute-stuff* :: *distributee-list*

Although REDISTRIBUTE is not an attribute and so cannot be used in a *combined-directive*, for convenience a *redistribute-directive* may be written in the style of attributed syntax, using "::" punctuation, so as to resemble a *distribute-directive*.

Either kind of directive mentions one or more *distributees* and some descriptive "stuff" that is taken to apply to each *distributee*. Each *distributee* (H307) must be either an *object-name* or a *template-name*.

The form of *dist-directive-stuff* (H305) is one of:

(*dist-format-list*)
(*dist-format-list*) ONTO *processors-name*

The form of *dist-attribute-stuff* (H306) is one of:

(*dist-format-list*)
(*dist-format-list*) ONTO *processors-name*
ONTO *dist-target*

The distinction between specification statement form and attributed form is merely that a parenthesized *dist-format* list *must* appear in the specification statement form, whereas it may be omitted in the attributed form if the ONTO clause appears. This admittedly arbitrary restriction forestalls syntactic ambiguity in the directive form.

(There are actually other possibilities for *dist-directive-stuff* and *dist-attribute-stuff* but they apply only to dummy arguments. Their complete syntax is discussed in Chapter 5.)

A *dist-format* (H309) may be one of:

BLOCK [(*int-expr*)]
CYCLIC [(*int-expr*)]
*

In a DISTRIBUTE or REDISTRIBUTE directive, the "formats" describe how each axis of an array or template is to be distributed and the ONTO clause, if present, specifies the particular abstract processor arrangement onto which the axes are distributed.

Rules and restrictions:
1. The DISTRIBUTE directive may appear only in the *specification-part* of a scoping unit.
2. The REDISTRIBUTE directive may appear only in the *execution-part* of a scoping unit.
3. An *object-name* mentioned as a *distributee* must be a simple name and not a subobject designator.
4. An *object-name* mentioned as a *distributee* may not appear as an *alignee* in an ALIGN or REALIGN directive.
5. A *distributee* that appears in a REDISTRIBUTE directive must have the DYNAMIC attribute (see Section 4.6).
6. If a *dist-format-list* is specified, its length must equal the rank of each *distributee*.

Data Mapping

7. If an **ONTO** clause is present, the *processors-name* must name a processors arrangement declared in a **PROCESSORS** directive (see Section 4.8).
8. If both a *dist-format-list* and a *processors-name* appear, the number of elements of the *dist-format-list* that are not "*" must equal the rank of the named processor arrangement.
9. If a *processors-name* appears but not a *dist-format-list*, the rank of each *distributee* must equal the rank of the named processor arrangement.
10. Any *int-expr* appearing after **BLOCK** or **CYCLIC** in a *dist-format* of a **DISTRIBUTE** directive must be a *specification-expr*.
11. The value of any *int-expr* appearing after **CYCLIC** in a *dist-format* of a **DISTRIBUTE** or **REDISTRIBUTE** directive must be a positive integer.
12. The value of any *int-expr* appearing after **BLOCK** in a *dist-format* of a **DISTRIBUTE** or **REDISTRIBUTE** directive must be a positive integer m such that, for every *distributee*, $m \times p \geq d$ (equivalently, $m \geq \lceil d/p \rceil$) where d is the extent of the corresponding dimension of the *distributee* and p is the corresponding dimension of the processors arrangement onto which the *distributee* is to be distributed.

The meanings of the alternatives for *dist-format* are given below. But first, some preliminaries.

Many of the formulas to come will use the subexpressions $\lceil \frac{j}{k} \rceil$ and $j - k \lceil \frac{j}{k} \rceil$ for some j and k. We note in passing that these play the role of integer division and remainder in the formulas (except that the division is rounded upwards rather than truncated as in standard Fortran usage). It is also true that this "remainder" is always negative or zero if j is nonnegative and k is positive.

The dimensions of a processor arrangement appearing in an **ONTO** clause are said to *correspond* in left-to-right order with those dimensions of a *distributee* for which the corresponding *dist-format* is not *. In the example

`!HPF$ DISTRIBUTE (BLOCK, *, BLOCK) ONTO SQUARE:: D1, D2`

the arrays **D1** and **D2** are three-dimensional (though not necessarily of the same shape), but the processor arrangement **SQUARE** must be two-dimensional. **SQUARE**'s first dimension corresponds to the first dimensions of **D1** and **D2** and its second dimension corresponds to the third dimensions of **D1** and **D2**.

Let d be the extent of a *distributee* in a certain dimension and let p be the extent of the processor arrangement in the corresponding dimension. For simplicity, assume all dimensions have a lower bound of 1. Then **BLOCK**(m) means that a *distributee* position whose index along that dimension is j is mapped to an abstract processor whose index along the corresponding dimension of the processor arrangement is $\lceil \frac{j}{m} \rceil$. Also, that element of the *distributee* is position number $m + j - m \lceil \frac{j}{m} \rceil$ (that is, $1 + (j \bmod m)$) among elements mapped to that abstract processor. The first *distributee* position in abstract processor k along that axis is position number $1 + m(k - 1)$.

BLOCK by definition means the same as **BLOCK**($\lceil \frac{d}{p} \rceil$).

CYCLIC(m) means that a *distributee* position whose index along that dimension is j is mapped to an abstract processor whose index along the corresponding dimension of the processor arrangement is $1 + (\frac{j}{m} \bmod p)$. Also, that *distributee* position is position number $1 + m \lfloor \frac{j}{pm} \rfloor + (j \bmod m)$ among positions mapped to that abstract processor. The first *distributee* position in abstract processor k along that axis is position number $1 + m(k - 1)$ (this formula is the same as for **BLOCK**(m)).

CYCLIC by definition means the same as **CYCLIC(1)**.

CYCLIC(m) and **BLOCK**(m) imply the same distribution when $m \times p \geq d$, but **BLOCK**(m) additionally asserts that the distribution will not wrap around in a cyclic manner, which a compiler cannot determine at compile time if m is not constant. Note that **CYCLIC** and **BLOCK** (without argument expressions) do not imply the same distribution unless $p \geq d$, a degenerate case in which the block size is 1 and the distribution does not wrap around.

The formulas for "position numbers" in the preceding paragraphs suggest a specific implementation of **BLOCK** and **CYCLIC** layouts. For simplicity, first consider one-dimensional arrays only. A one-dimensional array of length d may be stored within p processors by reserving a block of space within each processor. Let b_i be the address of the block of space within processor i (an implementation might or might not require the b_i to have the same value for all i). Then:

- For a **BLOCK**(m) distribution, element j of the array might be stored within processor $\lceil \frac{j}{m} \rceil$ at address $b_{\lceil j/m \rceil} + (j \bmod m)$.
- For a **CYCLIC**(m) distribution, element j of the array might be stored within processor $1 + (\lceil \frac{j}{m} \rceil - 1) \bmod p$ at address $b_{1+(\lceil j/m \rceil -1) \bmod p} + m \lfloor \frac{j}{pm} \rfloor + (j \bmod m)$.

For multidimensional arrays, one can separately apply the appropriate formula to each dimension and then combine processor numbers (on the one hand) and position numbers (on the other hand) in the same manner as one would combine ordinary subscripts for a Fortran multidimensional array to produce a linear processor number and a linear memory offset within that processor.

While these formulas are highly suggestive, HPF does not require this particular organization of processors or this particular memory layout within processors.

Data Mapping

Example 4.2 Suppose that we have 16 abstract processors and an array of length 100:

```
!HPF$ PROCESSORS SEDECIM(16)
      REAL CENTURY(100)
```

Distributing the array BLOCK (which in this case would mean the same as BLOCK(7)):

```
!HPF$ DISTRIBUTE CENTURY(BLOCK) ONTO SEDECIM
```

results in this mapping of array elements onto abstract processors:

	1	2	3	4	5	6	7	8	9	10	11	12	13	14	15	16
1	8	15	22	29	36	43	50	57	64	71	78	85	92	99		
2	9	16	23	30	37	44	51	58	65	72	79	86	93	100		
3	10	17	24	31	38	45	52	59	66	73	80	87	94			
4	11	18	25	32	39	46	53	60	67	74	81	88	95			
5	12	19	26	33	40	47	54	61	68	75	82	89	96			
6	13	20	27	34	41	48	55	62	69	76	83	90	97			
7	14	21	28	35	42	49	56	63	70	77	84	91	98			

Distributing the array BLOCK(8):

```
!HPF$ DISTRIBUTE CENTURY(BLOCK(8)) ONTO SEDECIM
```

results in this mapping of array elements onto abstract processors:

	1	2	3	4	5	6	7	8	9	10	11	12	13	14	15	16
1	9	17	25	33	41	49	57	65	73	81	89	97				
2	10	18	26	34	42	50	58	66	74	82	90	98				
3	11	19	27	35	43	51	59	67	75	83	91	99				
4	12	20	28	36	44	52	60	68	76	84	92	100				
5	13	21	29	37	45	53	61	69	77	85	93					
6	14	22	30	38	46	54	62	70	78	86	94					
7	15	23	31	39	47	55	63	71	79	87	95					
8	16	24	32	40	48	56	64	72	80	88	96					

Distributing the array BLOCK(6) is not HPF-conforming because $6 \times 16 < 100$.

Distributing the array CYCLIC (which means exactly the same as CYCLIC(1)):

`!HPF$ DISTRIBUTE CENTURY(CYCLIC) ONTO SEDECIM`

results in this mapping of array elements onto abstract processors:

1	2	3	4	5	6	7	8	9	10	11	12	13	14	15	16
1	2	3	4	5	6	7	8	9	10	11	12	13	14	15	16
17	18	19	20	21	22	23	24	25	26	27	28	29	30	31	32
33	34	35	36	37	38	39	40	41	42	43	44	45	46	47	48
49	50	51	52	53	54	55	56	57	58	59	60	61	62	63	64
65	66	67	68	69	70	71	72	73	74	75	76	77	78	79	80
81	82	83	84	85	86	87	88	89	90	91	92	93	94	95	96
97	98	99	100												

Distributing the array CYCLIC(3):

`!HPF$ DISTRIBUTE CENTURY(CYCLIC(3)) ONTO SEDECIM`

results in this mapping of array elements onto abstract processors:

1	2	3	4	5	6	7	8	9	10	11	12	13	14	15	16
1	4	7	10	13	16	19	22	25	28	31	34	37	40	43	46
2	5	8	11	14	17	20	23	26	29	32	35	38	41	44	47
3	6	9	12	15	18	21	24	27	30	33	36	39	42	45	48
49	52	55	58	61	64	67	70	73	76	79	82	85	88	91	94
50	53	56	59	62	65	68	71	74	77	80	83	86	89	92	95
51	54	57	60	63	66	69	72	75	78	81	84	87	90	93	96
97	100														
98															
99															

Thus different distributions may require the reservation of differing amounts of space within each processor. □

A DISTRIBUTE or REDISTRIBUTE directive must not cause any data object associated with the *distributee* via storage association (COMMON or EQUIVALENCE) to be mapped such that storage units of a scalar data object are split across more than one abstract processor. See Section 4.10.2 for further discussion of storage association.

Data Mapping

The statement form of a **DISTRIBUTE** or **REDISTRIBUTE** directive may be considered an abbreviation for an attributed form that happens to mention only one *alignee*; for example,

!HPF$ DISTRIBUTE *distributee* (*dist-format-list*) ONTO *dist-target*

is equivalent to

!HPF$ DISTRIBUTE (*dist-format-list*) ONTO *dist-target* :: *distributee*

Note that, to prevent syntactic ambiguity, the *dist-format-list* must be present (with its surrounding parentheses) in the statement form. But if a *dist-format-list* is present, at least one *dist-format* must appear, in which case each *distributee* must be an array. It follows that the statement form of the directive may not be used to specify the mapping of scalars; the attributed form must be used:

!HPF$ DISTRIBUTE ONTO SCALARPROC :: REALSCALAR, INTSCALAR

If the *dist-format-list* is omitted from the attributed form, then the language processor may make an arbitrary choice of distribution formats for each template or array. So the directive

!HPF$ DISTRIBUTE ONTO P :: D1, D2, D3

means the same as

!HPF$ DISTRIBUTE ONTO P :: D1
!HPF$ DISTRIBUTE ONTO P :: D2
!HPF$ DISTRIBUTE ONTO P :: D3

to which a compiler, perhaps taking into account patterns of use of D1, D2, and D3 within the code, might choose to supply three distinct distributions such as, for example,

!HPF$ DISTRIBUTE D1(BLOCK, BLOCK) ONTO P
!HPF$ DISTRIBUTE D2(CYCLIC, BLOCK) ONTO P
!HPF$ DISTRIBUTE D3(BLOCK(43),CYCLIC) ONTO P

Then again, the compiler might happen to choose the same distribution for all three arrays.

In either the statement form or the attributed form, if the **ONTO** clause is present, it specifies the processor arrangement that is the target of the distribution. If the **ONTO** clause is omitted, then a system-dependent processor arrangement is chosen arbitrarily for each *distributee*. So, for example,

```
      REAL, DIMENSION(1000) :: ARTHUR, ARNOLD, LINUS, LUCY
!HPF$ PROCESSORS EXCALIBUR(32)
!HPF$ DISTRIBUTE (BLOCK) ONTO EXCALIBUR :: ARTHUR, ARNOLD
!HPF$ DISTRIBUTE (BLOCK) :: LINUS, LUCY
```

causes the arrays **ARTHUR** and **ARNOLD** to have the same mapping, so that corresponding elements reside in the same abstract processor, because they are the same size and distributed in the same way (**BLOCK**) onto the same processor arrangement (**EXCALIBUR**). However, **LUCY** and **LINUS** do not necessarily have the same mapping because they might, depending on the implementation, be distributed onto differently chosen processor arrangements; so corresponding elements of **LUCY** and **LINUS** might not reside on the same abstract processor. (The **ALIGN** directive provides a way to ensure that two arrays have the same mapping without having to specify an explicit processor arrangement.)

4.5 ALIGN and REALIGN Directives

The **ALIGN** directive is used to specify that certain data objects are to be mapped in the same way as certain other data objects. Operations between aligned data objects are likely to be more efficient than operations between data objects that are not known to be aligned (because two objects that are aligned are intended to be mapped to the same abstract processor). The **ALIGN** directive is designed to make it particularly easy to specify explicit mappings for all the elements of an array at once. While objects can be aligned in some cases through careful use of matching **DISTRIBUTE** directives, **ALIGN** is more general and frequently more convenient.

The **REALIGN** directive is similar to the **ALIGN** directive but is considered executable. An array (or template) may be realigned at any time, provided it has been declared **DYNAMIC** (see Section 4.6) Unlike redistribution (see Section 4.4), realigning a data object does not cause any other object to be remapped. (However, realignment of even a single object, if it is large, could require a lot of computational and communication effort at run time; the programmer must take care when using this feature.)

The **ALIGN** directive may appear only in the *specification-part* of a scoping unit. The **REALIGN** directive is similar but may appear only in the *execution-part* of a scoping unit. The principal difference between **ALIGN** and **REALIGN** is that **ALIGN** must contain only a *specification-expr* as a *subscript* or in a *subscript-triplet*, whereas in **REALIGN** such subscripts may be any integer expressions. Another difference is that **ALIGN** is an attribute, and so can be combined with other attributes as part of a *combined-directive*, whereas **REALIGN** is not an attribute (although a **REALIGN** statement may be written in the style of attributed syntax, using "::" punctuation).

Data Mapping

The form of an *align-directive* (H312) is:

ALIGN *alignee align-directive-stuff*
ALIGN *align-attribute-stuff* :: *alignee-list*

(Note that the second form is a special case of a *combined-directive* (H301).)

The form of a *realign-directive* (H313) is:

REALIGN *alignee align-directive-stuff*
REALIGN *align-attribute-stuff* :: *alignee-list*

Although **REALIGN** is not an attribute and so cannot be used in a *combined-directive*, for convenience a *realign-directive* may be written in the style of attributed syntax, using "::" punctuation, so as to resemble an *align-directive*.

Either kind of directive mentions one or more alignees and some descriptive "stuff" that is taken to apply to each alignee.

The form of an *alignee* (H316) is:

object-name

The form of *align-directive-stuff* (H314) is:

(*align-source-list*) *align-with-clause*

whereas the form of an *align-attribute-stuff* (H315) is:

[(*align-source-list*)] *align-with-clause*

The distinction between directive form and attributed form is merely that the *align-source-list* with its enclosing parentheses must appear in the directive form, whereas it may be omitted in the attributed form. (This admittedly arbitrary restriction forestalls syntactic ambiguity in the directive form.) One important consequence of this restriction is that alignees that are not arrays require the use of the attributed form.

The form of each *align-source* (H317) is one of:

:
*
align-dummy

where an *align-dummy* (H318) is a *scalar-int-variable*.

Rules and restrictions:
1. An *object-name* mentioned as an *alignee* may not appear as a *distributee* in a **DISTRIBUTE** or **REDISTRIBUTE** directive.

2. Any *alignee* that appears in a `REALIGN` directive must have the `DYNAMIC` attribute (see Section 4.6).
3. The *align-source-list* (and its surrounding parentheses) must be omitted if the *alignee* is scalar. (In some cases this will preclude the use of the statement form of the directive.)
4. If the *align-source-list* is present, its length must equal the rank of the alignee.
5. An *align-dummy* must be a named variable.
6. An object may not have both the `INHERIT` attribute and the `ALIGN` attribute. (However, an object with the `INHERIT` attribute may appear as an *alignee* in a `REALIGN` directive, provided that it does not appear as a *distributee* in a `DISTRIBUTE` or `REDISTRIBUTE` directive.)

The statement form of an `ALIGN` or `REALIGN` directive may be considered an abbreviation of an attributed form that happens to mention only one *alignee*:

`!HPF$ ALIGN` *alignee* `(` *align-source-list* `) WITH` *align-spec*

is equivalent to

`!HPF$ ALIGN (` *align-source-list* `) WITH` *align-spec* `::` *alignee*

If the *align-source-list* is omitted from the attributed form and the *alignees* are not scalar, the *align-source-list* is assumed to consist of a parenthesized list of ":" entries, equal in number to the rank of the *alignees*. Similarly, if the *align-subscript-list* is omitted from the *align-spec* in either form, it is assumed to consist of a parenthesized list of ":" entries, equal in number to the rank of the *align-target*. So the directive

`!HPF$ ALIGN WITH B :: A1, A2, A3`

means

`!HPF$ ALIGN (:,:) WITH B(:,:) :: A1, A2, A3`

which in turn means the same as

`!HPF$ ALIGN A1(:,:) WITH B(:,:)`
`!HPF$ ALIGN A2(:,:) WITH B(:,:)`
`!HPF$ ALIGN A3(:,:) WITH B(:,:)`

because an attributed-form directive that mentions more than one *alignee* is equivalent to a series of identical directives, one for each *alignee*; all *alignees* must have the same rank. With this understanding, we will assume below, for the sake of simplifying the description, that an `ALIGN` or `REALIGN` directive has a single *alignee*.

Each *align-source* corresponds to one axis of the *alignee*, and is specified as either ":" or "*" or a dummy variable:

- If it is ":", then positions along that axis will be spread out across the matching axis of the *align-spec* (see below).
- If it is "*", then that axis is *collapsed*: positions along that axis make no difference in determining the corresponding position within the *align-target*. (Replacing the "*" with a dummy variable name not used anywhere else in the directive would have the same effect; "*" is merely a convenience that saves the trouble of inventing a variable name and makes it clear that no dependence on that dimension is intended.)
- A dummy variable is considered to range over all valid index values for that dimension of the *alignee*.

The form of an *align-with-clause* (H319) is:

WITH *align-target* [(*align-subscript-list*)]

There is actually another possibility for an *align-with-clause* but it applies only to dummy arguments. The complete syntax for an *align-with-clause* is discussed in Chapter 5.

An *align-target* (H321) must be an *object-name* or a *template-name*.

The form of an *align-subscript* (H322) is:

int-expr
align-subscript-use
subscript-triplet
*

An *align-subscript-use* is an integer expression that mentions some *align-dummy* variable exactly once as a manifestly linear function of that variable. The form of an *align-subscript-use* (H323) is one of:

[[*int-level-two-expr*] *add-op*] *align-add-operand*
align-subscript-use *add-op* *int-add-operand*

where an *align-add-operand* (H324) is one of:

[*int-add-operand* *] *align-primary*
align-add-operand * *int-mult-operand*

and an *align-primary* (H325) is one of:

align-dummy
(*align-subscript-use*)

An *int-add-operand* (H326) is simply a Fortran 90 *add-operand* (R706) of integer type. Similarly, a *int-mult-operand* (H327) is a *mult-operand* (R705) of integer type and a *int-level-two-expr* (H328) is an *level-2-expr* (R707) of integer type.

Rules and restrictions:
1. Each *align-dummy* may appear at most once in an *align-subscript-list*.
2. An *align-subscript-use* expression may contain at most one occurrence of an *align-dummy*.
3. An *align-dummy* may not appear anywhere in the *align-spec* except where explicitly permitted to appear by virtue of the grammar shown above. Paraphrased, one may construct an *align-subscript-use* by starting with an *align-dummy* and then doing additive and multiplicative things to it with any integer expressions that contain no *align-dummy*.
4. A *subscript* in an *align-subscript* may not contain occurrences of any *align-dummy*.
5. An *int-add-operand*, *int-mult-operand*, or *int-level-two-expr* must be of type integer.

The syntax rules for an *align-subscript-use* take account of operator precedence issues, but the basic idea is simple: an *align-subscript-use* is intended to be a linear function of a single occurrence of an *align-dummy*.

For example, the following *align-subscript-use* expressions are valid, assuming that J, K, and M are *align-dummy* names and N is not an *align-dummy*:

```
J       J+1       3-K       2*M       N*M       100-3*M
-J      +J        -K+3      M+2**3    M+N       -(4*7+IOR(6,9))*K-(13-5/3)
M*2     N*(M-N)   2*(J+1)   5-K+3     10000-M*3 2*(3*(K-1)+13)-100
```

The following expressions are not valid *align-subscript-use* expressions:

```
J+J     J-J       3*K-2*K   M*(N-M)   2*J-3*J+J 2*(3*(K-1)+13)-K
J*J     J+K       3/K       2**M      M*K       K-3*M
K-J     IOR(J,1)  -K/3      M*(2+M)   M*(M-N)   2**(2*J-3*J+J)
```

The *align-spec* must contain exactly as many *subscript-triplets* as the number of colons (":") appearing in the *align-source-list*. These are matched up in corresponding left-to-right order, ignoring, for this purpose, any *align-source* that is not a colon and any *align-subscript* that is not a *subscript-triplet*. Consider a dimension of the *alignee* for which a colon appears as an *align-source* and let the lower and upper bounds of that array be LA and UA. Let the corresponding subscript triplet be $LT : UT : ST$ or its equivalent. Then the colon could be replaced by a new, as-yet-unused dummy variable, say J, and the subscript triplet by the expression (J$-LA$)$*ST+LT$ without affecting the meaning of the directive. Moreover, the axes must conform, which means that

Data Mapping

$$\max(0, UA - LA + 1) = \max\left(0, \left\lceil \frac{UT - LT + 1}{ST} \right\rceil \right)$$

must be true. (This is entirely analogous to the treatment of array assignment.)

To simplify the remainder of the discussion, we assume that every colon in the *align-source-list* has been replaced by new dummy variables in exactly the fashion just described, and that every "*" in the *align-source-list* has likewise been replaced by an otherwise unused dummy variable. For example,

```
!HPF$ ALIGN A(:,*,K,:,:,*) WITH B(31:,:,K+3,20:100:3)
```

may be transformed into its equivalent

```
!HPF$ ALIGN A(I,J,K,L,M,N) WITH B(I-LBOUND(A,1)+31,      &
!HPF$           L-LBOUND(A,4)+LBOUND(B,2),K+3,(M-LBOUND(A,5))*3+20)
```

with the attached requirements

```
         SIZE(A,1) .EQ. UBOUND(B,1)-30
         SIZE(A,4) .EQ. SIZE(B,2)
         SIZE(A,5) .EQ. (100-20+3)/3
```

Thus we need consider further only the case where every *align-source* is a dummy variable and no *align-subscript* is a *subscript-triplet*.

Each dummy variable is considered to range over all valid index values for the corresponding dimension of the *alignee*. Every combination of possible values for the index variables selects an element of the *alignee*. The *align-spec* indicates a corresponding element (or section) of the *align-target* with which that element of the *alignee* should be aligned; this indication may be a function of the index values, but the nature of this function is syntactically restricted (as discussed above) to linear functions in order to limit the complexity of the implementation. Each *align-dummy* variable may appear at most once in the *align-spec* and only in certain rigidly prescribed contexts. The result is that each *align-subscript* expression may contain at most one *align-dummy* variable and the expression is constrained to be a linear function of that variable. (Therefore skew alignments are not possible.)

An asterisk "*" as an *align-subscript* indicates a replicated representation. Each element of the *alignee* is aligned with every position along that axis of the *align-target*. It is as if the compiler were, for each "*" *align-subscript*, to replace the "*" by a new dummy variable, automatically to add an extra dimension to the *alignee*, and then use the same new dummy variable as the *align-source* for the new dimension. Thus the replicating alignment

```
!HPF$ ALIGN A(J) WITH D(J,*)
```

roughly results in implementing **A** as a two-dimensional array with the specification

```
!HPF$ ALIGN A(J,K) WITH D(J,K)
```

The compiler then generates code that ensures that all the copies of the original **A** along the extra dimension are updated consistently; for example, a piece of code such as

```
DO I = 1, 200
   A(I) = 3.7 ** I
END DO
```

is compiled roughly as if it were first transformed into

```
DO I = 1, 200
   A(I, :) = 3.7 ** I
END DO
```

By applying the transformations given above, all cases of an *align-subscript* may be conceptually reduced to either an *int-expr* (not involving an *align-dummy*) or an *align-subscript-use*, and the *align-source-list* may be reduced to a list of index variables with no "*" or ":". An *align-subscript-list* may then be evaluated for any specific combination of values for the *align-dummy* variables simply by evaluating each *align-subscript* as an expression. The resulting subscript values must be legitimate subscripts for the *align-target*. (This implies that the *alignee* is not allowed to "wrap around" or "extend past the edges" of an *align-target*.) The selected element of the *alignee* is then considered to be aligned with the indicated element of the *align-target*; more precisely, the selected element of the *alignee* is considered to be ultimately aligned with the same object with which the indicated element of the *align-target* are currently ultimately aligned (possibly itself).

Once a relationship of ultimate alignment is established, it persists, even if the ultimate *align-target* is redistributed, unless and until the *alignee* is realigned by a **REALIGN** directive, which is permissible only if the *alignee* has the **DYNAMIC** attribute.

More examples of **ALIGN** directives follow:

```
      INTEGER D1(N)
      LOGICAL D2(N,N)
      REAL, DIMENSION(N,N):: X, A, B, C, AR1, AR2A, P, Q, R, S
!HPF$ ALIGN X(:,*) WITH D1(:)
!HPF$ ALIGN (:,*) WITH D1:: A, B, C, AR1, AR2A
!HPF$ ALIGN WITH D2, DYNAMIC:: P,Q,R,S
```

Note that, in a *alignee-list*, the alignees must all have the same rank but need not all have the same shape; the extents need match only for dimensions that correspond to colons in the *align-source-list*. This turns out to be an extremely important convenience; one of the most common cases in current practice is aligning arrays that match in distributed ("parallel") dimensions but may differ in collapsed ("on-processor") dimensions:

```
      REAL A(3,N), B(4,N), C(43,N), Q(N)
!HPF$ DISTRIBUTE Q(BLOCK)
!HPF$ ALIGN (*,:) WITH Q:: A, B, C
```

Here there are processors (perhaps N of them) and arrays of different sizes (3, 4, 43) within each processor are required. As far as HPF is concerned, the numbers 3, 4, and 43 may be different, because those axes will be collapsed. Thus array elements with indices differing only along that axis will all be aligned with the same element of Q (and thus be specified as residing in the same processor).

In the following examples, each directive in the group means the same thing, assuming that corresponding axis upper and lower bounds match:

```
!Second axis of X is collapsed
!HPF$ ALIGN X(:,*) WITH D1(:)
!HPF$ ALIGN X(J,*) WITH D1(J)
!HPF$ ALIGN X(J,K) WITH D1(J)

!Replicated representation along second axis of D3
!HPF$ ALIGN X(:,:) WITH D3(:,*,:)
!HPF$ ALIGN X(J,K) WITH D3(J,*,K)

!Transposing two axes
!HPF$ ALIGN X(J,K) WITH D2(K,J)
!HPF$ ALIGN X(J,:) WITH D2(:,J)
!HPF$ ALIGN X(:,K) WITH D2(K,:)
!But there isn't any way to get rid of *both* index variables;
! the subscript-triplet syntax alone cannot express transposition.

!Reversing both axes
!HPF$ ALIGN X(J,K) WITH D2(M-J+1,N-K+1)
!HPF$ ALIGN X(:,:) WITH D2(M:1:-1,N:1:-1)
```

```
!Simple case
!HPF$ ALIGN X(J,K) WITH D2(J,K)
!HPF$ ALIGN X(:,:) WITH D2(:,:)
!HPF$ ALIGN (J,K) WITH D2(J,K):: X
!HPF$ ALIGN (:,:) WITH D2(:,:):: X
!HPF$ ALIGN WITH D2:: X
```

4.6 DYNAMIC Directive

The **DYNAMIC** attribute specifies that an object may be dynamically realigned or redistributed. The form of a *dynamic-directive* (H329) is:

DYNAMIC *alignee-or-distributee-list*

where each *alignee-or-distributee* (H330) must be either an *alignee* (H316) or a *distributee* (H307).

Rules and restrictions:
1. An object in **COMMON** may not be declared **DYNAMIC** and may not be aligned to an object (or template) that is **DYNAMIC**. (To get this kind of effect, Fortran 90 modules must be used instead of **COMMON** blocks.)
2. An object with the **SAVE** attribute may not be declared **DYNAMIC** and may not be aligned to an object (or template) that is **DYNAMIC**.

A **REALIGN** directive may not be applied to an *alignee* that does not have the **DYNAMIC** attribute. A **REDISTRIBUTE** directive may not be applied to a *distributee* that does not have the **DYNAMIC** attribute.

A **DYNAMIC** directive may be combined with other directives, with the attributes stated in any order, consistent with the Fortran 90 attribute syntax.

Example 4.3 The following two directives mean exactly the same thing:

```
!HPF$ DYNAMIC A, B, C, D, E
!HPF$ DYNAMIC :: A, B, C, D, E
```

□

Example 4.4 The following two directives mean exactly the same thing:

```
!HPF$ DYNAMIC, ALIGN WITH SNEEZY :: X, Y, Z
!HPF$ ALIGN WITH SNEEZY, DYNAMIC :: X, Y, Z
```

Data Mapping

□

Example 4.5 The following two directives mean exactly the same thing:

```
!HPF$ DYNAMIC, DISTRIBUTE(BLOCK, BLOCK) :: X, Y
!HPF$ DISTRIBUTE(BLOCK, BLOCK), DYNAMIC :: X, Y
```

□

Example 4.6 The three directives

```
!HPF$ TEMPLATE A(64,64), B(64,64), C(64,64), D(64,64)
!HPF$ DISTRIBUTE(BLOCK, BLOCK) ONTO P:: A, B, C, D
!HPF$ DYNAMIC A, B, C, D
```

may be combined into a single directive as follows:

```
!HPF$ TEMPLATE, DISTRIBUTE(BLOCK, BLOCK) ONTO P,    &
!HPF$    DIMENSION(64,64), DYNAMIC :: A, B, C, D
```

□

4.7 Allocatable Arrays and Pointers

A variable with the **POINTER** or **ALLOCATABLE** attribute may appear as an *alignee* in an **ALIGN** directive or as a *distributee* in a **DISTRIBUTE** directive. Such directives do not take effect immediately, however; they take effect each time the array is allocated by an **ALLOCATE** statement, rather than on entry to the scoping unit. The values of all specification expressions in such a directive are determined once on entry to the scoping unit and may be used multiple times (or not at all). For example:

```
      SUBROUTINE MILLARD_FILLMORE(N,M)
      REAL, ALLOCATABLE, DIMENSION(:) :: A, B
!HPF$ ALIGN B(I) WITH A(I+N)
!HPF$ DISTRIBUTE A(BLOCK(M*2))
      N = 43
      M = 91
      ALLOCATE(A(27))
      ALLOCATE(B(13))
      ...
```

The values of the expressions N and M*2 on entry to the subprogram are conceptually retained by the ALIGN and DISTRIBUTE directives for later use at allocation time. When the array A is allocated, it is distributed with a block size equal to the retained value of M*2, not the value 182. When the array B is allocated, it is aligned relative to A according to the retained value of N, not its new value 43.

Note that it would have been incorrect in the MILLARD_FILLMORE example to perform the two ALLOCATE statements in the opposite order. In general, when an object X is created it may be aligned to another object Y only if Y has already been created or allocated. The following example illustrates several other incorrect cases.

```
      SUBROUTINE WARREN_HARDING(P,Q)
      REAL P(:)
      REAL Q(:)
      REAL R(SIZE(Q))
      REAL, ALLOCATABLE :: S(:),T(:)
!HPF$ ALIGN P(I) WITH T(I)       !*** Nonconforming!
!HPF$ ALIGN Q(I) WITH *T(I)      !*** Nonconforming!
!HPF$ ALIGN R(I) WITH T(I)       !*** Nonconforming!
!HPF$ ALIGN S(I) WITH T(I)
      ALLOCATE(S(SIZE(Q)))       !*** Nonconforming!
      ALLOCATE(T(SIZE(Q)))
```

The ALIGN directives are not HPF-conforming because the array T has not yet been allocated at the time that the various alignments must take place. The four cases differ slightly in their details. The arrays P and Q already exist on entry to the subroutine, but because T is not yet allocated, one cannot correctly prescribe the alignment of P or describe the alignment of Q relative to T. (See Section 5.5 for a discussion of prescriptive and descriptive directives.) The array R is created on subroutine entry and its size can correctly depend on the SIZE of Q, but the alignment of R cannot be specified in terms of the alignment of T any more than its size can be specified in terms of the size of T. It *is* permitted to have an alignment directive for S in terms of T, because the alignment action does not take place until S is allocated; however, the first ALLOCATE statement is nonconforming because S needs to be aligned but at that point in time T is still unallocated.

If an ALLOCATE statement is immediately followed by REDISTRIBUTE and/or REALIGN directives, the meaning in principle is that the array is first created with the statically declared alignment, then immediately remapped. In practice there is an obvious optimization: create the array in the processors to which it is about to be remapped, in a single step. HPF implementors are strongly encouraged to implement this optimization and HPF programmers are encouraged to rely upon it. Here is an example:

```
      REAL, ALLOCATABLE(:,:)      :: TINKER, EVERS
!HPF$ DYNAMIC                     :: TINKER, EVERS
      REAL, POINTER               :: CHANCE(:)
!HPF$ DISTRIBUTE(BLOCK), DYNAMIC  :: CHANCE
      ...
      READ 6,M,N
      ALLOCATE(TINKER(N*M,N*M))
!HPF$ REDISTRIBUTE TINKER(CYCLIC, BLOCK)
      ALLOCATE(EVERS(N,N))
!HPF$ REALIGN EVERS(:,:) WITH TINKER(M::M,1::M)
      ALLOCATE(CHANCE(10000))
!HPF$ REDISTRIBUTE CHANCE(CYCLIC)
```

While CHANCE is by default always allocated with a BLOCK distribution, it should be possible for a compiler to notice that it will immediately be remapped to a CYCLIC distribution. Similar remarks apply to TINKER and EVERS. (Note that EVERS is mapped in a thinly-spread-out manner onto TINKER; adjacent elements of EVERS are mapped to elements of TINKER separated by a stride M. This thinly-spread-out mapping is put in the lower left corner of TINKER, because EVERS(1,1) is mapped to TINKER(M,1).)

An array pointer may be used in REALIGN and REDISTRIBUTE as an *alignee*, *align-target*, or *distributee* if and only if it is currently associated with a whole array, not an array section. One may remap an object by using a pointer as an *alignee* or *distributee* only if the object was created by ALLOCATE but is not an ALLOCATABLE array.

Any directive that remaps an object constitutes an assertion on the part of the programmer that the remainder of program execution would be unaffected if all pointers associated with any portion of the object were instantly to acquire undefined pointer association status, except for the one pointer, if any, used to indicate the object in the remapping directive.

If HPF directives were ever to be absorbed as actual Fortran statements, the previous paragraph could be written as "Remapping an object causes all pointers associated with any portion of the object to have undefined pointer association status, except for the one pointer, if any, used to indicate the object in the remapping directive." The more complicated wording here is intended to avoid any implication that the remapping directives, in the form of structured comment annotations, have any effect on the execution semantics, as opposed to the execution speed, of the annotated program.)

When an array is allocated, it will be aligned to an existing template if there is an explicit ALIGN directive for the allocatable variable. If there is no explicit ALIGN directive, then the array will be ultimately aligned with itself. It is forbidden for any other object to be ultimately aligned to an array at the time the array becomes undefined by reason of deallocation. All this applies regardless of whether the name originally used in the **ALLOCATE** statement when the array was created had the **ALLOCATABLE** attribute or the **POINTER** attribute.

4.8 PROCESSORS Directive

The **PROCESSORS** directive declares one or more rectilinear processor arrangements, specifying for each one its name, its rank (number of dimensions), and the extent in each dimension. It may appear only in the *specification-part* of a scoping unit. Every dimension of a processor arrangement must have nonzero extent; therefore a processor arrangement cannot be empty.

In the language of Section 14.1.2 of the Fortran 90 standard, processor arrangements are local entities of class (1); therefore a processor arrangement may not have the same name as a variable, named constant, internal procedure, etc., in the same scoping unit. Names of processor arrangements obey the same rules for host and use association as other names in the long list in Section 12.1.2.2.1 of the Fortran 90 standard.

If two processor arrangements have the same shape, then corresponding elements of the two arrangements are understood to refer to the same abstract processor. (It is anticipated that system-dependent directives provided by some HPF implementations could overrule the default correspondence of processor arrangements that have the same shape.)

If directives collectively specify that two objects be mapped to the same abstract processor at a given instant during the program execution, the intent is that the two objects be mapped to the same physical processor at that instant.

The intrinsic functions **NUMBER_OF_PROCESSORS** and **PROCESSORS_SHAPE** may be used to inquire about the total number of actual physical processors used to execute the program. This information may then be used to calculate appropriate sizes for the declared abstract processor arrangements.

The form of a *processors-directive* (H331) is:

PROCESSORS *processors-decl-list*

where the form of a *processors-decl* (H332) is:

processors-name [(*explicit-shape-spec-list*)]

and a *processors-name* (H333) is simply an *object-name*.

Data Mapping

Examples:

```
!HPF$ PROCESSORS P(N)
!HPF$ PROCESSORS Q(NUMBER_OF_PROCESSORS()),       &
!HPF$             R(8,NUMBER_OF_PROCESSORS()/8)
!HPF$ PROCESSORS BIZARRO(1972:1997,-20:17)
!HPF$ PROCESSORS SCALARPROC
```

If no shape is specified, then the declared processor arrangement is conceptually scalar.

A scalar processor arrangement may be useful as a way of indicating that certain scalar data should be kept together but need not interact strongly with distributed data. Depending on the implementation architecture, data distributed onto such a processor arrangement may reside in a single "control" or "host" processor (if the machine has one), or may reside in an arbitrarily chosen processor, or may be replicated over all processors. For target architectures that have a set of computational processors and a separate scalar host computer, a natural implementation is to map every scalar processor arrangement onto the host processor. For target architectures that have a set of computational processors but no separate scalar "host" computer, data mapped to a scalar processor arrangement might be mapped to some arbitrarily chosen computational processor or replicated onto all computational processors.

An HPF compiler is required to accept any **PROCESSORS** declaration in which the product of the extents of each declared processor arrangement is equal to the number of physical processors that would be returned by the call **NUMBER_OF_PROCESSORS()**. It must also accept all declarations of scalar **PROCESSOR** arrangements. Other cases may be handled as well, depending on the implementation.

For compatibility with the Fortran 90 attribute syntax, an optional "::" may be inserted. The shape may also be specified with the **DIMENSION** attribute:

```
!HPF$ PROCESSORS :: RUBIK(3,3,3)
!HPF$ PROCESSORS, DIMENSION(3,3,3) :: RUBIK
```

As in Fortran 90, an *explicit-shape-spec-list* in a *processors-decl* will override an explicit **DIMENSION** attribute:

```
!HPF$ PROCESSORS, DIMENSION(3,3,3) ::         &
!HPF$             RUBIK, RUBIKS_REVENGE(4,4,4), SOMA
```

Here **RUBIKS_REVENGE** is $4 \times 4 \times 4$ while **RUBIK** and **SOMA** are each $3 \times 3 \times 3$. (By the rules enunciated above, however, such a statement may not be completely portable because no HPF language processor is required to handle shapes of total sizes 27 and 64 simultaneously.)

Returning from a subprogram causes all processor arrangements declared local to that subprogram to become undefined. It is not HPF-conforming for any array or template to be distributed onto a processor arrangement at the time the processor arrangement becomes undefined unless at least one of two conditions holds:

- The array or template itself becomes undefined at the same time by virtue of returning from the subprogram.
- Whenever the subprogram is called, the processor arrangement is always locally defined in the same way, with identical lower bounds, and identical upper bounds.

Note that second condition is slightly less stringent than requiring all expressions to be constant. This allows calls to **NUMBER_OF_PROCESSORS** or **PROCESSORS_SHAPE** to appear without violating the condition.

Variables in **COMMON** or having the **SAVE** attribute may be mapped to a locally declared processor arrangement, but because the first condition cannot hold for such variables (they don't become undefined), the second condition must be observed. This allows **COMMON** variables to work properly through the customary strategy of putting identical declarations in each scoping unit that needs to use them, while allowing the processor arrangements to which they may be mapped to depend on the value returned by **NUMBER_OF_PROCESSORS**.

It may be desirable to have a way for the user to specify at compile time the number of physical processors on which the program is to be executed. This might be specified either by a compiler-dependent directive, for example, or through the programming environment (for example, as a UNIX command-line argument). Such facilities are beyond the scope of the HPF specification, but as food for thought we offer the following illustrative hypothetical examples:

```
!Declaration for multiprocessor by ABC Corporation
!ABC$ PHYSICAL PROCESSORS(8)
!Declaration for mpp by XYZ Incorporated
!XYZ$ PHYSICAL PROCESSORS(65536)
!Declaration for hypercube machine by PDQ Limited
!PDQ$ PHYSICAL PROCESSORS(2,2,2,2,2,2,2)
!Declaration for two-dimensional grid machine by TLA GmbH
!TLA$ PHYSICAL PROCESSORS(128,64)
!One of the preceding might affect the following
!HPF$ PROCESSORS P(NUMBER_OF_PROCESSORS())
```

It may furthermore be desirable to have a way for the user to specify the precise mapping of the processor arrangement declared in a **PROCESSORS** statement to the physical

Data Mapping   127

processors of the executing hardware. Again, this might be specified either by a compiler-dependent directive or through the programming environment (for example, as a UNIX command-line argument); such facilities are beyond the scope of the HPF specification, but as food for thought we offer the following illustrative hypothetical example:[1]

```
!PDQ$ PHYSICAL PROCESSORS(2,2,2,2,2,2,2,2,2,2,2,2,2)
!HPF$ PROCESSORS G(8,64,16)
!PDQ$ MACHINE LAYOUT G(:GRAY(0:2),:GRAY(6:11),:BINARY(3:5,12))
```

This might specify that the first dimension of G should use hypercube axes 0, 1, 2 with a Gray-code ordering; the second dimension should use hypercube axes 6 through 11 with a Gray-code ordering; and the third dimension should use hypercube axes 3, 4, 5, and 12 with a binary ordering.

4.9 TEMPLATE Directive

The **TEMPLATE** directive declares one or more templates, specifying for each the name, the rank (number of dimensions), and the extent in each dimension. It must appear in the *specification-part* of a scoping unit.

In the language of section 14.1.2 of the Fortran 90 standard, templates are local entities of class (1); therefore a template may not have the same name as a variable, named constant, internal procedure, etc., in the same scoping unit. Template names obey the rules for host and use association as other names in the list in section 12.1.2.2.1 of the Fortran 90 standard.

A template is simply an abstract space of indexed positions; it can be considered as an "array of nothings" (as compared to an "array of integers," say). A template may be used as an abstract *align-target* that may then be distributed.

The form of a *template-directive* (H334) is:

TEMPLATE *template-decl-list*

where the form of a *template-decl* (H335) is:

template-name [(*explicit-shape-spec-list*)]

and a *template-name* (H336) is simply an *object-name*.

---

[1] This example assumes that PDQ Limited has extended Fortran to allow arrays of rank greater than seven.

Some examples follow:

```
!HPF$ TEMPLATE A(N)
!HPF$ TEMPLATE B(N,N), C(N,2*N)
!HPF$ TEMPLATE DOPEY(100,100),SNEEZY(24),GRUMPY(17,3,5)
```

If the "::" syntax is used, then the declared templates may optionally be distributed in the same *combined-directive*. In this case all templates declared by the directive must have the same rank so that the DISTRIBUTE attribute will be meaningful. The DIMENSION attribute may also be used.

```
!HPF$ TEMPLATE, DISTRIBUTE(BLOCK,*) :: WHINEY(64,64), MOPEY(128,128)&
!HPF$ TEMPLATE, DIMENSION(91,91) :: BORED, WHEEZY, PERKY
```

Templates are useful in the particular situation where one must align several arrays relative to one another but there is no need to declare a single array that spans the entire index space of interest. For example, one might want four $N \times N$ arrays aligned to the four corners of a template of size $(N+1) \times (N+1)$:

```
!HPF$ TEMPLATE, DISTRIBUTE(BLOCK, BLOCK) :: EARTH(N+1,N+1)
      REAL, DIMENSION(N,N) :: NW, NE, SW, SE
!HPF$ ALIGN NW(I,J) WITH EARTH( I  , J  )
!HPF$ ALIGN NE(I,J) WITH EARTH( I  ,J+1)
!HPF$ ALIGN SW(I,J) WITH EARTH(I+1, J  )
!HPF$ ALIGN SE(I,J) WITH EARTH(I+1,J+1)
```

Templates may also be useful in making assertions about the mapping of dummy arguments (see Section 5.5).

Unlike arrays, templates cannot be in COMMON. So two templates declared in different scoping units will always be distinct, even if they are given the same name. The only way for two program units to refer to the same template is to declare the template in a module that is then used by the two program units.

Templates are not passed through the subprogram argument interface. The template to which a dummy argument is aligned is always distinct from the template to which the actual argument is aligned, though it may be a copy (see Section 5.4). On exit from a subprogram, an HPF implementation arranges that the actual argument is aligned with the same template with which it was aligned before the call.

Returning from a subprogram causes all templates declared local to that subprogram to become undefined. It is not HPF-conforming for any variable to be aligned to a template at the time the template becomes undefined unless at least one of two conditions holds:

- The variable itself becomes undefined at the same time by virtue of returning from the subprogram.
- Whenever the subprogram is called, the template is always locally defined in the same way, with identical lower bounds, identical upper bounds, and identical distribution information (if any) onto identically defined processor arrangements (see Section 4.8).

(Note that this second condition is slightly less stringent than requiring all expressions to be constant. This allows calls to NUMBER_OF_PROCESSORS or PROCESSORS_SHAPE to appear without violating the condition.)

Variables in COMMON or having the SAVE attribute may be mapped to a locally declared template, but because the first condition cannot hold for such variable (they don't become undefined), the second condition must be observed.

4.10 Fortran Storage Association and HPF

So far our discussion, with the exception of some fine print, might lead the reader to think that all variables are candidates for the mapping directives. For some codes this may be true, but there are important restrictions that are covered in this section.

For most of the lifetime of the Fortran language, efficient use of memory has been very important. One use of COMMON and EQUIVALENCE in Fortran programs has been to conserve memory space. This is called *storage association*: storage units used for one set of variables in one section of code that are reused for another set of variables elsewhere. More formally stated:

> *Storage association is the association of two or more data objects that occurs when two or more storage sequences share or are aligned with one or more storage units.*
> — Fortran Standard (14.6.3.1)

It should not surprise the reader that this multiple use of storage has great potential for mischief if mapping directives are applied, either explicitly or implicitly. The (useful) Fortran tradition of separate compilation makes the problem worse because the compiler may not know where and how the multiple use is taking place. For this reason, HPF introduces certain rules that restrict the use of storage association. We first examine the issues informally; in Section 4.10.2 we present a more formal and detailed discussion.

4.10.1 Informal Introduction to Storage Association

First, we want to assure the reader that it is still okay to use COMMON and EQUIVALENCE in an HPF program. It is necessary, however, to sort out the safe uses of COMMON and

```
      SUBROUTINE ONE
      COMMON /A_OK/ X(128,10), Y(256), INX(128)
      COMMON /DANGER/ TEMP(10, 100), DEPTH(1000), LOC(1000,2)
      COMMON /PELIGRO/ A(10,10), B(20,10), C(30,10)
      . . .
      END SUBROUTINE ONE

      SUBROUTINE TWO
      COMMON /A_OK/ WORK(128,10), TEST(256), INX(128)
      COMMON /DANGER/ L1(10,2), L2(200), FILL(1780), LOC(1000,2)
      COMMON /PELIGRO/ A1(100), B1(200), C1(300)
      . . .
      END SUBROUTINE TWO
```

Figure 4.6
Checking COMMON blocks

EQUIVALENCE from the uses that have the potential to cause trouble. We strongly recommend that programmers writing new Fortran 90 code use features like MODULE with the *rename* feature (R1108), derived types (structures), and allocatable storage to avoid the use of COMMON and EQUIVALENCE completely in new code.

When is it safe to use common blocks? If COMMON is used solely as a way to create global variables, rather than as a mechanism of storage reuse, then common variables can safely be distributed. To be more specific, when a given common block is used for the same set of variables (same size, same type, and same shape) everywhere it appears, then it is okay to map the variables in the COMMON, but the mappings must also be the same everywhere. Only the variable names may differ. When an INCLUDE statement is used to introduce the declaration of COMMON and its variables, this rule is relatively straight forward for the programmer to observe. Figure 4.6 gives a very simple example of some good and bad uses of COMMON. The variables in common block /A_OK/ are the same shape, size, and type. They may be mapped, either explicitly by the user or implicitly by the compiler. The common blocks /DANGER/ and /PELIGRO/ both have problems. In SUBROUTINE TWO the programmer has violated the rule in multiple ways. LOC is the same, and in the same place in /DANGER/ in both subroutines, but the other variables in /DANGER/ are different in number, type, size and shape. In /PELIGRO/ it is just the shape that differs. It is still okay to have common blocks like /DANGER/ and /PELIGRO/ in a code. But they must be marked as *sequential* everywhere they occur. The SEQUENCE directive is supplied for this purpose. The following directive should appear in both subroutines for this code to be used in HPF.

```
!HPF$ SEQUENCE /DANGER/, /PELIGRO/
```

The notion *sequential* and *nonsequential* along with the form of the SEQUENCE directive is given in the next section.

It should be fairly obvious why we require that the explicit mappings be the same everywhere the COMMON is used. If this were not the case, a check for dynamic redistribution would be required on entry to every subroutine and that overhead would be unacceptable. The requirement for the variables to be the same shape comes from the need to guarantee that the compiler can use the same method to access the (potentially distributed) variable everywhere. If some component were a different shape or type, the compiler might apply different default distributions.

What about EQUIVALENCE? As with COMMON, there are some uses of EQUIVALENCE that are relatively benign such as a simple rename of a variable while other uses create complex relationships between variables that inhibit mapping. In HPF, it is the case that any use of EQUIVALENCE with (or overlapping) a variable causes that variable to be *sequential*. It is not difficult to check the basic rule that applies to mapping a variable involved in EQUIVALENCE: if there is one variable that is as big as (or bigger than) all of the other variables related by EQUIVALENCE, this variable is called a *cover*. If this cover is a 1-dimensional variable, it may be mapped. The precise definition of a cover is given in the next section.

Why restrict covers to 1-dimensional for mapping? If a variable is a multi-dimensional array, the mapping access functions can get quite sophisticated for some distributions. Suppose this variable were a cover. If the other variables associated with this variable via EQUIVALENCE were also multi-dimensioned, the access to these equivalenced variables might be a very messy composite function. On the other hand, if the distributed cover is a single dimensional array, the mapping is straightforward for all equivalenced variables.

4.10.2 Storage Association in More Detail

In this section we will define the notions of *sequential* and *nonsequential* as they apply to variables and common blocks. But first we will introduce the form of the directives supplied to designate the sequentiality of data. It is also useful to give the formal definition of *cover* as used with EQUIVALENCE before discussing the sequentiality of variables.

Sequence Directives A SEQUENCE directive is defined to allow a user to declare explicitly that variables or common blocks are to be treated by the compiler as sequential. The form of a *sequence-directive* (H701) is one of:

```
SEQUENCE
SEQUENCE [::] association-name-list
NO SEQUENCE
NO SEQUENCE [ :: ] association-name-list
```

and an *association-name* (H702) is one of:

```
variable name
/ [common-block-name] /
```

Rules and restrictions:
1. A variable or common block name may appear at most once in a *sequence-directive* within any scoping unit.
2. A *sequence-directive* belongs in the specification part of a program unit.
3. The result variable of an array-valued function that is not an intrinsic function is a nonsequential array. It may not appear in any HPF SEQUENCE directive.

A *sequence-directive* with an empty *association-name-list* is treated as if it contained the name of all implicitly mapped variables and common blocks in the scoping unit that cannot otherwise be determined to be sequential or nonsequential by their language context.

Normally, only the SEQUENCE directive is required, however some implementations may supply an optional compilation environment where variables are sequential by default. For completeness in such an environment, HPF defines the NO SEQUENCE directive to allow a user to establish that the usual nonsequential default should apply to a scoping unit, or selected variables and common blocks within the scoping unit.

Covers and Aggregates Often EQUIVALENCE is used simply to rename a variable or to give a new name to a part of a variable. However, it is possible in Fortran to link an elaborate string of variables together by overlapping the storage of multiple variables with one or more EQUIVALENCE statements. In HPF we call this an *aggregate variable group*. If there is a member variable that is exactly as big as the aggregate variable group, we call it a *cover*. The reader is encouraged to look at the examples in Figure 4.7 to get an informal idea what these terms mean before reading the next paragraph which gives a definition of the terms using some formal Fortran 90 terminology with reference numbers from the Fortran 90 standard.

An *aggregate variable group* is a collection of variables whose individual storage sequences are parts of a single storage sequence. Variables associated by EQUIVALENCE statements or by some combination of EQUIVALENCE and COMMON statements form an aggregate variable group. The *size* of an aggregate variable group is the number of storage

Data Mapping

```
      IMPLICIT REAL (A-Z)
      COMMON /FOO/ A(100), B(100), C(100), D(100), E(100)
      DIMENSION X(100), Y(150), Z(200)

!Example 1:  showing a simple cover of two variables
      EQUIVALENCE ( A(1), Z(1) )
!Four components: (A, B), C, D, E with sizes 200, 100, 100, 100
!Z is a cover of A, B

!Example 2: showing how an aggregate group consumes variables
      EQUIVALENCE ( B(100), Y(1) )
!Three components A, (B, C, D), E with sizes 100, 300, 100
!B, C, and D are an aggregate variable group but there is no cover

!Example 3: showing that a group can extend the length of common
      EQUIVALENCE ( E(1), Y(1) )
!Five components: A, B, C, D, E with sizes 100, 100, 100, 100, 150
!Y is a cover of E

!Example 4: showing how a group may be a composite of groups
      EQUIVALENCE ( A(51), X(1) )
      EQUIVALENCE ( B(100), Y(1) )
!Two components (A, B, C, D), E with sizes 400, 100
!There is no cover for the group with A, B, C, D, X and Y

!Example 5: showing local variables making an aggregate group
      EQUIVALENCE (Y(100), Z(1))
!One aggregate variable group (Y, Z) with size 299
!No COMMON block involved and no cover

!Example 6: showing how a common block becomes sequential
!HPF$ SEQUENCE /FOO/
!The COMMON has one component, (A, B, C, D, E) with size 500
```

Figure 4.7
Examples of aggregate variable groups and covers

units in the group's storage sequence (14.6.3.1). If there is a member in an aggregate variable group whose storage sequence is totally associated (14.6.3.3) with the storage sequence of the aggregate variable group, that variable is called an *aggregate cover* or simply a *cover*.

Sequential and Nonsequential Common Blocks In HPF a common block is *nonsequential* by definition, unless there is an explicit **SEQUENCE** directive to specify that it is *sequential*. All of the common blocks in Figure 4.7 are nonsequential except Example 6. A *sequential common block* has a single common block storage sequence (5.5.2.1). The variables of a sequential common block are defined to form a single aggregate variable group.

A common block contains a sequence of *components*. Each component is either an aggregate variable group, or a variable that is not a member of any aggregate variable group. Sequential common blocks contain a single component. Nonsequential common blocks may contain multiple components that may be nonsequential or sequential variables or aggregate variable groups.

As an aid to porting old FORTRAN programs, some implementations may provide a compilation environment where the default definition of a common block is *sequential*.

Sequential and Nonsequential Variables HPF variables are either sequential or nonsequential as determined by their context in a program or by explicit directives. A variable is *sequential* if and only if any of the following holds:

- It appears in a sequential common block;
- It is a member of an aggregate variable group;
- It is an assumed-size array;
- It is a component of a derived type with the Fortran 90 **SEQUENCE** attribute; or
- It is declared to be sequential in an HPF **SEQUENCE** directive.

A sequential variable can be storage associated or sequence associated (see Section 5.9); nonsequential variables cannot.

We say a variable is *explicitly mapped* if it appears in an HPF alignment or distribution directive within the scoping unit in which it is declared; otherwise it is *implicitly mapped*.

Storage Association Rules There are some rules about storage association to which HPF programs must conform:

- A sequential variable may not be explicitly mapped unless it is a scalar or rank-one array that is an aggregate cover. If there is more than one aggregate cover for an aggregate variable group, only one may be explicitly mapped.

- No explicit mapping may be given for a component of a derived type having the Fortran 90 **SEQUENCE** attribute. (By its definition, this attribute demands storage association.)

If a common block is nonsequential, then all of the following must hold:

- Every occurrence of the common block has exactly the same number of components with each corresponding component having a storage sequence of exactly the same size;
- If a component is a nonsequential variable in *any* occurrence of the common block, then it must be nonsequential with identical type, shape, and mapping attributes in *every* occurrence of the common block;
- If a component is sequential and explicitly mapped (either a variable or an aggregate variable group with an explicitly mapped aggregate cover) in any occurrence of the common block, then it must be sequential and explicitly mapped with identical mapping attributes in *every* occurrence of the common block. In addition, the type and shape of the explicitly mapped variable must be identical in all occurrences; and
- Every occurrence of the common block must be nonsequential.

If any of these constraints are not met, it is the programmer's responsibility to declare every instance of the common block as sequential using a **SEQUENCE** directive.

Under these rules, variables in a common block can be mapped as long as the components of the common block are the same in every scoping unit that declares the common block. The rules above also allow variables involved in an **EQUIVALENCE** statement to be mapped by the mechanism of declaring a rank-one array to cover exactly the aggregate variable group and mapping that array. Notice in Figure 4.7 that every example has a different set of components for **/FOO/**. If these examples all came from the same source program and each example were in a different subroutine, the programmer would have to declare **/FOO/** sequential everywhere it is used, as was done in Example 6. This is required even though the actual set of variables in the common block are identical everywhere.

As a reminder, an HPF program is nonconforming if it specifies any mapping that would cause a scalar data object to be mapped onto more than one abstract processor (Section 4.4, page 110). This puts a constraint on the sequential variables and aggregate covers that can be mapped. In particular, a program is nonconforming if it directs double precision or complex arrays to be mapped such that the storage units of a single array element are split because of some **EQUIVALENCE** statement or common block layout.

In Figure 4.8 we give an example of a common block with a mix of sequential and nonsequential variables. **/MIX/** in both subroutines is a nonsequential common block with an identical set of four components. Components one and four are sequential and

```
      SUBROUTINE ALPHA
      COMMON /MIX/ A(20,40),E(10,10),G(10,100,10),H(100),P(100)
      REAL   COVER (200)
      EQUIVALENCE (COVER(1), H(1))
!HPF$   SEQUENCE :: A
!HPF$   ALIGN E ...
!HPF$   DISTRIBUTE COVER (CYCLIC(2))
          .....
      END SUBROUTINE ALPHA

      SUBROUTINE BETA
      COMMON /MIX/ A(800), E(10,10), G(10,100,10), Z(200)
!HPF$   SEQUENCE :: A, Z
!HPF$   ALIGN E ...
!HPF$   DISTRIBUTE Z (CYCLIC(2))
          ....
      END SUBROUTINE BETA
```

Figure 4.8
Examples of mapping covers

components two and four are explicitly mapped, with the same type, shape and mapping attributes.

The first component, **A**, is declared sequential in both subroutines because its shape is different. It may not be explicitly mapped in either because it is not rank-one or scalar in **ALPHA**. The second component, **E**, is explicitly mapped, while the third component, **G** is implicitly mapped. **E** and **G** agree in type and shape in both occurrences. **E** must have the same explicit mapping and **G** must have no explicit mapping in both occurrences, since they are nonsequential variables.

The last component in **BETA**, **Z**, must be declared sequential because there is an **EQUIVALENCE** statement in **ALPHA**. The variable **COVER** in **ALPHA** provides an aggregate cover of the aggregate variable group (**H, P**). It is 1-dimensional so it is eligible for mapping. Notice that **Z** and **COVER** are the same shape, size, and type. Notice also that the mapping specified is the same in each subroutine.

As a summary, we give a check-list for a programmer to determine the status of a variable or common block. The following questions can be applied, in order:

- Does the variable appear in some explicit language context which dictates sequential (e.g., **EQUIVALENCE**) or nonsequential (e.g., array-valued function result variable)?
- If not, does the variable or common block name appear in the list of names on a **SEQUENCE** or **NO SEQUENCE** directive?
- If not, does the variable appear in an explicit mapping directive?
- If not, does the scoping unit contain a nameless **SEQUENCE** or **NO SEQUENCE**?
- If not, is the compilation affected by some special implementation-dependent environment which dictates that names default to **SEQUENCE**?
- If not, then the compiler will consider the variable or common block name nonsequential and is free to apply data mapping optimizations disregarding Fortran sequence and storage association.

5 Data Mapping for Procedure Arguments

The rules for data mapping are more complicated when procedure calls are involved. The HPF alignment and distribution directives have extra features that apply only to dummy arguments: a directive for a dummy argument may be *prescriptive*, *descriptive*, or *transcriptive*, and the template for a dummy argument may be *natural* or *inherited*. There are also some restrictions on the use of sequence association.

5.1 Data Mapping for Dummy Variables

A general principle of the design of HPF is that a subprogram cannot permanently alter the mappings of data visible to its caller. (This restriction is intended to allow a compiler to generate more efficient code, because the compiler can rely on declared data mappings throughout the body of a scoping unit without concern for the possibility that a call to a subprogram might rearrange data.)

On the other hand, it is useful to allow a subprogram to remap data received through a dummy argument. As a simple example, a subroutine might receive two array arguments A and B and apply an algorithm that is much more efficient when A and B are aligned. But generality demands that the subroutine operate correctly even when the actual array arguments are not aligned.

The solution adopted in HPF is that a subprogram may include HPF directives that prescribe the alignment or distribution of dummy arguments. Such directives are identical to those for non-dummy variables. For example:

`!HPF$ DISTRIBUTE Z(BLOCK,*,CYCLIC)`

If the actual argument does not satisfy the directives, then an implicit remapping must occur so as to satisfy the directives. Such an implicit remapping is not visible to the caller; when execution resumes following the call, everything must be as if no remapping had occurred.

On yet another hand, remapping a large piece of data may impose a large run-time execution cost, so it is not desirable to *require* remapping on entry to a subprogram. HPF allows a subprogram to specify, for a given dummy argument, that the corresponding actual argument should *never* be implicitly remapped; instead, the subroutine should be able to operate on the actual argument data however it happens to be distributed.

`!HPF$ INHERIT Z`

This avoids the overhead of remapping actual argument data, but the subprogram itself may execute more slowly because it must handle the generality of arbitrary data mappings.

Therefore HPF provides one more option: the subprogram may specify no remapping of an actual argument but also *assert* that the actual argument will have a particular alignment or distribution.

```
!HPF$ DISTRIBUTE *Z(BLOCK,*,CYCLIC)
```

This allows maximal efficiency but requires the caller to provide an actual argument that satisfies the assertion.

Let us examine some more specific illustrations of these concepts. As we will see, if *explicit interfaces* are used, then directives need not match in the caller and callee, because the HPF compiler will have the necessary information at compile time to perform a remapping. If explicit interfaces are not used, everything is still okay if the actual mapping of the actual argument matches the declared mapping of the dummy argument, or if the callee admits remapping of the actual argument.

Figure 5.1 shows five subroutines: KOVACS, WOOD, ELDER, and CLARKE each call MINGO. Now subroutine MINGO prefers to receive its argument M with (BLOCK,BLOCK) distribution (perhaps this minimizes communications costs within the subroutine) so it contains a DISTRIBUTE directive for its dummy argument. This is called a *prescriptive* directive: it *prescribes* a mapping for the dummy argument.

Subroutine KOVACS has a local array K that it declares to be (*,CYCLIC). When it passes array K to MINGO, the data must be implicitly remapped so that the dummy argument has a (BLOCK,BLOCK) distribution. When subroutine KOVACS resumes execution on return from the call to MINGO, the array K within KOVACS still has (*,CYCLIC) distribution.

Subroutine WOOD has a local array W that it declares to be (BLOCK,BLOCK). When it passes array W to MINGO, nothing needs to be done. (However, in some implementations there might be a small run-time cost simply for testing *whether* remapping might be necessary.)

Subroutine ELDER, like KOVACS, has a local array that it declares to be (*,CYCLIC). But ELDER also contains a Fortran 90 interface block describing MINGO. When it passes array E to MINGO, the data must be implicitly remapped so that the dummy argument has a (BLOCK,BLOCK) distribution. If ELDER is compiled separately from MINGO, the information in the interface block may allow the compiler to generate more efficient remapping code. When subroutine ELDER resumes execution on return from the call to MINGO, the array E within ELDER still has (*,CYCLIC) distribution.

Subroutine CLARKE, like WOOD, has a local array C that it declares to be (BLOCK,BLOCK). But CLARKE also contains a Fortran 90 interface block describing MINGO. When it passes array C to MINGO, nothing needs to be done. The information in the interface block allows a compiler to determine at compile time that no remapping will be required.

```
          SUBROUTINE KOVACS                         SUBROUTINE WOOD
          REAL K(100,100)                           REAL W(100,100)
    !HPF$ DISTRIBUTE K(*,CYCLIC)               !HPF$ DISTRIBUTE W(BLOCK,BLOCK)
          ...                                       ...
          CALL MINGO(K)                             CALL MINGO(W)
          ...                                       ...
          END                                       END
```

              implicit remapping   no remapping required

```
          SUBROUTINE ELDER                          SUBROUTINE CLARKE
          REAL E(100,100)                           REAL C(100,100)
    !HPF$ DISTRIBUTE E(*,CYCLIC)               !HPF$ DISTRIBUTE C(BLOCK,BLOCK)
          INTERFACE                                 INTERFACE
            SUBROUTINE MINGO(M)                       SUBROUTINE MINGO(M)
              REAL M(100,100)                           REAL M(100,100)
    !HPF$     DISTRIBUTE M(BLOCK,BLOCK)       !HPF$     DISTRIBUTE M(BLOCK,BLOCK)
            END SUBROUTINE MINGO                      END SUBROUTINE MINGO
          END INTERFACE                             END INTERFACE
          ...                                       ...
          CALL MINGO(E)                             CALL MINGO(C)
          ...                                       ...
          END                                       END
```

          implicit remapping   no remapping required
       (known at compile time)   (known at compile time)

```
          SUBROUTINE MINGO(M)
          REAL M(100,100)
    !HPF$ DISTRIBUTE M(BLOCK,BLOCK))
          ...
          END
```

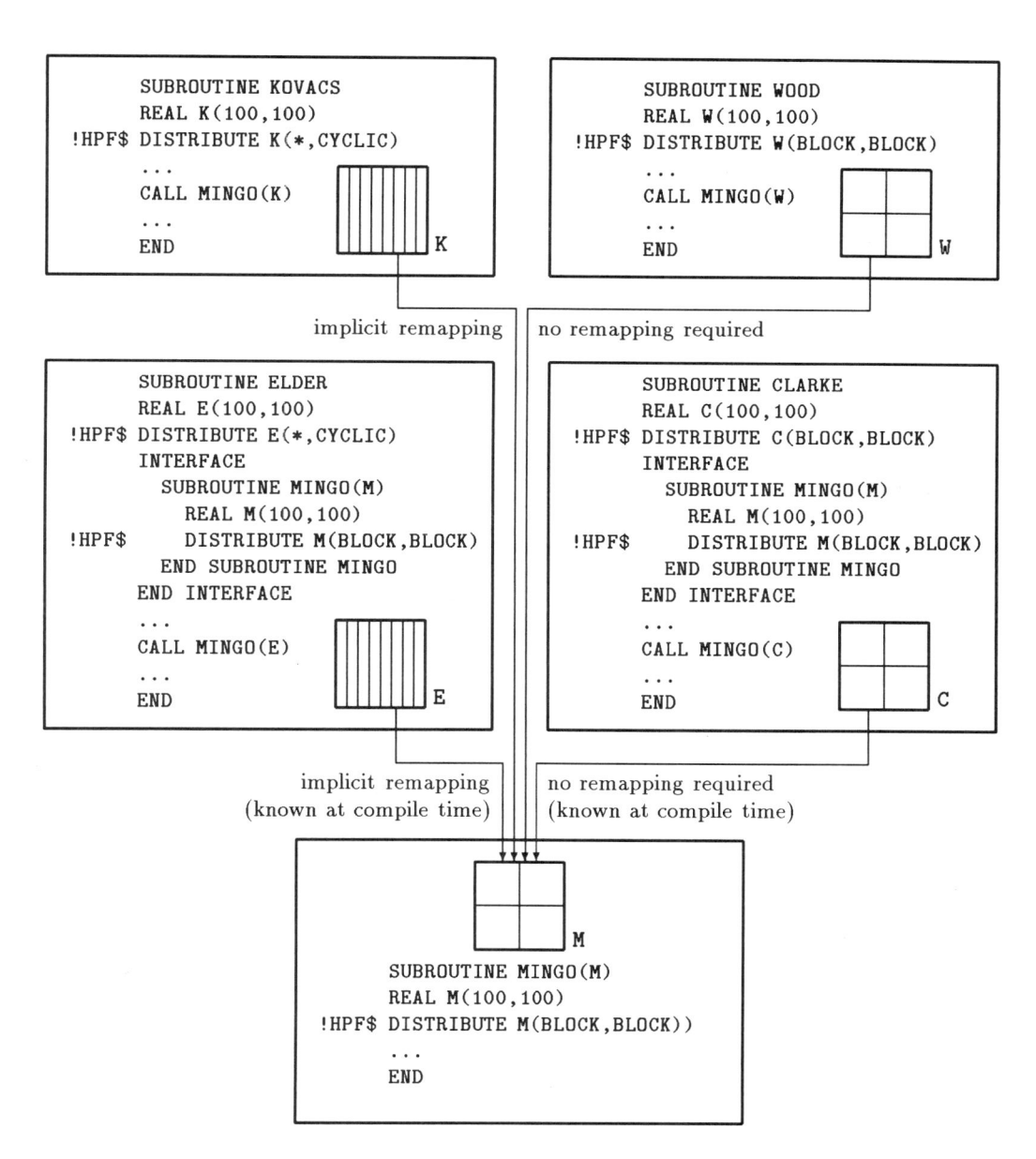

Figure 5.1
Treatment of a prescriptive directive for a dummy argument

Figure 5.2 shows five more subroutines: `PROHIAS`, `BERG`, `DAVIS`, and `GAINES` each call `JAFFEE`. Now subroutine `JAFFEE` is willing to receive its argument `J` with any distribution, so it contains a `DISTRIBUTE` directive for its dummy argument that has simply asterisks "*" in place of a distribution format list and processors arrangement. This is called a *transcriptive* directive: the mapping of the dummy is simply copied, or *transcribed*, from the mapping of the actual argument. The intent is that if the argument is passed by reference, no movement of the data will be necessary at run time. Note, by the way, that transcriptive directives are not included in Subset HPF.

(Asterisks may be used in two different ways in a `DISTRIBUTE` directive: *within* a *dist-format-list* to indicate on-processor distribution, or to *replace* a *dist-format-list* and its surrounding parentheses. Thus, if `HUMOR` is a dummy argument, then

`!HPF$ DISTRIBUTE HUMOR (*)`

is a *prescriptive* specification of `HUMOR` as residing within a single abstract processor, whereas

`!HPF$ DISTRIBUTE HUMOR *`

is a *transcriptive* specification indicating that any distribution is acceptable and that the actual argument should not be remapped.)

Subroutine `PROHIAS` has a local array `P` that it declares to be `(*,CYCLIC)`. When it passes array `P` to `JAFFEE`, no remapping occurs. Subroutine `JAFFEE` must be prepared to handle its dummy argument `J` with `(*,CYCLIC)` distribution.

Subroutine `BERG` has a local array `B` that it declares to be `(BLOCK,BLOCK)`. When it passes array `B` to `JAFFEE`, no remapping occurs. Subroutine `JAFFEE` must be prepared to handle its dummy argument `J` with `(*,CYCLIC)` distribution.

Subroutine `DAVIS`, like `PROHIAS`, has a local array that it declares to be `(*,CYCLIC)`. But `DAVIS` also contains a Fortran 90 interface block describing `JAFFEE`. When it passes array `D` to `JAFFEE`, no remapping occurs. If `DAVIS` is compiled separately from `JAFFEE`, the information in the interface block informs the compiler that `JAFFEE` will accept any distribution, which may allow the compiler to generate more efficient code for the call.

Subroutine `GAINES`, like `BERG`, has a local array `G` that it declares to be `(BLOCK,BLOCK)`. But `GAINES` also contains a Fortran 90 interface block describing `JAFFEE`. When it passes array `G` to `JAFFEE`, no remapping occurs. As with `DAVIS`, the information in the interface block may allow the compiler to generate more efficient code.

Observe that subroutine `JAFFEE` specifies the `INHERIT` attribute for its dummy argument `J`. If it did not, then it might be necessary to remap the actual argument after all, for the following subtle technical reason: for any given system (and the choices that system might make concerning default mappings), it must be possible to describe the

Data Mapping for Procedure Arguments

```
          SUBROUTINE PROHIAS                    SUBROUTINE BERG
          REAL P(100,100)                       REAL B(100,100)
!HPF$     DISTRIBUTE P(*,CYCLIC)       !HPF$    DISTRIBUTE B(BLOCK,BLOCK)
          ...                                   ...
          CALL JAFFEE(P)                        CALL JAFFEE(B)
          ...                                   ...
          END                    P              END                    B
```

            no remapping occurs   no remapping occurs

```
          SUBROUTINE DAVIS                      SUBROUTINE GAINES
          REAL D(100,100)                       REAL G(100,100)
!HPF$     DISTRIBUTE D(*,CYCLIC)       !HPF$    DISTRIBUTE G(BLOCK,BLOCK)
          INTERFACE                             INTERFACE
            SUBROUTINE JAFFEE(J)                  SUBROUTINE JAFFEE(J)
              REAL J(100,100)                       REAL J(100,100)
!HPF$         DISTRIBUTE J * ONTO *    !HPF$        DISTRIBUTE J * ONTO *
!HPF$         INHERIT J                !HPF$        INHERIT J
            END SUBROUTINE JAFFEE                 END SUBROUTINE JAFFEE
          END INTERFACE                         END INTERFACE
          ...                                   ...
          CALL JAFFEE(D)                        CALL JAFFEE(G)
          ...                                   ...
          END                    D              END                    G
```

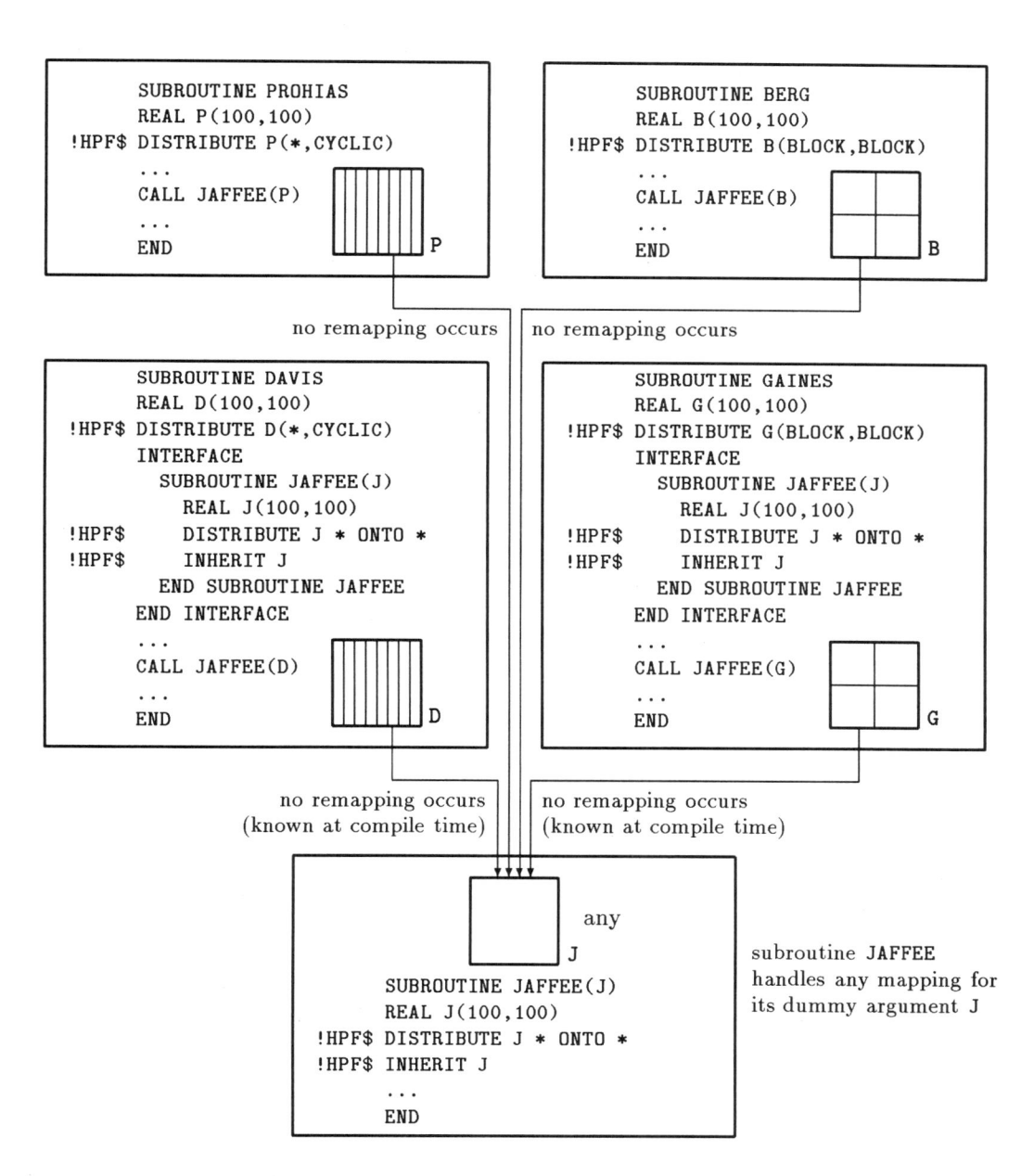

          no remapping occurs   no remapping occurs
          (known at compile time)   (known at compile time)

```
                              any
                               J
              SUBROUTINE JAFFEE(J)           subroutine JAFFEE
              REAL J(100,100)                handles any mapping for
!HPF$         DISTRIBUTE J * ONTO *          its dummy argument J
!HPF$         INHERIT J
              ...
              END
```

Figure 5.2
Treatment of a transcriptive directive for a dummy argument

mapping of every data object through the use of HPF directives to that system. It is always possible to describe the mapping of a dummy argument by means of an inherited template or its equivalent, but not every possible data mapping can be specified by use of a natural template. See Section 5.4 for further discussion of natural and inherited templates and of the INHERIT directive.

For now, suffice it to remark that the INHERIT attribute always implies the default distribution DISTRIBUTE * ONTO *, so it is convenient and perhaps stylistically pleasant simply to omit transcriptive DISTRIBUTE directives such as

```
!HPF$ DISTRIBUTE J * ONTO *
```

and use INHERIT by itself to indicate transcriptive acceptance of any data mapping:

```
      SUBROUTINE JAFFEE(J)
      REAL J(100,100)
!HPF$ INHERIT J              ! Implies DISTRIBUTE J * ONTO *
```

Figure 5.3 shows one more set of five subroutines: ARAGONES, NORTH, SIEGEL, and TORRES each call RICKARD. Now subroutine RICKARD prefers to receive its argument R with (BLOCK,BLOCK) distribution and furthermore asserts that the caller will provide an actual argument that is so distributed. Therefore RICKARD contains a DISTRIBUTE directive for its dummy argument that has an asterisk—meaning that no remapping will be required—*followed by* a distribution format list. This is called a *descriptive* directive: it *describes* the mapping of the dummy argument and claims that no remapping of the actual will be required to satisfy this description. (The intent is that if the argument is passed by reference, no movement of the data will be necessary at run time. All this is under the assumption that the language processor has in fact observed all other directives. While a conforming HPF language processor is not required to obey mapping directives, it should handle descriptive directives with the understanding that their implied assertions are relative to this assumption.)

Subroutine ARAGONES has a local array A that it declares to be (*,CYCLIC). When it passes array A to RICKARD, the mapping of A does not satisfy the description for the dummy R. This call is **nonconforming** and the behavior of the program is not specified by HPF.

Subroutine NORTH has a local array N that it declares to be (BLOCK,BLOCK). When it passes array N to RICKARD, nothing needs to be done; the mapping of N satisfies the description for the dummy R.

Subroutine SIEGEL, like ARAGONES, has a local array that it declares to be (*,CYCLIC). But SIEGEL also contains a Fortran 90 interface block describing RICKARD. When it passes array S to RICKARD, the data must be implicitly remapped to the (BLOCK,BLOCK)

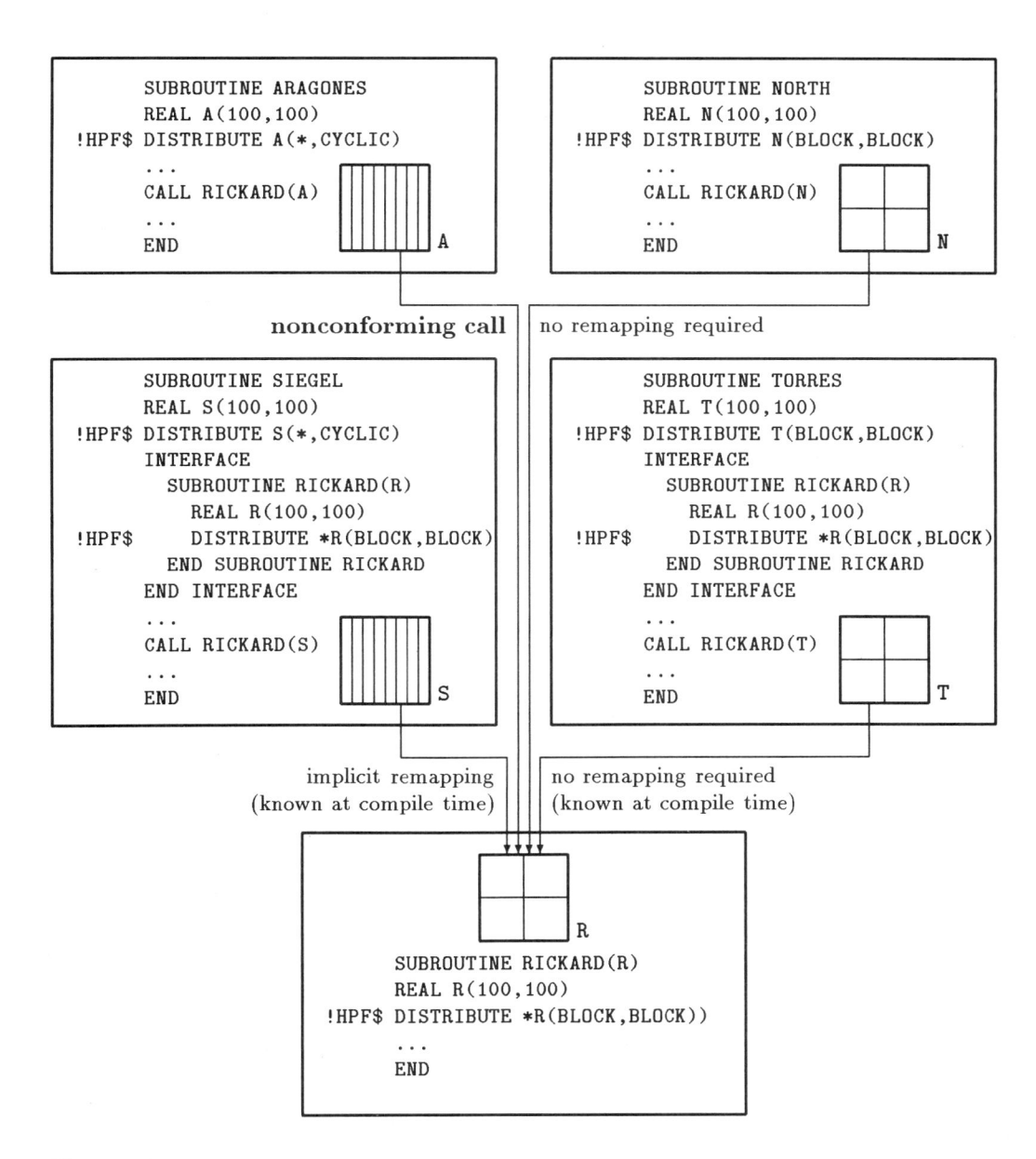

```
SUBROUTINE ARAGONES
    REAL A(100,100)
!HPF$ DISTRIBUTE A(*,CYCLIC)
    ...
    CALL RICKARD(A)
    ...
    END                        A
```

```
SUBROUTINE NORTH
    REAL N(100,100)
!HPF$ DISTRIBUTE N(BLOCK,BLOCK)
    ...
    CALL RICKARD(N)
    ...
    END                        N
```

nonconforming call | no remapping required

```
SUBROUTINE SIEGEL
    REAL S(100,100)
!HPF$ DISTRIBUTE S(*,CYCLIC)
    INTERFACE
      SUBROUTINE RICKARD(R)
        REAL R(100,100)
!HPF$   DISTRIBUTE *R(BLOCK,BLOCK)
      END SUBROUTINE RICKARD
    END INTERFACE
    ...
    CALL RICKARD(S)
    ...
    END                        S
```

```
SUBROUTINE TORRES
    REAL T(100,100)
!HPF$ DISTRIBUTE T(BLOCK,BLOCK)
    INTERFACE
      SUBROUTINE RICKARD(R)
        REAL R(100,100)
!HPF$   DISTRIBUTE *R(BLOCK,BLOCK)
      END SUBROUTINE RICKARD
    END INTERFACE
    ...
    CALL RICKARD(T)
    ...
    END                        T
```

implicit remapping | no remapping required
(known at compile time) | (known at compile time)

```
                               R
SUBROUTINE RICKARD(R)
    REAL R(100,100)
!HPF$ DISTRIBUTE *R(BLOCK,BLOCK))
    ...
    END
```

Figure 5.3
Treatment of a descriptive directive for a dummy argument

distribution specified in the interface block. In other words, descriptive directives *in an interface block* must be treated as if they were prescriptive. This is discussed further in Section 5.5.

Subroutine TORRES, like NORTH, has a local array that it declares to be (BLOCK,BLOCK). But TORRES also contains a Fortran 90 interface block describing RICKARD. When it passes array T to RICKARD, nothing needs to be done. The information in the interface block allows a compiler to confirm at compile time that the mapping of the actual argument will satisfy the description of the dummy.

These examples, while perhaps exhausting, are not exhaustive. Some additional points to observe:

- It is likely most helpful to an HPF compiler to specify, where possible, not only the distribution formats for dummy arguments but the specific processors arrangement(s) onto which they are distributed.
- Conversely, it is best to specify DISTRIBUTE * ONTO * (or INHERIT), rather than simply *, to ensure that an actual argument will not be remapped.
- The examples show only arrays of fixed shape (100, 100). There is no reason why assumed-shape arrays, for example, cannot be specified.
- It is permitted to use an ALIGN directive instead of a DISTRIBUTE directive on a dummy argument; ALIGN directives have both prescriptive and descriptive forms (but not transcriptive).

As an illustration of some of these points, consider this code:

```
      SUBROUTINE MELVIN(AXOLOTL,POIUYT)
      REAL AXOLOTL(:,:),POIUYT(:,:)
!HPF$ INHERIT, DISTRIBUTE *(BLOCK,BLOCK) :: AXOLOTL
!HPF$ ALIGN POIUYT(:,:) WITH *AXOLOTL(:,:)
```

The two arguments are assumed-shape arrays. The HPF directives convey some interesting information about them:

- The INHERIT attribute for AXOLOTL implies the default distribution DISTRIBUTE * ONTO *. Part of this default is then explicitly overridden, so the resulting specification is DISTRIBUTE *(BLOCK,BLOCK) ONTO *. Therefore the actual argument for AXOLOTL is never remapped.
- It is asserted that the template of the actual argument for AXOLOTL will already be distributed (BLOCK,BLOCK).
- It is asserted that the actual argument for POIUYT will already be aligned with AXOLOTL; this actual also should not be remapped.

- It is asserted that `AXOLOTL` and `POIUYT` will have the same shape (though they may have a different shared shape on each entry to `MELVIN`). (Note that the alternative

    `!HPF$ ALIGN POIUYT(I,J) WITH *AXOLOTL(I,J)`

would allow the possibility that `POIUYT` not have the same shape as `AXOLOTL`—it might be smaller along any or all dimensions—but still be aligned with the "upper left corner" of `AXOLOTL`.

5.2 DISTRIBUTE Directives and Dummy Arguments

The syntax for the `DISTRIBUTE` directive given in Section 4.4 omitted certain options relevant only to dummy arguments. The complete syntax for these options is explained here. Note that the options related to dummy arguments may be used only in `DISTRIBUTE` directives, not in `REDISTRIBUTE` directives.

The form of a *distribute-directive* (H303) is:

`DISTRIBUTE` *distributee dist-directive-stuff*
`DISTRIBUTE` *dist-attribute-stuff* `::` *distributee-list*

(Note that the second form is a special case of a *combined-directive* (H301).)

The form of *dist-directive-stuff* (H305) is one of

dist-format-clause
dist-format-clause dist-onto-clause

The form of *dist-attribute-stuff* (H306) is one of:

dist-format-clause
dist-format-clause dist-onto-clause
dist-onto-clause

The form of a *dist-format-clause* (H308) is:

(*dist-format-list*)
* (*dist-format-list*)
*

These forms are prescriptive, descriptive, and transcriptive, respectively; the last two may be used only for dummy arguments.

A *dist-format* (H309) is one of:

```
BLOCK [ ( int-expr ) ]
CYCLIC [ ( int-expr ) ]
*
```

An asterisk as a *dist-format* indicates on-processor distribution.

The form of a *dist-onto-clause* (H310) is:

`ONTO` *dist-target*

where the *dist-target* (H311) is one of:

processors-name
`*` *processors-name*
`*`

where *processors-name* is defined by a **PROCESSORS** directive. These forms are prescriptive, descriptive, and transcriptive, respectively; the last two may be used only for dummy arguments.

Rules and restrictions:
1. If either the *dist-format-clause* or the *dist-target* in a **DISTRIBUTE** directive begins with "`*`" then every *distributee* must be a dummy argument.
2. Neither the *dist-format-clause* nor the *dist-target* in a **REDISTRIBUTE** directive may begin with "`*`".
3. If an **ONTO** clause is present and mentions a *processors-name*, it must name a processors arrangement declared in a **PROCESSORS** directive (see Section 4.8).
4. The other rules given in Section 4.4 also apply.

5.3 ALIGN Directives and Dummy Arguments

The syntax for the **ALIGN** directive given in Section 4.5 omitted certain options relevant only to dummy arguments. The complete syntax for these options is explained here. Note that the options related to dummy arguments may be used only in **ALIGN** directives, not in **REALIGN** directives.

The form of an *align-with-clause* (H319) is:

`WITH` *align-spec*

where the form of an *align-spec* (H320) is one of:

align-target [(*align-subscript-list*)]
`*` *align-target* [(*align-subscript-list*)]

Data Mapping for Procedure Arguments   149

These forms are prescriptive and descriptive respectively; the descriptive form may be used only for dummy arguments. (To get the effect of a transcriptive **ALIGN** specification, simply use **INHERIT**—see Section 5.4.)

Rules and restrictions:
1. If the *align-spec* in an **ALIGN** directive begins with "*" then every *alignee* must be a dummy argument.
2. The *align-spec* in a **REALIGN** may not begin with "*".
3. The other rules given in Section 4.5 also apply.

5.4 INHERIT Directive

The **INHERIT** attribute specifies that the template for a dummy argument should be a copy of the template of the corresponding actual argument. This template may not have the same size and shape as the dummy argument; the dummy argument is aligned to the template copy in the same way that the actual argument is aligned to its original template.

The form of an *inherit-directive* (H337) is:

INHERIT *dummy-argument-name-list*

The **INHERIT** directive causes the named subprogram dummy arguments to have the **INHERIT** attribute.

Rules and restrictions:
1. Only dummy arguments may have the **INHERIT** attribute.
2. An object may not have both the **INHERIT** attribute and the **ALIGN** attribute.
3. The **INHERIT** directive may appear only in a *specification-part* of a scoping unit.

The **INHERIT** attribute specifies that the template for a dummy argument should be inherited, by making a copy of the template of the actual argument. Moreover, the **INHERIT** attribute implies a default distribution of **DISTRIBUTE * ONTO ***. Note that this default distribution is not part of Subset HPF; if a program uses **INHERIT**, it *must* override the default distribution with an explicit mapping directive in order to conform to Subset HPF. If an explicit mapping directive appears for the dummy argument, thereby overriding the default distribution, then the actual argument must be a whole array or a regular array section; it may not be an expression of any other form.

If none of the attributes **INHERIT**, **ALIGN**, and **DISTRIBUTE** is specified explicitly for a dummy argument, then the template of the dummy argument has the same shape as the dummy itself and the dummy argument is aligned to its template by the identity mapping.

An **INHERIT** directive may be combined with other directives as part of a *combined-directive* (H301).

Consider the following example:

```
      REAL DOUGH(100)
!HPF$ DISTRIBUTE DOUGH( BLOCK(10) )
      CALL PROBATE( DOUGH(7:23:2) )
       ...
      SUBROUTINE PROBATE(BREAD)
      REAL BREAD(9)
!HPF$ INHERIT BREAD
```

The template of **BREAD** (a copy of the template for **DOUGH**) has shape [100]. Element **BREAD(I)** is aligned with element **5 + 2*I** of the inherited template. Since **BREAD** does not appear in a prescriptive **DISTRIBUTE** directive, the new template is not remapped and therefore has a **BLOCK(10)** distribution. Thus **BREAD(1)** and **BREAD(2)** reside on the first abstract processor (of at least ten), **BREAD(3:7)** resides on the second abstract processor, and **BREAD(8:9)** resides on the third abstract processor.

5.5 Rules for Explicit Interfaces

If, in a caller, there is an explicit interface for the called subprogram and that interface contains mapping directives (whether prescriptive or descriptive) for the dummy argument in question, the actual argument will be remapped if necessary to conform to the directives in the explicit interface. The template of the dummy will then satisfy any constraints imposed by the declared interface.

The caller is required to treat descriptive directives in an explicit interface as if they were prescriptive so that the directives in the interface may be an exact textual copy of the directives appearing in the subprogram. If the *caller* enforces descriptive directives as if they were prescriptive, then the descriptive directives in the *called* routine will in fact be correct descriptions.

There are two subtle points to be remarked upon.

1. The term "explicit interface" is used here in the Fortran 90 sense. An interface block is not the only way to specify an explicit interface; for example, module procedures and internal procedures also are considered to have explicit interfaces.

2. If there is an explicit interface, the remapping rule stated above applies even if there are no explicit HPF directives associated with the explicit interface. Where the programmer has not specified directives explicitly, the compiler is required to supply suitable defaults, and to do so in a consistent manner so that the same defaulted specifications are provided for a procedure and for any explicit interface for that procedure.

If there is no explicit interface, then actual arguments that are whole arrays or array sections are not remapped before the call; the values of other expressions may be mapped in any manner at the discretion of the language processor. (It follows that an HPF program is nonconforming if all the following hold:

1. Some procedure P is called from some scoping unit S.
2. P has a descriptive declaration for a dummy.
3. The corresponding actual is not a whole array or array section.
4. S has no explicit interface for P.

The reasoning is that the descriptive declaration cannot provably describe the mapping of the actual argument, as that mapping depends on the language processor.)

5.6 Descriptive DISTRIBUTE Directives

In order to specify explicitly the distribution of a dummy argument, whether prescriptively or descriptively, the template that is subject to distribution must be determined. A dummy argument does not have the same template as the corresponding actual argument (this is why remappings of dummies by a subroutine or function have no effect on the actual arguments as viewed by the caller). Its template is determined in one of three ways:

1. If the dummy argument appears explicitly as an *alignee* in an **ALIGN** directive, its template is specified by the *align-target*.
2. If the dummy argument is not explicitly aligned and does not have the **INHERIT** attribute, then it has a brand-new, freshly created template that has the same shape and bounds as the dummy argument; this is called the *natural template* for the dummy. In this case the dummy is ultimately aligned with itself.
3. If the dummy argument is not explicitly aligned and does have the **INHERIT** attribute, then the template is "inherited" from the actual argument as follows:

- If the actual argument is a whole array, the template of the dummy is a *copy* of the template with which the actual argument is ultimately aligned.

- If the actual argument is a regular array section of array A, then the template of the dummy is a *copy* of the template with which A is ultimately aligned.
- If the actual argument is any other expression, a freshly created template is used, the shape and distribution of which may be chosen arbitrarily by the language processor (and therefore the programmer cannot know anything *a priori* about its distribution).

Then we say that the dummy has an *inherited template* rather than a natural template.

Consider the following example:

```
      LOGICAL FRUG(128), TWIST(128)
!HPF$ PROCESSORS DANCE_FLOOR(16)
!HPF$ DISTRIBUTE (BLOCK) ONTO DANCE_FLOOR :: FRUG, TWIST
      CALL TERPSICHORE(FRUG(1:40:3), TWIST(1:40:3))
```

The two array sections `FRUG(1:40:3)` and `TWIST(1:40:3)` are mapped onto abstract processors in the same manner:

	1	2	3	4	5	6	7	8	9	10	11	12	13	14	15	16
	1			25												
		10			34											
			19													
	4			28												
		13			37											
			22													
	7			31												
		16			40											

However, the subroutine `TERPSICHORE` will view them in different ways because it inherits the template for the second dummy but not the first:

```
      SUBROUTINE TERPSICHORE(FOXTROT, TANGO)
      LOGICAL FOXTROT(:), TANGO(:)
!HPF$ INHERIT TANGO
```

Therefore the template of `TANGO` is a copy of the 128 element template of the whole array `TWIST`. The template is mapped like this:

Data Mapping for Procedure Arguments   153

	1	2	3	4	5	6	7	8	9	10	11	12	13	14	15	16
1	9	17	25	33	41	49	57	65	73	81	89	97	105	113	121
2	10	18	26	34	42	50	58	66	74	82	90	98	106	114	122
3	11	19	27	35	43	51	59	67	75	83	91	99	107	115	123
4	12	20	28	36	44	52	60	68	76	84	92	100	108	116	124
5	13	21	29	37	45	53	61	69	77	85	93	101	109	117	125
6	14	22	30	38	46	54	62	70	78	86	94	102	110	118	126
7	15	23	31	39	47	55	63	71	79	87	95	103	111	119	127
8	16	24	32	40	48	56	64	72	80	88	96	104	112	120	128

TANGO(I) is aligned with element **3*I-2** of the template. But the template of **FOXTROT** has the same size 14 as **FOXTROT** itself. The actual argument, **FRUG(1:40:3)** is mapped to the 16 processors in this manner:

Abstract processor	Elements of FRUG
1	1, 2, 3
2	4, 5, 6
3	7, 8
4	9, 10, 11
5	12, 13, 14
6–16	none

It would seem reasonable to understand the mapping of the template of **FOXTROT** to coincide in like manner with the layout of the array section:

	1	2	3	4	5	6	7	8	9	10	11	12	13	14	15	16
1			9												
	4		12												
		7													
2			10												
	5		13												
		8													
3			11												
	6		14												

but we shall see that this cannot properly be described in HPF. Within subroutine **TERPSICHORE** it would be correct to make the descriptive assertion

```
!HPF$ DISTRIBUTE TANGO *(BLOCK)
```

but it would not be correct to declare

```
!HPF$ DISTRIBUTE FOXTROT *(BLOCK)       ! *** Nonconforming
```

Each of these asserts that the template of the specified dummy argument is already distributed **BLOCK** on entry to the subroutine. The shape of the template for **TANGO** is [128], inherited (copied) from the array **TWIST**, whose section was passed as the corresponding actual argument, and that template does indeed have a **BLOCK** distribution. But the shape of the template for **FOXTROT** is [14]; the layout of the elements of the actual argument **FRUG(1:40:3)** (3 on the first processor, 3 on the second processor, 2 on the third processor, 3 on the fourth processor, ...) cannot properly be described as a **BLOCK** distribution of a length-14 template, so the **DISTRIBUTE** declaration for **FOXTROT** shown above would indeed be erroneous.

On the other hand, the layout of **FRUG(1:40:3)** can be specified in terms of an alignment to a length-128 template which, can be described by an explicit **TEMPLATE** declaration (see Section 4.9), so the directives

```
!HPF$ PROCESSORS DANCE_FLOOR(16)
!HPF$ TEMPLATE, DISTRIBUTE(BLOCK) ONTO DANCE_FLOOR :: GURF(128)
!HPF$ ALIGN FOXTROT(J) WITH *GURF(3*J-2)
```

could be correctly included in **TERPSICHORE** to describe the layout of **FOXTROT** on entry to the subroutine without using an inherited template.

Descriptive directives allow the programmer to make claims about the pre-existing distribution of a dummy based on knowledge of the mapping of the actual argument. But what claims may the programmer correctly make?

If the dummy argument has an inherited template, then the subprogram may contain directives corresponding to the directives describing the actual argument. Sometimes it is necessary, as an alternative, to introduce an explicit named template (using a **TEMPLATE** directive) rather than inheriting a template; an example of this (**GURF**) appears above.

If the dummy argument has a natural template (no **INHERIT** attribute) then things are more complicated. In certain situations the programmer is justified in inferring a pre-existing distribution for the natural template from the distribution of the actual's template, that is, the template that would have been inherited if the **INHERIT** attribute had been specified. In all these situations, the actual argument must be a whole array or array section, and the template of the actual must be coextensive with the array along any axes having a distribution format other than "*."

If the actual argument is a whole array, then the pre-existing distribution of the natural template of the dummy is identical to that of the actual argument.

If the actual argument is an array section, then, from each *section-subscript* and the distribution format for the corresponding axis of the array being subscripted, one constructs an axis distribution format for the corresponding axis of the natural template:

- If the *section-subscript* is scalar and the array axis is collapsed (as by an **ALIGN** directive) then no entry should appear in the distribution for the natural template.
- If the *section-subscript* is a *subscript-triplet* and the array axis is collapsed (as by an **ALIGN** directive), then * should appear in the distribution for the natural template.
- If the *section-subscript* is scalar and the array axis corresponds to an actual template axis distributed *, then no entry should appear in the distribution for the natural template.
- If the *section-subscript* is a *subscript-triplet* and the array axis corresponds to an actual template axis distributed *, then * should appear in the distribution for the natural template.
- If the *section-subscript* is a *subscript-triplet* $l:u:s$ and the array axis corresponds to an actual template axis distributed **BLOCK**(n) (which might have been specified as simply **BLOCK**, but there will be some n that describes the resulting distribution) and LB is the lower bound for that axis of the array, then **BLOCK**(n/s) should appear in the distribution for the natural template, *provided* that s divides n evenly and that $l - LB < s$.
- If the *section-subscript* is a *subscript-triplet* $l:u:s$ and the array axis corresponds to an actual template axis distributed **CYCLIC**(n) (which might have been specified as simply **CYCLIC**, in which case $n = 1$) and LB is the lower bound for that axis of the array, then **CYCLIC**(n/s) should appear in the distribution for the natural template, *provided* that s divides n evenly and that $l - LB < s$.

If the situation of interest is not described by the cases listed above, no assertion about the distribution of the natural template of a dummy is HPF-conforming.

Here is a typical example of the use of this feature. The main program has a two-dimensional array **TROGGS**, which is to be processed by a subroutine one column at a time. (Perhaps processing the entire array at once would require prohibitive amounts of temporary space.) Each column is to be distributed across many processors.

```
      REAL TROGGS(1024,473)
!HPF$ DISTRIBUTE TROGGS(BLOCK,*)
      DO J = 1, 473
```

```
      CALL WILD_THING(TROGGS(:,J))
    END DO
```

Each column of **TROGGS** has a **BLOCK** distribution. The rules listed above justify the programmer in saying so:

```
      SUBROUTINE WILD_THING(GROOVY)
      REAL GROOVY(:)
!HPF$ DISTRIBUTE GROOVY *(BLOCK) ONTO *
```

Consider now the **ALIGN** directive. The presence or absence of an asterisk at the start of an *align-spec* has the same meaning as in a *dist-format-clause*: it specifies whether the **ALIGN** directive is descriptive or prescriptive, respectively.

If an *align-spec* that does not begin with * is applied to a dummy argument, the meaning is that the dummy argument will be forced to have the specified alignment on entry to the subprogram (which may require temporarily remapping the data of the actual argument or a copy thereof).

Note that a dummy argument may also be used as an *align-target*.

```
      SUBROUTINE NICHOLAS(TSAR,CZAR)
      REAL, DIMENSION(1918) :: TSAR,CZAR
!HPF$ INHERIT :: TSAR
!HPF$ ALIGN WITH TSAR :: CZAR
```

In this example the first dummy argument, **TSAR**, is allowed to remain aligned with the corresponding actual argument, while the second dummy argument, **CZAR**, is forced to be aligned with the first dummy argument. If the two actual arguments are already aligned, no remapping of the data will be required at run time; but the subprogram will operate correctly even if the actual arguments are not already aligned, at the cost of remapping the data for the second dummy argument at run time.

If the *align-spec* begins with "*", then the *alignee* must be a dummy argument and the directive must be **ALIGN** and not **REALIGN**. The "*" indicates that the **ALIGN** directive constitutes a guarantee on the part of the programmer that, on entry to the subprogram, the indicated alignment will already be satisfied by the dummy argument, without any action to remap it required at run time. For example:

```
      SUBROUTINE GRUNGE(PLUNGE, SPONGE)
      REAL, DIMENSION(1000) :: PLUNGE, SPONGE
!HPF$ ALIGN PLUNGE WITH *SPONGE
```

This asserts that, for every J in the range 1:1000, on entry to subroutine GRUNGE, the directives in the program have specified that PLUNGE(J) is currently mapped to the same abstract processor as SPONGE(J). (The intent is that if the language processor has in fact honored the directives, then no interprocessor communication will be required to achieve the specified alignment.)

The alignment of a general expression is up to the language processor and therefore unpredictable by the programmer; but the alignment of whole arrays and array sections is predictable. In the code fragment

```
      REAL FIJI(5000), SQUEEGEE(2000)
!HPF$ ALIGN SQUEEGEE(K) WITH FIJI(2*K)
      CALL GRUNGE(FIJI(2002:4000:2), SQUEEGEE(1001:))
```

it is true that every element of the array section SQUEEGEE(1001:) is aligned with the corresponding element of the array section FIJI(2002:4000:2), so the claim made in subroutine GRUNGE is satisfied by this particular call.

It is not permitted to say simply "ALIGN WITH *"; an *align-target* must follow the asterisk. (The proper way to say "accept any alignment" is INHERIT.)

If a dummy argument has no explicit ALIGN or DISTRIBUTE attribute, then the compiler provides an implicit alignment and distribution specification, one that could have been described explicitly without any "assertion asterisks".

5.7 Examples of DISTRIBUTE Directives for Dummy Arguments

A DISTRIBUTE directive for a dummy argument may have a *dist-format-list* and an ONTO clause, and each one may be prescriptive, descriptive, transcriptive, or omitted. The following examples of DISTRIBUTE directives for dummy arguments illustrate many of the possible combinations:

Example 5.1 Prescriptive format, prescriptive processors arrangement:

```
!HPF$ DISTRIBUTE URANIA (CYCLIC) ONTO GALILEO
```

The language processor should do whatever it takes to cause URANIA to have a CYCLIC distribution on the processor arrangement GALILEO. □

Example 5.2 Transcriptive format, prescriptive processors arrangement:

```
!HPF$ DISTRIBUTE POLYHYMNIA * ONTO ELVIS
```

The language processor should do whatever it takes to cause **POLYHYMNIA** to be distributed onto the processor arrangement **ELVIS**, using whatever distribution format it currently has (which might be on some other processor arrangement). (You can't say this in Subset HPF.) □

Example 5.3 Descriptive format, prescriptive processors arrangement:

    !HPF$ DISTRIBUTE THALIA *(CYCLIC) ONTO FLIP

The language processor should do whatever it takes to cause **THALIA** to have a **CYCLIC** distribution on the processor arrangement **FLIP**; **THALIA** already has a cyclic distribution, though it might be on some other processor arrangement. □

Example 5.4 Prescriptive format, descriptive processors arrangement:

    !HPF$ DISTRIBUTE CALLIOPE (CYCLIC) ONTO *HOMER

The language processor should do whatever it takes to cause **CALLIOPE** to have a **CYCLIC** distribution on the processor arrangement **HOMER**; **CALLIOPE** is already distributed onto **HOMER**, though it might be with some other distribution format. □

Example 5.5 Transcriptive format, descriptive processors arrangement:

    !HPF$ DISTRIBUTE MELPOMENE * ONTO *EURIPIDES

MELPOMENE is asserted to already be distributed onto **EURIPIDES**; use whatever distribution format the actual argument had so, if possible, no data movement should occur. (You can't say this in Subset HPF.) □

Example 5.6 Descriptive format, descriptive processors arrangement:

    !HPF$ DISTRIBUTE CLIO *(CYCLIC) ONTO *HERODOTUS

CLIO is asserted to already be distributed **CYCLIC** onto **HERODOTUS** so, if possible, no data movement should occur. □

Example 5.7 Prescriptive format, transcriptive processors arrangement:

    !HPF$ DISTRIBUTE EUTERPE (CYCLIC) ONTO *

The language processor should do whatever it takes to cause **EUTERPE** to have a **CYCLIC** distribution onto whatever processor arrangement the actual was distributed onto. (You can't say this in Subset HPF.) □

Example 5.8 Transcriptive format, transcriptive processors arrangement:

    !HPF$ DISTRIBUTE ERATO * ONTO *

The mapping of **ERATO** should not be changed from that of the actual argument. (You can't say this in Subset HPF.) You're probably better off just saying

    !HPF$ INHERIT ERATO

which implies `DISTRIBUTE ERATO * ONTO *` as the default distribution. □

Example 5.9 Descriptive format, transcriptive processors arrangement:

    !HPF$ DISTRIBUTE ARTHUR_MURRAY *(CYCLIC) ONTO *

ARTHUR_MURRAY is asserted to already be distributed **CYCLIC** onto whatever processor arrangement the actual argument was distributed onto, and no data movement should occur. (You can't say this in Subset HPF.) □

Please note that `DISTRIBUTE ERATO * ONTO *` does not mean the same thing as

    !HPF$ DISTRIBUTE ERATO *(*) ONTO *

This latter means: **ERATO** is asserted to already be distributed * (that is, on-processor) onto whatever processor arrangement the actual was distributed onto. Note that the processor arrangement is necessarily scalar in this case.

One may omit either the *dist-format-clause* or the *dist-target-clause* for a dummy argument. If such a clause is omitted and the dummy argument has the **INHERIT** attribute, then the compiler must handle the directive as if * or **ONTO** * had been specified explicitly. If such a clause is omitted and the dummy does not have the **INHERIT** attribute, then the compiler may choose the distribution format or a target processor arrangement arbitrarily.

Example 5.10 Descriptive format, defaulted processors arrangement:

    !HPF$ DISTRIBUTE WHEEL_OF_FORTUNE *(CYCLIC)

WHEEL_OF_FORTUNE is asserted to already be **CYCLIC**. As long as it is kept **CYCLIC**, it may be remapped it onto some other processor arrangement, but there is no reason to. □

Example 5.11 Defaulted format, descriptive processors arrangement:

    !HPF$ DISTRIBUTE ONTO *TV :: DAVID_LETTERMAN

DAVID_LETTERMAN is asserted to already be distributed on TV in some fashion. The distribution format may be changed as long as DAVID_LETTERMAN is kept on TV. (Note that this declaration must be made in attributed form; the statement form

```
!HPF$ DISTRIBUTE DAVID_LETTERMAN ONTO *TV     ! *** Nonconforming
```

does not conform to the syntax for a DISTRIBUTE directive.) □

5.8 Explicit Dynamic Remapping of Dummy Arguments

The rules on the interaction of the REALIGN and REDISTRIBUTE directives with a subprogram argument interface are:

1. A dummy argument may be declared DYNAMIC. However, it is subject to the general restrictions concerning the use of the name of an array to stand for its associated template.
2. If an array or any section thereof is accessible by two or more paths, it is not HPF-conforming to remap it through any of those paths. For example, if an array is passed as an actual argument, it is forbidden to realign that array, or to redistribute an array or template to which it was aligned at the time of the call, until the subprogram has returned from the call. This prevents nasty aliasing problems. An example follows:

```
      MODULE FOO
      REAL A(10,10)
!HPF$ DYNAMIC ::  A
      END

      PROGRAM MAIN
      USE FOO
      CALL SUB(A(1:5,3:9))
      END

      SUBROUTINE SUB(B)
      USE FOO
      REAL B(:,:)
      ...
!HPF$ REDISTRIBUTE A            ! *** Nonconforming
      ...
      END
```

Situations such as this are forbidden, for the same reasons that an assignment to **A** at the statement marked "Nonconforming" would also be forbidden. In general, in *any* situation where assignment to a variable would be nonconforming by reason of aliasing, remapping of that variable by an explicit **REALIGN** or **REDISTRIBUTE** directive is also forbidden.

An overriding principle is that any mapping or remapping of arguments is not visible to the caller. This is true whether such remapping is implicit (in order to conform to prescriptive directives, which may themselves be explicit or implicit) or explicit (specified by **REALIGN** or **REDISTRIBUTE** directives). When the subprogram returns and the caller resumes execution, all objects accessible to the caller after the call are mapped exactly as they were before the call. It is not possible for a subprogram to change the mapping of any object in a manner visible to its caller, not even by means of **REALIGN** and **REDISTRIBUTE**.

The implicit remapping of dummy arguments can be implemented in several ways. One is for the subprogram to make a copy of the argument data and remap the copy for use within the subprogram. Another is to remap the actual argument on entry to the subprogram and later to perform a second remapping on exit from the subprogram to restore the data to its original layout.

5.9 Argument Passing and Sequence Association

This section is primarily about making old codes work, but it is also important for programmers writing new codes to understand. In the previous discussion there was an assumption that the dummy argument and the actual argument matched in size and shape. From its beginnings Fortran has allowed considerable flexibility across the boundaries of a call. The basic rule is summarized in this statement from the standard:

> *The rank and shape of the actual argument need not agree with the rank and shape of the dummy argument, ...*
> — Fortran Standard (12.4.1.4)

This works in Fortran programs because of *sequence association*: the order of array elements that Fortran requires when an array, array expression, or array element is associated with a dummy array argument. As with storage association, sequence association is a natural concept only in systems with a linearly addressed memory.

As an aid to porting FORTRAN 77 codes, HPF allows codes that rely on sequence association to be valid HPF; however, each argument must be checked and the programmer may have to insert sequence directives (Section 4.10.2) to instruct the HPF compiler to support the linear sequencing of memory.

Actual argument	Dummy argument requirements
Scalar name	The dummy argument must be a scalar.
Scalar expression or constant	The dummy argument must be a scalar.
Array element	If dummy argument is an array both arrays must be declared sequential.
Array section	The dummy argument must match in size and shape or both arrays must be declared sequential.
Array name	The dummy argument must match in size and shape or both arrays must be declared sequential.
Array expression	The dummy argument must match in size and shape. If this is not true, the actual argument expression must first be stored in a sequential array and the array name can be passed.
Assumed-size array	The dummy argument must be declared sequential.
Character variable	The explicit-length of the dummy argument must match the length of the actual argument, in addition to matching shape. Otherwise both the actual and the dummy must be declared sequential.

Table 5.1
Matching procedure arguments

5.9.1 Argument Requirements

In order to give a direct way to check all of the kinds of arguments for sequence association, the different possibilities for actual arguments are listed in Table 5.1.

There are some very common FORTRAN 77 cases that must be examined carefully. The practice of passing a portion of an array (e.g., a column) by passing an array element which is treated as the starting address of a dummy array argument is incompatible with distributed data. Fortran 90 provides the array section mechanism to accomplish this same thing. When the shape of the array section conforms to the shape declared by the dummy argument, then data mapping is still permitted.

Another special case to note is an array expression as an actual argument. HPF provides no mechanism for the programmer to specify the mapping of an expression and also no mechanism to specify that an expression is sequential. In this case, the dummy argument may not be a sequential array. The programmer will have to create an explicit (sequential) temporary to hold the expression value and pass that temporary as the argument.

Assumed size arrays are listed as one of the kinds of argument that require the associated dummy argument to be sequential. Assumed size arrays are themselves sequential (see Section 4.10.2). It is easy to confuse assumed-size arrays and assumed shape arrays, so we will take a step back to review what they are.

Assumed shape dummy arguments are of the form DIMENSION A(:,:,:). The rank of the actual argument is reflected exactly in the associated dummy argument. Assumed size arguments are of the form DIMENSION A(20, 10, *); they are a different story. By their definition, storage and sequence association apply to the values of the array. The programmer dictates a shape that the dummy argument assumes, regardless of the shape of the actual argument. It is only the size of the last dimension that is left unspecified. We treat these assumed-size variables as sequential. If such a variable is, in turn, passed on to another subroutine, the associated dummy must be declared sequential.

The reader should notice that a single case of an argument that requires sequence association and needs a sequential declaration can have a wider impact. If the actual argument is in COMMON this will entail finding all instances of the common block to mark that component sequential. In the long run, it is much better to correct a problem, such as the mismatch in shape, wherever possible.

5.9.2 Sequence Association Examples

Figure 5.4 gives some code segments to illustrate sequence association in arguments. The two calls to SEQ_ARGS and GOOD_ARGS look very similar. But on close examination, all of the actual arguments in the call to GOOD_ARGS in subroutine TWO match the shape and size of the corresponding dummy arguments exactly. The programmer will have to worry a bit about the proper distribution for B because of the section used as an actual, but there are no issues related to sequence association. The call to SEQ_ARGS in subroutine ONE, on the other hand, illustrates sequence association requirements for every argument. The reader will notice that we have inserted a SEQUENCE directive for each actual argument and each dummy argument. Let's just check them one at a time. The first argument uses a very common FORTRAN 77 method to pass a column of the array A. The address of the first element of the column is passed. The second and third arguments both illustrate cases where the dummy argument is a different rank than the corresponding actual arguments. The last argument is another common case where the programmer passes in an array of one size, but only uses part of the array. In this example, the programmer wishes to send in a Fortran 90 array expression D+E, but is required by the

```
       SUBROUTINE ONE
         REAL A(100,100), B(100), C(10,100), D(100), E(100)
         REAL TEMP(100)
!HPF$    SEQUENCE A, B, C, TEMP
         ...
         TEMP = D + E
         CALL SEQ_ARGS(A(1,I), B(11:35), C, TEMP)
       END SUBROUTINE ONE

       SUBROUTINE SEQ_ARGS(COL, SQUARE, FLAT, PART)
         REAL COL(100), SQUARE(5,5), FLAT(1000), PART(20)
!HPF$    SEQUENCE COL, SQUARE, FLAT, PART
         ...
       END SUBROUTINE SEQ_ARGS

       SUBROUTINE TWO
         REAL A(100,100), B(100), C(10,100), D(100), E(100)
         ...
         CALL GOOD_ARGS(A(1,I), B(11:35), C, D+E)
         ...
       END SUBROUTINE TWO

       SUBROUTINE GOOD_ARGS(SCALAR, X25, MATCH_C, MATCH_D)
         REAL X25(25), MATCH_C(10,100), MATCH_D(100)
         ...
       END SUBROUTINE GOOD_ARGS
```

Figure 5.4
Checking sequence association for arguments

```
      CHARACTER (LEN=44) A_LONG_WORD
!HPF$ SEQUENCE A_LONG_WORD
      A_LONG_WORD='Chargoggagoggmanchaugagoggchaubunagungamaugg'
      CALL WEBSTER(A_LONG_WORD)

      SUBROUTINE WEBSTER(SHORT_DICTIONARY)
      CHARACTER (LEN=4) SHORT_DICTIONARY (11)
      !Note that short_dictionary(3) is 'agog'
!HPF$ SEQUENCE SHORT_DICTIONARY
```

Figure 5.5
Character sequence association

rules to store the value into a temporary location first in order to designate that it is sequential. As an alternative to using the **SEQUENCE** directives, the programmer might have replaced the call to **SEQ_ARGS** with the following call.

```
CALL SEQ_ARGS(A((*,I)), RESHAPE(B(11:35),(/5,5/)),           &
              RESHAPE(C, (/1000/)), TEMP(1:20))
```

This uses the Fortran 90 **RESHAPE** intrinsic to pass the exact shapes and sizes required to the subroutine. It avoids the use of the **SEQUENCE** directives on either side of the call. While the **SEQUENCE** directive is certainly easier to use, and this is not backwards compatible with FORTRAN 77, there may be performance reasons for avoiding the **SEQUENCE** directives.

Figure 5.5 gives an example of the additional sequence association issue for character variables. This code segment where the data is treated both as a single long character and an array of short characters is legal in both FORTRAN 77 and Fortran 90. However in HPF, both the actual argument and dummy argument must be sequential. (By the way, "Chargoggagoggmanchaugagoggchaubunagungamaugg" is the original Nipmuc name for what is now called "Lake Webster" in Massachusetts.)

Figure 5.6 shows the case of an assumed-size argument. In subroutine **ONE**, the declared shape of **WHAT_SIZE** may match that of the incoming actual argument in its first two dimensions, but the compiler does not know for sure. **WHAT_SIZE** is sequential. When it is passed on to subroutine **TWO**, it doesn't matter how **WHO_KNOWS** is declared. It must be declared sequential. If the declaration in subroutine **ONE** were **WHAT_SIZE(:,:,:)** instead then no directive would be required in subroutine **TWO**.

```
      SUBROUTINE ONE (WHAT_SIZE)
        REAL WHAT_SIZE(10,50,*)
        ...
        CALL TWO (WHAT_SIZE)
        ...
      END SUBROUTINE ONE

      SUBROUTINE TWO (WHO_KNOWS)
        INTEGER WHO_KNOWS(10,50,5)
!HPF$   SEQUENCE WHO_KNOWS
        ...
      END SUBROUTINE TWO
```

Figure 5.6
Assumed size arguments

5.9.3 Formal Sequence Association Rules

For completeness, the formal rules about sequence association from the HPF document are listed here.

1. When an array element or the name of an assumed-size array is used as an actual argument, the associated dummy argument must be a scalar or specified to be a sequential array.

   An array-element designator of a nonsequential array must not be associated with a dummy array argument.

2. When an actual argument is an array or array section and the corresponding dummy argument differs from the actual argument in shape, then the dummy argument must be declared sequential and the actual array argument must be sequential.

3. A variable of type character (scalar or array) is nonsequential if it conforms to the requirements of Section 4.10.2. If the length of an explicit-length character dummy argument differs from the length of the actual argument, then both the actual and dummy arguments must be sequential.

6 Data Parallelism

As explained in Chapter 2, the High Performance Fortran programming model considers two factors—parallelism and communication. Chapters 4 and 5 describe the data mapping mechanisms that determine the communication in a program. This chapter looks at some data parallel features of HPF. Other parallel features appear in Chapter 3 (array assignments), Chapter 7 (HPF library functions), and Chapter 8 (EXTRINSIC procedures).

6.1 Overview of Data Parallelism

This chapter describes three features of HPF: the FORALL statement, the PURE attribute, and the INDEPENDENT directive. Of these, FORALL and INDEPENDENT are parallel in and of themselves. PURE is not parallel by itself, but can be used in conjunction with the FORALL statement to increase the generality of that construct.

The FORALL statement, described in Section 6.2, generalizes the Fortran 90 array assignment to handle new shapes of arrays. In the process, the FORALL statement ends up looking a bit like a DO loop. (Note, however, that the FORALL statement is not itself a loop—it assigns to a block of array elements, but does not iterate over them in any specific order.) The meaning is the same as for array assignments: compute all right-hand sides before making any assignments. For example, Figure 6.1 shows how a FORALL statement can shift elements of the main diagonal of an array along the diagonal. There is also a multi-statement FORALL, in which the array assignment semantics are applied to each statement in turn. Figure 6.2 shows this form of the FORALL. As you can see, FORALL statements can be nested and can have mask expressions.

The intent in defining the FORALL is to create a parallel construct with determinate semantics. That is, the statement can execute in parallel, and the results are identical if it is re-executed with the same data. Identical results will hold even if the number of processors or the entire machine architecture changes (up to the differences in machine arithmetic, such as floating-point precision, permitted by the Fortran 90 standard). To ensure this level of determinacy, the FORALL has a number of constraints. It is important to realize that, because of these constraints, the FORALL is *not* the general "parallel loop" that some other languages have; in particular, there is no way (and no need) to perform explicit synchronization, schedule tasks, or pass messages in a FORALL.

The FORALL can apply a user-defined function to every element of an array if the function is PURE, as defined in Section 6.3. Figure 6.3 shows a FORALL applying EQN_OF_STATE to elements of the arrays V, N, and T to produce array P. This is similar to using Fortran 90 elemental intrinsics, except that PURE functions can be user-defined. A PURE

FORALL (I = 2:5) A(I,I) = A(I-1,I-1)

$$\begin{bmatrix} 11 & 12 & 13 & 14 & 15 \\ 21 & 22 & 23 & 24 & 25 \\ 31 & 32 & 33 & 34 & 35 \\ 41 & 42 & 43 & 44 & 45 \\ 51 & 52 & 53 & 54 & 55 \end{bmatrix} \rightarrow \begin{bmatrix} 11 & 12 & 13 & 14 & 15 \\ 21 & 11 & 23 & 24 & 25 \\ 31 & 32 & 22 & 34 & 35 \\ 41 & 42 & 43 & 33 & 45 \\ 51 & 52 & 53 & 54 & 44 \end{bmatrix}$$

A before A after

Figure 6.1
A single-statement FORALL

```
FORALL (I = 1:8)
  A(I,I) = SQRT(A(I,I))
  FORALL (J = I-3:I+3, J/=I .AND. J>=1 .AND. J<=8)
    A(I,J) = A(I,I) * A(J,J)
  END FORALL
END FORALL
```

$$\begin{bmatrix} 1 & 0 & 0 & 0 & 0 & 0 & 0 & 0 \\ 0 & 4 & 0 & 0 & 0 & 0 & 0 & 0 \\ 0 & 0 & 9 & 0 & 0 & 0 & 0 & 0 \\ 0 & 0 & 0 & 16 & 0 & 0 & 0 & 0 \\ 0 & 0 & 0 & 0 & 25 & 0 & 0 & 0 \\ 0 & 0 & 0 & 0 & 0 & 36 & 0 & 0 \\ 0 & 0 & 0 & 0 & 0 & 0 & 49 & 0 \\ 0 & 0 & 0 & 0 & 0 & 0 & 0 & 64 \end{bmatrix} \rightarrow \begin{bmatrix} 1 & 2 & 3 & 4 & 0 & 0 & 0 & 0 \\ 2 & 2 & 6 & 8 & 10 & 0 & 0 & 0 \\ 3 & 6 & 3 & 12 & 15 & 18 & 0 & 0 \\ 4 & 8 & 12 & 4 & 20 & 24 & 28 & 0 \\ 0 & 10 & 15 & 20 & 5 & 30 & 35 & 40 \\ 0 & 0 & 18 & 24 & 30 & 6 & 42 & 48 \\ 0 & 0 & 0 & 28 & 35 & 42 & 7 & 56 \\ 0 & 0 & 0 & 0 & 40 & 48 & 56 & 8 \end{bmatrix}$$

A before A after

Figure 6.2
A multi-statement FORALL

```
    INTERFACE
      PURE REAL FUNCTION EQN_OF_STATE(VOL, MOLES, TEMP)
        REAL VOL, MOLES, TEMP
      END FUNCTION EQN_OF_STATE
    END INTERFACE
    ...
    FORALL (I = 1:NUM, J = 1:NUM)
      P(I,J) = EQN_OF_STATE(V(I,J), N(I,J), T(I,J))
    END FORALL
```

Figure 6.3
A PURE function declaration and use

```
!HPF$ INDEPENDENT, NEW (J, N1)
      DO I = 1, NBLACK
        N1 = IBLACK_PT(I)
        DO J = INITIAL_RED(N1), LAST_RED(N1)
          X(N1) = X(N1) + A(J)*X(IRED_PT(J))
        END DO
      END DO
```

Figure 6.4
An INDEPENDENT directive

function cannot have side effects on global data or on its arguments; thus, it behaves like a mathematically pure function. HPF puts some rather heavy restrictions on the function before it can be declared PURE to ensure that the compiler can check for the lack of side effects. Like the constraints on FORALL, these restrictions ensure determinate execution at some cost in generality.

Sometimes the programmer knows that a loop is parallel in cases where the compiler cannot detect the parallelism. HPF introduces the INDEPENDENT directive for just such situations. The INDEPENDENT directive is a promise by the user that the results of the DO loop will be the same even if its iterations are executed in some other order or asynchronously in parallel. Figure 6.4 shows how an INDEPENDENT directive allows NBLACK sums to be computed in parallel. Without the INDEPENDENT directive, the compiler would have to assume that some elements of X were referenced as both X(N1) and X(IRED_PT(J)), forcing the loop to run serially. Note the difference in philosophy from the **FORALL** statement. The **FORALL** is a new statement, with a different meaning from the similar-looking **DO** loop. The **INDEPENDENT** directive is a statement about the behavior of the program as it is written.

6.2 The FORALL Statement

The **FORALL** is a generalization of the Fortran 90 array assignment and **WHERE** statements. It provides for more array shapes to be assigned, particularly when nested **FORALL** statements are used. In addition, when used with **PURE** functions (see Section 6.3) it provides a form of user-defined elemental functions. An HPF-conforming **FORALL** statement always has a well-defined meaning; no nondeterminacy is provided in the construct, and most of the restrictions to ensure this can be checked by the compiler.

A **FORALL** statement is *not* a loop, nor is it a "parallel loop" as defined in some languages. We say this for a very simple reason: the **FORALL** does not iterate in any well-defined order. Parallel loops are often defined to express nondeterminate execution, or as a basis for expressing arbitrary parallel computations. The **FORALL**, when used in an HPF-conforming way, cannot do either of those things.

HPF defines two forms of the **FORALL** statement—the *single-statement FORALL* (called the *forall-stmt* (H401) in the grammar) and the *multi-statement FORALL* (called the *forall-construct* (H405)). We will use the term *FORALL statement* to refer to both forms. Explanations of the few details where they differ will clearly identify either the single-statement or multi-statement form. Note that the single-statement **FORALL** is included in Subset HPF, but the multi-statement **FORALL** is not.

6.2.1 Form of the FORALL Statement

The form of the *forall-stmt* (H401) is:

    FORALL (*forall-triplet-spec-list* [, *scalar-mask-expr*]) *forall-assignment*

The form of the *forall-construct* (H405) is:

    FORALL (*forall-triplet-spec-list* [, *scalar-mask-expr*])
    forall-body-stmt
    [*forall-body-stmt*] ...
    END FORALL

The following rules and restrictions apply to both the *forall-stmt* and *forall-construct*.

Rules and restrictions:
1. Any procedure referenced in the *scalar-mask-expr* of a FORALL must be PURE, as defined in Section 6.3.
2. The evaluation of any expression in the *forall-triplet-spec-list* or *scalar-mask-expr* of a FORALL must not affect the result of computing any other expression in the *forall-triplet-spec-list* or the *scalar-mask-expr*.
3. If a FORALL is nested within a *forall-construct* (a multi-statement FORALL), then the inner FORALL may not redefine any *index-name* used in the outer *forall-construct*. Note that a FORALL may not be nested within a *forall-stmt*, (a single-statement FORALL).
4. Each assignment or pointer assignment nested within a FORALL assigns to data objects specified by the statement for permitted values of the *index-name* variables. (Note that even for deeply nested FORALL statements, an innermost statement is always an assignment or pointer assignment.) A single assignment of this type may not cause multiple values to be assigned to the same atomic object. (Recall that an atomic data object is a Fortran 90 object which has no subobjects.) An HPF-conforming program may, however, assign to the same atomic objects in different assignment statements.

The form of a *forall-triplet-spec* (H403) is:

index-name = *subscript* : *subscript* [: *stride*]

Rules and restrictions:
1. The *index-name* must be a scalar integer variable.
2. If *stride* is present, it must not have the value 0.
3. A *subscript* or *stride* in a *forall-triplet-spec-list* must not contain a reference to any *index-name* in the *forall-triplet-spec-list* in which it appears.

Note that Fortran 90 restricts *subscript* (R617) and *stride* (R620) to be scalar integers as well.

A *forall-assignment* (H404) is one of:

assignment-stmt
pointer-assignment-stmt

A *forall-body-stmt* (H406) is one of:

forall-assignment
where-stmt
where-construct
forall-stmt
forall-construct

The following rules apply to both the *forall-assignment* and the *forall-body-stmt*.

Rules and restrictions:
1. Any procedure referenced in a *forall-assignment* or *forall-body-stmt*, including one referenced by a defined operation or assignment, must be **PURE** (see Section 6.3).

See Section 6.2.3 for many examples of **FORALL** syntax.

6.2.2 Meaning of the FORALL Statement

A multi-statement **FORALL** is interpreted essentially as a series of single-statement **FORALL** statements. We therefore describe the single-statement **FORALL**'s interpretation first, and then the complications of the multi-statement form.

The descriptions below speak of the "index values" of a **FORALL** statement rather than "iterations" or any other term that might suggest an order to the operations. We hope this helps the reader break out of the habit of thinking in terms of looping through a space, with the corresponding implied serialization.

Part of the semantics of the **FORALL** statement depends on the concept of an *atomic object*. Recall that this is a Fortran *data object* which contains no subobjects. For example, an integer variable is an atomic object, but an array of integers is an object that is not atomic.

Interpretation of a Single-statement FORALL A single-statement **FORALL** is executed in four stages.

1. Compute the *valid set* of index values. This is the set of values defined by the forall index range(s), not considering the mask expression. If there is more than one index, then the valid set is a set of tuples, where each tuple contains a value for each index. The range of valid values for each index is computed separately. For the *forall-triplet-spec*

    INDEX = *lb* : *ub* : *step*

let $max = \left\lceil \frac{ub-lb+1}{step} \right\rceil$. If *step* is missing, it is as if it were present with the value 1. Then the set of valid values for **INDEX** is $lb + (k-1) \times step$, $k = 1, 2, ..., max$. The valid set for the whole **FORALL** is the Cartesian product of the active sets for the individual indices. If $max \leq 0$ for some index, the **FORALL** is not executed.

2. Compute the *active set* of index values. This is the set of index values for which the *forall-assignment* is actually executed. The active set is constructed by evaluating the *scalar-mask-expr* for each element of the valid set. The mask elements may be calculated in any order or perhaps in parallel. The active set of index values is the subset of the valid index values for which the *scalar-mask-expr* evaluates to .TRUE. If there is no mask expression, then it is as if it were present with the constant value .TRUE., and so the active set equals the valid set.

3. For each index value tuple in the active set, compute the right-hand side for the body of the FORALL; the tuple specifies the values for the index variables. (Note that in a single-statement FORALL, the body will be either an assignment or a pointer assignment. In the case of an assignment statement (including array assignment), this step is a standard expression evaluation. In the case of pointer assignment, it may involve evaluating a pointer-valued expression or constructing a pointer to an object (depending on the type of the right-hand side).) At the same time, evaluate and save any subexpressions in the left-hand side (such as array subscripts). The evaluations for different index values may be done in any order or perhaps in parallel.

4. For each index value tuple in the active set, assign the right-hand side value computed in the previous step to the left-hand side. Depending on the statement type, this may be either a normal assignment or a pointer assignment. The left-hand side is determined from the saved subexpression values, rather than being computed while assignments are in progress. The assignments may be performed in any order or perhaps in parallel. (Remember that it is nonconforming for execution of a FORALL assignment to assign multiple values to the same memory location.)

The scope of a FORALL index is the FORALL statement itself. In other words, the value of the FORALL index variable becomes undefined after the termination of the FORALL.

The importance of computing both the right-hand sides and the left-hand subexpressions in step 3 is that it prevents them from being overwritten. Thus, the order of assignments cannot affect either the values being assigned or the locations to which they are assigned. Similarly, computing the bounds and mask elements first ensures that they are not affected by any assignments within the FORALL body.

Interpretation of a Multi-statement FORALL The multi-statement FORALL is conceptually a sequence of single-statement FORALLs. Its interpretation is therefore similar, with suitable elaborations for sequences of statements and nesting.

1. Compute the valid set of index values. This is done precisely as for the single-statement FORALL and has the same meaning.

2. Compute the active set of index values. This is done precisely as for the single-statement **FORALL** and has the same meaning.
3. Execute the statements in the **FORALL** body in the order given according to the rules below. Effectively, the rules specify that each statement takes effect for all active index values before any following statements begin.

- An assignment or pointer assignment statement is executed as if it were within a single-statement **FORALL**: the right-hand side is computed for all active index values, then the computed values are assigned to the left-hand side for all active index values.
- A **FORALL** statement modifies the active set of index values; the new active set is then used for executing the statements in the inner **FORALL** body. The process is more complicated than simply computing a single range for each of the inner indices and then taking a simple Cartesian product, because the ranges for the inner variables can depend on outer **FORALL** index variables. Consider, as an example, this code:

```
FORALL (I=1:3, J=1:3, I > J)
  FORALL(K=1:3, L=1:J, K+L > I)
    A(I,J,K,L) = J*K + L
  END FORALL
END FORALL
```

The (I, J) tuples in the active set for the outer **FORALL** are:

{ (2,1),
  (3,1),
  (3,2), }

For each index value tuple in the *outer active set*, a new valid set is computed for the inner **FORALL** statement. Each tuple in the new active set includes all the index values from the outer tuple as well as values for the index variables newly introduced by the inner **FORALL**. In our example, there are three pairs in the outer active set, so three new valid sets of (I,J,K,L) tuples are computed:

{ (2,1,1,1), (2,1,2,1), (2,1,3,1) }
{ (3,1,1,1), (3,1,2,1), (3,1,3,1) }
{ (3,2,1,1), (3,2,1,2), (3,2,2,1), (3,2,2,2), (3,2,3,1), (3,2,3,2) }

The union of all the new valid sets, one for each tuple in the outer active set, forms the *inner valid set* of (I,J,K,L) tuples:

{ (2,1,1,1),   (2,1,2,1),   (2,1,3,1)
   (3,1,1,1),   (3,1,2,1),   (3,1,3,1)
   (3,2,1,1),   (3,2,1,2),   (3,2,2,1),   (3,2,2,2),   (3,2,3,1),   (3,2,3,2)   }

The inner **FORALL** then computes the *inner active set* of index tuples by evaluating its mask expression for all index values in the inner valid set and discarding index value tuples that result in a **.FALSE.** mask value. In our example, inner active value tuples must satisfy **K+L > I**:

{   (2,1,2,1),   (2,1,3,1)
              (3,1,3,1)
                           (3,2,2,2),   (3,2,3,1),   (3,2,3,2)   }

Statements in the inner **FORALL** body are then executed using the inner active set of index values. At the end of the inner **FORALL**, the active set reverts to the outer active set.

- A **WHERE** statement or construct masks the array assignments in its body. The **WHERE** first evaluates its mask expression for all active index values. The assignments within the **WHERE** branch of the construct (or the single assignment in the one-line **WHERE** statement) are then executed in order using the interpretation of array assignments above. However, the only array elements assigned are those selected by both the active set of index values and the **WHERE** mask. Finally, the assignments in the **ELSEWHERE** branch are executed (if it is present). The assignments here are also treated as array assignments, but elements are assigned only if they are selected by both the active set of index values and by the negation of the **WHERE** mask.

6.2.3 Discussion of the FORALL Statement

The purpose of this section is to give some concrete examples of the **FORALL** statement and suggest how it can be used in practical programs. Before that, however, we digress to give a more visual explanation of the meaning of a **FORALL**.

Visualizing a FORALL The execution of the **FORALL** can be visualized by showing its *precedence graph*. Such a graph shows all the computations performed in a **FORALL** and tells when one computation must finish before another one starts. Figure 6.5 shows the precedence graph for a small **FORALL** statement. For comparison, Figure 6.6 shows the precedence graph for a **DO** statement with the same body.

In a precedence graph, the computations are shown as ellipses. The "Begin" ellipse contains the computation of the **FORALL** active set and the **DO** loop bounds. There are two computations for each assignment statement in the construct body—the right-hand side

```
                Begin

    b(1)        b(2)        b(3)


    a(1)        a(2)        a(3)


    d(1)        d(2)        d(3)


    c(1)        c(2)        c(3)

                 End
```

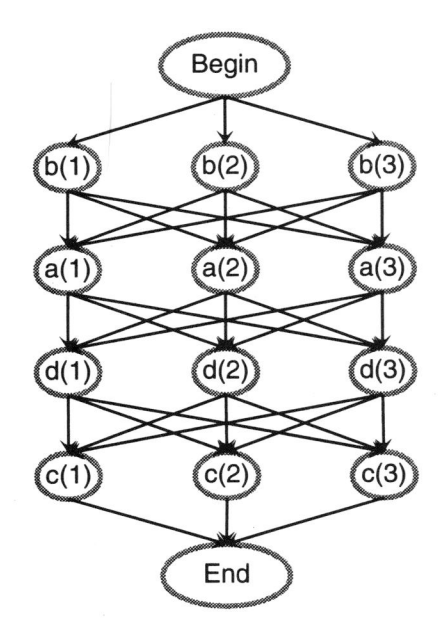

```
FORALL (I = 1:3)
   a(I) = b(I)
   c(I) = d(I)
END FORALL
```

Figure 6.5
Precedence graph for a FORALL statement

computation and the assignment to the left-hand side. The "End" ellipse does not contain any computation; it simply shows when the construct is complete. If two computations may have to be done in order, then there is an arrow from the earlier computation to the later one. The variables used in the FORALL in the figure are only for labeling; the arrows do not represent the actual dependences for a computation using only those variables. Instead, an arrow between, for example, b(1) and a(2) means that the right-hand side of the first statement for index value 1 may need to be completed before updating the left-hand side of the same statement for index value 2. Arrows from right-hand sides (b and d labels) to left-hand sides (a and c) are there because the left-hand update could overwrite some data needed to compute the right-hand side. Arrows from left-hand sides to right-hand sides are easier to understand; they mean that the assigned value might be used in a right-hand side computation.

The key point to note about Figure 6.5 is that every statement in the body essentially has two synchronization points—one after the right-hand side is computed, and one after the assignment to the left-hand side. An operation near the end of a FORALL (such as the operation c(1)) may depend on an operation near the top for *any* index value. Note

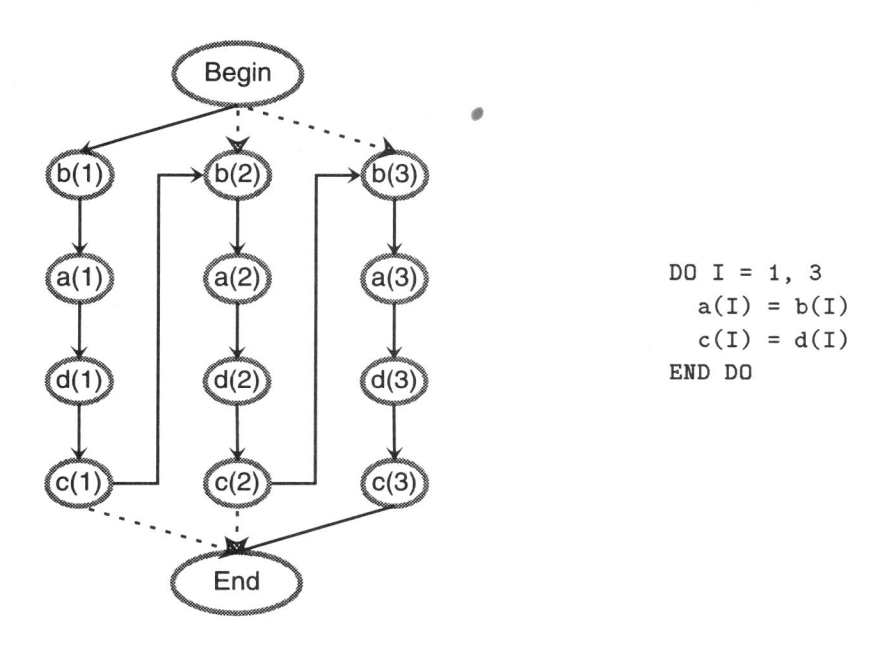

Figure 6.6
Precedence graph for a DO statement

```
DO I = 1, 3
  a(I) = b(I)
  c(I) = d(I)
END DO
```

how this differs from the DO loop. There, a dependence goes from the last operation in each iteration to the first operation in the next, forming a single continuous chain. The effect of this is that every row in the FORALL dependence diagram can be executed in parallel, while no operations in the DO can execute in parallel.

In practice, many of the dependences shown in these diagrams do not actually occur for a particular FORALL or DO statement. That is, Figures 6.5 and 6.6 are worst-case scenarios as far as parallelism is concerned. For example, if the computation in d does not use any elements from the array assigned in a, then none of the arrows from the second to the third row in the FORALL diagram actually occur. In simple cases (like the one we just described), a compiler may be able to detect that some dependences are not needed. Section 6.4.3 shows how the INDEPENDENT directive can make assertions about some DO and FORALL statements.

The precedence graph for nested FORALL statements is (not surprisingly) a bit more complex. Figure 6.7 shows one small example. The key point to notice is the mass of dependences between operations in the inner FORALL statement. Every c operation potentially depends on every d operation, even those with different I values. The remarks

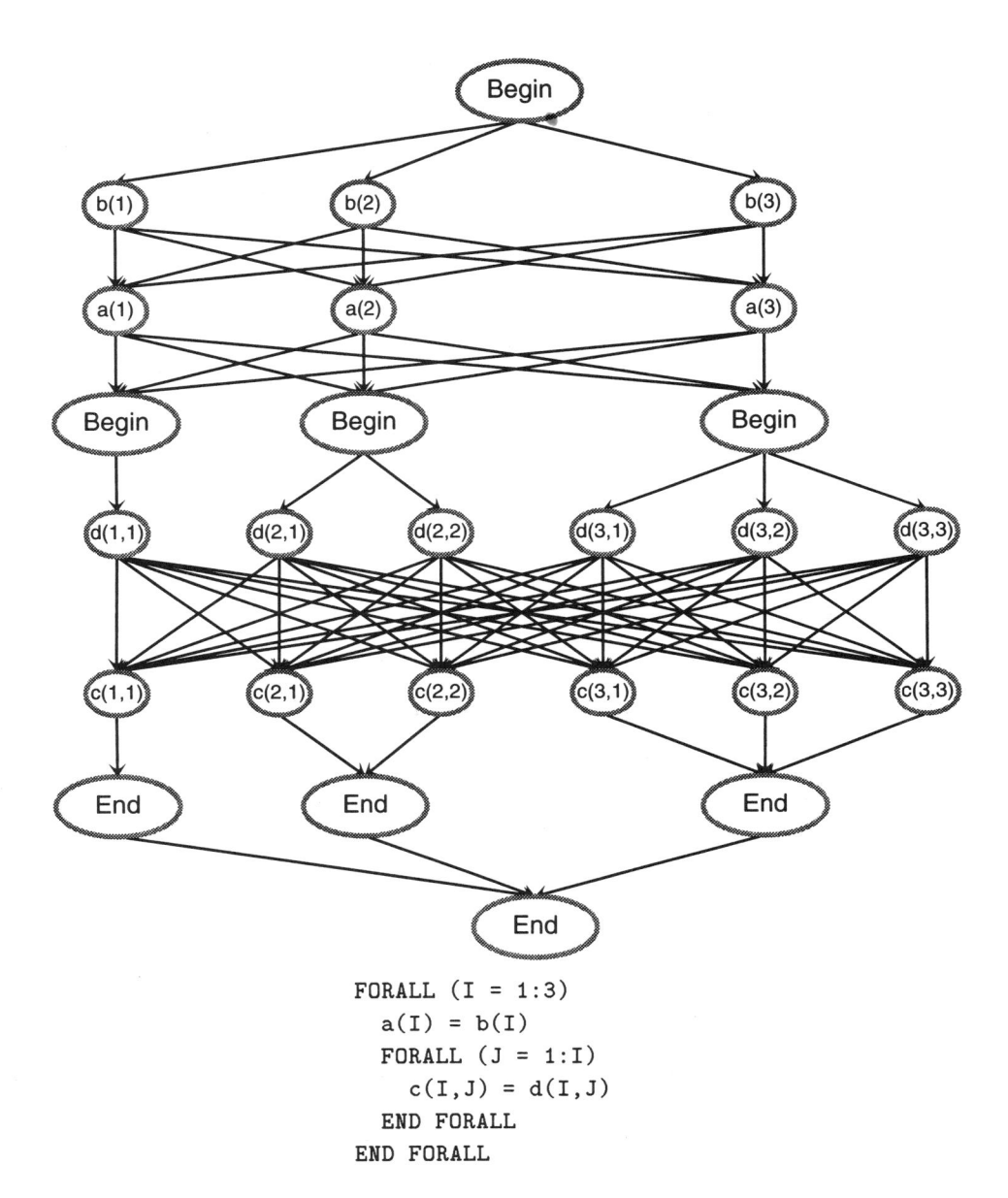

```
FORALL (I = 1:3)
  a(I) = b(I)
  FORALL (J = 1:I)
    c(I,J) = d(I,J)
  END FORALL
END FORALL
```

Figure 6.7
Precedence graph for nested FORALL statements

Data Parallelism

about dependences not occurring in practice apply doubly here. For example, in the statement

```
FORALL (I = 1:100)
  FORALL (J = 1:I)
    A(I,J) = A(J,I) * A(I,I)
  END FORALL
END FORALL
```

the worst-case diagram has 25,502,500 dependences between left- and right-hand sides; the number that actually occur is 5050. (The triangular index value space eliminates dependences between different values of I, and the only dependences in the FORALL J construct are from J=I to every value of J.) As before, every row in the FORALL precedence diagram can be executed in parallel. Although we don't show it, the diagram for a nested DO loop is a long chain of operations, snaking its way through the inner loops.

FORALL Examples Examples 6.1 and 6.2 go through the interpretation of two FORALL statements in some detail. The other examples in this section suggest ways that the FORALL can be useful, as well as illustrating some subtleties of the definitions in Sections 6.2.1 and 6.2.2.

Example 6.1 First, we consider the FORALL in Figure 6.1, reproduced below.

```
FORALL (I = 2:5) A(I, I) = A(I-1, I-1)
```

It is interpreted as follows:

1. The bounds are evaluated (trivially) to determine that the valid set of the FORALL is $\{2, 3, 4, 5\}$.
2. Since there is no mask expression, the active set is the same as the valid set.
3. The value of A(I-1, I-1) is computed for every index value in the active set. Using the values shown in Figure 6.1 produces the values $\{11, 22, 33, 44\}$.
4. The values are assigned to the elements $\{A(2,2), A(3,3), A(4,4), A(5,5)\}$.

Figure 6.1 shows the overall effect of the FORALL statement. □

Example 6.2 We next consider the code in Figure 6.2, reproduced below.

```
FORALL (I = 1:8)
  A(I, I) = SQRT(A(I,I))
  FORALL (J = I-3: I+3, J/=I .AND. J>=1 .AND. J<=9)
    A(I, J) = A(I, I) * A(J, J)
```

```
            END FORALL
        END FORALL
```

The interpretation is only slightly more complex than the last example.

1. The valid set for the **FORALL I** statement is easily computed as $\{1,2,3,4,5,6,7,8\}$.
2. The active set for the **FORALL I** statement is the same as the valid set.
3. The expression `SQRT(A(I,I))` is computed for every active index value. Using the values `A(I,I) = I**2`, as shown in Figure 6.2, produces the values $\{1,2,3,4,5,6,7,8\}$.
4. The values are assigned to elements `A(I, I)` for all elements of the active set. After this, **A** is the following matrix.

$$\begin{bmatrix} 1 & 0 & 0 & 0 & 0 & 0 & 0 & 0 \\ 0 & 2 & 0 & 0 & 0 & 0 & 0 & 0 \\ 0 & 0 & 3 & 0 & 0 & 0 & 0 & 0 \\ 0 & 0 & 0 & 4 & 0 & 0 & 0 & 0 \\ 0 & 0 & 0 & 0 & 5 & 0 & 0 & 0 \\ 0 & 0 & 0 & 0 & 0 & 6 & 0 & 0 \\ 0 & 0 & 0 & 0 & 0 & 0 & 7 & 0 \\ 0 & 0 & 0 & 0 & 0 & 0 & 0 & 8 \end{bmatrix}$$

5. The valid set for the **FORALL J** is computed. The (I, J) values for that set are

{ (1,-2), (1,-1), (1,0), (1,1), (1,2), (1,3), (1,4),
  (2,-1), (2, 0), (2,1), (2,2), (2,3), (2,4), (2,5),
  (3,0), (3,1), (3,2), (3,3), (3,4), (3,5), (3,6),
  (4,1), (4,2), (4,3), (4,4), (4,5), (4,6), (4,7),
  (5,2), (5,3), (5,4), (5,5), (5,6), (5,7), (5,8),
  (6,3), (6,4), (6,5), (6,6), (6,7), (6,8), (6,9),
  (7,4), (7,5), (7,6), (7,7), (7,8), (7,9), (7,10),
  (8,5), (8,6), (8,7), (8,8), (8,9), (8,10), (8,11) }

6. The active set for the **FORALL J** is computed. The (I, J) values for that set are

{   (1,2), (1,3), (1,4),
                        (2,1),   (2,3), (2,4), (2,5),
                (3,1), (3,2),   (3,4), (3,5), (3,6),
         (4,1), (4,2), (4,3),   (4,5), (4,6), (4,7),
         (5,2), (5,3), (5,4),   (5,6), (5,7), (5,8),
         (6,3), (6,4), (6,5),   (6,7), (6,8),
         (7,4), (7,5), (7,6),   (7,8),

Data Parallelism

(8,5), (8,6), (8,7)   }

From the valid set, the J/=I condition masks out the middle column, and the J>=1 and J<=8 conditions remove the upper left and lower right corners.

7. The values of A(I,I) * A(J,J) are computed for the active index value tuples. This gives the values

{
			2,	3,	4,
		2,	6,	8,	10,
	3,	6,	12,	15,	18,
4,	8,	12,	20,	24,	28,
10,	15,	20,	30,	35,	40,
18,	24,	30,	42,	48,	
28,	35,	42,	56,		
40,	48,	56			
}

8. The computed values are assigned to the elements A(I,J) for all active index value tuples. The list of elements is identical to the list of active index values shown above.

Figure 6.2 shows the overall effect of the FORALL statement. □

Since the semantics of FORALL statements parallel the semantics of array assignment, it is not surprising that some FORALL statements can be translated fairly directly to array assignments or WHERE statements.

Example 6.3 The following FORALL statements

```
FORALL (I = 2:N-1) X(I) = X(I-1) + X(I) + X(I+1)          ! Ex.1
FORALL (I = 1:N)   X(INDX(I)) = X(I)                       ! Ex.2
FORALL (I = 1:N, J=1:M, B(I,J)/=0.0) A(I,J) = 1.0/B(I,J)   ! Ex.3
FORALL (J = 1:M, I=1:N) A(I,J) = B(J,I)                    ! Ex.4
FORALL (I = 2:N-1, J = 2:M-1)
   A(I,J) = A(I,J-1) + A(I,J+1) + A(I-1,J) + A(I+1,J)      ! Ex.5a
   B(I,J) = A(I,J)                                         ! Ex.5b
END FORALL
```

are equivalent to the following Fortran 90 statements.

```
X(2:N-1) = X(1:N-2) + X(2:N-1) + X(3:N)                        ! Ex.1
X(INDX(1:N)) = X(1:N)                                           ! Ex.2
WHERE (Y(1:N,1:M) /= 0.0) X(1:N,1:M) = 1.0/Y(1:N,1:M)          ! Ex.3
A(1:N,1:M) = TRANSPOSE(B(1:M,1:N))                              ! Ex.4
```

```
A(2:N-1,2:M-1) = A(2:N-1,1:M-2) + A(2:N-1,3:M)     &  ! Ex.5a
              + A(1:N-2,2:M-1) + A(3:N,2:M-1)         ! Ex.5a
B(2:N-1,2:M-1) = A(2:N-1,2:M-1)                       ! Ex.5b
```

A few details of these statements should be mentioned.

1. Statement **Ex.1** uses the original values in the array **X** for all its computations. For example, if X(I)=1 for all I initially, then after the statement X(I)=3 for elements 2 through N-1. Note that it does *not* have the same effect as the Fortran 90 loop

```
DO I = 2, N-1
  X(I) = X(I-1) + X(I) + X(I+1)
END DO
```

which produces X(I)=2*I+1 (for 2<=I<=N-1) from the same data.

2. Statement **Ex.2**, performs a permutation of the array **X** if **INDX** contains the integers from 1 to **N** in some order. If **INDX** contains repeated values, neither the behavior of the **FORALL** nor the equivalent array assignment is defined.

3. Statement **Ex.3** takes the reciprocal of each nonzero element of array B(1:N,1:M). Elements that are zero are filtered out before the computation is done, so the statement is safe from "division by zero" errors.

The reader can make up his or her own mind whether the **FORALL** or the array assignment forms of these statements are more readable. Both forms have fans and detractors. □

Not all **FORALL** statements have simple translations to Fortran 90. Translations sometimes become complex due to the shapes of array sections assigned, or because the **FORALL** indices are used in computations besides subscripts.

Example 6.4 The following **FORALL** statements are difficult to translate to Fortran 90:

```
! Forall 1
FORALL (I = 1:N) A(I,INDX(I)) = X(I)
! Forall 2
FORALL (I = 1:N, J = 1:N) A(I,J) = 1.0 / REAL(I+J-1)
```

The shortest Fortran 90 equivalents we know of using array operations are below.

```
! Forall 1
WHERE (SPREAD((/(I,I=1,N)/),DIM=2,NCOPIES=N) = &
       SPREAD((/(I,I=1,N)/),DIM=1,NCOPIES=N))
  A(1:N,INDX(1:N)) = SPREAD(X(1:N), DIM=2, NCOPIES=N)
END WHERE
! Forall 2
A(1:N,1:M) = 1.0 / REAL(SPREAD((/(I,I=1,N)/),DIM=2,NCOPIES=M) &
             + SPREAD((/(J,J=1,M)/),DIM=1,NCOPIES=N) - 1 )
```

Equivalent DO loops are shorter. However, if the right-hand sides used the array A then the translations to DO loops would be more complex. Example 6.1, for example, requires either using two DO loops or changing the natural iteration order. □

Example 6.5 The ability to nest a WHERE statement in a FORALL is sometimes useful.

```
FORALL (I = 1:5)
  WHERE (A(I,:) /= 0.0 )
    A(I,:) = A(I-1,:) + A(I+1,:)
  ELSEWHERE
    B(I,:) = A(6-I,:)
  END WHERE
END FORALL
```

This FORALL construct, when executed with the input arrays

$$A = \begin{bmatrix} 0.0 & 0.0 & 0.0 & 0.0 & 0.0 \\ 1.0 & 1.0 & 1.0 & 0.0 & 1.0 \\ 2.0 & 2.0 & 0.0 & 2.0 & 2.0 \\ 3.0 & 0.0 & 3.0 & 3.0 & 3.0 \\ 0.0 & 0.0 & 0.0 & 0.0 & 0.0 \end{bmatrix}, B = \begin{bmatrix} 0.0 & 0.0 & 0.0 & 0.0 & 0.0 \\ 10.0 & 10.0 & 10.0 & 10.0 & 10.0 \\ 20.0 & 20.0 & 20.0 & 20.0 & 20.0 \\ 30.0 & 30.0 & 30.0 & 30.0 & 30.0 \\ 40.0 & 40.0 & 40.0 & 40.0 & 40.0 \end{bmatrix}$$

will produce as results

$$A = \begin{bmatrix} 0.0 & 0.0 & 0.0 & 0.0 & 0.0 \\ 2.0 & 2.0 & 0.0 & 0.0 & 2.0 \\ 4.0 & 1.0 & 0.0 & 3.0 & 4.0 \\ 2.0 & 0.0 & 0.0 & 2.0 & 2.0 \\ 0.0 & 0.0 & 0.0 & 0.0 & 0.0 \end{bmatrix}, B = \begin{bmatrix} 0.0 & 0.0 & 0.0 & 0.0 & 0.0 \\ 10.0 & 10.0 & 10.0 & 2.0 & 10.0 \\ 20.0 & 20.0 & 0.0 & 20.0 & 20.0 \\ 30.0 & 2.0 & 30.0 & 30.0 & 30.0 \\ 0.0 & 0.0 & 0.0 & 0.0 & 0.0 \end{bmatrix}$$

Note that, as with WHERE statements in ordinary Fortran 90, assignments in the WHERE branch may affect computations in the ELSEWHERE branch. □

Example 6.6 The `FORALL` statement also allows pointer assignments in its body, which is a clear extension of Fortran 90 array assignments.

```
TYPE MONARCH
  INTEGER, POINTER :: P
END TYPE MONARCH
TYPE(MONARCH), DIMENSION(8)   :: PATTERN
INTEGER, DIMENSION(8), TARGET :: OBJECT

! Set up a butterfly pattern
FORALL (J = 1:N)  PATTERN(J)%P => OBJECT(1+IEOR(J-1,2))
```

This `FORALL` statement sets the elements 1 through 8 of array `PATTERN` to point to elements $[3, 4, 1, 2, 7, 8, 5, 6]$ of `OBJECT`. (`IEOR` is allowed because all intrinsic functions are `PURE`; see Section 6.3.) □

Example 6.7 Functions returning arrays can also be `PURE`, as Section 6.3 discusses. This allows the programmer to think of subarrays as "elements" to be assigned, as in the following code.

```
INTERFACE
  PURE FUNCTION F(X)
    REAL, DIMENSION(3) :: F
    REAL, DIMENSION(3), INTENT(IN) :: X
  END FUNCTION F
END INTERFACE
REAL, DIMENSION(3,L,M,N) :: V
...
FORALL (I = 1:L, J = 1:M, K = 1:N)  V(:,I,J,K) = F(V(:,I,J,K))
```

Computations of this form are common in some areas of physics, such as quantum chromodynamics. □

6.3 The PURE Attribute

The `PURE` attribute applies to functions and subroutines, in much the same way as the Fortran 90 `RECURSIVE` attribute. It constrains the statements allowed in the procedure so that the procedure cannot have any side effects, except to return a value (in the case of a `PURE` function) or modify `INTENT(OUT)` and `INTENT(INOUT)` parameters (in the case of a `PURE` subroutine). This makes `PURE` functions safe for use in a `FORALL` statement; in fact, this is intended to be the major use of **PURE** procedures. **PURE** subroutines are mainly intended to be called from other **PURE** procedures; they cannot be called from a **FORALL** statement directly. A **PURE** procedure may also be used anywhere that a procedure of the same type can be called.

The **PURE** attribute is not a part of Subset HPF. However, intrinsic functions are still considered **PURE** in Subset HPF. This allows (single-statement) **FORALL** statement bodies to call intrinsic functions, but not user-defined functions. Thus, Example 6.11 is not Subset-conforming, but Example 6.12 is allowed in Subset HPF.

6.3.1 Form of the PURE Attribute

The **PURE** attribute is specified in the *function-stmt* (H409) or *subroutine-stmt* (H411) by the *prefix* (H407) part. The new form of a *prefix* (H407) is:

prefix-spec [*prefix-spec*] ...

where a *prefix-spec* (H408) is one of:

type-spec
RECURSIVE
PURE
extrinsic-prefix

See Chapter 8 for the definition of *extrinsic-prefix* (H601). The form of a *function-stmt* (H409)) is not changed from rule R1217 of the Fortran 90 standard, but is rewritten here for clarity:

[*prefix*] **FUNCTION** *function-name* ([*dummy-arg-name-list*]) [**RESULT**(*result-name*)]

Similarly, the form of a *subroutine-stmt* (H411) is the same as Rule R1220 of the Fortran 90 standard, and is rewritten here:

[*prefix*] **SUBROUTINE** *subroutine-name* [([*dummy-arg-list*])]

Rules and restrictions:
1. A *prefix* must contain at most one of each variety of *prefix-spec*.
2. The *prefix* of a *subroutine-stmt* must not contain a *type-spec*.
3. Intrinsic functions, including the HPF intrinsic functions, are always **PURE** and require no explicit declaration of this fact. Intrinsic subroutines are **PURE** if they are elemental (i.e., **MVBITS**) but not otherwise.
4. A statement function is **PURE** if and only if all functions that it references are **PURE**.

Functions in the HPF library are **PURE**.

In addition to the new definition of *prefix*, the **PURE** attribute adds a number of constraints to other Fortran 90 rules when they use a **PURE** function. When the constraints mention "a **PURE** procedure" they mean a procedure that is declared **PURE** by the above rules.

Add the following rules and restrictions to the definitions of *function-subprogram* (R1215) and *subroutine-subprogram* (R1219) from the Fortran 90 standard:

Rules and restrictions:
1. The *specification-part* of a **PURE** function must specify that all dummy arguments have **INTENT(IN)** except procedure arguments and arguments with the **POINTER** attribute.
2. The *specification-part* of a **PURE** subroutine must specify the **INTENT** of all dummy arguments except procedure arguments and arguments that have the **POINTER** attribute.
3. A local variable declared in a **PURE** procedure (including a variable declared in an internal procedure) must not have the **SAVE** attribute.
4. A local variable declared in a **PURE** procedure (including a variable declared in an internal procedure) cannot be initialized in a type declaration statement or a **DATA** statement, since such initializations imply the **SAVE** attribute.
5. A **PURE** procedure (or its internal procedures) may not use global variables, dummy arguments with **INTENT(IN)**, or objects that are storage associated with any part of a global variable in any operation that might cause their value to change. In addition, a **PURE** function may not use any dummy argument, even without a declared **INTENT** attribute, in these contexts. In particular, those variables cannot be used as:

   - The left-hand side of an assignment statement or pointer assignment statement.
   - An actual argument associated with an dummy argument with **INTENT (OUT)** or **INTENT(INOUT)** or with the **POINTER** attribute.
   - An index variable in a **DO** statement, **FORALL** statement, or an implied **DO** clause.
   - The variable in an **ASSIGN** statement.
   - An input item in a **READ** statement.
   - An internal file unit in a **WRITE** statement.
   - The object to be allocated in an **ALLOCATE**, the object to be deallocated in a **DEALLOCATE** statement, or the pointer to be nullified in a **NULLIFY** statement.
   - An **IOSTAT=** or **SIZE=** specifier in an I/O statement, or the **STAT=** specifier in a **ALLOCATE** or **DEALLOCATE** statement.

6. A **PURE** procedure (or its internal procedures) may not use global variables, dummy arguments with **INTENT(IN)**, or objects that are storage associated with any part

Data Parallelism

of a global variable in any operation that could create a pointer to that variable. In addition, a **PURE** function may not use any dummy argument, even without a declared **INTENT** attribute, in these contexts. In particular, those variables cannot be used as:

- The target (right-hand side) of a pointer assignment statement.
- The right-hand side of an assignment to a derived-type variable (including a variable that is a pointer to a derived type) if the derived type has a pointer component at any level of component selection.

7. If a **PURE** procedure calls another procedure, then the called procedure must also be **PURE**.
8. If a dummy argument to a **PURE** procedure or the dummy result of a **PURE** function is explicitly mapped, then:

    - If the dummy appears in an **ALIGN** directive as the *alignee* (H316) (i.e., as the variable being aligned with something), then the *align-target* (H321) (i.e., the thing being aligned to) must be another dummy argument or the dummy result.
    - The dummy cannot appear in a **DISTRIBUTE** directive.
    - The dummy cannot have the **INHERIT** attribute.
    - The dummy cannot have the **DYNAMIC** attribute.

9. If a local variable in a **PURE** procedure is explicitly mapped, then:

    - If the variable appears in an **ALIGN** directive as the *alignee* (H316) (i.e., as the variable being aligned with something), then the *align-target* (H321) (i.e., the thing being aligned to) must be another local variable, a dummy argument or the dummy result.
    - The variable may not appear in a **DISTRIBUTE** directive.
    - The variable cannot have the **DYNAMIC** attribute.

10. A global variable that appears in a **PURE** procedure must not be used in a **REALIGN** or **REDISTRIBUTE** directive.
11. A **PURE** procedure may not contain any external input/output statement. The list of external I/O statements includes the **PRINT**, **OPEN**, **CLOSE**, **BACKSPACE**, **ENDFILE**, **REWIND**, and **INQUIRE** statements. It also includes **READ** and **WRITE** statements whose I/O unit is an external file unit number or *.
12. A **PURE** function must not contain a **PAUSE** or **STOP** statement.

Add the following rules to the definition of *interface-body* (R1204).

Rules and restrictions:
1. In an `INTERFACE` block, the interface specification of a `PURE` procedure must specify the `INTENT` of all dummy arguments except `POINTER` and procedure arguments.
2. A procedure that is declared `PURE` at its definition may be declared `PURE` in an `INTERFACE` block, but this is not required.
3. A procedure that is not declared `PURE` at its definition must not be declared `PURE` in an `INTERFACE` block.

6.3.2 Meaning of the PURE Attribute

A call to a `PURE` procedure has exactly the same interpretation as a call to any other procedure. However, it is legal to call a `PURE` procedure in contexts where an arbitrary procedure is not allowed. In particular,

- A `PURE` function may be used in the mask expression or the body of a `FORALL` statement.
- A `PURE` function or subroutine may be called from a `PURE` procedure.
- A `PURE` function or subroutine may be passed as an actual parameter to a dummy parameter that is declared `PURE`.

If a procedure is used in any of these contexts, then its interface must be explicit and the `PURE` attribute must be part of that interface. Note that all the restrictions on `PURE` can be checked statically, that is, they refer to the syntax of the function, not to its behavior. (Consistency of the declarations between compilation units cannot be checked directly, unfortunately; however, it can be checked when the units are linked into a single program.)

6.3.3 Discussion of the PURE Attribute

We first give some examples of functions that are (or are not) `PURE`, then illustrate their use.

Example 6.8 The following statement functions are `PURE`:

```
REAL :: MY_EXP, MY_SINH, STD_SINH
MY_EXP(X) = 1 + X + X*X/2.0 + X**3/6.0
MY_SINH(X) = (MY_EXP(X) - MY_EXP(-X)) / 2.0
STD_SINH(X) = (EXP(X) - EXP(-X)) / 2.0
```

`MY_EXP` references no functions, so it cannot reference any non-`PURE` functions. The other two functions reference only the `PURE` user-defined function `MY_EXP` and the intrinsic `EXP`. □

Example 6.9 The following function is correctly declared to be **PURE**.

```
PURE INTEGER FUNCTION MANDELBROT(X)

    COMPLEX, INTENT(IN) :: X
    COMPLEX             :: XTMP
    INTEGER             :: K
    ! Assume SHARED_DEFS includes the declaration
    ! INTEGER ITOL
    USE SHARED_DEFS

    K = 0
    XTMP = -X
    DO WHILE (ABS(XTMP)<2.0 .AND. K<ITOL)
      XTMP = XTMP * XTMP - X
      K = K + 1
    END DO
    ITER = K

END FUNCTION
```

Example 6.11 shows how a **FORALL** might call this function to update all the elements of an array. We expect that this will be a common use for **PURE** functions. A suitable **INTERFACE** block for **MANDELBROT** would be as follows.

```
INTERFACE
   PURE INTEGER FUNCTION MANDELBROT(X)
      COMPLEX, INTENT(IN) :: X
   END FUNCTION MANDELBROT
END INTERFACE
```

We note a few interesting points about this function.

- It uses shared data (**ITOL**), but does not assign to it. Read-only use of shared data is allowed in **PURE** functions.
- It contains a loop construct. Arbitrary flow control is allowed in **PURE** functions.

These features make **PURE** functions quite useful, although they also make compilation somewhat more complex. □

Example 6.10 The following function is **not** **PURE**. Any one of the commented statements is enough to disqualify it from being **PURE**.

```
      REAL FUNCTION IMPURE_FCN(W, X, Y)  ! *IMPURE* - No PURE attribute

      ! Assume SHARED_DEFS contains the declarations
      ! INTEGER, PARAMETER         :: N = 1000
      ! INTEGER                    :: NUM_CALLS
      ! REAL, DIMENSION(N), TARGET :: LOOKUP_TABLE
      USE SHARED_DEFS

      REAL, INTENT(IN)                 :: W
      REAL, DIMENSION(10), INTENT(IN)  :: X
      REAL, DIMENSION(N), TARGET       :: Y    ! *IMPURE* - No INTENT

      INTEGER, SAVE              :: LAST = 1 ! *IMPURE* - Has SAVE
      REAL, DIMENSION(10), POINTER :: Z

      INTERFACE
        PURE SUBROUTINE BINARY_SEARCH(A, B, I)
          REAL, INTENT(IN)                     :: A
          REAL, INTENT(INOUT), DIMENSION(N)    :: B
          INTEGER, INTENT(INOUT)               :: I
        END PROCEDURE BINARY_SEARCH
      END INTERFACE

      ! *IMPURE* - Passing global to INTENT(INOUT) parameter
      CALL BINARY_SEARCH(W, LOOKUP_TABLE, LAST)
      Z => Y(LAST:LAST+9)        ! *IMPURE* - Pointer to dummy
      NUM_CALLS = NUM_CALLS + 1 ! *IMPURE* - Assignment to global
      IMPURE_FCN = SUM(X * Z)
      END FUNCTION IMPURE_FCN
```

Notice that many of the "impurities" in this function do not actually cause side effects.

- Leaving out the PURE attribute is purely a syntactic matter.
- Although Y is not declared INTENT(IN), it is not assigned in the procedure.
- Assuming that BINARY_SEARCH does what its name implies, its second parameter will not be modified. A more appropriate INTERFACE block might be

```
      INTERFACE
        PURE SUBROUTINE BINARY_SEARCH(A, B, I)
```

```
          REAL, INTENT(IN)              :: A
          REAL, INTENT(IN), DIMENSION(N) :: B
          INTEGER, INTENT(INOUT)        :: I
        END PROCEDURE BINARY_SEARCH
      END INTERFACE
```

which would make the CALL statement legal in a PURE function.

- Although Z points to Y, there are no assignments to Z that modify Y.

The rules for PURE ensure that no side effects occur; it is not the case that every subroutine without side effects is PURE. □

Example 6.11 This FORALL applies the MANDELBROT function defined in Example 6.9 to fill an array.

```
      FORALL (I = 1:N, J = 1:M)
        A(I,J) = MANDELBROT(COMPLX((I-1)*1.0/(N-1), (J-1)*1.0/(M-1))
      END FORALL
```

Note that because of the control flow inside MANDELBROT this computation could not be written as a FORALL statement without the PURE function. One of the major advantages of PURE functions is that they allow more complex operations to be done in parallel by FORALL statements. □

Example 6.12 Since intrinsic functions are PURE, they can be always be called from FORALL statements. For example,

```
      FORALL (K = 1:9) X(K) = SUM(X(1:10:K))
```

computes nine sums of subarrays of X. If X has the value

$[1, 2, 3, 4, 5, 6, 7, 8, 9, 10]$

before the FORALL, then it have the value

$[55, 25, 22, 15, 7, 8, 9, 10, 11, 10]$

afterwards. Note that, since SUM is not an elemental function, it cannot be applied elementally in this way. □

6.4 The INDEPENDENT Directive

The **INDEPENDENT** directive is an assertion that the programmer makes about the behavior of a **DO** loop or **FORALL** statement. In particular, **INDEPENDENT** asserts that the iterations of a **DO** or the computations for different active index values of a **FORALL**, do not interfere with each other in any way. This implies that the **DO** or **FORALL** will produce exactly the same answers if its iterations or computations are executed in parallel (or, for that matter, in any sequential order). The compiler can use this information to produce more efficient code.

Note that **INDEPENDENT** is providing *new information* to the compiler, not *defining a new meaning* for the code. If it is used correctly, **INDEPENDENT** will not change the meaning of a program. If it is misused (i.e., if the programmer is mistaken deliberately lies about the interactions between iterations), then the program is not HPF-conforming.

While **FORALL** statements technically do not have "iterations" because they are not loops, for simplicity of exposition in this section we use the term "iteration" to describe either an iteration of a **DO** loop or the execution of the body of a **FORALL** for a single active index value tuple.

Subset HPF includes the **INDEPENDENT** directive applied to both **DO** loops and **FORALL** statements.

6.4.1 Form of the INDEPENDENT Directive

The **INDEPENDENT** directive precedes the **DO** loop or **FORALL** statement for which it is asserting behavior, and is said to apply to that loop or statement. The form of the *independent-directive* (H413) is:

INDEPENDENT [, NEW (*variable-list*)]

Rules and restrictions:
1. The first non-comment line following an **INDEPENDENT** directive must be a **DO** or **FORALL** statement.
2. If the **NEW** option is present, then the directive must apply to a **DO** loop.
3. A **NEW** option cannot name a pointer or dummy argument in its *variable-list*.
4. A *variable* named in the **NEW** option must not have the **SAVE** or **TARGET** attribute.
5. The **DO** or **FORALL** to which the **INDEPENDENT** directive applies must behave as described in Section 6.4.2.

6.4.2 Meaning of the INDEPENDENT Directive

A **DO** loop with an **INDEPENDENT** assertion applied to it is called a *DO INDEPENDENT* loop. The interpretation of a **DO INDEPENDENT** is identical to the interpretation of the corresponding **DO** loop with no **INDEPENDENT**. That is, **INDEPENDENT** (when correctly applied) does not change the results computed by the **DO** to which it applies. Similarly, a **FORALL** statement with an **INDEPENDENT** assertion applied to it is called a *FORALL INDEPENDENT*. The interpretation of a **FORALL INDEPENDENT** is identical to the corresponding **FORALL**'s interpretation. The importance of the **INDEPENDENT** directive is that it gives the compiler more information that may be used to optimize the program. Thus, although the meaning of the program does not change, its performance is likely to be better because the compiler can make less restrictive assumptions.

The interpretation of **INDEPENDENT** itself is essentially an explanation of what the directive asserts. In short, it asserts two things:

- *Bernstein's conditions* [8]: If R_i is the set of locations "read" in iteration i of a construct, and W_i is the set of locations "written" in iteration i, then for any $i \neq j$ it must be true that

$$(R_i \cap W_j) \cup (W_i \cap R_j) \cup (W_i \cap W_j) = \phi$$

The effect of this is that no atomic data object may be read in one iteration and written in another, nor may any atomic object be written in more than one iteration.

- *No control dependence*: Once the construct begins execution, it will execute to completion.

Note that, unlike the restrictions on **PURE** functions, these are assertions about the behavior of the **INDEPENDENT** construct, not about its syntax. For example, a **DO INDEPENDENT** could legally contain a **STOP** statement, provided that statement was in a branch of an **IF** that was never executed.

It is important to define precisely the terms "read" and "written" in Bernstein's conditions. Given that, we have the following:

- An assignment to an object is a write to all the atomic objects that it contains. For example, an assignment to an integer variable is a write to one atomic object; an array assignment to an integer array can be many atomic writes. Note that this is considered a write *even if the value does not change*.
- Similarly, using an object as a **DO** or implied **DO** index; as **FORALL** index; as an input item in a **READ** statement; as an internal file unit in a **WRITE** statement; as the variable in an **ASSIGN** statement; as the pointer in an **ALLOCATE**, **DEALLOCATE** or **NULLIFY** statement; or as a **IOSTAT=**, **SIZE=** or **STAT=** specifier is a write to all atomic objects in that object.
- A use of a variable in an expression (not including "use" in modifying that variable, as detailed above) is a read of every atomic object in the (fully-qualified) use. For example,

```
TYPE EXAMPLE
  REAL, DIMENSION(3) :: X, Y
END TYPE EXAMPLE
REAL, DIMENSION(10) :: A, B
TYPE(EXAMPLE)        :: C
...
A(1) = A(10)
B(2:9) = B(1:8)
C%X(1) = C%Y(3)
```

contains reads of A(10), B(1), B(2), B(3), B(4), B(5), B(6), B(7), B(8), and C%Y(3). It does not contain reads of (among other things) A(1), B(9), B(10), or C%Y taken as a whole.

- Any file I/O statement except INQUIRE both reads and writes that file, where the file itself is considered to be an object. (This is due to Fortran's definition of how the file position is affected by I/O statements; the position is defined after every operation, even for direct access files.) An INQUIRE operation performs a read from its file.

- A REALIGN or REDISTRIBUTE directive reads and writes a variable and every atomic object that it contains. (This is because the operation may change the processor storing every array element, which interferes with any assignment or use of those elements.) In addition, a REDISTRIBUTE directive reads and writes every element of any array aligned to the array being distributed.

Obviously, some of these points do not apply to FORALL statements, which cannot contain (for example) ASSIGN statements.

A construct has *control dependence* if the execution of one iteration determines whether other iterations are executed. The following cases constitute control dependence in HPF programs:

- A transfer of control (by a GO TO, alternate procedure return, or ERR= branch) to a branch target statement outside the body of the loop.
- Any execution of an EXIT, STOP, or PAUSE statement.

A FORALL statement cannot be affected by either of these conditions.

The NEW clause modifies the meaning of the INDEPENDENT directive by restricting the variables considered for inclusion in the read and write sets. The technical definition is that it changes the INDEPENDENT directive where it appears and all surrounding INDEPENDENT directives to mean that those assertions would be true *if* new objects were created for the named variables for each iteration of the DO loop. In other words, it asserts that the remainder of program execution is unaffected if all variables in the variable list and any variables associated with them were to become undefined immediately before execution of every iteration of the loop, and also become undefined immediately after the completion of each iteration of the loop.

The English translation of the above definition is that the variables named in the **NEW** clause should be treated as being private in the loop body. Effectively, the variables lose their values at the end of each iteration. The reason for the strange circumlocution has to do with the fact that **NEW** is part of a directive, rather than a first-class statement in the language. Since directives can't change the meaning of the program, they can't allocate new objects or make existing objects undefined. Therefore, the official definition has to be phrased as a series of "what ifs."

NEW variables provide the means to declare temporaries in **INDEPENDENT** loops. Without this feature, many conceptually independent loops would need substantial rewriting (including expansion of scalars into arrays) to meet the rather strict requirements for **INDEPENDENT**. Note that a temporary need only be declared **NEW** at the innermost lexical level at which it is assigned, since all enclosing **INDEPENDENT** assertions must take that **NEW** into account. Note also that index variables for nested **DO** loops must be declared **NEW**; the alternative was to limit the scope of an index variable to the loop itself, which changes Fortran semantics. **FORALL** indices, however, have scopes restricted by the semantics of the **FORALL** statement; they require no **NEW** declarations.

The compiler is justified in producing a warning if it can prove that an **INDEPENDENT** assertion is incorrect. It is not required to do so, however. Indeed, since deciding whether a loop is **INDEPENDENT** is an undecidable problem, it is always possible to write an assertion that the compiler cannot fully check. A program containing any false assertion of this type is not HPF-conforming, thus is not defined by HPF, and the compiler may take any action it deems appropriate.[1]

6.4.3 Discussion of the INDEPENDENT Directive

Like the **FORALL** statement, there is a good graphical representation of a **DO INDEPENDENT** loop. We show that in Figure 6.8, and then give some examples of loops that are (and are not) **INDEPENDENT**.

Visualizing INDEPENDENT Figure 6.8 shows the precedence graph for a **DO INDEPENDENT** loop. If the **INDEPENDENT** assertion were applied to a **FORALL** statement, the picture would look exactly the same. **INDEPENDENT** means that only the dependences shown may occur, rather than the full sets of arrows from Figures 6.5 and 6.6. The

---

[1] At one point the HPF language draft suggested executing the programmer if such an error was found, but that sentence was eventually removed.

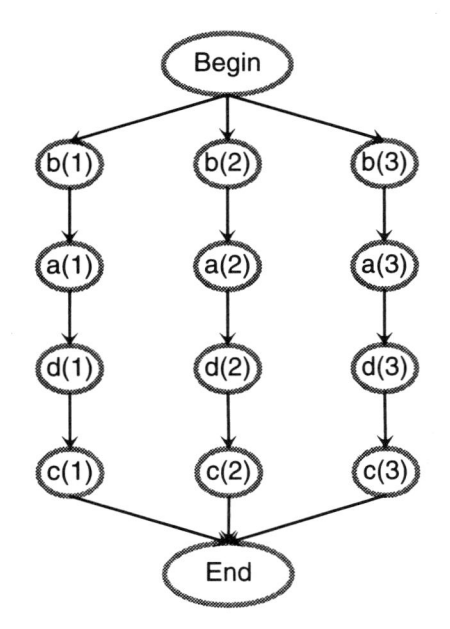

```
!HPF$ INDEPENDENT
      DO I = 1, 3
         a(I) = b(I)
         c(I) = d(I)
      END DO
```

Figure 6.8
Precedence graph for a DO INDEPENDENT loop

assertion essentially tells the compiler that this particular statement is not a worst case; in fact, it is far from the worst. It is clear from the figure that any operation in one iteration can be performed in parallel with any operation from any other iteration. The only ordering that needs to be enforced is within the same iteration. (Sometimes even this ordering may be unnecessary—in particular, when the statements in the body do not depend on each other. HPF has no way to express such fine control, however.)

Figure 6.9 shows a **FORALL INDEPENDENT** with a nested **FORALL**. Replacing the outer **FORALL** statement with a **DO** loop would produce the same picture. We show it to point out that the **INDEPENDENT** assertion does mean that **FORALL** statements (or **DO** loops) nested within the **INDEPENDENT** statement are also **INDEPENDENT**. Compared to Figure 6.7, however, it is clear that removing the dependences between iterations in the outer **FORALL** is still a substantial improvement.

INDEPENDENT Examples For simplicity, our explanations in this section assume there is no storage, sequence, or pointer association between any variables used in the code. **INDEPENDENT** can be used when variables are associated, but only if the association does not cause one of the rules in Section 6.4.2 to be violated.

Example 6.13 The following loop is **INDEPENDENT** regardless of the values of the variables involved.

```
!HPF$ INDEPENDENT
      DO I = 2, N-1
         X(I) = Y(I-1) + Y(I) + Y(I+1)
      END DO
```

This is, of course, trivial to see—all iterations read from one array and write to another, so there can be no interference. Note that many elements of Y are used repeatedly; this is allowed by the definition of **INDEPENDENT**. The other conditions relate to constructs not used in the loop. The loop could be written equivalently as follows.

```
!HPF$ INDEPENDENT
      FORALL (I = 2:N-1) X(I) = Y(I-1) + Y(I) + Y(I+1)
```

It is always the case that a **FORALL INDEPENDENT** can be directly rewritten as a **DO INDEPENDENT**. The converse is not true, due to the restrictions on the body of a **FORALL** statement. □

```
!HPF$ INDEPENDENT
      FORALL (I = 1:3)
        a(I) = b(I)
        FORALL (J = 1:I)
          c(I,J) = d(I,J)
        END FORALL
      END FORALL
```

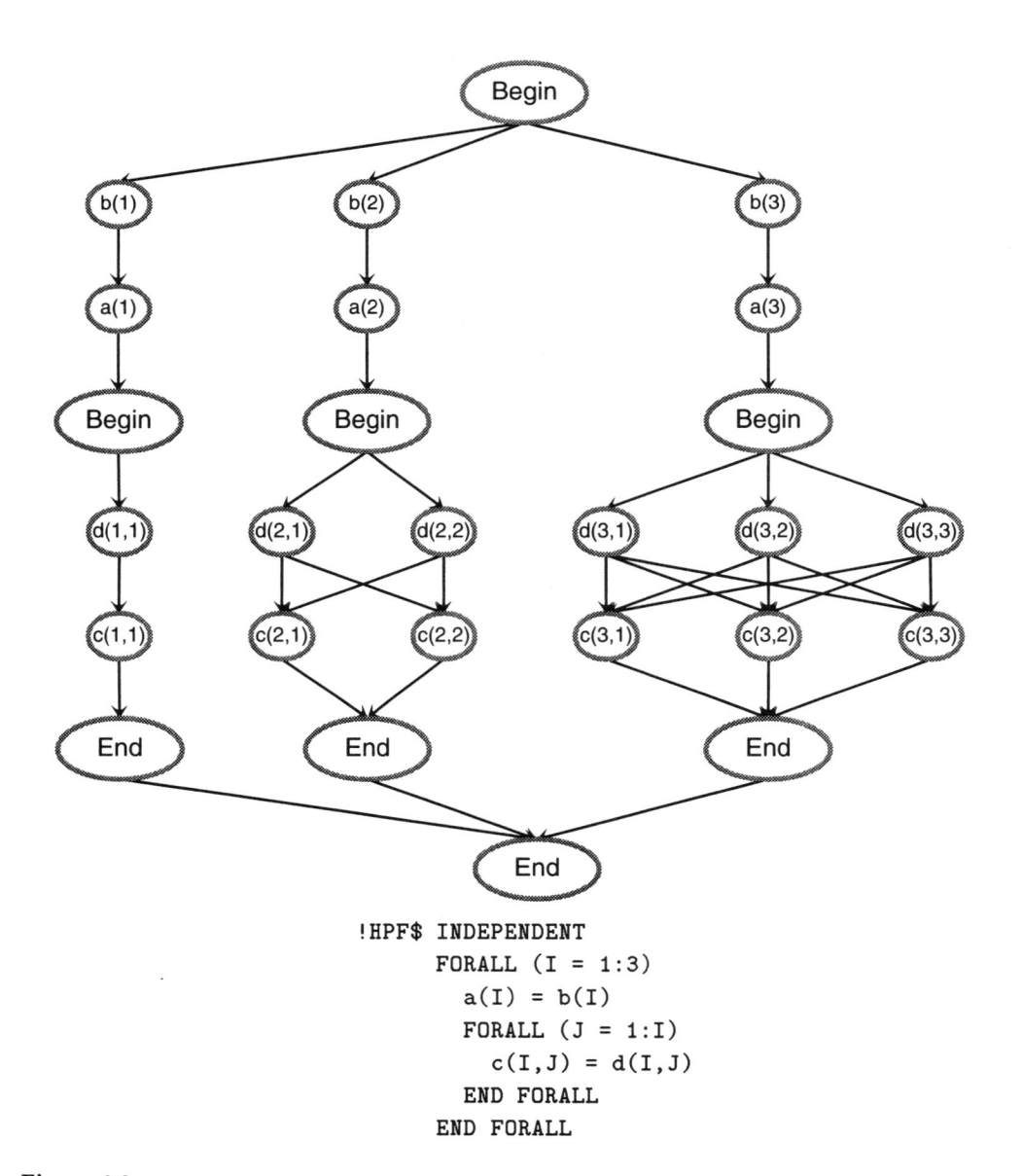

Figure 6.9
Precedence graph for **INDEPENDENT** with nested statements

Example 6.14 The following loops are **INDEPENDENT** regardless of the data values used.

```
!HPF$ INDEPENDENT, NEW (I)
      DO J = 2, M-1, 2
!HPF$   INDEPENDENT, NEW(VL, VR, UL, UR)
        DO I = 2 , N-1, 2
          VL = A(I,J) - A(I-1,J)
          VR = A(I+1,J) - A(I,J)
          UL = A(I,J) - A(I,J-1)
          UR = A(I,J+1) - A(I,J)
          A(I,J) = B(I,J) + A(I,J) + 0.25 * (VR - VL + UR - UL)
        END DO
      END DO
```

There is no interference due to accesses of the array **X** because of the stride of the **DO** loop (i.e., **I** and **J** are always even, therefore **I-1**, etc. are always odd.) Some compilers can detect this independence without a directive, but the reasoning to do so is clearly harder than in Example 6.13. Good discussions of compiler dependence tests can be found in books by Wolfe [31] and Zima and Chapman [33]. Since different compilers will perform different analyses, we recommend using explicit **INDEPENDENT** assertions whenever portability to other systems is important.

Without the **NEW** clause on the **I** loop, neither **INDEPENDENT** assertion would be correct. For intuition why, consider an interleaved execution of loop iterations, that is, performing one statement from one iteration, followed by a statement from another iteration. It is easy to see that this might cause some iteration to use values of **VL**, **VR**, **UL**, and **UR** in the assignment to **A(I,J)** that another iteration computed. The **NEW** option, however, specifies that this is not true if distinct storage units are used in each iteration of the loop. □

Example 6.15 The truth of some **INDEPENDENT** assertions depends on the data used in the construct.

```
!HPF$ INDEPENDENT
      DO I = 1, N
        X(INDX(I)) = Y(I)
      END DO
```

This directive asserts that the array **INDX** does not have any repeated entries in its first **N** elements. If there were repeated entries, at least one element of **X** would receive two values from **Y**, thus violating the Bernstein conditions. In general, there is no way for the compiler to know the values variables will have at runtime. When a loop is INDEPENDENT because of properties of the input data, it is almost always advisable to use the explicit directive. (Unfortunately, we cannot say it is always advisable—reports of directives causing pathological behavior in compilers are legion.) □

Example 6.16 INDEPENDENT loops may contain loops with dependences, so long as those dependences do not "escape" the INDEPENDENT loop. The code from Figure 6.4 is an example of this.

```
!HPF$ INDEPENDENT, NEW (J, N1)
      DO I = 1, NBLACK
        N1 = IBLACK_PT(I)
        DO J = INITIAL_RED(N1), LAST_RED(N1)
          X(N1) = X(N1) + A(J)*X(IRED_PT(J))
        END DO
      END DO
```

As in the last example, the correctness of the INDEPENDENT assertion depends on the data. Essentially, the assertion says that no element is both "black" (i.e., referenced by IBLACK_PT) and "red" (i.e., referenced by IRED_PT). It is clear, however, that the DO J loop is not INDEPENDENT, since it repeatedly uses the value of and assigns to the same element of X. □

Example 6.17 Although we have concentrated on assignments in the previous examples, a DO INDEPENDENT can contain arbitrary code if its behavior obeys the restrictions in Section 6.4.2.

```
!HPF$ INDEPENDENT, NEW(K, L, N, ROOT)
L1:   DO J = 1, 10
L2:     DO
          READ (J, '(2I6,I3)') K, L, N
          IF (K<=0 .OR. L<=0 .OR. N<3) EXIT L2
          ROOT = (K**N + L**N) ** (1.0 / N)
          WRITE(J+10, 'E18.6) ROOT
          IF (ROOT_M = FLOOR(ROOT)) THEN
            PRINT 'Fermat was wrong!'
            EXIT L1
          END IF
        END DO
      END DO
```

Data Parallelism

The **READ** and **WRITE** operations use different I/O units on every iteration. According to standard Fortran, different I/O units must be associated with different files, so there is no cross-iteration interference. The **PRINT** statement would cause an interference if it were executed, and the **EXIT** statement would likewise invalidate the **INDEPENDENT** assertion. However, those statements are only executed if there are four positive integers K, L, M, N (with $N > 2$) such that

$$K^N + L^N = M^N$$

Fermat's Last Theorem, which was recently proved, guarantees that such integers do not exist. □

The next three examples contain incorrect code. Be careful!

Example 6.18 The following loop is *not* a correct use of **INDEPENDENT**:

```
!HPF$ INDEPENDENT            ! *** Nonconforming!!! ***
      DO I = 1, N
         SCALAR = SCALAR + X(I)*Y(I)
      END DO
```

The reason is that **SCALAR** is both read and written by every iteration of the loop, creating almost **N**∗∗2 violations of the Bernstein conditions. Placing **SCALAR** in a **NEW** clause is not correct either, since the results of the loop would change rather drastically if the value of **SCALAR** was forgotten at the end of each iteration. In short, you cannot use a **DO INDEPENDENT** to accumulate sums (or products, or other reduction operations), even though there are parallel algorithms for such accumulations. The intrinsics in Chapter 7 are the correct way to perform these operations. □

Example 6.19 The following program is *not* correct usage of **INDEPENDENT**:

```
      ERR = ERR_TOL + 1
      DO WHILE (ERR > ERR_TOL)
!HPF$    INDEPENDENT, NEW(J)  ! *** Nonconforming!!! ***
         DO J = 2, M-1
!HPF$       INDEPENDENT        ! *** Nonconforming!!! ***
            DO I = 2, N-1
               B(I,J) = A(I,J)
               A(I,J) = 0.25*(A(I-1,J)+A(I+1,J)+A(I,J-1)+A(I,J+1))
               B(I,J) = ABS(A(I,J) - B(I,J))
            END DO
```

```
      END DO
      ERR = MAXVAL(B(2:N-1,2:M-1))
   END DO
```

As just one example of why the **INDEPENDENT** assertion is incorrect, consider **A(3,3)**. It is assigned by iteration **(I,J) = (3,3)**, and is used in iterations **(I,J) = (4,3)**, **(2,3)**, **(3,4)** and **(3,2)**. It is true that the outer **DO WHILE** will produce the same answer if the inner loops are executed in parallel, in the sense that it will terminate with answers that are very close to the sequential execution. However, changing the order of iterations does change the exact answer, which is what the Fortran and HPF language specifications define. □

Example 6.20 The following loop is **not** a correct use of **INDEPENDENT** if **SCALAR** is ever found in **X**.

```
   !HPF$ INDEPENDENT              ! *** Possibly Nonconforming!!! ***
   L1:   DO I = 1, N
            IF (X(I) = SCALAR) THEN
               I_ANSWER = I
               EXIT L1
            END IF
         END DO
```

When the **IF** condition is true for some value of **I** some iterations are not executed. This constitutes control dependence, and makes the **INDEPENDENT** assertion invalid. As in the last example, it does not matter that the answer will be the same if the loop is executed in parallel. Note, however, that if the **EXIT** statement is deleted then the loop may be **INDEPENDENT**, depending on the input data. Without the **EXIT** statement an **INDEPENDENT** assertion would mean that there was at most one **I** such that **X(I)=SCALAR**. □

7 Intrinsic and Library Procedures

An important feature of Fortran 90 is the rich set of intrinsic functions and subroutines with which it is endowed. These allow the coding of data parallel programs at a higher level, and potentially with greater efficiency, than if their functions were programmed by the users. HPF includes Fortran 90's intrinsic procedures. Two of them, MAXLOC and MINLOC, are enhanced in HPF. Three new intrinsic functions are included in HPF: two system inquiry functions, and one new computational function.

In addition to the new intrinsic functions, HPF defines a library module, HPF_LIBRARY, that adds further to the power of the language. Intrinsic procedures are unlike ordinary procedures in that their interfaces are automatically known to the compiler. Some can take arbitrarily many arguments (MAX, for example). These special features of intrinsic procedures were judged unnecessary for most of the HPF procedures, which were therefore included in the HPF library module, where a USE statement is required to access them. Note that the library is not part of subset HPF. The library contains a large group of additional functions and subroutines. One of the most important facilities these provide is the ability to query the alignment and distribution attributes of arrays or templates at run-time. The library also includes some important data parallel programming primitives: new reduction operations, combining scatter operations, prefix and suffix operations, and sorting.

Detailed specifications of the intrinsic and library procedures appear in Appendix B.

In order to make them more readable, the examples of this section use T and F to denote the logical values .TRUE. and .FALSE.

7.1 System Inquiry Functions

In a multi-processor computer, the physical processors may be arranged in a multi-dimensional processor array. The system inquiry functions return values that describe the size and shape of the underlying processor array. NUMBER_OF_PROCESSORS returns the total number of processors available to the program or the number of processors available to the program along a specified dimension of the processor array. PROCESSORS_SHAPE returns the shape of the processor array. Therefore, SIZE(PROCESSORS_SHAPE()) returns the rank of the processor array.

The values returned by the system inquiry intrinsic functions remain constant for the duration of one program execution. For this reason, NUMBER_OF_PROCESSORS and PROCESSORS_SHAPE may be used wherever Fortran 90 requires a *specification-expr*. In particular, references to system inquiry functions may occur in array declarations and in HPF directives.

Function	Value returned
`NUMBER_OF_PROCESSORS`	Number of executing processors (intrinsic)
`PROCESSORS_SHAPE`	Shape of the executing processor array (intrinsic)

Table 7.1
System inquiry functions

Example 7.1 The code

```
      INTEGER, DIMENSION(SIZE(PROCESSORS_SHAPE())) :: PSHAPE
      REAL, DIMENSION(3*NUMBER_OF_PROCESSORS())    :: A
!HPF$ TEMPLATE, DIMENSION(NUMBER_OF_PROCESSORS()) :: T
```

declares `PSHAPE` to have one element for each dimension of the processor array. It is therefore the correct shape to contain the value of `PROCESSORS_SHAPE()`, for example. The array `A` has a size dependent on the number of physical processors; this helps ensure that the data values in `A` are spread evenly between processors when `A` is explicitly mapped. (It is still possible to unbalance the load due to `A` by choosing a bad parameter to a `CYCLIC(K)` distribution.) The template `T` has one element per processor; this may be convenient for defining some mappings, but is usually not necessary. □

The values of system inquiry functions may not occur in an *initialization-expr*, because they may not be assumed to be constants. HPF programs may be compiled to run on machines whose configurations are not known at compile time. We hope that vendors will supply HPF compilers and linkers that allow an executable program to run on a range of machines of varying size, using the system inquiry intrinsics to determine the machine size and shape at run time.

Note that the system inquiry functions query the physical machine, and have nothing to do with any `PROCESSORS` directive that may occur.

Table 7.1 summarizes the system inquiry functions.

7.2 Mapping Inquiry Subroutines

HPF provides data mapping directives that are advisory in nature. The mapping inquiry library subroutines allow the program to determine the actual mapping of an array at run time. For example, if `REALIGN` or `REDISTRIBUTE` are used the mapping inquiry procedures can tell which data mapping is actually in effect. It may be especially important to know the exact mapping when an `EXTRINSIC` subprogram is invoked. For these reasons, HPF includes mapping inquiry subroutines that describe how an array is actually mapped onto the machine. To keep the number of routines small, the inquiry procedures are structured as subroutines with optional **INTENT(OUT)** arguments.

Example 7.2 The distribution in effect may affect the choice of algorithm.

```
        SUBROUTINE GAUSS(A, X)
          REAL, DIMENSION(1:,1:)        :: A
          REAL, DIMENSION(1:SIZE(A,2)) :: X
!HPF$     INHERIT :: A, X
          LOGICAL SIMPLE
          CHARACTER*10 DISTS(2)
          INTEGER BLOCKS(2)

          CALL HPF_ALIGNMENT(A, IDENTITY_MAP=SIMPLE)
          IF (SIMPLE) THEN
            CALL HPF_DISTRIBUTE(A, AXIS_TYPE=DISTS, AXIS_INFO=BLOCKS)
            IF (DISTS(1)=='COLLAPSED' .AND. DISTS(2)=='CYCLIC') THEN
              CALL FACTOR_NORMAL_ORDER(A, X, BLOCKS(2))      ! Cyclic
            ELSE IF (DISTS(1)=='COLLAPSED' .AND. DISTS(2)=='BLOCK') THEN
              CALL FACTOR_PERMUTED_ORDER(A, X, BLOCKS(2))    ! Block
            ELSE
              CALL REDIST_THEN_FACTOR(A, X)    ! Other distributions
            END IF
          ELSE
            CALL REDIST_THEN_FACTOR(A, X)      ! Other alignments
          END IF
        END SUBROUTINE GAUSS
```

This code checks the mapping of **A**, and calls one of three other subroutines to perform the real work. For a Gaussian elimination routine (as the names here suggest), the different routines might use different elimination orders to keep the computational load balanced among processors. Another use might be to allow the called routines to use descriptive mapping directives; some compilers may produce more efficient code from these directives than from a simple **INHERIT**. □

Table 7.2 summarizes the mapping inquiry subroutines.

Subroutine	Effect
HPF_ALIGNMENT	Returns information about the alignment of an array in optional INTENT(OUT) arguments
HPF_TEMPLATE	Returns information about the template or array to which an array is ultimately aligned in optional INTENT(OUT) arguments
HPF_DISTRIBUTION	Returns information about the distribution of the template or array to which an array is ultimately aligned in optional INTENT(OUT) arguments

Table 7.2
Mapping inquiry subroutines

7.3 Computational Functions

7.3.1 Array Location Functions

HPF generalizes the Fortran 90 MAXLOC and MINLOC intrinsic functions with an optional DIM parameter for finding the locations of maximum or minimum elements along a given dimension. This is analogous to the optional DIM argument in the MAXVAL and MINVAL intrinsics. Table 7.3 summarizes the array location functions.

Function	Value returned
MAXLOC	Location of a maximum value in an array (intrinsic)
MINLOC	Location of a minimum value in an array (intrinsic)

Table 7.3
Array location functions

7.3.2 Bit Manipulation Functions

HPF adds an elemental intrinsic function, ILEN, that computes the number of bits needed to store an integer value. ILEN was included as an intrinsic because of its use in rounding an integer up or down to the nearest power of two, a role that was deemed quite important. Three other elemental, bit-manipulation functions are included in the library: LEADZ computes the number of leading zero bits in an integer's representation; POPCNT counts the number of one bits in an integer; POPPAR computes the parity of an integer. Table 7.4 summarizes the new bit manipulation functions.

Intrinsic and Library Procedures

Function	Value returned
ILEN	Number of bits to store an integer (intrinsic)
LEADZ	Number of leading zeros
POPCNT	Number of one bits
POPPAR	Parity of an integer

Table 7.4
Bit manipulation functions

7.3.3 Array Reduction Functions

HPF adds additional array reduction functions that operate in the same manner as the Fortran 90 SUM and ANY intrinsic functions. The new reduction functions are IALL, IANY, IPARITY, and PARITY, which correspond to the commutative, associative binary operations IAND, IOR, IEOR, and .NEQV. respectively. Thus:

- IALL((/ 7,3,10 /)) has the value 2.
- IANY((/ 7,3,10 /)) has the value 15.
- IPARITY((/ 7,3,10 /)) has the value 14.
- PARITY((/ T,F,F,T,T /)) has the value .TRUE.
- PARITY((/ T,F,F,T,F /)) has the value .FALSE.

In the specifications of these functions and the prefix, suffix, and combining scatter functions in Appendix B, the terms "XXX reduction" are used, where XXX is one of the reduction functions defined above or the Fortran 90 array reduction intrinsics. These are defined by means of an example. The IAND reduction of all the elements of ARRAY for which the corresponding elements of MASK are true is the scalar integer computed in RESULT by

```
RESULT = IAND_IDENTITY_ELEMENT
DO I_1 = LBOUND(ARRAY,1), UBOUND(ARRAY,1)
  ...
    DO I_N = LBOUND(ARRAY,N), UBOUND(ARRAY,N)
      IF ( MASK(I_1,I_2,...,I_N) ) &
        RESULT = IAND( RESULT, ARRAY(I_1,I_2,...,I_N) )
    END DO
  ...
END DO
```

Function	Value returned
IALL	Bitwise logical AND reduction
IANY	Bitwise logical OR reduction
IPARITY	Bitwise logical EOR reduction
PARITY	Logical EOR reduction

Table 7.5
Array reduction functions

Here, N is the rank of ARRAY and IAND_IDENTITY_ELEMENT is the integer that has all bits equal to one. (The interpretation of an integer as a sequence of bits is given in Section 13.5.7 of the Fortran 90 standard.) The other three reductions are similarly defined. The identity elements for IOR and IEOR are zero. The identity element for PARITY is .FALSE.

Table 7.5 lists the new array reduction functions.

7.3.4 Array Combining Scatter Functions

Suppose that A is the array [10 20 30], X is the array [1 2 3 4], and V is the array [3 2 1]. In Fortran 90, one may write the array assignment

    X(V) = A

after which X has the value [30 20 10 4]. If, however, the elements of V are not all different, the assignment is not standard-conforming in Fortran 90 (or HPF). The combining scatter functions, in effect, allow duplicated indices and provide a means of specifying how elements sent to the same position in the result are to be combined. Thus, the combining scatter functions are generalized array reductions in which completely general, but nonoverlapping, subsets of array elements can be combined.

There is a scatter function for each of twelve reduction operations. These functions all have the form

    XXX_SCATTER(ARRAY, BASE, INDX1, ..., INDXn, MASK)

The allowed values of XXX are ALL, ANY, COPY, COUNT, IALL, IANY, IPARITY, MAXVAL, MINVAL, PARITY, PRODUCT, and SUM.

The result has the same shape and type as BASE. In fact, the result is equal to BASE in positions for which no elements of ARRAY arrive.

The source data come from ARRAY, and the integer INDX arguments must be conformable with it. The number of INDX arguments must equal the rank of BASE. For example, if ARRAY has rank two and BASE has rank three, then for all valid subscripts

I and J, `ARRAY(I,J)` contributes to element (`INDX1(I,J)`, `INDX2(I,J)`, `INDX3(I,J)`) of the result.

Except for `COUNT_SCATTER`, `ARRAY` and `BASE` are arrays of the same type. (Because it returns the number of true elements of `ARRAY`, `COUNT_SCATTER` has a logical `ARRAY` and an integer `BASE`.)

The optional, logical `MASK` argument selects elements of `ARRAY` for inclusion in the reduction. Only elements of `ARRAY` in positions for which `MASK` is true can contribute to the result. (For `ALL_SCATTER`, `ANY_SCATTER`, `COUNT_SCATTER`, and `PARITY_SCATTER`, `ARRAY` must be logical. These functions do not have an optional `MASK` argument.)

Here is a more precise description of the way the result is computed. For every element a in `ARRAY` for which the `MASK` element is true there is a corresponding element in each of the `INDX` arrays. Let s_1 be the value of the element of `INDX1` that is indexed by the same subscripts as element a of `ARRAY`. More generally, for each $j = 1, 2, ..., n$, let s_j be the value of the element of `INDXj` that corresponds to element a in `ARRAY`, where n is the rank of `BASE`. The integers $s_j, j = 1, ..., n$, form a subscript selecting an element of `BASE`: `BASE`$(s_1, s_2, ..., s_n)$. Unless element a is masked out by the optional `MASK` argument, $(s_1, s_2, ..., s_n)$ must be a valid subscript for `BASE`.

Thus the `INDX` arrays establish a mapping from all the elements of `ARRAY` onto selected elements of `BASE`. Viewed in the other direction, this mapping associates with each element b of `BASE` a set S of elements from `ARRAY`.

Because `BASE` and the result are conformable, for each element of `BASE` there is a corresponding element of the result.

If S is empty, then the element of the result corresponding to the element b of `BASE` has the same value as b.

If S is non-empty, then the elements of S will be combined with element b to produce an element of the result. For every combining-scatter function except `COPY_SCATTER`, this combining is done by the corresponding reduction function. As an example, for `SUM_SCATTER`, if the elements of S are $a_1, ..., a_m$, then the element of the result corresponding to the element b of `BASE` is the result of evaluating `SUM`$((/a_1, a_2, \ldots, a_m, b/))$. For `COPY_SCATTER`, one of the elements of S is chosen in a system-dependent way.

Note that, since a scalar is conformable with any array, a scalar may be used in place of an `INDX` array, in which case one hyperplane of the result is selected. See the example below.

Example 7.3 If

$$A \text{ is the array } \begin{bmatrix} 1 & 2 & 3 \\ 4 & 5 & 6 \\ 7 & 8 & 9 \end{bmatrix}; \qquad B \text{ is the array } \begin{bmatrix} -1 & -2 & -3 \\ -4 & -5 & -6 \\ -7 & -8 & -9 \end{bmatrix};$$

$$\text{I1 is the array } \begin{bmatrix} 1 & 1 & 1 \\ 2 & 1 & 1 \\ 3 & 2 & 1 \end{bmatrix}; \qquad \text{I2 is the array } \begin{bmatrix} 1 & 2 & 3 \\ 1 & 1 & 2 \\ 1 & 1 & 1 \end{bmatrix}.$$

then

$$\text{SUM\_SCATTER(A, B, I1, I2) has the value } \begin{bmatrix} 14 & 6 & 0 \\ 8 & -5 & -6 \\ 0 & -8 & -9 \end{bmatrix};$$

$$\text{SUM\_SCATTER(A, B, 2, I2) has the value } \begin{bmatrix} -1 & -2 & -3 \\ 30 & 3 & -3 \\ -7 & -8 & -9 \end{bmatrix};$$

$$\text{SUM\_SCATTER(A, B, I1, 2) has the value } \begin{bmatrix} -1 & 24 & -3 \\ -4 & 7 & -6 \\ -7 & -1 & -9 \end{bmatrix};$$

$$\text{SUM\_SCATTER(A, B, 2, 2) has the value } \begin{bmatrix} -1 & -2 & -3 \\ -4 & 40 & -6 \\ -7 & -8 & -9 \end{bmatrix}.$$

□

Table 7.6 lists the combining scatter functions.

7.3.5 Array Prefix and Suffix Functions

In a prefix function, or scan, of a vector, each element of the result is a function of the elements of the vector that precede it. Similarly, in a suffix function each element of the result is a function of the elements in the vector that follow it. For instance, SUM_PREFIX((/ 1, 2, 3, 4 /)) has the value [1 3 6 10]. Parallel implementations of these functions are possible. They are important in building efficient parallel algorithm on graphs and other general data structures. Because they are so useful, and because their efficient parallel implementation may best be done for some machines at programming levels below that of HPF, they have been included in the library.

These functions provide prefix and suffix operations on arrays and subarrays. The functions all have the form

Function	Value returned
ALL_SCATTER	Scatter of logical array, combining with logical AND
ANY_SCATTER	Scatter of logical array, combining with logical OR
COPY_SCATTER	Scatter of array, combining by (processor-dependent) selection
COUNT_SCATTER	Scatter of logical array, counting number of .TRUE. elements
IALL_SCATTER	Scatter of integer array, combining with bitwise AND
IANY_SCATTER	Scatter of integer array, combining with bitwise OR
IPARITY_SCATTER	Scatter of integer array, combining with bitwise EOR
MAXVAL_SCATTER	Scatter of array, combining by taking the maximum
MINVAL_SCATTER	Scatter of array, combining by taking the minimum
PARITY_SCATTER	Scatter of logical array, combining with logical EOR
PRODUCT_SCATTER	Scatter of array, combining by taking the product
SUM_SCATTER	Scatter of array, combining by taking the sum

Table 7.6
Combining scatter functions

```
XXX_PREFIX(ARRAY, DIM, MASK, SEGMENT, EXCLUSIVE)
XXX_SUFFIX(ARRAY, DIM, MASK, SEGMENT, EXCLUSIVE)
```

The allowed values of XXX are ALL, ANY, COPY, COUNT, IALL, IANY, IPARITY, MAXVAL, MINVAL, PARITY, PRODUCT, and SUM.

A detailed and precise description of these routines will be given below. But to begin, we give some examples to convey the general idea. In all of them we assume that:

$$\text{B has the value } \begin{bmatrix} 1 & 2 & 3 & 4 & 5 \\ 6 & 7 & 8 & 9 & 10 \\ 11 & 12 & 13 & 14 & 15 \end{bmatrix};$$

$$\text{M has the value } \begin{bmatrix} T & T & T & T & T \\ F & F & T & T & T \\ T & F & T & F & F \end{bmatrix};$$

$$\text{S has the value } \begin{bmatrix} T & T & F & F & F \\ F & T & T & F & F \\ T & T & T & T & T \end{bmatrix}.$$

The elements of ARRAY are scanned in increasing (prefix) or decreasing (suffix) array element order.

Example 7.4 SUM_PREFIX(B) has the value $\begin{bmatrix} 1 & 20 & 42 & 67 & 95 \\ 7 & 27 & 50 & 76 & 105 \\ 18 & 39 & 63 & 90 & 120 \end{bmatrix}$.

SUM_SUFFIX(B) has the value $\begin{bmatrix} 120 & 102 & 81 & 57 & 30 \\ 119 & 100 & 78 & 53 & 25 \\ 113 & 93 & 70 & 44 & 15 \end{bmatrix}$. □

If DIM is present, one dimensional scans occur along the indicated dimension.

Example 7.5 SUM_PREFIX(B, DIM=2) has the value $\begin{bmatrix} 1 & 3 & 6 & 10 & 15 \\ 6 & 13 & 21 & 30 & 40 \\ 11 & 23 & 36 & 50 & 65 \end{bmatrix}$. □

If MASK is present, only the elements of ARRAY corresponding to true elements of MASK can contribute to the result.

Example 7.6 SUM_PREFIX(B, MASK=M) has the value $\begin{bmatrix} 1 & 14 & 17 & 42 & 56 \\ 1 & 14 & 25 & 51 & 66 \\ 12 & 14 & 38 & 51 & 66 \end{bmatrix}$. □

If SEGMENT is present, then it divides ARRAY up into subarrays that are scanned independently. Each such subarray corresponds to a run of contiguous identical values in SEGMENT.

Example 7.7 SUM_PREFIX(B, SEGMENT=S) returns $\begin{bmatrix} 1 & 13 & 3 & 4 & 5 \\ 6 & 20 & 8 & 13 & 15 \\ 11 & 32 & 21 & 14 & 15 \end{bmatrix}$. □

If EXCLUSIVE is present and is true, then an element of ARRAY does not contribute to the corresponding element of the result; only elements that precede (prefix) or succeed (suffix) it can contribute to the corresponding element of the result.

Example 7.8 SUM_PREFIX(B, SEGMENT=S, EXCLUSIVE=.TRUE.) has the value
$\begin{bmatrix} 0 & 11 & 0 & 0 & 0 \\ 0 & 13 & 0 & 4 & 5 \\ 0 & 20 & 8 & 0 & 0 \end{bmatrix}$. □

Here is a precise discussion of how these routines function. When comments below apply to both prefix and suffix forms of the routines, we will refer to them as YYYFIX functions.

The arguments DIM, MASK, SEGMENT, and EXCLUSIVE are optional. The COPY_YYYFIX functions do not have MASK or EXCLUSIVE arguments. The ALL_YYYFIX, ANY_YYYFIX,

COUNT_YYYFIX, and PARITY_YYYFIX functions do not have MASK arguments. Their ARRAY argument must be of type logical; it is denoted MASK in their specifications in Appendix B.

The arguments MASK and SEGMENT must be of type logical. SEGMENT must have the same shape as ARRAY. MASK must be conformable with ARRAY. EXCLUSIVE is a logical scalar. DIM is a scalar integer between one and the rank of ARRAY.

The result has the same shape as ARRAY, and, with the exception of COUNT_YYYFIX, the same type and kind type parameter as ARRAY. (The result of COUNT_YYYFIX is default integer.)

In all cases, every element of the result is determined by combining the values of certain selected elements of ARRAY. For prefix and suffix functions based on array reduction functions, the combining is done by the named reduction. For example, SUM_PREFIX combines elements by addition. COPY_PREFIX chooses one of the selected elements in a system-dependent way. The optional arguments affect the selection of elements of ARRAY for each element of the result; the selected elements of ARRAY are said to contribute to the result element. This section describes fully which elements of ARRAY contribute to a given element of the result.

If no elements of ARRAY are selected for a given element of the result, that result element is set to a default value that is specific to the particular function and is described in its specification.

For any given element r of the result, let a be the corresponding element of ARRAY. Every element of ARRAY contributes to r unless disqualified by one of the following rules.

1. If the function is XXX_PREFIX, no element that follows a in the array element ordering of ARRAY contributes to r. If the function is XXX_SUFFIX, no element that precedes a in the array element ordering of ARRAY contributes to r.
2. If the DIM argument is provided, an element z of ARRAY does not contribute to r unless all its indices, excepting only the index for dimension DIM, are the same as the corresponding indices of a. (It follows that if the DIM argument is omitted, then ARRAY, MASK, and SEGMENT are processed in array element order, as if temporarily regarded as rank-one arrays. If the DIM argument is present, then a family of completely independent scan operations is carried out along the selected dimension of ARRAY.)
3. If the MASK argument is provided, an element z of ARRAY contributes to r only if the element of MASK corresponding to z is true. (It follows that array elements corresponding to positions where the MASK is false do not contribute anywhere to the result. However, the result is nevertheless defined at all positions, even positions where the MASK is false.)
4. If the SEGMENT argument is provided, an element z of ARRAY does not contribute if there is some intermediate element w of ARRAY, possibly z itself, with all of the following properties:

- If the function is **XXX_PREFIX**, w does not precede z but does precede a in the array element ordering; if the function is **XXX_SUFFIX**, w does not follow z but does follow a in the array element ordering.
- If the **DIM** argument is present, all the indices of w, excepting only the index for dimension **DIM**, are the same as the corresponding indices of a.
- The element of **SEGMENT** corresponding to w does not have the same value as the element of **SEGMENT** corresponding to a. (In other words, z can contribute only if there is an unbroken string of **SEGMENT** values, all alike, extending from z through a.)

5. If the **EXCLUSIVE** argument is provided and is true, then a itself does not contribute to r.

These general rules lead to the following important cases:

Case (i): If **ARRAY** has rank one, element i of the result of **XXX_PREFIX(ARRAY)** is determined by the first i elements of **ARRAY**; element $SIZE(ARRAY) - i + 1$ of the result of **XXX_SUFFIX(ARRAY)** is determined by the last i elements of **ARRAY**.

Case (ii): If **ARRAY** has rank greater than one, then each element of the result of **XXX_PREFIX(ARRAY)** has a value determined by the corresponding element a of the **ARRAY** and all elements of **ARRAY** that precede a in array element order. For **XXX_SUFFIX**, a is determined by the elements of **ARRAY** that correspond to or follow a in array element order.

Case (iii): Each element of the result of **XXX_PREFIX(ARRAY,MASK=MASK)** is determined by selected elements of **ARRAY**, namely the corresponding element a of the **ARRAY** and all elements of **ARRAY** that precede a in array element order, but an element of **ARRAY** may contribute to the result only if the corresponding element of **MASK** is true. If this restriction results in selecting no array elements to contribute to some element of the result, then that element of the result is set to the default value for the given function.

Case (iv): Each element of the result of **XXX_PREFIX(ARRAY,DIM=DIM)** is determined by selected elements of **ARRAY**, namely the corresponding element a of the **ARRAY** and all elements of **ARRAY** that precede a along dimension **DIM**; for example, in **SUM_PREFIX(A(1:N, 1:N), DIM=2)**, result element (i_1, i_2) could be computed as **SUM(A(i_1,1 : i_2))**. More generally, in **SUM_PREFIX(ARRAY, DIM)**, result element $i_1, i_2, \ldots, i_{DIM}, \ldots, i_n$ could be computed as **SUM(ARRAY($i_1, i_2, \ldots, :i_{DIM}, \ldots, i_n$))** . (Note the colon before i_{DIM} in that last expression.)

Case (v): If **ARRAY** has rank one, then element i of the result of **XXX_PREFIX(ARRAY, EXCLUSIVE=.TRUE.)** is determined by the first $i - 1$ elements of **ARRAY**.

Case (vi): The options may be used in any combination.

A new segment begins at every *transition* from false to true or true to false; thus a segment is indicated by a maximal contiguous subsequence of like logical values:

```
(/T,T,T,F,T,F,F,F,T,F,F,T/)
 -----   - -   -----   - ---   -     seven segments
```

This organization deserves some comment. One library that influenced HPF delimited the segments by indicating the *start* of each segment. Another delimited the segments by indicating the *stop* of each segment. Each method had its advantages. There was also the question of whether the convention should change when performing a suffix rather than a prefix. HPF adopted the symmetric representation above for two reasons:

1. It is symmetrical, in that the same segment specifier may be meaningfully used for prefix and suffix without changing its interpretation (start versus stop).

2. The start-bit or stop-bit representation is easily converted to this form by using **PARITY_PREFIX** or **PARITY_SUFFIX**. These might be standard idioms for a compiler to recognize:

```
SUM_PREFIX(FOO,SEGMENT=PARITY_PREFIX(START_BITS))
SUM_PREFIX(FOO,SEGMENT=PARITY_SUFFIX(STOP_BITS))
SUM_SUFFIX(FOO,SEGMENT=PARITY_SUFFIX(START_BITS))
SUM_SUFFIX(FOO,SEGMENT=PARITY_PREFIX(STOP_BITS))
```

Table 7.7 lists the new array prefix and suffix functions.

7.3.6 Array Sorting Functions

HPF includes procedures for sorting multidimensional arrays. These are structured as functions that return sorting permutations. An array can be sorted along a given axis, or the whole array may be viewed as a sequence in array element order. The sorts are stable, allowing for convenient sorting of structures by major and minor keys.

Suppose that ARRAY has shape $\begin{bmatrix} 4 & 5 & 6 \end{bmatrix}$.

```
S = GRADE_DOWN(ARRAY)
```

returns an integer array of shape $\begin{bmatrix} 3 & 120 \end{bmatrix}$ in S. It is such that if $j < k$ then the element ARRAY(S(1,j), S(2,j), S(3,j)) is greater than or equal to ARRAY(S(1,k), S(2,k), S(3,k)). And if these two elements are equal, then ARRAY(S(1,j),S(2,j),S(3,j)) precedes ARRAY(S(1,k),S(2,k),S(3,k)) in the array element ordering of ARRAY.

If ARRAY has shape $\begin{bmatrix} 4 & 5 & 6 \end{bmatrix}$, and the optional argument is present, as in

```
S = GRADE_DOWN(ARRAY, DIM=2)
```

Function	Value returned (for each element)
ALL_PREFIX	Logical AND of preceding elements in array
ALL_SUFFIX	Logical AND of following elements in array
ANY_PREFIX	Logical OR of preceding elements in array
ANY_SUFFIX	Logical OR of following elements in array
COPY_PREFIX	Selected (processor-dependent) value from preceding array elements
COPY_SUFFIX	Selected (processor-dependent) value from following array elements
COUNT_PREFIX	Number of preceding .TRUE. elements in array
COUNT_SUFFIX	Number of following .TRUE. elements in array
IALL_PREFIX	Bitwise AND of preceding elements in array
IALL_SUFFIX	Bitwise AND of following elements in array
IANY_PREFIX	Bitwise OR of preceding elements in array
IANY_SUFFIX	Bitwise OR of following elements in array
IPARITY_PREFIX	Bitwise EOR of preceding elements in array
IPARITY_SUFFIX	Bitwise EOR of following elements in array
MAXVAL_PREFIX	Maximum of preceding elements in array
MAXVAL_SUFFIX	Maximum of following elements in array
MINVAL_PREFIX	Minimum of preceding elements in array
MINVAL_SUFFIX	Minimum of following elements in array
PARITY_PREFIX	Logical EOR of preceding elements in array
PARITY_SUFFIX	Logical EOR of following elements in array
PRODUCT_PREFIX	Product of preceding elements in array
PRODUCT_SUFFIX	Product of following elements in array
SUM_PREFIX	Sum of preceding elements in array
SUM_SUFFIX	Sum of following elements in array

Table 7.7
Prefix and suffix functions

then the result has the same shape as `ARRAY:` [4 5 6]. For every *i* and *k* the vector `ARRAY( i, S(i, :, k), k )` is sorted in descending order. Stability means that if `ARRAY( i, S(i, m, k), k )` is equal to `ARRAY( i, S(i, m+1, k), k )` then `S(i, m, k)` must be smaller than `S(i, m+1, k)`.

Because of the stability requirement, `GRADE_DOWN(A(1:N))` does not, in general, equal `GRADE_UP(A(N:1:-1))`. Indeed, these results are equal if and only if A contains no duplicate values.

Example 7.9 The stability requirement allows one to cascade grading operations in order to sort on multiple fields. For example, consider the following code:

```
TYPE PERSON
  INTEGER AGE
  CHARACTER (LEN=50) NAME
END TYPE PERSON
TYPE(PERSON), DIMENSION(100000) :: MEMBERS, ROSTER
INTEGER, DIMENSION(100000)      :: V
...
V = GRADE_UP(MEMBERS%AGE, DIM=1)
V = V(GRADE_UP(MEMBERS(V)%NAME, DIM=1))
ROSTER = MEMBERS(V)
```

This would cause `ROSTER` to be a rearrangement of `MEMBERS` that is sorted primarily by name and secondarily by age (that is, members with the same name are grouped together in order of ascending age). Note that the minor sort field is graded first, and that more statements like the second one may be inserted to sort on additional fields. Without the use of the `DIM` argument, `GRADE_UP` returns a rank-two result of shape [1 100000], which would make the example more cumbersome.

To list members with the same name in descending order of age, change the first `GRADE_UP` to `GRADE_DOWN`:

```
V = GRADE_DOWN(MEMBERS%AGE, DIM=1)
V = V(GRADE_UP(MEMBERS(V)%NAME, DIM=1))
ROSTER = MEMBERS(V)
```

□

Table 7.8 summarizes the sorting functions.

Function	Value returned
GRADE_DOWN	Permutation that sorts into descending order
GRADE_UP	Permutation that sorts into ascending order

Table 7.8
Sorting functions

7.4 Alphabetical List of Intrinsic and Library Procedures

Tables 7.9 through 7.11 contain an alphabetical listing of all HPF library procedures and the intrinsics that are new to HPF or changed from Fortran 90. Intrinsic procedures are marked with an asterisk (*); subroutines are marked with a dagger (†) The arguments shown are the names that must be used for keywords when using the keyword form for actual arguments. Many of the argument keywords have names that are indicative of their usage, as is the case in Fortran 90. Detailed descriptions of all the procedures appear in Appendix B.

Intrinsic and Library Procedures

Function	Optional arguments
ALL_PREFIX(MASK, DIM, SEGMENT, EXCLUSIVE)	DIM, SEGMENT, EXCLUSIVE
ALL_SCATTER(MASK, BASE, INDX1 ..., INDXn)	
ALL_SUFFIX(MASK, DIM, SEGMENT, EXCLUSIVE)	DIM, SEGMENT, EXCLUSIVE
ANY_PREFIX(MASK, DIM, SEGMENT, EXCLUSIVE)	DIM, SEGMENT, EXCLUSIVE
ANY_SCATTER(MASK, BASE, INDX1, ..., INDXn)	
ANY_SUFFIX(MASK, DIM, SEGMENT, EXCLUSIVE)	DIM, SEGMENT, EXCLUSIVE
COPY_PREFIX(ARRAY, DIM, SEGMENT)	DIM, SEGMENT
COPY_SCATTER(ARRAY, BASE, INDX1, ..., INDXn, MASK)	MASK
COPY_SUFFIX(ARRAY, DIM, SEGMENT)	DIM, SEGMENT
COUNT_PREFIX(MASK, DIM, SEGMENT, EXCLUSIVE)	DIM, SEGMENT, EXCLUSIVE
COUNT_SCATTER(ARRAY, BASE, INDX1, ..., INDXn, MASK)	MASK
COUNT_SUFFIX(MASK, DIM, SEGMENT, EXCLUSIVE)	DIM, SEGMENT, EXCLUSIVE
GRADE_DOWN(ARRAY, DIM)	DIM
GRADE_UP(ARRAY, DIM)	DIM
HPF_ALIGNMENT(ALIGNEE, LB, UB, STRIDE, AXIS_MAP, IDENTITY_MAP, DYNAMIC, NCOPIES) †	LB, UB, STRIDE, AXIS_MAP, IDENTITY_MAP, DYNAMIC, NCOPIES
HPF_DISTRIBUTION(DISTRIBUTEE, AXIS_TYPE, AXIS_INFO, PROCESSORS_RANK, PROCESSORS_SHAPE) †	AXIS_TYPE, AXIS_INFO, PROCESSORS_RANK, PROCESSORS_SHAPE
HPF_TEMPLATE(ALIGNEE, TEMPLATE_RANK, LB, UB, AXIS_TYPE, AXIS_INFO, NUMBER_ALIGNED, DYNAMIC) †	TEMPLATE_RANK, LB, UB, AXIS_TYPE, AXIS_INFO, NUMBER_ALIGNED, DYNAMIC
IALL(IARRAY, DIM, MASK)	DIM, MASK

Table 7.9
HPF intrinsic and library procedures

Function	Optional arguments
IALL_PREFIX(ARRAY, DIM, MASK, SEGMENT, EXCLUSIVE)	DIM, MASK, SEGMENT, EXCLUSIVE
IALL_SCATTER(ARRAY, BASE, INDX1, ..., INDXn, MASK)	MASK
IALL_SUFFIX(ARRAY, DIM, MASK, SEGMENT, EXCLUSIVE)	DIM, MASK, SEGMENT, EXCLUSIVE
IANY(IARRAY, DIM, MASK)	DIM, MASK
IANY_PREFIX(ARRAY, DIM, MASK, SEGMENT, EXCLUSIVE)	DIM, MASK, SEGMENT, EXCLUSIVE
IANY_SCATTER(ARRAY, BASE, INDX1, ..., INDXn, MASK)	MASK
IANY_SUFFIX(ARRAY, DIM, MASK, SEGMENT, EXCLUSIVE)	DIM, MASK, SEGMENT, EXCLUSIVE
ILEN(I) *	
IPARITY(IARRAY, DIM, MASK)	DIM, MASK
IPARITY_PREFIX(ARRAY, DIM, MASK, SEGMENT, EXCLUSIVE)	DIM, MASK, SEGMENT, EXCLUSIVE
IPARITY_SCATTER(ARRAY, BASE, INDX1, ..., INDXn, MASK)	MASK
IPARITY_SUFFIX(ARRAY, DIM, MASK, SEGMENT, EXCLUSIVE)	DIM, MASK, SEGMENT, EXCLUSIVE
LEADZ(I)	
MAXLOC(ARRAY, DIM, MASK) *	DIM, MASK
MAXVAL_PREFIX(ARRAY, DIM, MASK, SEGMENT, EXCLUSIVE)	DIM, MASK, SEGMENT, EXCLUSIVE
MAXVAL_SCATTER(ARRAY, BASE, INDX1, ..., INDXn, MASK)	MASK
MAXVAL_SUFFIX(ARRAY, DIM, MASK, SEGMENT, EXCLUSIVE)	DIM, MASK, SEGMENT, EXCLUSIVE
MINLOC(ARRAY, DIM, MASK) *	DIM, MASK

Table 7.10
HPF intrinsic and library procedures (continued)

Function	Optional arguments
MINVAL_PREFIX(ARRAY, DIM, MASK, SEGMENT, EXCLUSIVE)	DIM, MASK, SEGMENT, EXCLUSIVE
MINVAL_SCATTER(ARRAY, BASE, INDX1, ..., INDXn, MASK)	MASK
MINVAL_SUFFIX(ARRAY, DIM, MASK, SEGMENT, EXCLUSIVE)	DIM, MASK, SEGMENT, EXCLUSIVE
NUMBER_OF_PROCESSORS(DIM) *	DIM
PARITY(MASK, DIM)	DIM
PARITY_PREFIX(MASK, DIM, SEGMENT, EXCLUSIVE)	DIM, SEGMENT, EXCLUSIVE
PARITY_SCATTER(MASK, BASE, INDX1, ..., INDXn)	
PARITY_SUFFIX(MASK, DIM, SEGMENT, EXCLUSIVE)	DIM, SEGMENT, EXCLUSIVE
POPCNT(I)	
POPPAR(I)	
PROCESSORS_SHAPE() *	
PRODUCT_PREFIX(ARRAY, DIM, MASK, SEGMENT, EXCLUSIVE)	DIM, MASK, SEGMENT, EXCLUSIVE
PRODUCT_SCATTER(ARRAY, BASE, INDX1, ..., INDXn, MASK)	MASK
PRODUCT_SUFFIX(ARRAY, DIM, MASK, SEGMENT, EXCLUSIVE)	DIM, MASK, SEGMENT, EXCLUSIVE
SUM_PREFIX(ARRAY, DIM, MASK, SEGMENT, EXCLUSIVE)	DIM, MASK, SEGMENT, EXCLUSIVE
SUM_SCATTER(ARRAY, BASE, INDX1, ..., INDXn, MASK)	MASK
SUM_SUFFIX(ARRAY, DIM, MASK, SEGMENT, EXCLUSIVE)	DIM, MASK, SEGMENT, EXCLUSIVE

Table 7.11
HPF intrinsic and library procedures (continued)

8 Extrinsic Procedures

Fortran, wonderful as it may be, is not the only programming language in the world; and HPF is not the only way to get good performance out of a parallel computer.

One important competing model is the so-called "SPMD style" in which many copies of the same program execute at the same time, one on each available processor. ("SPMD" stands for "Single Program Multiple Data.") Communication of data among the various running copies of the program is managed explicitly by the programmer, perhaps through the use of common data in a shared memory or through a library of subroutines that send and receive messages (packets of data).

It is beyond the scope of HPF to define all the facilities needed for SPMD programming. However, HPF provides a mechanism by which HPF programs may call procedures written in other parallel programming styles or other programming languages. Because such procedures are themselves outside HPF, they are called *extrinsic procedures*. HPF simply provides a way of labeling external procedures as being non-HPF; indeed, there may be several different labels indicating several different kinds of extrinsic procedure. This allows an HPF compiler to generate the right kind of subroutine linkage, to convert data formats if necessary, and to rely on specific features of the "contract" between HPF routines and any specific kind of non-HPF procedure.

A called procedure that is written in a language other than HPF should be declared **EXTRINSIC** within an HPF program that calls it. The **EXTRINSIC** prefix declares what sort of interface should be used when calling indicated subprograms. For example:

```
      INTERFACE
        EXTRINSIC(COBOL) SUBROUTINE PRINT_REPORT(DATA_ARRAY)
          REAL DATA_ARRAY(:,:)
        END SUBROUTINE PRINT_REPORT
      END INTERFACE
```

might be used to indicate the use of a subroutine written in COBOL. Note, however, that this is merely an illustrative example; the keyword **COBOL** itself is not actually defined by HPF. Exactly which keywords are supported depends on the particular HPF language processor.

Here is a perhaps more realistic example:

```
      INTERFACE
        EXTRINSIC(C_LOCAL) SUBROUTINE MUNCH_COLUMNS(A)
          REAL A(:,:)
!HPF$     DISTRIBUTE A(*,BLOCK)
        END SUBROUTINE MUNCH_COLUMNS
```

```
      END INTERFACE
```

Here the called routine is presumably SPMD code written in C. If the actual argument for a call to `MUNCH_COLUMNS` is 100×100 and there are four processors, then each copy of the C procedure, one on each processor, will receive a 100×25 portion of the array, namely the elements that are mapped to the processor running that copy of `MUNCH_COLUMNS`. If there were instead 8 processors, then the first seven processors would receive 100×13 portions of the actual argument and the last processor a 100×9 portion, again exactly the elements mapped to that processor.

An extrinsic procedure might indeed be written in any of a number of languages and programming styles:

- A single-thread-of-control language where *one* copy of the procedure is conceptually executing and there is a single locus of control within the program text. Such a language might be specifically designed for parallel implementation (C* is one example). On the other hand, it might be a perfectly ordinary sequential language; a plausible scenario is an HPF program calling user interface code (perhaps for X Windows) written in C.

- A multiple-thread-of-control language, perhaps with dynamic assignment of loop iterations to processors or explicit dynamic process forking. When a procedure in such a language is first called, a single thread of control enters it, but it may spawn additional threads, resulting in multiple loci of control within the procedure or multiple copies of the procedure running on different processors. It is permissible for an extrinsic procedure to use any sequential or parallel control discipline within itself, and to remap or rearrange data among the processors as it pleases, so long as it leaves things in good order and reverts to a single conceptual thread of control on return to its HPF caller. (Exactly what this means is described more carefully in Section 8.1.2.)

- Any programming language targeted to a single processor, with the understanding that, the instant a procedure is called, there will be many copies of the procedure executing, one on each processor ("SPMD mode"). HPF refers to a procedure written in this fashion as a *local* procedure, because there is a local copy on each processor that operates principally on the data in that processor's local memory. A local procedure might be written in FORTRAN 77, Fortran 90, C, C++, Ada, or Pascal, for example. A particularly interesting possibility is that a local procedure might be written in (a special subset of) HPF! In this situation we sometimes call ordinary HPF code *global code* in order to distinguish it from local code written in HPF.

Extrinsic Procedures

```
      EXTRINSIC(HPF_LOCAL) SUBROUTINE MUNCH_COLUMNS(A)
      REAL A(:,:)
!HPF$ INDEPENDENT, NEW( I )
      INTEGER I, J
      DO J = 1, UBOUND(A,2)
        I = 1
        SEARCH: DO WHILE (I <= UBOUND(A,1))
          IF (A(I,J) /= 0.0) THEN      ! Found a nonzero element
            A(1:I-1,J) = A(I,J)
            EXIT SEARCH
          END IF
          I = I + 1
        END DO SEARCH
      END DO
      END SUBROUTINE MUNCH_COLUMNS
```

Figure 8.1
Local HPF code for the MUNCH_COLUMNS example

```
      SUBROUTINE MUNCH_COLUMNS(A)
      REAL A(:,:)
!HPF$ DISTRIBUTE A(*,BLOCK)
      INTEGER I(UBOUND(A,2)), J, K
      FORALL (J = 1:UBOUND(A,2))
        I(J) = MINLOC( (/ (K, K = 1, UBOUND(A,1)) /), MASK = A(:,J) )
        A(1:I(J)-1) = A(I(J))
      END FORALL
      END SUBROUTINE MUNCH_COLUMNS
```

Figure 8.2
Global HPF code for the MUNCH_COLUMNS example

The previous example of an interface to local C code is easily changed to indicate an interface to local code written in HPF:

```
      INTERFACE
        EXTRINSIC(HPF_LOCAL) SUBROUTINE MUNCH_COLUMNS(A)
          REAL A(:,:)
!HPF$     DISTRIBUTE A(*,BLOCK)
        END SUBROUTINE MUNCH_COLUMNS
      END INTERFACE
```

If the task of MUNCH_COLUMNS is to find the first nonzero element in each column and overwrite the leading zeros with that value, then the code for the local routine might appear as in Figure 8.1. (Note the use of an **INDEPENDENT** directive on a **DO** loop and of array assignment, both of which are permitted in local HPF code. While these constructs might not execute on multiple processors, use of these features could help a compiler to generate good vector code, for example. A **DISTRIBUTE** directive is *not* included, despite the fact that one appears in the interface block in the caller.)

While MUNCH_COLUMNS could be expressed as global HPF code (see Figure 8.2), the local version might be faster because it expresses and exploits the idea that only a prefix of each column needs to be examined and processed. Each processor might take a different amount of time to process its first column; the local code clearly indicates that the processors synchronize only after processing all columns, not after processing each column. (A *really smart* HPF compiler might be able to exploit the same trick when compiling the global code shown in Figure 8.2, but we doubt that HPF implementations will achieve that level of optimization in the near future.)

The next section describes the extrinsic procedure interface as seen by a calling routine written in HPF. This interface is used when calling *any* extrinsic procedure. The remainder of the chapter discusses the more specific topic of coding an extrinsic procedure in the SPMD (local) style. This latter topic is not a required part of the HPF language specification.

8.1 Definition and Invocation of Extrinsic Procedures

An explicit interface must be provided for each extrinsic procedure entry in the scope where it is called, using an interface block. This interface defines the "HPF view" of the extrinsic procedure.

8.1.1 EXTRINSIC Prefix Syntax

The form of an *extrinsic-prefix* (H601) is:

EXTRINSIC (*extrinsic-kind-keyword*)

where an *extrinsic-kind-keyword* (H602) is one of:

HPF
HPF_LOCAL

or perhaps some other, system-dependent, keyword. (Only the two keywords **HPF** and **HPF_LOCAL** are defined by the HPF language specification.)

An *extrinsic-prefix* may appear in a *subroutine-stmt* or *function-stmt* (as defined in the Fortran 90 standard) in the same place that the keyword **RECURSIVE** might appear. See Section 6.3.1 for the extended forms of the grammar rules for *function-stmt* and *subroutine-stmt* covering this case.

The *extrinsic-kind-keyword* indicates the kind of extrinsic interface to be used. (It may be helpful to compare this to Fortran 90 **KIND** parameters for numeric types. However, an *extrinsic-kind* is not integer-valued; it is merely a keyword.) HPF defines two such keywords: **HPF** and **HPF_LOCAL**. The keyword **HPF_LOCAL** is intended for use in calling routines coded in the "local HPF" style described in section 8.4. The keyword **HPF** refers to the interface normally used for calling ordinary HPF routines. Thus, writing **EXTRINSIC(HPF)** in an HPF program has exactly the same effect as not using an **EXTRINSIC** prefix at all.

(HPF defines the *extrinsic-kind-keyword* **HPF** primarily to set an example for other programming languages that might adopt this style of interface specification. For example, in an extended Fortran 90 compiler it would not be redundant to specify **EXTRINSIC(HPF)**, though it might be redundant to specify **EXTRINSIC(F90)**. The C++ language already adds a *linkage-specification* feature to the C **extern** declaration; the result is quite similar to (and predates) the HPF **EXTRINSIC** syntax. It would be quite plausible for a declaration such as

```
extern "HPF" crunch_numbers(HPF_matrix<float> a);
```

to appear in a C++ program.)

Note that any particular HPF implementation is free to support any selection of extrinsic kind keywords, or none at all except for **HPF** itself. (While HPF defines the meaning of the *extrinsic-kind* keyword **HPF_LOCAL**, a conforming implementation is not required to support it.)

A subprogram with an extrinsic interface lies outside the scope of HPF. However, explicit interfaces to such subprograms must conform to HPF in all respects. HPF data mapping directives may appear in interface blocks for extrinsic procedures even though such extrinsic procedures might not be written in HPF; the point is that the caller, which *is* written in HPF, may be bound to observe and enforce such mapping directives.

Example 8.1 An interface for an ordinary function:

```
       INTERFACE
         EXTRINSIC(HPF_LOCAL) FUNCTION BAGEL(X)
           REAL X(:)
           REAL BAGEL(100)
!HPF$      DISTRIBUTE (CYCLIC) :: X, BAGEL
         END FUNCTION BAGEL
       END INTERFACE
```

Function `BAGEL` is declared to use the interface appropriate for local procedures coded in HPF. The caller should ensure that the actual argument has been mapped to a `CYCLIC` distribution. The returned result will be of size 100 and also have a `CYCLIC` distribution.
□

Example 8.2 An interface for an operator:

```
       INTERFACE OPERATOR (+)
         EXTRINSIC(C_LOCAL) FUNCTION LATKES(X, Y)    RESULT(Z)
           REAL, DIMENSION(:,:) :: X
           REAL, DIMENSION(SIZE(X,1), SIZE(X,2)) :: Y, Z
!HPF$      ALIGN WITH X :: Y, Z
!HPF$      DISTRIBUTE (BLOCK, BLOCK) X
         END FUNCTION LATKES
       END INTERFACE
```

The addition operator on real matrices is redefined to use a local SPMD procedure, coded in C, whose name is `LATKES`. The arguments must have the same shape. This local procedure expects its arguments to be aligned with a `BLOCK,BLOCK` distribution; the result will be mapped in the same way and will have the same shape as the arguments.
□

Example 8.3 An interface for a generic function:

```
       INTERFACE KNISH

         FUNCTION RKNISH(X)                           !normal HPF interface
```

```
            REAL X(:), RKNISH
        END FUNCTION RKNISH

        EXTRINSIC(SISAL) FUNCTION CKNISH(X)           !extrinsic interface
            COMPLEX X(:), CKNISH
        END FUNCTION CKNISH

    END INTERFACE
```

A generic procedure named **KNISH** is declared with two instantiations. The implementation for a **REAL** argument is an ordinary HPF procedure, but the implementation for a **COMPLEX** argument is an extrinsic routine, presumably coded in SISAL. □

Overall, the intent is that a call to an extrinsic subprogram should behave, as observed by a calling program coded in HPF, exactly as if the subprogram had been coded in HPF. This is an obligation placed on the implementation of the interface and perhaps on the programmer when coding an extrinsic routine. However, it is also desirable to grant a certain freedom of implementation strategy so long as the obligation is satisfied. To this end an implementation may place certain restrictions on the programmer; moreover, each *extrinsic-kind-keyword* may call for a different set of restrictions. For example, an implementation on a parallel processor may find it convenient to replicate scalar arguments so as to provide a copy on every processor. This is permitted so long as this process is invisible to the caller. One way to achieve this is to place a restriction on the programmer who codes the called procedure: on return from the subprogram, all the copies of this scalar argument must have the same value. This implies that if the dummy argument has **INTENT(OUT)** or **INTENT(INOUT)**, then all copies must have been updated consistently by the time of subprogram return.

8.1.2 Requirements on the Called Extrinsic Procedure

HPF requires a called extrinsic procedure to satisfy the following behavioral requirements:

1. The overall implementation must behave as if all actions of the caller preceding the subprogram invocation are completed before any action of the subprogram is executed; and as if all actions of the subprogram are completed before any action of the caller following the subprogram invocation is executed.
2. **IN/OUT** intent restrictions declared in the interface for the extrinsic subroutine must be obeyed.
3. Replicated variables, if updated, must be updated consistently. More precisely, if a variable accessible to a local subprogram has a replicated representation and is updated

by (one or more copies of) the local subroutine, then all copies of the replicated data must have identical values when the last processor returns from the local procedure.

4. No HPF variable is modified unless it could be modified by an HPF procedure with the same explicit interface.

5. When a subprogram returns and the caller resumes execution, all objects accessible to the caller after the call are mapped exactly as they were before the call. (Note that, as with a non-extrinsic (that is, ordinary HPF) subprogram, actual arguments may be copied or remapped in any way, so long as the effect is undone on return from the subprogram.)

6. Exactly the same set of processors is visible to the HPF environment before and after the subprogram call.

The call to an extrinsic procedure that fulfills these rules is semantically equivalent to the execution of an ordinary HPF procedure.

8.2 Coding Local Procedures

The remainder of this chapter defines a mechanism for coding single-processor local "per-node" code in single-processor Fortran 90 or in a single-processor subset of HPF; the idea is that only data that is mapped to a given physical processor is accessible to that processor. This allows the programming of MIMD multiprocessor machines in a single-program multiple-data (SPMD) style. Implementation-specific libraries may be provided to facilitate communication between the physical processors that are independently executing this code, but the specification of such libraries is outside the scope of HPF and outside the scope of this book.

From the caller's standpoint, an invocation of an extrinsic procedure from a "global" HPF program has the same semantics as an invocation of a regular procedure. The callee may see a different picture. This chapter describes a particular set of conventions for coding callees in the "local" style in which a copy of the subprogram executes on each processor (of which there may be one or many).

An extrinsic procedure can be defined as explicit SPMD code by specifying the local procedure code that is to execute on each processor. HPF provides a mechanism for defining local procedures in a subset of HPF that excludes only data mapping directives, which are not relevant to local code. If a subprogram definition or interface uses the *extrinsic-kind-keyword* **HPF_LOCAL**, then an HPF compiler should assume that the subprogram is coded as a local procedure. Because local procedures written in HPF are thus syntactically distinguished, they may be intermixed unambiguously with global HPF code if the implementor of an HPF language processor chooses to support such intermixing. (Thus global and local HPF code might reside together within a single source file, for example. An alternate implementation strategy might require the two kinds of code to reside in separate files and to be compiled separately. Such implementation and programming environment details are not specified by HPF.)

The following sections cover three distinct topics:

1. The contract between the caller and a callee that is a local procedure.

2. A specific version of this interface for the case where the callee is a local procedure coded in HPF (*extrinsic-kind-keyword* HPF_LOCAL). Such local procedures may be compiled separately or included as part of the text of a global HPF program.

3. A specific version of this interface for the case where extrinsic procedures are defined as explicit SPMD code with each local procedure coded in Fortran 90 (the *extrinsic-kind-keyword* might be, for instance, F90_LOCAL). Ideally these local procedures may be separately compiled by a Fortran 90 compiler and then linked with HPF code, though this depends on implementation details.

8.3 Conventions for Local Subprograms

All HPF arrays accessible to an extrinsic procedure (arrays passed as arguments) are logically carved up into pieces; the local procedure executing on a particular physical processor sees an array containing just those elements of the global array that are mapped to that physical processor.

It is important not to confuse the extrinsic procedure, which is conceptually a single procedural entity called from the HPF program, with the local procedures, which are executed on each node, one apiece. An *invocation* of an extrinsic procedure results in a separate invocation of a local procedure on each processor. The *execution* of an extrinsic procedure consists of the concurrent execution of a local procedure on each executing processor. Each local procedure invocation may terminate at any time by executing a RETURN statement. However, the extrinsic procedure as a whole terminates only after every local procedure has terminated; in effect, the processors are synchronized before return to a global HPF caller.

With the exception of returning from a local procedure to the global caller that initiated local execution, there is no implicit synchronization of the locally executing processors. A local procedure may use any control structure whatsoever. To access data outside the processor requires either preparatory communication to copy data into the processor before running the local code, or communication among the separately executing copies of the local procedure. Individual implementations may provide implementation-dependent means for communicating, for example through a message-passing library or a shared-memory mechanism. Such communication mechanisms are beyond the scope of HPF and of this book. Note, however, that many useful portable algorithms that require only independence of control structure can take advantage of local routines, without requiring a communication facility.

This model assumes only that array axes are mapped independently to axes of a rectangular processor grid, each array axis to at most one processor axis (no "skew" distributions) and no two array axes to the same processor axis. This restriction suffices to ensure that each physical processor contains a subset of array elements that can be locally arranged in a rectangular configuration. (To compute the global indices of an element given its local indices, or vice versa, may be quite a tangled computation—but it will be possible. See Section 8.4.3 for a description of recommended library routines for performing these index transformations.)

It is recommended that if, in any given implementation, an interface kind does not obey the conventions described in this section, then the name of that interface kind should not end in "_LOCAL".

8.3.1 Conventions for Calling Local Subprograms

The default mapping of scalar dummy arguments and of scalar function results is such that the argument is replicated on each physical processor. These mappings may, optionally, be explicit in the interface, but any other explicit mapping of a scalar dummy argument or of a scalar function result is not HPF-conforming.

As in the case of non-extrinsic subprograms, actual arguments may be mapped in any way; if necessary, they are copied automatically to correctly mapped temporaries before invocation of and after return from the extrinsic procedure.

8.3.2 Calling Sequence

The actions detailed below have to occur prior to the invocation of the local procedure on each processor. These actions are enforced by the compiler of the calling routine, and are not the responsibility of the programmer, nor do they impact the local procedure. (The next section discusses restrictions on the local procedure.)

1. The processors are synchronized. In other words, all actions that logically precede the call are completed.
2. Each actual argument is remapped, if necessary, according to the directives (explicit or implicit) in the declared interface for the extrinsic procedure. Thus, HPF mapping directives appearing in the interface are binding—the compiler must obey these directives in calling local extrinsic procedures. (The reason for this rule is that data mapping is explicitly visible in local routines). Actual arguments corresponding to scalar dummy

arguments are replicated (by broadcasting, for example) in all processors.

3. If a variable accessible to the called routine has a replicated representation, then all copies are updated prior to the call to contain the correct current value according to the sequential semantics of the source program.

After these actions have occurred, the local procedure is invoked on each processor. The information available to the local invocation is described below in Section 8.3.3.

The following actions must occur before control is transferred back to the caller.

1. All processors are synchronized after the call. In other words, execution of every copy of the local routine is completed before execution in the caller is resumed.

2. The original distribution of arguments (and of the result of an extrinsic function) is restored, if necessary.

An implementation might check, before returning from the local subprogram, to make sure that replicated variables have been updated consistently by the subprogram. However, there is certainly no requirement—perhaps not even any encouragement—to do so. This is merely a tradeoff between speed and, for instance, debuggability.

8.3.3 Information Available to the Local Procedure

The local procedure invoked on each processor is passed a *local argument* for each *global argument* passed by the caller to the (global) extrinsic procedure interface. Each global argument is a distributed HPF array or a replicated scalar. The corresponding local argument is the part of the global array stored locally, or the local copy of a scalar argument. An array actual argument passed by an HPF caller is called a *global array*; the subgrid of that global array passed to one copy of a local routine (because it resides in that processor) is called a *local array*.

If the extrinsic procedure is a function, then the local procedure is also a function. Each local invocation of that function will return the local part of the extrinsic function return value. If the extrinsic function is scalar-valued then the implicit mapping of the return value is replicated; in this case, all executed copies of the local function must return the same value. If it is desired to return one, possibly distinct, value per processor, then the extrinsic function should be declared to return a distributed rank-one array of size NUMBER_OF_PROCESSORS().

The run-time interface should provide enough information that each local function can discover for each local argument the mapping of the corresponding global argument, translate global indices to local indices, and vice-versa. A specific set of procedures that provide this information is described in Section 8.4.3. The manner in which this information is made available to the local routine depends on the implementation and the programming language used for the local routine.

8.4 Local Routines Written in HPF

This section provides a specific design for providing the required information to local procedures in the case these procedures are written in HPF. (This design is merely a recommendation; a conforming HPF implementation is not required to support it.)

A local procedure may be declared within an HPF program (and be compiled by an HPF compiler). The *subroutine-stmt* or *function-stmt* that begins the subprogram must contain the prefix **EXTRINSIC(HPF_LOCAL)**.

8.4.1 Restrictions

There are some restrictions on what HPF features may be used in writing a local, per-processor procedure. These restrictions are detailed here.

> (Look out! Here comes a pun!) The restricted language used for coding local HPF procedures is sometimes called "HPF Lite" because it is lo-cal.

A local HPF program unit may invoke other local program units or internal procedures, but it may not invoke an ordinary, "global" HPF routine. If a global HPF program calls local subprogram **A** with an actual array argument **X**, and **A** receives a portion of array **X** as dummy argument **P**, then **A** may call another local subprogram **B** and pass **P** or a section of **P** as an actual argument to **B**.

A local HPF program unit may not access global HPF data other than data that is accessible, either directly or indirectly, via the actual arguments. In particular, a local HPF program unit does not have access to global HPF **COMMON** blocks; **COMMON** blocks appearing in local HPF program units are not identified with global HPF **COMMON** blocks. The same name may not be used to identify a **COMMON** block within both a local HPF program unit and an HPF program unit in the same executable program.

Local program units can use all HPF constructs except for **DISTRIBUTE**, **REDISTRIBUTE**, **ALIGN**, **REALIGN**, **DYNAMIC**, **INHERIT**, **PROCESSORS**, and **TEMPLATE** directives (and attributes). The distribution query library subroutines **HPF_ALIGNMENT**, **HPF_TEMPLATE**, and **HPF_DISTRIBUTION** may be applied to local arrays. Their outcome is the same as for a global array that happens to have all its elements on a single node.

Scalar dummy arguments must be mapped so that each processor has a copy of the argument. This holds true, by convention, if no mapping is specified for the argument in the interface. Thus, the constraint disallows only explicit alignment and distribution directives in an explicit interface that imply that a scalar dummy argument is not replicated on all processors.

An EXTRINSIC(HPF_LOCAL) routine may not be RECURSIVE.

An EXTRINSIC(HPF_LOCAL) routine may not have alternate returns.

An EXTRINSIC(HPF_LOCAL) routine may not be invoked, either directly or indirectly, in the body of a FORALL construct or in the body of an INDEPENDENT loop.

The attributes (type, kind, rank, optional, intent) of the dummy arguments must match the attributes of the corresponding dummy arguments in the explicit interface. A dummy argument of an EXTRINSIC(HPF_LOCAL) routine may not be a procedure name.

A dummy argument of an EXTRINSIC(HPF_LOCAL) routine may not have the POINTER attribute.

A dummy argument of an EXTRINSIC(HPF_LOCAL) routine must be nonsequential.

A dummy array argument of an EXTRINSIC(HPF_LOCAL) routine must have assumed shape, even when it is explicit shape in the interface. Note that, in general, the shape of a dummy array argument differs from the shape of the corresponding actual argument, unless there is a single executing processor.

Explicit mapping directives for dummy arguments and function result variables may not appear in a local procedure, although they may appear (in the case of the result of an array-valued function, they must appear) in the required explicit interface accessible to the caller.

A local procedure may have several ENTRY points. A global HPF caller must contain a separate extrinsic interface for each entry point that can be invoked from the HPF program.

8.4.2 Argument Association

If a dummy argument of an EXTRINSIC(HPF_LOCAL) routine is an array, then the corresponding dummy argument in the explicit interface for the local procedure must be an array of the same rank, type, and type parameters. When the extrinsic procedure is invoked, the local dummy argument is associated with the local array that consists of the subgrid of the global array that is stored locally. This local array will be a valid HPF array.

If a dummy argument of an EXTRINSIC(HPF_LOCAL) routine is a scalar then the corresponding dummy argument of the local procedure must be a scalar of the same type. When the extrinsic procedure is invoked then the local procedure is passed an argument that consists of the local copy of the replicated scalar. This copy will be a valid HPF scalar.

If an EXTRINSIC(HPF_LOCAL) routine is a function, then the local procedure is a function that returns a scalar of the same type and type parameters, or an array of the same rank, type, and type parameters, as the HPF extrinsic function. The value returned by each local invocation is the local part of the value returned by the HPF invocation.

Each physical processor has at most one copy of each HPF variable.
Consider the following extrinsic interface:

```
      INTERFACE
        EXTRINSIC(HPF_LOCAL) FUNCTION MATZOH(X, Y) RESULT(Z)
          REAL, DIMENSION(:,:) :: X
          REAL, DIMENSION(SIZE(X,1)) :: Y, Z
!HPF$     ALIGN WITH X(:,*) :: Y(:), Z(:)
!HPF$     DISTRIBUTE X(BLOCK, CYCLIC)
        END FUNCTION
      END INTERFACE
```

The corresponding local HPF procedure is specified as follows.

```
      EXTRINSIC(HPF_LOCAL) FUNCTION MATZOH(XX, YY) RESULT(ZZ)
        REAL, DIMENSION(:,:) :: XX
        REAL, DIMENSION(5:)  :: YY, ZZ
        NX1 = SIZE(XX, 1)
        LX1 = LBOUND(XX, 1)
        UX1 = UBOUND(XX, 1)
        NX2 = SIZE(XX, 2)
        LX2 = LBOUND(XX, 2)
        UX2 = UBOUND(XX, 2)
        NY  = SIZE(YY, 1)
        LY  = LBOUND(YY, 1)
        UY  = UBOUND(YY, 1)
        ...
      END FUNCTION
```

Assume that the function is invoked with an actual (global) array X of shape 3×3 and an actual vector Y of length 3 on a 4-processor machine, using a 2×2 processor arrangement (assuming one abstract processor per physical processor).

Then the various local invocations of the function MATZOH receive actual arguments as shown here:

Extrinsic Procedures

Processor (1,1)

X(1,1)	X(1,3)
X(2,1)	X(2,3)

Y(1)
Y(2)

Processor (1,2)

X(1,2)
X(2,2)

Y(1)
Y(2)

Processor (2,1)

X(3,1)	X(3,3)

Y(3)

Processor (2,2)

X(3,2)

Y(3)

Each local invocation of **MATZOH** sees its own set of dummy arguments as shown here:

Processor (1,1)

XX(1,1)	XX(1,2)
XX(2,1)	XX(2,2)

YY(5)
YY(6)

Processor (1,2)

XX(1,1)
XX(2,1)

YY(5)
YY(6)

Processor (2,1)

XX(1,1)	XX(1,2)

YY(5)

Processor (2,2)

XX(1,1)

YY(5)

Thus when processor (1,1) refers to its dummy argument element XX(1,2), it sees the value of actual argument element X(1,3). But when processor (2,1) refers to *its* dummy argument element XX(1,2), it sees the value of actual argument element X(3,3).

Here are the values to which each processor would set NX1, LX1, UX1, NX2, LX2, UX2, NY, LY, and UY:

Processor (1,1)

NX1 = 2 LX1 = 1 UX1 = 2
NX2 = 2 LX2 = 1 UX2 = 2
NY = 2   LY = 5   UY = 6

Processor (1,2)

NX1 = 2 LX1 = 1 UX1 = 2
NX2 = 1 LX2 = 1 UX2 = 1
NY = 2   LY = 5   UY = 6

Processor (2,1)

NX1 = 1 LX1 = 1 UX1 = 1
NX2 = 2 LX2 = 1 UX2 = 2
NY = 1   LY = 5   UY = 5

Processor (2,2)

NX1 = 1 LX1 = 1 UX1 = 1
NX2 = 1 LX2 = 1 UX2 = 1
NY = 1   LY = 5   UY = 5

The return array `ZZ` is distributed identically to `YY` and therefore has a partially replicated representation. Processors (1,1) and (1,2) should return identical rank-one arrays of size 2; processors (2,1) and (2,2) should return identical rank-one arrays of size 1.

An actual argument to an extrinsic procedure may be a pointer. Since the corresponding dummy argument may not have the `POINTER` attribute, the dummy argument becomes associated with the target of the HPF global pointer. In no way may a local pointer become pointer associated with a global HPF target. Therefore, an actual argument may not be of a derived type containing a pointer component. (It is expected that global pointer variables will have a different representation from that of local pointer variables, at least on distributed memory machines, because of the need to carry additional information for global addressing. This restriction could be lifted in the future.)

Other inquiry intrinsics, such as `ALLOCATED` or `PRESENT`, should also behave as expected. Note that when a global array is passed to a local routine, some processors may receive an empty subarray. Such argument is `PRESENT` and has `SIZE` zero.

8.4.3 HPF Local Routine Library

Local HPF procedures can use any HPF intrinsic or library procedure. (The arguments to such procedures will be local arrays. Depending on the implementation, the actual code for the intrinsic and library routines used by local HPF procedures may or may not be the same code used when called from global HPF code.)

In addition, several local library procedures are provided to query the global mapping of an actual argument to an extrinsic function. These library procedures take as input the name of a dummy argument and return information on the corresponding global HPF actual argument. They may be invoked only by a local procedure that was directly invoked by global HPF code. If module facilities are available, they reside in a module called `HPF_LOCAL_LIBRARY`; a local routine that calls them should include the statement

```
USE HPF_LOCAL_LIBRARY
```

or some functionally appropriate variant thereof.

The local HPF library also provides a new derived type `PROCID`, to be used for processor identifiers. Each physical processor has a distinct identifier of type `PROCID`. It is assumed that a function is available to find the identifier of each executing processor—the syntax for calling such a function is beyond the scope of HPF and of this book. (It is likely that in many implementations type `PROCID` will be effectively identical to type `INTEGER`—perhaps a derived type with a single integer component.)

GLOBAL_ALIGNMENT(ARRAY, ...) This has the same interface and behavior as the HPF inquiry subroutine `HPF_ALIGNMENT`, but it returns information about the *global* HPF array actual argument associated with the local dummy argument **ARRAY**, rather than returning information about the local array.

GLOBAL_DISTRIBUTION(ARRAY, ...)   This has the same interface and behavior as the HPF inquiry subroutine **HPF_DISTRIBUTION**, but it returns information about the *global* HPF array actual argument associated with the local dummy argument **ARRAY**, rather than returning information about the local array.

GLOBAL_TEMPLATE(ARRAY, ...)   This has the same interface and behavior as the HPF inquiry subroutine **HPF_TEMPLATE**, but it returns information about the *global* HPF array actual argument associated with the local dummy argument **ARRAY**, rather than returning information about the local array.

ABSTRACT_TO_PHYSICAL(ARRAY, INDEX, PROC)

Description. Returns processor identification for the physical processor associated with a specified abstract processor relative to a global actual argument array.

Class. Subroutine.

Arguments.

ARRAY   may be of any type; it must be a dummy array that is associated with a global HPF array actual argument. It is an **INTENT(IN)** argument.

INDEX   must be a rank-1 integer array containing the coordinates of an abstract processor in the processors arrangement onto which the global HPF array is mapped. It is an **INTENT(IN)** argument. The size of **INDEX** must equal the rank of the processors arrangement.

PROC   must be scalar and must be of type **PROCID**. It is an **INTENT(OUT)** argument. It receives the identifying value for the physical processor associated with the abstract processor specified by **INDEX**.

PHYSICAL_TO_ABSTRACT(ARRAY, PROC, INDEX)

Description. Returns coordinates for an abstract processor, relative to a global actual argument array, corresponding to a specified physical processor.

Class. Subroutine.

Arguments.

ARRAY may be of any type; it must be a dummy array that is associated with a global HPF array actual argument. It is an INTENT(IN) argument.

PROC must be scalar and must be of type PROCID. It is an INTENT(IN) argument. It contains an identifying value for a physical processor.

INDEX must be a rank-1 integer array. It is an INTENT(OUT) argument. The size of INDEX must equal the rank of the processor arrangement onto which the global HPF array is mapped. INDEX receives the coordinates within this processors arrangement of the abstract processor associated with the physical processor specified by PROC.

This procedure can be used only on systems where there is a one-to-one correspondence between abstract processors and physical processors. On systems where this correspondence is one-to-many an equivalent, system-dependent procedure should be provided.

LOCAL_TO_GLOBAL(ARRAY, L_INDEX, G_INDEX)

Description. Converts a set of local coordinates within a local dummy array to an equivalent set of global coordinates within the associated global HPF actual argument array.

Class. Subroutine.

Arguments.

ARRAY may be of any type; it must be a dummy array that is associated with a global HPF array actual argument. It is an INTENT(IN) argument.

L_INDEX must be a rank-1 integer array whose size is equal to the rank of ARRAY. It is an INTENT(IN) argument. It contains the coordinates of an element within the local dummy array ARRAY.

G_INDEX must be a rank-1 integer array whose size is equal to the rank of ARRAY. It is an INTENT(OUT) argument. It receives the coordinates within the global HPF array actual argument of the element identified within the local array by L_INDEX.

GLOBAL_TO_LOCAL(ARRAY, G_INDEX, L_INDEX, LOCAL)

Optional arguments. L_INDEX, LOCAL

Description. Converts a set of global coordinates within a global HPF actual argument array to an equivalent set of local coordinates within the associated local dummy array.

Class. Subroutine.

Arguments.

ARRAY   may be of any type; it must be a dummy array that is associated with a global HPF array actual argument. It is an INTENT(IN) argument.

G_INDEX   must be a rank-1 integer array whose size is equal to the rank of ARRAY. It is an INTENT(IN) argument. It contains the coordinates of an element within the global HPF array actual argument associated with the local dummy array ARRAY.

L_INDEX   (optional) must be a rank-1 integer array whose size is equal to the rank of ARRAY. It is an INTENT(OUT) argument. It receives the coordinates within the local dummy array of the element identified within the global actual argument array by G_INDEX. However, the values in L_INDEX are undefined if the value returned (or that would be returned) in LOCAL is false.

LOCAL   (optional) must be scalar and must be of type LOGICAL. It is an INTENT(OUT) argument. It is set to .TRUE. if the local array contains a copy of the global array element and to .FALSE. otherwise.

8.5 Local Routines Written in Fortran 90

The suggested interface to local SPMD routines written in Fortran 90 is the same as that for HPF local routines, with these few exceptions:

• Only Fortran 90 constructs should be used; it may not be possible to use extensions peculiar to HPF such as FORALL and the HPF intrinsic library procedures.

• It is recommended that Fortran 90 language processors to be used for this purpose be extended to support the HPF local distribution query routines GLOBAL_ALIGNMENT, GLOBAL_TEMPLATE, and GLOBAL_DISTRIBUTION and the PROCID derived type as described in Section 8.4.3. It is also recommended that these facilities be defined in a Fortran 90 module named HPF_LOCAL_LIBRARY.

• Assuming that the intent is to compile such routines with a non-HPF Fortran 90 compiler, the Fortran 90 program text should be in separate files rather than incorporated into HPF source code.

• The suggested *extrinsic-kind-keyword* for this calling interface is F90_LOCAL.

The restrictions listed in Section 8.4.1 ought to apply as well to local routines written in Fortran 90.

The local HPF code example in Figure 8.1 could also serve as an example of local Fortran 90 code simply by changing the keyword **HPF_LOCAL** in the first line to **F90_LOCAL**.

8.5.1 Argument Association

If a dummy argument in the HPF explicit extrinsic interface is an array, then the corresponding dummy argument in the specification of the local procedure must be an array of the same rank, type, and type parameters. When the extrinsic procedure is invoked, the local dummy argument is associated with the local array that consists of the subgrid of the global array that is stored locally. This local array will be a valid Fortran 90 array.

If a dummy argument in the HPF explicit extrinsic interface is a scalar then the corresponding dummy argument of the local procedure must be a scalar of the same type. When the extrinsic procedure is invoked then the local procedure is passed an argument that consists of the local copy of the replicated scalar. This copy will be a valid Fortran 90 scalar.

If an HPF explicit extrinsic interface defines a function, then the local procedure should be a Fortran 90 function that returns a scalar of the same type and type parameters, or an array of the same rank, type, and type parameters, as the HPF extrinsic function. The value returned by each local invocation is the local part of the value returned by the HPF invocation.

8.6 Example HPF Extrinsic Procedures

Figure 8.3 shows an **INTERFACE** block, call, and subroutine definition for matrix multiplication coded as a local subroutine.

Figure 8.4 shows an **INTERFACE** block, call, and subroutine definition for sum reduction coded as a local function.

```
! The caller:
!     The NEWMATMULT routine computes C=A*B. Before calling NEWMATMULT,
!     the ALIGN directives require broadcasting copies of row A(I,*)
!     and column B(*,J) to the processor that computes C(I,J).
      INTERFACE
         EXTRINSIC(HPF_LOCAL) SUBROUTINE NEWMATMULT(A, B, C)
            REAL, DIMENSION(:,:), INTENT(IN)  ::  A, B
            REAL, DIMENSION(:,:), INTENT(OUT) ::  C
!HPF$       ALIGN A(I,J) WITH *C(I,*)
!HPF$       ALIGN B(I,J) WITH *C(*,J)
         END SUBROUTINE NEWMATMULT
      END INTERFACE
      REAL P(100,93), Q(93,47), R(100,47)
      ...
      CALL NEWMATMULT(P,Q,R)
      ...
! The local subroutine definition:
!     Each processor is passed 3 arrays of rank 2. Assume that the
!     global HPF arrays A, B, and C have dimensions LxM, MxN and LxN,
!     respectively. The local array CC is (a copy of) a rectangular
!     subarray of C. For each position (I,J) in this local array,
!     the local array AA contains an entire row of A as AA(I,:) and
!     the local array BB contains an entire column of B as BB(:,J).
!     C may have a replicated representation, in which case copies
!     of C(I,J) will be consistently updated at various processors.
      EXTRINSIC(HPF_LOCAL) SUBROUTINE NEWMATMULT(AA, BB, CC)
      REAL, DIMENSION(:,:), INTENT(IN)  ::  AA, BB
      REAL, DIMENSION(:,:), INTENT(OUT) ::  CC
!     The loops use local indices into AA, BB, and CC.
      DO I = LBOUND(CC,1), UBOUND(CC,1)
        DO J = LBOUND(CC,2), UBOUND(CC,2)
           CC(I,J) = DOT_PRODUCT(AA(I,:), BB(:,J))
        END DO
      END DO
      END SUBROUTINE NEWMATMULT
```

Figure 8.3
Matrix multiplication coded as a local HPF subroutine

```
!       The SREDUCE routine computes at each processor the sum of
!       the local elements of an array of rank 1. It returns an
!       array that consists of one sum per processor. The sum
!       reduction is completed by reducing this array of partial sums.
!       The function calls an error routine if the array is replicated.
!       (Replicated arrays could be handled by a more complicated code.)

        INTERFACE
          EXTRINSIC(HPF_LOCAL) FUNCTION SREDUCE(A) RESULT(R)
            REAL, DIMENSION(NUMBER_OF_PROCESSORS()) :: R
!HPF$       DISTRIBUTE (BLOCK) :: R
            REAL, DIMENSION(:), INTENT(IN) :: A
          END FUNCTION SREDUCE
        END INTERFACE
        ...
        TOTAL = SUM(SREDUCE(A))
        ...


! The local subroutine definition
        EXTRINSIC(HPF_LOCAL) FUNCTION SREDUCE(AA) RESULT R
        REAL, DIMENSION(:) :: R
        REAL, DIMENSION(:), INTENT(IN) :: AA

        CALL GLOBAL_ALIGNMENT(AA, NUMBER_N= N)
        IF (COPIES > 1) THEN
          CALL ERROR       ! Array is replicated--call error routine
        ELSE
          R = 0            ! Array is not replicated--compute local sum
          DO J = 1, UBOUND(AA)
            R(1) = R(1) + A(J)
          END DO
        END IF
        END SUBROUTINE SREDUCE
```

Figure 8.4
Sum reduction coded as a local HPF function

9 Subset High Performance Fortran

This subset of HPF is intended to define a minimal starting set of features from Fortran 90 and HPF. We will give the list of the HPF extensions that are in Subset HPF, followed by the definition of the Fortran 90 subset. The purpose of a subset is to encourage early release of compilers with HPF features. Actual HPF Subset implementations may include more features than are listed here. The programmer should check the specific details of each Subset compiler used.

9.1 HPF Extensions and Subset High Performance Fortran

The HPF extensions have been divided into two parts, those in Subset HPF, and those not in Subset HPF. This division was primarily done on the basis of expected implementation difficulty.

9.1.1 HPF Features in the Subset

The static data mapping features of HPF are in the subset. These include: the directives for **ALIGN, DISTRIBUTE, TEMPLATE,** and **PROCESSORS**, as well as the *combined-directive*.

The **INHERIT** directive is part of the subset, but only the descriptive and prescriptive forms. That is, the programmer must specify what the distribution to be inherited is, either by asserting its form or by instructing the compiler to convert to a specific distribution.

The single-statement **FORALL** is part of the subset. The **INDEPENDENT** directive as applied both to **DO** and **FORALL** is also part of the subset.

The three new HPF intrinsic functions are part of the subset: **NUMBER_OF_PROCESSORS, PROCESSORS_SHAPE** and **ILEN**.

9.1.2 HPF Features Not in the Subset

For completeness, we also list the HPF extensions that are not required as part of Subset HPF.

The dynamic mapping features are not part of the subset. These include the **REALIGN, REDISTRIBUTE,** and **DYNAMIC** directives.

The transcriptive ("lone star") form of the **DISTRIBUTE** directive and **INHERIT** directive is not part of the subset.

The **PURE** function attribute is not part of the subset. This means that only HPF and Fortran 90 intrinsic functions can be called from the **FORALL** statement. No other subprograms can be called.

The *forall-construct* (multi-statement) `FORALL` is not in the subset.

The HPF library and the `HPF_LIBRARY` module are not part of the subset.

The `EXTRINSIC` function attribute is not in the subset. By implication, this means that the optional `HPF_LOCAL` interface is not part of the subset.

9.2 Fortran 90 and Subset High Performance Fortran

The set of Fortran 90 features selected for Subset HPF is most definitely not an ideal subset of the language. Features were selected either because they were already in common use or because they contributed to the performance-oriented goal of HPF. There are numerous useful and popular features omitted from this subset.

9.2.1 Fortran 90 Features in the Subset

The Fortran 90 features listed here are the features of Subset HPF For reference, the section numbers from the Fortran 90 standard are given along with the related syntax rule numbers:

- All FORTRAN 77 standard conforming features, except for storage and sequence association. (See Sections 4.10 and 5.9 for detailed discussion of the exception.)
- The Fortran 90 definitions of MIL-STD-1753 features:

  - `DO WHILE` statement (8.1.4.1.1 / R821)
  - `END DO` statement (8.1.4.1.1 / R825)
  - `IMPLICIT NONE` statement (5.3 / R540)
  - `INCLUDE` line (3.4)
  - Scalar bit manipulation intrinsic procedures: `IOR`, `IAND`, `NOT`, `IEOR`, `ISHFT`, `ISHFTC`, `BTEST`, `IBSET`, `IBCLR`, `IBITS`, `MVBITS` (13.13)
  - Binary, octal and hexadecimal constants for use in `DATA` statements (4.3.1.1 / R407 and 5.2.9 / R533)

- Arithmetic and logical array features:

  - Array sections (6.2.2.3 / R618–621) using subscript triplet notation (6.2.2.3.1) and vector-valued subscripts (6.2.2.3.2)
  - Array constructors limited to one level of implied `DO` (4.5 / R431)
  - Arithmetic and logical operations on whole arrays and array sections (2.4.3, 2.4.5, and 7.1)
  - Array assignment (2.4.5, 7.5, 7.5.1.4, and 7.5.1.5)

Subset High Performance Fortran

- Masked array assignment (7.5.3) using the WHERE statement (7.5.3 / R738) and the block WHERE ... ELSEWHERE construct (7.5.3 / R739)
- Array-valued external functions (12.5.2.2)
- Automatic arrays (5.1.2.4.1)
- ALLOCATABLE arrays and the ALLOCATE and DEALLOCATE statements (5.1.2.4.3, 6.3.1 / R622, and 6.3.3 / R631)
- Assumed-shape arrays (5.1.2.4.2 / R516)

- Intrinsic procedures: The list of intrinsic functions and subroutines below is a combination of (a) routines that are entirely new to Fortran and (b) routines that have always been part of Fortran, but now have been extended to new argument and result types. The new or extended definitions of these routines are part of the subset. If a FORTRAN 77 routine is not included in this list, then only the original FORTRAN 77 definition is part of the subset.

  - The argument presence inquiry function: PRESENT (13.10.1)
  - All the numeric elemental functions: ABS, AIMAG, AINT, ANINT, CEILING, CMPLX, CONJG, DBLE, DIM, DPROD, FLOOR, INT, MAX, MIN, MOD, MODULO, NINT, REAL, SIGN (13.10.2)
  - All mathematical elemental functions: ACOS, ASIN, ATAN, ATAN2, COS, COSH, EXP, LOG, LOG10, SIN, SINH, SQRT, TAN, TANH (13.10.3)
  - All the bit manipulation elemental functions : BTEST, IAND, IBCLR, IBITS, IBSET, IEOR, IOR, ISHFT, ISHFTC, NOT (13.10.10)
  - All the vector and matrix multiply functions: DOT_PRODUCT, MATMUL (13.10.13)
  - All the array reduction functions: ALL†, ANY†, COUNT†, MAXVAL†, MINVAL†, PRODUCT†, SUM†(13.10.14)
  - All the array inquiry functions: ALLOCATED, LBOUND†, SHAPE, SIZE†, UBOUND†(13.10.15)
  - All the array construction functions: MERGE, PACK, SPREAD†, UNPACK (13.10.16)
  - The array reshape function: RESHAPE (13.10.17)
  - All the array manipulation functions: CSHIFT†, EOSHIFT†, TRANSPOSE (13.10.18)
  - All array location functions: MAXLOC†, MINLOC†(13.10.19)
  - All the intrinsic subroutines: DATEANDTIME, MVBITS, RANDOMNUMBER, RANDOMSEED, SYSTEMCLOCK (3.11)

For all of the intrinsics that have an optional argument DIM, only actual argument expressions for DIM that are initialization expressions are part of the subset. The intrinsics with this constraint are marked with a dagger (†) in the list above.

- Declarations:

- Type declaration statements, with all forms of *type-spec* except *kind-selector* and TYPE(*type-name*), and all forms of *attr-spec* except *access-spec*, TARGET, and POINTER. (5.1 / R501-503, R510)
- Attribute specification statements: ALLOCATABLE, INTENT, OPTIONAL, PARAMETER, SAVE (5.2)

- Procedure features: Interface blocks are included in the subset in order to facilitate use of the HPF directives across subroutine boundaries. Interface blocks provide a mechanism to specify the expected mapping of data, in addition to the types and intents of the arguments.

  - INTERFACE blocks with no *generic-spec* or *module-procedure-stmt* (12.3.2.1)
  - Optional arguments (5.2.2)
  - Keyword argument passing (12.4.1 /R1212)

- Syntax improvements:

  - Long (31 character) names (3.2.2)
  - Lower case letters (3.1.7)
  - Use of "_" in names (3.1.3)
  - "!" initiated comments, both full line and trailing (3.3.2.1)

9.2.2 Fortran 90 Features Not in the Subset

We will not attempt a precise list of the Fortran 90 features not included in the subset, but for the reader's aid, we do give a short summary of features here. The following are omitted: the free form source; control features such as CASE, CYCLE and EXIT; the numeric precision KIND feature; the character array language, and full form of array constructors; POINTER and TARGET; derived type and operator definitions; generic procedures and internal subprograms; MODULE and USE; extensions to I/O such as additional clauses for OPEN and INQUIRE, NAMELIST formatting, and non-advancing, stream I/O.

A Definition of Terms

abstract processors: A rectilinear arrangement of processors that may be defined by a `PROCESSORS` directive. The mapping of the abstract processors to physical processors is system-dependent.

aggregate cover: A member of an aggregate variable group whose storage is totally associated with the storage sequence of the aggregate variable group. Informally stated, this is a variable that is exactly the same size as the entire aggregate variable group.

aggregate variable group: A collection of variables whose individual storage sequences are parts of a single storage sequence.

align target: A data object name or template name whose distribution serves as a pattern for the distribution of the index space of other data objects.

alignee: A data object that is associated with an align target by an `ALIGN` or `REALIGN` directive, for the purpose of determining the distribution of the index space.

alignment: An attribute of a data object that establishes the relationship between data objects for distribution.

atomic object: A data object that contains no subobjects. These may not be split across processors as a result of distribution. They also define the basic unit of write and read operations for defining independent.

collapsed: A term used to describe a dimension of an array where every element of the dimension is aligned to the same element of another array or template.

communication: The overhead incurred when an operation on one processor uses a data object stored on a different processor.

component: Either a single variable or an aggregate variable group in a common block.

cover: See aggregate cover.

data locality: A term used to describe the likelihood that a processor operation uses data objects stored in its local memory.

data parallel: A description of parallelism potentially obtained when the same operation is applied to many elements of an array or data object. The data parallel model is a single-threaded control structure, global name space, and loosely synchronous parallel execution

descriptive mapping: A method used to establish the mapping attributes of a dummy procedure argument where the attribute of the actual argument is asserted to be of a specified kind and thus requires no data motion.

directive: A special Fortran comment that suggests implementation strategies or asserts facts about a program to the compiler.

distributee: A data object named in a `DISTRIBUTE` directive.

distribution: The partition of the index space of a data object among a set of abstract processors according to a given pattern.

dynamic mapping: A mapping that may change during execution as a result of a `REDISTRIBUTE` or `REALIGN` directive.

explicit interface: A definition of a procedure interface that is visible to the scoping unit of a reference (call) to the procedure, e.g. via an interface block or `MODULE` procedure definition.

explicit mapping: A mapping attribute specified in an `ALIGN`, `DISTRIBUTE`, or `DYNAMIC` directive.

extrinsic procedure: A routine that is not properly part of HPF. It may be written in a different programming paradigm and possibly in a different language.

extrinsic kind keyword: Description of the extrinsic interface. HPF defines `HPF` and `HPF_LOCAL`.

global name space: Programming model where a data object name can be accessed by more than one processor. This is the usual model on shared memory systems, but also supported on distributed memory systems in languages such as HPF.

global variable: A variable accessible from more than one procedure.

HPF conforming: A program that obeys all of the syntax and semantic rules of the HPF language specification.

immediately aligned: Two data objects with an alignment established by a specific `ALIGN` directive.

implicit mapping: A mapping attribute selected by the compiler when no explicit mapping is given.

independent: A property of a `DO` loop or `FORALL` statement where the results are the same whether executed serially or in parallel. This may be established by the compiler or may be asserted by the programmer with an `INDEPENDENT` directive.

inherited template: A template for a dummy argument that is a copy of the template of the corresponding actual argument. Note that the shape and size of this template may differ from the shape and size of the dummy argument.

load balance: Refers to program optimization to give each processor approximately the same amount of work.

local name space: Programming model where a data object name is accessibly only by the local processor.

local variable: A variable that is accessible only within the procedure where it is declared.

local procedure: A procedure from a programming model where each processor is potentially executing different code.

loosely synchronous: Refers to an execution model where the processors are not necessarily processing the exact same instruction (as in the SIMD model), but are forced by periodic synchronization events (such as message communication) to stay in the same general location in the program, possibly on the same line or control structure from the source program.

mapping: The combination of alignment and distribution attributes used to describe how a data object is allocated to an abstract processor arrangement.

mapping inquiry subroutines: Subroutines to allow a program to determine the actual mapping of an array at run time.

MIMD: Stands for Multiple Instruction stream, Multiple Data stream, meaning that the processors can all be executing different instructions at the same time.

natural template: A freshly created template for a dummy argument that is not explicitly aligned and does not have the **INHERIT** attribute. Causes the dummy argument to be ultimately aligned with itself.

node program: See local procedure.

nonconforming: A program that does not obey one or more syntax and semantic rules of the HPF language specification. The results of execution of the program are not defined. The compiler may not detect all instances of a nonconforming program.

nonsequential variable: A variable that does not occur in a context involving storage association and is not named on a **SEQUENCE** directive.

prescriptive mapping: A method used to establish the mapping attributes of a dummy procedure argument where the attribute is explicitly specified and the incoming mapping of the actual argument must be modified to match if it does not already conform.

processor arrangement: See abstract processor arrangement.

pure: An attribute of a procedure that constrains the statements allowed in the procedure so that the procedure cannot have any side effects other than modification of output arguments or the function value.

rank: The number of dimensions of an array. A scalar value has rank zero.

replication: A means of creating copies of a data object on more than one processor by establishing a special alignment of the data object.

sequence association: The element sequence order of array elements that is required when an array, array expression, or array element is associated with a dummy argument in a call to a subprogram.

Definition of Terms

sequential common: A common block that is named in a `SEQUENCE` directive. Required for any common block whose components do not match exactly in shape, type, mapping and sequentiality in every occurrence of the common block.

sequential variable: A variable that is involved in storage association or is named in a `SEQUENCE` directive.

shape: For an array, the rank and extent of each dimension.

SIMD: Stands for Single Instruction stream, Multiple Data stream, meaning that all processors execute exactly the same instruction at the same time (unless they have been turned off).

SPMD: Stands for Single Program, Multiple Data, meaning that all processors are executing the same program.

static mapping: Mapping attributes that stay the same throughout program execution, except for possible remapping across procedure boundaries that are restored to their original state on return from the procedure. Required for all variables in `COMMON`.

storage association: The association of two or more data objects that occurs when two or more storage sequences share or are aligned with one or more storage units.

storage sequence: Contiguous storage units.

stride: An array increment specified in subscript triplet notation.

synchronization: A point in a program where the processor cannot proceed without a result or event from another processor and must wait for it to happen.

system inquiry functions: Functions that return values to describe attributes of the physical computing resource, including the size and shape of the processor array.

template: An index space associated with an array. This may be an array or an explicit `TEMPLATE` defined by a directive.

totally associated: Term referring to entities which have the same storage sequence.

transcriptive mapping: A method used to establish the mapping attributes of a dummy procedure argument where the attribute is to be copied from the actual argument and code is produced to adapt to the possibility that the attribute may be different from call to call.

ultimately aligned: The final alignment target in a set of related alignments. An object not explicitly aligned with another object is ultimately aligned with itself.

B Description of HPF Library and Intrinsic Procedures

Procedures not marked "Intrinsic" are HPF library procedures. In order to save space and enhance readability, the examples of this appendix use `T` and `F` to denote the logical values `.TRUE.` and `.FALSE.`. Optional arguments are marked with an asterisk (*).

B.1 ALL_PREFIX

Synopsis. ALL_PREFIX(MASK, DIM, SEGMENT, EXCLUSIVE)

Optional Arguments. DIM, SEGMENT, EXCLUSIVE

Description. Computes a segmented logical AND scan along dimension `DIM` of `MASK`.

Class. Transformational function.

Arguments.

MASK   must be of type logical. It must not be scalar.

DIM*   must be scalar and of type integer with a value in the range $1 \leq$ `DIM` $\leq n$, where n is the rank of `MASK`.

SEGMENT*   must be of type logical and have the same shape as `MASK`.

EXCLUSIVE*   must be of type logical and must be scalar.

Result Type, Type Parameter, and Shape. Same as `MASK`.

Result Value. Element r of the result has the value ALL((/ $a_1, \ldots, a_m$ /)) where $(a_1, \ldots, a_m)$ is the (possibly empty) set of elements of `MASK` selected to contribute to r by the rules stated in Chapter 7.

Example. ALL_PREFIX((/T,F,T,T,T/), SEGMENT= (/F,F,F,T,T/)) is $[\text{T F F T T}]$.

B.2 ALL_SCATTER

Synopsis. ALL_SCATTER(MASK, BASE, INDX1, ..., INDXn)

Description. Scatters elements of **MASK** to positions of the result indicated by index arrays **INDX1**, ..., **INDXn**. An element of the result is true if and only if the corresponding element of **BASE** and all elements of **MASK** scattered to that position are true.

Class. Transformational function.

Arguments.

MASK   must be of type logical. It must not be scalar.

BASE   must be of type logical with the same kind type parameter as **MASK**. It must not be scalar.

INDX1,...,INDXn must be of type integer and conformable with **MASK**. The number of **INDX** arguments must be equal to the rank of **BASE**.

Result Type, Type Parameter, and Shape. Same as **BASE**.

Result Value. The element of the result corresponding to the element b of **BASE** has the value ALL((/$a_1, a_2, \ldots, a_m, b$/)), where $(a_1, \ldots, a_m)$ are the elements of **MASK** associated with b as described in Chapter 7.

Example. ALL_SCATTER((/T, T, T, F/), (/T, T, T/), (/1, 1, 2, 2/)) is [T F T].

B.3 ALL_SUFFIX

Synopsis. ALL_SUFFIX(MASK, DIM, SEGMENT, EXCLUSIVE)

Optional Arguments. DIM, SEGMENT, EXCLUSIVE

Description. Computes a reverse, segmented logical AND scan along dimension DIM of **MASK**.

Class. Transformational function.

Arguments.

MASK   must be of type logical. It must not be scalar.

DIM*   must be scalar and of type integer with a value in the range $1 \leq$ DIM $\leq n$, where n is the rank of **MASK**.

Description of HPF Library and Intrinsic Procedures   257

SEGMENT* must be of type logical and have the same shape as MASK.

EXCLUSIVE* must be of type logical and must be scalar.

Result Type, Type Parameter, and Shape. Same as MASK.

Result Value. Element r of the result has the value ALL((/ $a_1, \ldots, a_m$ /)) where $(a_1, \ldots, a_m)$ is the (possibly empty) set of elements of MASK selected to contribute to r by the rules stated in Chapter 7.

Example. ALL_SUFFIX((/T,F,T,T,T/), SEGMENT= (/F,F,F,T,T/)) is $\begin{bmatrix} F & F & T & T & T \end{bmatrix}$.

B.4 ANY_PREFIX

Synopsis. ANY_PREFIX(MASK, DIM, SEGMENT, EXCLUSIVE)

Optional Arguments. DIM, SEGMENT, EXCLUSIVE

Description. Computes a segmented logical OR scan along dimension DIM of MASK.

Class. Transformational function.

Arguments.

MASK   must be of type logical. It must not be scalar.

DIM*   must be scalar and of type integer with a value in the range $1 \leq$ DIM $\leq n$, where n is the rank of MASK.

SEGMENT*   must be of type logical and have the same shape as MASK.

EXCLUSIVE* must be of type logical and must be scalar.

Result Type, Type Parameter, and Shape. Same as MASK.

Result Value. Element r of the result has the value ANY((/ $a_1, \ldots, a_m$ /)) where $(a_1, \ldots, a_m)$ is the (possibly empty) set of elements of MASK selected to contribute to r by the rules stated in Chapter 7.

Example. ANY_PREFIX((/F,T,F,F,F/), SEGMENT= (/F,F,F,T,T/)) is $\begin{bmatrix} F & T & T & F & F \end{bmatrix}$.

B.5 ANY_SCATTER

Synopsis. `ANY_SCATTER(MASK, BASE, INDX1, ..., INDXn)`

Description. Scatters elements of `MASK` to positions of the result indicated by index arrays `INDX1, ..., INDXn`. An element of the result is true if and only if the corresponding element of `BASE` or any element of `MASK` scattered to that position is true.

Class. Transformational function.

Arguments.

MASK   must be of type logical. It must not be scalar.

BASE   must be of type logical with the same kind type parameter as `MASK`. It must not be scalar.

INDX1,...,INDXn must be of type integer and conformable with `MASK`. The number of `INDX` arguments must be equal to the rank of `BASE`.

Result Type, Type Parameter, and Shape. Same as `BASE`.

Result Value. The element of the result corresponding to the element b of `BASE` has the value `ANY(` $(/a_1, a_2, \ldots, a_m, b/)$ `)`, where $(a_1, \ldots, a_m)$ are the elements of `MASK` associated with b as described in Chapter 7.

Example. `ANY_SCATTER( (/T, F, F, F/), (/F, F, T/), (/1, 1, 2, 2/) )` is $\begin{bmatrix} T & F & T \end{bmatrix}$.

B.6 ANY_SUFFIX

Synopsis. `ANY_SUFFIX(MASK, DIM, SEGMENT, EXCLUSIVE)`

Optional Arguments. `DIM, SEGMENT, EXCLUSIVE`

Description. Computes a reverse, segmented logical OR scan along dimension `DIM` of `MASK`.

Class. Transformational function.

Arguments.

Description of HPF Library and Intrinsic Procedures 259

MASK   must be of type logical. It must not be scalar.

DIM*   must be scalar and of type integer with a value in the range $1 \leq$ DIM $\leq n$, where n is the rank of MASK.

SEGMENT* must be of type logical and have the same shape as MASK.

EXCLUSIVE* must be of type logical and must be scalar.

Result Type, Type Parameter, and Shape. Same as MASK.

Result Value. Element r of the result has the value ANY((/ $a_1, \ldots, a_m$ /)) where $(a_1, \ldots, a_m)$ is the (possibly empty) set of elements of MASK selected to contribute to r by the rules stated in Chapter 7.

Example. ANY_SUFFIX((/F,T,F,F,F/), SEGMENT= (/F,F,F,T,T/)) is
$\begin{bmatrix} T & T & F & F & F \end{bmatrix}$.

B.7 COPY_PREFIX

Synopsis. COPY_PREFIX(ARRAY, DIM, SEGMENT)

Optional Arguments. DIM, SEGMENT

Description. Computes a segmented copy scan along dimension DIM of ARRAY.

Class. Transformational function.

Arguments.

ARRAY   may be of any type. It must not be scalar.

DIM*   must be scalar and of type integer with a value in the range $1 \leq$ DIM $\leq n$, where n is the rank of ARRAY.

SEGMENT* must be of type logical and have the same shape as ARRAY.

Result Type, Type Parameter, and Shape. Same as ARRAY.

Result Value. Element r of the result has the value a_1 where $(a_1, \ldots, a_m)$ is the set, in array element order, of elements of ARRAY selected to contribute to r by the rules stated in Chapter 7.

Example. COPY_PREFIX((/1,2,3,4,5/), SEGMENT= (/F,F,F,T,T/)) is
$\begin{bmatrix} 1 & 1 & 1 & 4 & 4 \end{bmatrix}$.

B.8 COPY_SCATTER

Synopsis. COPY_SCATTER(ARRAY,BASE,INDX1, ..., INDXn, MASK)

Optional Argument. MASK

Description. Scatters elements of ARRAY selected by MASK to positions of the result indicated by index arrays INDX1, ..., INDXn. Each element of the result is equal to one of the elements of ARRAY scattered to that position or, if there is none, to the corresponding element of BASE.

Class. Transformational function.

Arguments.

ARRAY   may be of any type. It must not be scalar.

BASE   must be of the same type and kind type parameter as ARRAY.

INDX1,...,INDXn must be of type integer and must be conformable with ARRAY. The number of INDX arguments must be equal to the rank of BASE.

MASK*   must be of type logical and must be conformable with ARRAY.

Result Type, Type Parameter, and Shape. Same as BASE.

Result Value. Let S be the set of elements of ARRAY associated with element b of BASE as described in Chapter 7.

If S is empty, then the element of the result corresponding to the element b of BASE has the same value as b.

If S is non-empty, then the element of the result corresponding to the element b of BASE is the result of choosing one element from S. HPF does not specify how the choice is to be made; the mechanism is processor dependent.

Example. COPY_SCATTER((/1, 2, 3, 4/), (/7, 8, 9/), (/1, 1, 2, 2/)) is [x, y, 9], where x is a member of the set $\{1, 2\}$ and y is a member of the set $\{3, 4\}$.

B.9 COPY_SUFFIX

Synopsis. COPY_SUFFIX(ARRAY, DIM, SEGMENT)

Optional Arguments. DIM, SEGMENT

Description. Computes a reverse, segmented copy scan along dimension DIM of ARRAY.

Class. Transformational function.

Arguments.

ARRAY   may be of any type. It must not be scalar.

DIM*   must be scalar and of type integer with a value in the range $1 \leq$ DIM $\leq n$, where n is the rank of ARRAY.

SEGMENT*   must be of type logical and have the same shape as ARRAY.

Result Type, Type Parameter, and Shape. Same as ARRAY.

Result Value. Element r of the result has the value a_m where $(a_1, \ldots, a_m)$ is the set, in array element order, of elements of ARRAY selected to contribute to r by the rules stated in Chapter 7.

Example. COPY_SUFFIX((/1,2,3,4,5/), SEGMENT= (/F,F,F,T,T/)) is $\begin{bmatrix} 3 & 3 & 3 & 5 & 5 \end{bmatrix}$.

B.10 COUNT_PREFIX

Synopsis. COUNT_PREFIX(MASK, DIM, SEGMENT, EXCLUSIVE)

Optional Arguments. DIM, SEGMENT, EXCLUSIVE

Description. Computes a segmented COUNT scan along dimension DIM of MASK.

Class. Transformational function.

Arguments.

MASK   must be of type logical. It must not be scalar.

DIM*   must be scalar and of type integer with a value in the range $1 \leq \text{DIM} \leq n$, where n is the rank of MASK.

SEGMENT*   must be of type logical and have the same shape as MASK.

EXCLUSIVE* must be of type logical and must be scalar.

Result Type, Type Parameter, and Shape. The result is of type default integer and of the same shape as MASK.

Result Value. Element r of the result has the value COUNT((/ $a_1, \ldots, a_m$ /)) where $(a_1, \ldots, a_m)$ is the (possibly empty) set of elements of MASK selected to contribute to r by the rules stated in Chapter 7.

Example. COUNT_PREFIX((/F,T,T,T,T/), SEGMENT= (/F,F,F,T,T/)) is $[\, 0 \;\; 1 \;\; 2 \;\; 1 \;\; 2 \,]$.

B.11 COUNT_SCATTER

Synopsis. COUNT_SCATTER(MASK, BASE, INDX1, ..., INDXn)

Description. Scatters elements of MASK to positions of the result indicated by index arrays INDX1, ..., INDXn. Each element of the result is the sum of the corresponding element of BASE and the number of true elements of MASK scattered to that position.

Class. Transformational function.

Arguments.

MASK   must be of type logical. It must not be scalar.

BASE   must be of type integer. It must not be scalar.

INDX1,...,INDXn must be of type integer and must be conformable with MASK. The number of INDX arguments must be equal to the rank of BASE.

Result Type, Type Parameter, and Shape. Same as BASE.

Result Value. The element of the result corresponding to the element b of BASE has the value b + COUNT((/$a_1, a_2, \ldots, a_m$/)), where $(a_1, \ldots, a_m)$ are the elements of MASK associated with b as described in Chapter 7.

Example. COUNT_SCATTER((/T, T, T, F/),(/1, -1, 0/),(/1, 1, 2, 2/)) is $[\, 3 \;\; 0 \;\; 0 \,]$.

B.12 COUNT_SUFFIX

Synopsis. COUNT_SUFFIX(MASK, DIM, SEGMENT, EXCLUSIVE)

Optional Arguments. DIM, SEGMENT, EXCLUSIVE

Description. Computes a reverse, segmented COUNT scan along dimension DIM of MASK.

Class. Transformational function.

Arguments.

MASK   must be of type logical. It must not be scalar.

DIM*   must be scalar and of type integer with a value in the range $1 \leq$ DIM $\leq n$, where n is the rank of MASK.

SEGMENT*   must be of type logical and have the same shape as MASK.

EXCLUSIVE* must be of type logical and must be scalar.

Result Type, Type Parameter, and Shape. The result is of type default integer and of the same shape as MASK.

Result Value. Element r of the result has the value COUNT((/ $a_1, \ldots, a_m$ /)) where $(a_1, \ldots, a_m)$ is the (possibly empty) set of elements of MASK selected to contribute to r by the rules stated in Chapter 7.

Example. COUNT_SUFFIX((/T,F,T,T,T/), SEGMENT= (/F,F,F,T,T/)) is $\begin{bmatrix} 2 & 1 & 1 & 2 & 1 \end{bmatrix}$.

B.13 GRADE_DOWN

Synopsis. GRADE_DOWN(ARRAY, DIM)

Optional Argument. DIM

Description. Produces a permutation of the indices of an array, sorted by descending array element values.

Class. Transformational function.

Arguments.

ARRAY   must be of type integer, real, or character.

DIM*   must be scalar and of type integer with a value in the range $1 \leq$ DIM $\leq n$, where n is the rank of ARRAY. The corresponding actual argument must not be an optional dummy argument.

Result Type, Type Parameter, and Shape. The result is of type default integer. If DIM is present, the result has the same shape as ARRAY. If DIM is absent, the result has shape (/ SIZE(SHAPE(ARRAY)), PRODUCT(SHAPE(ARRAY)) /).

Result Value.

Case (i):   The result of S = GRADE_DOWN(ARRAY) has the property that if one computes the rank-one array B of size PRODUCT(SHAPE(ARRAY)) by FORALL(K=1:SIZE(B,1))B(K)=ARRAY(S(1,K),S(2,K),...,S(N,K)) where N has the value SIZE(SHAPE(ARRAY)), then B is sorted in descending order; moreover, all of the columns of S are distinct, that is, if $j \neq m$ then ALL(S(:,j) .EQ. S(:,m)) will be false. The sort is stable; if $j \leq m$ and B(j) = B(m), then ARRAY(S(1,j), S(2,j), ..., S(n,j)) precedes ARRAY(S(1,m),S(2,m),...,S(n,m)) in the array element ordering of ARRAY.

Case (ii):   The result of R = GRADE_DOWN(ARRAY,DIM=K) has the property that if one computes the array B($i_1, i_2, \ldots, i_k, \ldots, i_n$) = ARRAY($i_1, i_2, \ldots,$ R($i_1, i_2, \ldots, i_k, \ldots, i_n$), $\ldots, i_n$) then for all $i_1, i_2, \ldots,$ (omit i_k), $\ldots, i_n$ the vector B($i_1, i_2, \ldots, :, \ldots, i_n$) is sorted in descending order; moreover, R($i_1, i_2, \ldots, :, \ldots, i_n$) is a permutation of all the integers in the range LBOUND(ARRAY,K):UBOUND(ARRAY,K). The sort is stable; that is, if $j \leq m$ and B($i_1, i_2, \ldots, j, \ldots, i_n$) = B($i_1, i_2, \ldots, m, \ldots, i_n$), then R($i_1, i_2, \ldots, j, \ldots, i_n$) $\leq$ R($i_1, i_2, \ldots, m, \ldots, i_n$).

Examples.

Case (i):   GRADE_DOWN((/30, 20, 30, 40, -10/)) is a rank two array of shape [1   5] with the value [4   1   3   2   5]. (To produce a rank-one result, the optional DIM = 1 argument must be used.)

Description of HPF Library and Intrinsic Procedures   265

If A is the array $\begin{bmatrix} 1 & 9 & 2 \\ 4 & 5 & 2 \\ 1 & 2 & 4 \end{bmatrix}$, then GRADE_DOWN(A) has the value

$\begin{bmatrix} 1 & 2 & 2 & 3 & 3 & 1 & 2 & 1 & 3 \\ 2 & 2 & 1 & 3 & 2 & 3 & 3 & 1 & 1 \end{bmatrix}$.

Case (ii): If A is the array $\begin{bmatrix} 1 & 9 & 2 \\ 4 & 5 & 2 \\ 1 & 2 & 4 \end{bmatrix}$, then GRADE_DOWN(A, DIM = 1) has the value $\begin{bmatrix} 2 & 1 & 3 \\ 1 & 2 & 1 \\ 3 & 3 & 2 \end{bmatrix}$.

B.14 GRADE_UP

Synopsis. GRADE_UP(ARRAY, DIM)

Optional Argument. DIM

Description. Produces a permutation of the indices of an array, sorted by ascending array element values.

Class. Transformational function.

Arguments.

ARRAY   must be of type integer, real, or character.

DIM*   must be scalar and of type integer with a value in the range $1 \leq$ DIM $\leq n$, where n is the rank of ARRAY. The corresponding actual argument must not be an optional dummy argument.

Result Type, Type Parameter, and Shape. The result is of type default integer. If DIM is present, the result has the same shape as ARRAY. If DIM is absent, the result has shape (/ SIZE(SHAPE(ARRAY)), PRODUCT(SHAPE(ARRAY)) /).

Result Value.

Case (i): The result of S = GRADE_UP(ARRAY) has the property that if one computes the rank-one array B of size PRODUCT(SHAPE(ARRAY)) by FORALL(K=1:SIZE(B,1))B(K)=ARRAY(S(1,K),S(2,K),...,S(N,K))

where N has the value SIZE(SHAPE(ARRAY)), then B is sorted in ascending order; moreover, all of the columns of S are distinct, that is, if $j \neq m$ then ALL(S(:,j) .EQ. S(:,m)) will be false. The sort is stable; if $j \leq m$ and $B(j) = B(m)$, then ARRAY(S(1,j), S(2,j), ..., S(n,j)) precedes ARRAY(S(1,m), S(2,m), ..., S(n,m)) in the array element ordering of ARRAY.

Case (ii): The result of R = GRADE_UP(ARRAY,DIM=K) has the property that if one computes the array $B(i_1, i_2, \ldots, i_k, \ldots, i_n)$ = ARRAY($i_1, i_2, \ldots, R(i_1, i_2, \ldots, i_k, \ldots, i_n), \ldots, i_n$) then for all $i_1, i_2, \ldots,$ (omit i_k), ..., i_n the vector $B(i_1, i_2, \ldots, :, \ldots, i_n)$ is sorted in ascending order; moreover, $R(i_1, i_2, \ldots, :, \ldots, i_n)$ is a permutation of all the integers in the range LBOUND(ARRAY,K):UBOUND(ARRAY,K). The sort is stable; that is, if $j \leq m$ and $B(i_1, i_2, \ldots, j, \ldots, i_n) = B(i_1, i_2, \ldots, m, \ldots, i_n)$, then $R(i_1, i_2, \ldots, j, \ldots, i_n) \leq R(i_1, i_2, \ldots, m, \ldots, i_n)$.

Examples.

Case (i): GRADE_UP((/30, 20, 30, 40, -10/)) is a rank two array of shape [1 5] with the value [5 2 1 3 4]. (To produce a rank-one result, the optional DIM = 1 argument must be used.)

If A is the array $\begin{bmatrix} 1 & 9 & 2 \\ 4 & 5 & 2 \\ 1 & 2 & 4 \end{bmatrix}$, then GRADE_UP(A) has the value $\begin{bmatrix} 1 & 3 & 3 & 1 & 2 & 2 & 3 & 2 & 1 \\ 1 & 1 & 2 & 3 & 3 & 1 & 3 & 2 & 2 \end{bmatrix}$.

Case (ii): If A is the array $\begin{bmatrix} 1 & 9 & 2 \\ 4 & 5 & 2 \\ 1 & 2 & 4 \end{bmatrix}$, then GRADE_UP(A, DIM = 1) has the value $\begin{bmatrix} 1 & 3 & 1 \\ 3 & 2 & 2 \\ 2 & 1 & 3 \end{bmatrix}$.

B.15 HPF_ALIGNMENT

Synopsis. HPF_ALIGNMENT(ALIGNEE, LB, UB, STRIDE, AXIS_MAP, IDENTITY_MAP, DYNAMIC, NCOPIES)

Optional Arguments. LB, UB, STRIDE, AXIS_MAP, IDENTITY_MAP, DYNAMIC, NCOPIES

Description. Returns information regarding the correspondence of a variable and the *align-target* (array or template) to which it is ultimately aligned.

Class. Mapping inquiry subroutine.

Arguments.

ALIGNEE   may be of any type. It may be scalar or array valued. It must not be an assumed-size array. It must not be a structure component. If it is a member of an aggregate variable group, then it must be an aggregate cover of the group. (See Chapter 4 for the definitions of "aggregate variable group" and "aggregate cover.") It must not be a pointer that is disassociated or an allocatable array that is not allocated. It is an INTENT (IN) argument.

If ALIGNEE is a pointer, information about the alignment of its target is returned. The target must not be an assumed-size dummy argument or a section of an assumed-size dummy argument. If the target is (a section of) a member of an aggregate variable group, then the member must be an aggregate cover of the group. The target must not be a structure component, but the pointer may be.

LB*   must be of type default integer and of rank one. Its size must be at least equal to the rank of ALIGNEE. It is an INTENT (OUT) argument. The first element of the ith axis of ALIGNEE is ultimately aligned to the LB(i)th *align-target* element along the axis of the *align-target* associated with the ith axis of ALIGNEE. If the ith axis of ALIGNEE is a collapsed axis, LB(i) is processor dependent.

UB*   must be of type default integer and of rank one. Its size must be at least equal to the rank of ALIGNEE. It is an INTENT (OUT) argument. The last element of the ith axis of ALIGNEE is ultimately aligned to the UB(i)th *align-target* element along the axis of the *align-target* associated with the ith axis of ALIGNEE. If the ith axis of ALIGNEE is a collapsed axis, UB(i) is processor dependent.

STRIDE*   must be of type default integer and of rank one. Its size must be at least equal to the rank of ALIGNEE. It is an INTENT (OUT) argument. The ith element of STRIDE is set to the stride used in aligning the elements of **ALIGNEE** along its ith axis. If the ith axis of **ALIGNEE** is a collapsed axis, **STRIDE**(i) is zero.

AXIS_MAP* must be of type default integer and of rank one. Its size must be at least equal to the rank of **ALIGNEE**. It is an **INTENT (OUT)** argument. The ith element of **AXIS_MAP** is set to the *align-target* axis associated with the ith axis of **ALIGNEE**. If the ith axis of **ALIGNEE** is a collapsed axis, **AXIS_MAP**(i) is 0.

IDENTITY_MAP* must be scalar and of type default logical. It is an **INTENT (OUT)** argument. It is set to true if the ultimate *align-target* associated with **ALIGNEE** has a shape identical to **ALIGNEE**, the axes are mapped using the identity permutation, and the strides are all positive (and therefore equal to 1, because of the shape constraint); otherwise it is set to false. If a variable has not appeared as an *alignee* in an **ALIGN** or **REALIGN** directive, and does not have the **INHERIT** attribute, then **IDENTITY_MAP** must be true; it can be true in other circumstances as well.

DYNAMIC* must be scalar and of type default logical. It is an **INTENT (OUT)** argument. It is set to true if **ALIGNEE** has the **DYNAMIC** attribute; otherwise it is set to false. If **ALIGNEE** has the pointer attribute, then the result applies to **ALIGNEE** itself rather than its target.

NCOPIES* must be scalar and of type default integer. It is an **INTENT (OUT)** argument. It is set to the number of copies of **ALIGNEE** that are ultimately aligned to *align-target*. For a non-replicated variable, it is set to one.

Examples. If **ALIGNEE** is scalar, then no elements of **LB**, **UB**, **STRIDE**, or **AXIS_MAP** are set.

Given the declarations

```
      REAL PI = 3.1415927
      POINTER P_TO_A(:)
      DIMENSION A(10,10),B(20,30),C(20,40,10),D(40)
!HPF$ TEMPLATE T(40,20)
!HPF$ DYNAMIC A
!HPF$ ALIGN A(I,:) WITH T(1+3*I,2:20:2)
!HPF$ ALIGN C(I,*,J) WITH T(J,21-I)
```

Description of HPF Library and Intrinsic Procedures

```
!HPF$ ALIGN D(I) WITH T(I,4)
!HPF$ PROCESSORS PROCS(4,2), SCALARPROC
!HPF$ DISTRIBUTE T(BLOCK,BLOCK) ONTO PROCS
!HPF$ DISTRIBUTE B(CYCLIC,BLOCK) ONTO PROCS
!HPF$ DISTRIBUTE ONTO SCALARPROC :: PI
      P_TO_A => A(3:9:2, 6)
```

the results of **HPF_ALIGNMENT** are, assuming that the actual mappings are as the directives specify:

	A	B	C	D	P_TO_A
LB	[4, 2]	[1, 1]	[1, N/A, 1]	[1]	[10]
UB	[31, 20]	[20, 30]	[20, N/A, 10]	[40]	[28]
STRIDE	[3, 2]	[1, 1]	[-1, 0, 1]	[1]	[6]
AXIS_MAP	[1, 2]	[1, 2]	[2, 0, 1]	[1]	[1]
IDENTITY_MAP	false	true	false	false	false
DYNAMIC	true	false	false	false	false
NCOPIES	1	1	1	1	1

where "N/A" denotes a processor-dependent result. To illustrate the use of **NCOPIES**, consider:

```
      LOGICAL BOZO(20,20),RONALD_MCDONALD(20)
!HPF$ TEMPLATE EMMETT_KELLY(100,100)
!HPF$ ALIGN RONALD_MCDONALD(I) WITH BOZO(I,*)
!HPF$ ALIGN BOZO(J,K) WITH EMMETT_KELLY(J,5*K)
```

CALL HPF_ALIGNMENT(RONALD_MCDONALD, NCOPIES = NC) sets NC to 20. Now consider:

```
      LOGICAL BOZO(20,20),RONALD_MCDONALD(20)
!HPF$ TEMPLATE WILLIE_WHISTLE(100)
!HPF$ ALIGN RONALD_MCDONALD(I) WITH BOZO(I,*)
!HPF$ ALIGN BOZO(J,*) WITH WILLIE_WHISTLE(5*J)
```

CALL HPF_ALIGNMENT(RONALD_MCDONALD, NCOPIES = NC) sets NC to one.

B.16 HPF_DISTRIBUTION

Synopsis. HPF_DISTRIBUTION(DISTRIBUTEE, AXISTYPE, AXISINFO, PROCESSORS_RANK, PROCESSORSSHAPE)

Optional Arguments. `AXIS_TYPE`, `AXIS_INFO`, `PROCESSORS_RANK`, `PROCESSORS_SHAPE`

Description. The `HPF_DISTRIBUTION` subroutine returns information regarding the distribution of the ultimate *align-target* associated with a variable.

Class. Mapping inquiry subroutine.

Arguments.

`DISTRIBUTEE` may be of any type. It may be scalar or array valued. It must not be an assumed-size array. It must not be a structure component. If it is a member of an aggregate variable group, then it must be an aggregate cover of the group. (See Chapter 4 for the definitions of "aggregate variable group" and "aggregate cover.") It must not be a pointer that is disassociated or an allocatable array that is not allocated. It is an `INTENT (IN)` argument.

If `DISTRIBUTEE` is a pointer, information about the distribution of its target is returned. The target must not be an assumed-size dummy argument or a section of an assumed-size dummy argument. If the target is (a section of) a member of an aggregate variable group, then the member must be an aggregate cover of the group. The target must not be a structure component, but the pointer may be.

`AXIS_TYPE*` must be a rank one array of type default character. It may be of any length, although it must be of length at least 9 in order to contain the complete value. Its elements are set to the values below as if by a character intrinsic assignment statement. Its size must be at least equal to the rank of the *align-target* to which `DISTRIBUTEE` is ultimately aligned; this is the value returned by `HPF_TEMPLATE` in `TEMPLATE_RANK`). It is an `INTENT (OUT)` argument. Its ith element contains information on the distribution of the ith axis of that *align-target*. The following values are defined by HPF (implementations may define other values):

'BLOCK' The axis is distributed `BLOCK`. The corresponding element of `AXIS_INFO` contains the block size.

'COLLAPSED' The axis is collapsed (distributed with the "*" specification). The value of the corresponding element of `AXIS_INFO` is processor dependent.

'CYCLIC' The axis is distributed CYCLIC. The corresponding element of AXIS_INFO contains the block size.

AXIS_INFO* must be a rank one array of type default integer, and size at least equal to the rank of the *align-target* to which DISTRIBUTEE is ultimately aligned (as returned by HPF_TEMPLATE in TEMPLATE_RANK). It is an INTENT (OUT) argument. The ith element of AXIS_INFO contains the block size in the block or cyclic distribution of the ith axis of the ultimate *align-target* of DISTRIBUTEE; if that axis is a collapsed axis, then the value is processor dependent.

PROCESSORS_RANK* must be scalar and of type default integer. It is set to the rank of the processor arrangement onto which DISTRIBUTEE is distributed. It is an INTENT (OUT) argument.

PROCESSORS_SHAPE* must be a rank one array of type default integer and of size at least equal to the value, m, returned in PROCESSORS_RANK. It is an INTENT (OUT) argument. Its first m elements are set to the shape of the processor arrangement to which DISTRIBUTEE is mapped. (It may be necessary to call HPF_DISTRIBUTION twice, the first time to obtain the value of PROCESSORS_RANK in order to allocate PROCESSORS_SHAPE.)

Example. Given the declarations in the example under HPF_ALIGN, and assuming that the actual mappings are as the directives specify, the results of HPF_DISTRIBUTION are:

	A	B	PI
AXIS_TYPE	['BLOCK', 'BLOCK']	['CYCLIC', 'BLOCK']	[ ]
AXIS_INFO	[10, 10]	[1, 15]	[ ]
PROCESSORS_SHAPE	[4, 2]	[4, 2]	[ ]
PROCESSORS_RANK	2	2	0

B.17 HPF_TEMPLATE

Synopsis. HPF_TEMPLATE(ALIGNEE, TEMPLATERANK, LB, UB, AXISTYPE, AXISINFO, NUMBER_ALIGNED, DYNAMIC)

Optional Arguments. LB, UB, AXIS_TYPE, AXIS_INFO, NUMBER_ALIGNED, TEMPLATE_RANK, DYNAMIC

Description. The HPF_TEMPLATE subroutine returns information regarding the ultimate *align-target* associated with a variable; HPF_TEMPLATE returns information concerning the variable from the template's point of view (assuming the alignment is to a template rather than to an array), while HPF_ALIGNMENT returns information from the variable's point of view.

Class. Mapping inquiry subroutine.

Arguments.

ALIGNEE   may be of any type. It may be scalar or array valued. It must not be an assumed-size array. It must not be a structure component. If it is a member of an aggregate variable group, then it must be an aggregate cover of the group. (See Chapter 4 for the definitions of "aggregate variable group" and "aggregate cover.") It must not be a pointer that is disassociated or an allocatable array that is not allocated. It is an INTENT (IN) argument.

If ALIGNEE is a pointer, information about the alignment of its target is returned. The target must not be an assumed-size dummy argument or a section of an assumed-size dummy argument. If the target is (a section of) a member of an aggregate variable group, then the member must be an aggregate cover of the group. The target must not be a structure component, but the pointer may be.

TEMPLATE_RANK*   must be scalar and of type default integer. It is an INTENT (OUT) argument. It is set to the rank of the ultimate *align-target*. This can be different from the rank of the ALIGNEE, due to collapsing and replicating.

LB*   must be of type default integer and of rank one. Its size must be at least equal to the rank of the *align-target* to which ALIGNEE is ultimately aligned; this is the value returned in TEMPLATE_RANK. It is an INTENT (OUT) argument. The ith element of LB contains the declared *align-target* lower bound for the ith template axis.

UB*   must be of type default integer and of rank one. Its size must be at least equal to the rank of the *clign-target* to which ALIGNEE is ultimately aligned; this is the value returned in TEMPLATE_RANK. It is an INTENT (OUT) argument. The ith element of UB contains the declared *align-target* upper bound for the ith template axis.

Description of HPF Library and Intrinsic Procedures   273

AXIS_TYPE* must be a rank one array of type default character. It may be of any length, although it must be of length at least 10 in order to contain the complete value. Its elements are set to the values below as if by a character intrinsic assignment statement. Its size must be at least equal to the rank of the *align-target* to which ALIGNEE is ultimately aligned; this is the value returned in the INTENT (OUT) argument TEMPLATE_RANK. The ith element of AXIS_TYPE contains information about the ith axis of the *align-target*. The following values are defined by HPF (implementations may define other values):

'NORMAL' An axis of ALIGNEE is aligned to the *align-target* axis. For elements of AXIS_TYPE assigned this value, the corresponding element of AXIS_INFO is set to the number of the axis of ALIGNEE aligned to this *align-target* axis.

'REPLICATED' ALIGNEE is replicated along this *align-target* axis. For elements of AXIS_TYPE assigned this value, the corresponding element of AXIS_INFO is set to the number of copies of ALIGNEE along this *align-target* axis.

'SINGLE' ALIGNEE is aligned with one coordinate of the *align-target* axis. For elements of AXIS_TYPE assigned this value, the corresponding AXIS_INFO element is set to the *align-target* coordinate to which ALIGNEE is aligned.

AXIS_INFO* must be of type default integer and of rank one. Its size must be at least equal to the rank of the *align-target* to which ALIGNEE is ultimately aligned; this is the value returned in TEMPLATE_RANK. It is an INTENT (OUT) argument. See the description of AXIS_TYPE above.

NUMBER_ALIGNED* must be scalar and of type default integer. It is an INTENT (OUT) argument. It is set to the total number of variables aligned to the ultimate *align-target*. This is the number of variables that are moved if the *align-target* is redistributed.

DYNAMIC* must be scalar and of type default logical. It is an INTENT (OUT) argument. It is set to true if the *align-target* has the DYNAMIC attribute, and to false otherwise.

Example. Given the declarations in the example under HPF_ALIGN, and assuming that the actual mappings are as the directives specify, the results of HPF_TEMPLATE are:

	A	C	D
LB	[1, 1]	[1, 1]	[1, 1]
UB	[40, 20]	[40, 20]	[40, 20]
AXIS_TYPE	['NORMAL', 'NORMAL']	['NORMAL', 'NORMAL']	['NORMAL', 'SINGLE']
AXIS_INFO	[1, 2]	[3, 1]	[1, 4]
NUMBER_ALIGNED	3	3	3
TEMPLATE_RANK	2	2	2
DYNAMIC	false	false	false

B.18 IALL

Synopsis. IALL(ARRAY, DIM, MASK)

Optional Arguments. DIM, MASK

Description. Computes a bitwise logical AND reduction along dimension DIM of ARRAY.

Class. Transformational function.

Arguments.

ARRAY   must be of type integer. It must not be scalar.

DIM*   must be scalar and of type integer with a value in the range $1 \leq \text{DIM} \leq n$, where n is the rank of ARRAY. The corresponding actual argument must not be an optional dummy argument.

MASK*   must be of type logical and must be conformable with ARRAY.

Result Type, Type Parameter, and Shape. The result is of type integer with the same kind type parameter as ARRAY. It is scalar if DIM is absent or if ARRAY has rank one; otherwise, the result is an array of rank $n-1$ and shape $(d_1, d_2, \ldots, d_{DIM-1}, d_{DIM+1}, \ldots, d_n)$ where $(d_1, d_2, \ldots, d_n)$ is the shape of ARRAY.

Result Value.

Case (i):   The result of IALL(ARRAY) is the IAND reduction of all the elements of ARRAY. If ARRAY has size zero, the result is equal to a processor-dependent integer value x with the property that IAND(I, x) = I for all integers I of the same kind type parameter as ARRAY.

Description of HPF Library and Intrinsic Procedures

Case (ii): The result of `IALL(ARRAY, MASK=MASK)` is the `IAND` reduction of all the elements of `ARRAY` corresponding to the true elements of `MASK`; if `MASK` contains no true elements, the result is equal to a processor-dependent integer value x (of the same kind type parameter as `ARRAY`) with the property that `IAND(I, x) = I` for all integers `I`.

Case (iii): If `ARRAY` has rank one, `IALL(ARRAY, DIM=1 [,MASK])` has a value equal to that of `IALL(ARRAY [,MASK])`. Otherwise, the value of element $(s_1, s_2, \ldots, s_{DIM-1}, s_{DIM+1}, \ldots, s_n)$ of `IALL(ARRAY, DIM=1 [,MASK])` is equal to `IALL(ARRAY`$(s_1, s_2, \ldots, s_{DIM-1}, :, s_{DIM+1}, \ldots, s_n)$ `[,MASK = MASK`$(s_1, s_2, \ldots, s_{DIM-1}, :, s_{DIM+1}, \ldots, s_n)$`)]`).

Examples.

Case (i): The value of `IALL((/7, 6, 3, 2/))` is 2.

Case (ii): The value of `IALL(C, MASK = BTEST(C,0))` is the `IAND` reduction of the odd elements of `C`.

Case (iii): If `B` is the array $\begin{bmatrix} 2 & 3 & 5 \\ 3 & 7 & 7 \end{bmatrix}$, then `IALL(B, DIM = 1)` is $\begin{bmatrix} 2 & 3 & 5 \end{bmatrix}$ and `IALL(B, DIM = 2)` is $\begin{bmatrix} 0 & 3 \end{bmatrix}$.

B.19 IALL_PREFIX

Synopsis. `IALL_PREFIX(ARRAY, DIM, MASK, SEGMENT, EXCLUSIVE)`

Optional Arguments. `DIM, MASK, SEGMENT, EXCLUSIVE`

Description. Computes a segmented bitwise logical AND scan along dimension `DIM` of `ARRAY`.

Class. Transformational function.

Arguments.

`ARRAY`   must be of type integer. It must not be scalar.

`DIM*`   must be scalar and of type integer with a value in the range $1 \leq$ `DIM` $\leq n$, where n is the rank of `ARRAY`.

`MASK*`   must be of type logical and must be conformable with `ARRAY`.

SEGMENT* must be of type logical and have the same shape as ARRAY.

EXCLUSIVE* must be of type logical and must be scalar.

Result Type, Type Parameter, and Shape. Same as ARRAY.

Result Value. Element r of the result has the value IALL((/ $a_1, \ldots, a_m$ /)) where $(a_1, \ldots, a_m)$ is the (possibly empty) set of elements of ARRAY selected to contribute to r by the rules stated in Chapter 7.

Example. IALL_PREFIX((/1,3,2,4,5/), SEGMENT= (/F,F,F,T,T/)) is $\begin{bmatrix} 1 & 1 & 0 & 4 & 4 \end{bmatrix}$.

B.20 IALL_SCATTER

Synopsis. IALL_SCATTER(ARRAY, BASE, INDX1, ..., INDXn, MASK)

Optional Argument. MASK

Description. Scatters elements of ARRAY selected by MASK to positions of the result indicated by index arrays INDX1, ..., INDXn. The jth bit of an element of the result is 1 if and only if the jth bits of the corresponding element of BASE and of the elements of ARRAY scattered to that position are all equal to 1.

Class. Transformational function.

Arguments.

ARRAY   must be of type integer. It must not be scalar.

BASE   must be of type integer with the same kind type parameter as ARRAY. It must not be scalar.

INDX1,...,INDXn must be of type integer and must be conformable with ARRAY. The number of INDX arguments must be equal to the rank of BASE.

MASK*   must be of type logical and must be conformable with ARRAY.

Result Type, Type Parameter, and Shape. Same as BASE.

Result Value. The element of the result corresponding to the element b of BASE has the value IALL((/$a_1, a_2, \ldots, a_m, b$/)), where $(a_1, \ldots, a_m)$ are the elements of ARRAY associated with b as described in Chapter 7.

Example. IALL_SCATTER((/1, 2, 3, 6/), (/1, 3, 7/), (/1, 1, 2, 2/)) is $\begin{bmatrix} 0 & 2 & 7 \end{bmatrix}$.

B.21 IALL_SUFFIX

Synopsis. IALL_SUFFIX(ARRAY, DIM, MASK, SEGMENT, EXCLUSIVE)

Optional Arguments. DIM, MASK, SEGMENT, EXCLUSIVE

Description. Computes a reverse, segmented bitwise logical AND scan along dimension DIM of ARRAY.

Class. Transformational function.

Arguments.

ARRAY   must be of type integer. It must not be scalar.

DIM*   must be scalar and of type integer with a value in the range $1 \leq$ DIM $\leq n$, where n is the rank of ARRAY.

MASK*   must be of type logical and must be conformable with ARRAY.

SEGMENT* must be of type logical and have the same shape as ARRAY.

EXCLUSIVE* must be of type logical and must be scalar.

Result Type, Type Parameter, and Shape. Same as ARRAY.

Result Value. Element r of the result has the value IALL((/ $a_1, \ldots, a_m$ /)) where $(a_1, \ldots, a_m)$ is the (possibly empty) set of elements of ARRAY selected to contribute to r by the rules stated in Chapter 7.

Example. IALL_SUFFIX((/1,3,2,4,5/), SEGMENT= (/F,F,F,T,T/)) is $\begin{bmatrix} 0 & 2 & 2 & 4 & 5 \end{bmatrix}$.

B.22 IANY

Synopsis. IANY(ARRAY, DIM, MASK)

Optional Arguments. DIM, MASK

Description. Computes a bitwise logical OR reduction along dimension DIM of ARRAY.

Class. Transformational function.

Arguments.

ARRAY   must be of type integer. It must not be scalar.

DIM*   must be scalar and of type integer with a value in the range $1 \leq \text{DIM} \leq n$, where n is the rank of ARRAY. The corresponding actual argument must not be an optional dummy argument.

MASK*   must be of type logical and must be conformable with ARRAY.

Result Type, Type Parameter, and Shape. The result is of type integer with the same kind type parameter as ARRAY. It is scalar if DIM is absent or if ARRAY has rank one; otherwise, the result is an array of rank $n-1$ and shape $(d_1, d_2, \ldots, d_{DIM-1}, d_{DIM+1}, \ldots, d_n)$ where $(d_1, d_2, \ldots, d_n)$ is the shape of ARRAY.

Result Value.

Case (i):   The result of IANY(ARRAY) is the IOR reduction of all the elements of ARRAY. If ARRAY has size zero, the result has the value zero.

Case (ii): The result of IANY(ARRAY, MASK=MASK) is the IOR reduction of all the elements of ARRAY corresponding to the true elements of MASK; if MASK contains no true elements, the result is zero.

Case (iii): If ARRAY has rank one, IANY(ARRAY, DIM=1 [,MASK]) has a value equal to that of IANY(ARRAY [,MASK]). Otherwise, the value of element $(s_1, s_2, \ldots, s_{DIM-1}, s_{DIM+1}, \ldots, s_n)$ of IANY(ARRAY, DIM=1 [,MASK]) is equal to IANY(ARRAY$(s_1, s_2, \ldots, s_{DIM-1}, :, s_{DIM+1}, \ldots, s_n)$ [,MASK = MASK$(s_1, s_2, \ldots, s_{DIM-1}, :, s_{DIM+1}, \ldots, s_n)$]).

Examples.

Case (i):   The value of IANY((/9, 8, 3, 2/)) is 11.

Case (ii): The value of IANY(C, MASK = BTEST(C,0)) is the IOR reduction of the odd elements of C.

Case (iii): If B is the array $\begin{bmatrix} 2 & 3 & 5 \\ 0 & 4 & 2 \end{bmatrix}$, then IANY(B, DIM = 1) is $\begin{bmatrix} 2 & 7 & 7 \end{bmatrix}$ and IANY(B, DIM = 2) is $\begin{bmatrix} 7 & 6 \end{bmatrix}$.

B.23 IANY_PREFIX

Synopsis. IANY_PREFIX(ARRAY, DIM, MASK, SEGMENT, EXCLUSIVE)

Optional Arguments. DIM, MASK, SEGMENT, EXCLUSIVE

Description. Computes a segmented bitwise logical OR scan along dimension DIM of ARRAY.

Class. Transformational function.

Arguments.

ARRAY   must be of type integer. It must not be scalar.

DIM*   must be scalar and of type integer with a value in the range $1 \leq$ DIM $\leq n$, where n is the rank of ARRAY.

MASK*   must be of type logical and must be conformable with ARRAY.

SEGMENT* must be of type logical and have the same shape as ARRAY.

EXCLUSIVE* must be of type logical and must be scalar.

Result Type, Type Parameter, and Shape. Same as ARRAY.

Result Value. Element r of the result has the value IANY((/ $a_1, \ldots, a_m$ /)) where $(a_1, \ldots, a_m)$ is the (possibly empty) set of elements of ARRAY selected to contribute to r by the rules stated in Chapter 7.

Example. IANY_PREFIX((/1,2,3,2,5/), SEGMENT= (/F,F,F,T,T/)) is $\begin{bmatrix} 1 & 3 & 3 & 2 & 7 \end{bmatrix}$.

B.24 IANY_SCATTER

Synopsis. IANY_SCATTER(ARRAY,BASE,INDX1,..., INDXn, MASK)

Optional Argument. MASK

Description. Scatters elements of ARRAY selected by MASK to positions of the result indicated by index arrays INDX1, ..., INDXn. The jth bit of an element of the result is 1 if and only if the jth bit of the corresponding element of BASE or of any of the elements of ARRAY scattered to that position is equal to 1.

Class. Transformational function.

Arguments.

ARRAY   must be of type integer. It must not be scalar.

BASE   must be of type integer with the same kind type parameter as ARRAY. It must not be scalar.

INDX1,...,INDXn must be of type integer and must be conformable with ARRAY. The number of INDX arguments must be equal to the rank of BASE.

MASK*   must be of type logical and must be conformable with ARRAY.

Result Type, Type Parameter, and Shape. Same as BASE.

Result Value. The element of the result corresponding to the element b of BASE has the value IANY((/$a_1, a_2, \ldots, a_m, b$/)), where $(a_1, \ldots, a_m)$ are the elements of ARRAY associated with b as described in Chapter 7.

Example. IANY_SCATTER((/1, 2, 3, 6/), (/1, 3, 7/), (/1, 1, 2, 2/)) is $\begin{bmatrix} 3 & 7 & 7 \end{bmatrix}$.

B.25 IANY_SUFFIX

Synopsis. IANY_SUFFIX(ARRAY, DIM, MASK, SEGMENT, EXCLUSIVE)

Optional Arguments. DIM, MASK, SEGMENT, EXCLUSIVE

Description. Computes a reverse, segmented bitwise logical OR scan along dimension DIM of ARRAY.

Class. Transformational function.

Arguments.

ARRAY   must be of type integer. It must not be scalar.

DIM*   must be scalar and of type integer with a value in the range $1 \leq$ DIM $\leq n$, where n is the rank of ARRAY.

MASK*   must be of type logical and must be conformable with ARRAY.

SEGMENT*   must be of type logical and have the same shape as ARRAY.

EXCLUSIVE* must be of type logical and must be scalar.

Result Type, Type Parameter, and Shape. Same as ARRAY.

Result Value. Element r of the result has the value IANY((/ $a_1, \ldots, a_m$ /)) where $(a_1, \ldots, a_m)$ is the (possibly empty) set of elements of ARRAY selected to contribute to r by the rules stated in Chapter 7.

Example. IANY_SUFFIX((/4,2,3,2,5/), SEGMENT= (/F,F,F,T,T/)) is [7 3 3 7 5].

B.26 ILEN

Synopsis. ILEN(I)

Description. Returns one less than the length, in bits, of the two's-complement representation of an integer.

Class. Elemental function. Intrinsic.

Argument. I must be of type integer.

Result Type and Type Parameter. Same as I.

Result Value. If I is nonnegative, ILEN(I) has the value $\lceil \log_2(\text{I}+1) \rceil$; if I is negative, ILEN(I) has the value $\lceil \log_2(-\text{I}) \rceil$.

Examples. ILEN(4) = 3. ILEN(-4) = 2. 2**ILEN(N-1) rounds N up to a power of 2 (for N > 0), whereas 2**(ILEN(N)-1) rounds N down to a power of 2. Compare with LEADZ.

The value returned is one *less* than the length of the two's-complement representation of I, as the following explains. The shortest two's-complement representation of 4 is 0100. The leading zero is the required sign bit. In 3-bit two's complement, 100 represents -4.

B.27 IPARITY

Synopsis. IPARITY(ARRAY, DIM, MASK)

Optional Arguments. DIM, MASK

Description. Computes a bitwise logical exclusive OR reduction along dimension DIM of ARRAY.

Class. Transformational function.

Arguments.

ARRAY   must be of type integer. It must not be scalar.

DIM*   must be scalar and of type integer with a value in the range $1 \leq$ DIM $\leq n$, where n is the rank of ARRAY. The corresponding actual argument must not be an optional dummy argument.

MASK*   must be of type logical and must be conformable with ARRAY.

Result Type, Type Parameter, and Shape. The result is of type integer with the same kind type parameter as ARRAY. It is scalar if DIM is absent or if ARRAY has rank one; otherwise, the result is an array of rank $n-1$ and shape $(d_1, d_2, \ldots, d_{DIM-1}, d_{DIM+1}, \ldots, d_n)$ where $(d_1, d_2, \ldots, d_n)$ is the shape of ARRAY.

Result Value.

Case (i):   The result of IPARITY(ARRAY) is the IEOR reduction of all the elements of ARRAY. If ARRAY has size zero, the result has the value zero.

Case (ii):   The result of IPARITY(ARRAY, MASK=MASK) is the IEOR reduction of all the elements of ARRAY corresponding to the true elements of MASK; if MASK contains no true elements, the result is zero.

Case (iii):   If ARRAY is rank one, IPARITY(ARRAY, DIM=1 [,MASK]) is equivalent to IPARITY(ARRAY [,MASK]). Otherwise, the value of element $(s_1, s_2, \ldots, s_{DIM-1}, s_{DIM+1}, \ldots, s_n)$ of IPARITY(ARRAY, DIM=1 [,MASK]) is equal to IPARITY(ARRAY$(s_1, s_2, \ldots, s_{DIM-1}, :, s_{DIM+1}, \ldots, s_n)$ [,MASK = MASK$(s_1, s_2, \ldots, s_{DIM-1}, :, s_{DIM+1}, \ldots, s_n)$])

Examples.

Case (i):   The value of IPARITY((/13, 8, 3, 2/)) is 4.

Case (ii):   The value of IPARITY(C, MASK = BTEST(C,0)) is the IEOR reduction of the odd elements of C.

Case (iii):   If B is the array $\begin{bmatrix} 2 & 3 & 7 \\ 0 & 4 & 2 \end{bmatrix}$, then IPARITY(B, DIM = 1) is $\begin{bmatrix} 2 & 7 & 5 \end{bmatrix}$ and IPARITY(B, DIM = 2) is $\begin{bmatrix} 6 & 6 \end{bmatrix}$.

B.28 IPARITY_PREFIX

Synopsis. IPARITY_PREFIX(ARRAY, DIM, MASK, SEGMENT, EXCLUSIVE)

Optional Arguments. DIM, MASK, SEGMENT, EXCLUSIVE

Description. Computes a segmented bitwise logical exclusive OR scan along dimension DIM of ARRAY.

Class. Transformational function.

Arguments.

ARRAY   must be of type integer. It must not be scalar.

DIM*   must be scalar and of type integer with a value in the range $1 \leq$ DIM $\leq n$, where n is the rank of ARRAY.

MASK*   must be of type logical and must be conformable with ARRAY.

SEGMENT*   must be of type logical and have the same shape as ARRAY.

EXCLUSIVE*   must be of type logical and must be scalar.

Result Type, Type Parameter, and Shape. Same as ARRAY.

Result Value. Element r of the result has the value IPARITY((/ $a_1, \ldots, a_m$ /)) where $(a_1, \ldots, a_m)$ is the (possibly empty) set of elements of ARRAY selected to contribute to r by the rules stated in Chapter 7.

Example. IPARITY_PREFIX((/1,2,3,4,5/), SEGMENT= (/F,F,F,T,T/)) is $\begin{bmatrix} 1 & 3 & 0 & 4 & 1 \end{bmatrix}$.

B.29 IPARITY_SCATTER

Synopsis. IPARITY_SCATTER(ARRAY, BASE, INDX1, ..., INDXn, MASK)

Optional Argument. MASK

Description. Scatters elements of ARRAY selected by MASK to positions of the result indicated by index arrays INDX1, ..., INDXn. The jth bit of an element of the result is 1 if and only if there are an odd number of ones among the jth bits of the corresponding element of BASE and the elements of ARRAY scattered to that position.

Class. Transformational function.

Arguments.

ARRAY   must be of type integer. It must not be scalar.

BASE   must be of type integer with the same kind type parameter as ARRAY. It must not be scalar.

INDX1,...,INDXn must be of type integer and must be conformable with ARRAY. The number of INDX arguments must be equal to the rank of BASE.

MASK*   must be of type logical and must be conformable with ARRAY.

Result Type, Type Parameter, and Shape. Same as BASE.

Result Value. The element of the result corresponding to the element b of BASE has the value IPARITY((/$a_1, a_2, \ldots, a_m, b$/)), where $(a_1, \ldots, a_m)$ are the elements of ARRAY associated with b as described in Chapter 7.

Example. IPARITY_SCATTER((/1,2,3,6/), (/1,3,7/), (/1,1,2,2/)) is [2 6 7].

B.30 IPARITY_SUFFIX

Synopsis. IPARITY_SUFFIX(ARRAY, DIM, MASK, SEGMENT, EXCLUSIVE)

Optional Arguments. DIM, MASK, SEGMENT, EXCLUSIVE

Description. Computes a reverse, segmented bitwise logical exclusive OR scan along dimension DIM of ARRAY.

Class. Transformational function.

Arguments.

ARRAY   must be of type integer. It must not be scalar.

DIM*   must be scalar and of type integer with a value in the range $1 \leq$ DIM $\leq n$, where n is the rank of ARRAY.

MASK*   must be of type logical and must be conformable with ARRAY.

SEGMENT*   must be of type logical and have the same shape as ARRAY.

EXCLUSIVE* must be of type logical and must be scalar.

Result Type, Type Parameter, and Shape. Same as ARRAY.

Result Value. Element r of the result has the value IPARITY(($/\ a_1,\ldots,a_m\ /$)) where $(a_1,\ldots,a_m)$ is the (possibly empty) set of elements of ARRAY selected to contribute to r by the rules stated in Chapter 7.

Example. IPARITY_SUFFIX((/1,2,3,4,5/), SEGMENT= (/F,F,F,T,T/)) is $\begin{bmatrix} 0 & 1 & 3 & 1 & 5 \end{bmatrix}$.

B.31 LEADZ

Synopsis. LEADZ(I)

Description. Return the number of leading zeros in an integer.

Class. Elemental function.

Argument. I must be of type integer.

Result Type and Type Parameter. Same as I.

Result Value. The result is a count of the number of leading 0-bits in the integer I. The model for the interpretation of an integer as a sequence of bits is in Section 13.5.7 of the Fortran 90 Standard. LEADZ(0) is BIT_SIZE(I). For nonzero I, if the leftmost one bit of I occurs in position $k-1$ (where the rightmost bit is bit 0) then LEADZ(I) is BIT_SIZE(I) - k.

Examples. LEADZ(3) has the value BIT_SIZE(3) - 2. For scalar I, LEADZ(I) == MINVAL((/ (J, J=0, BIT_SIZE(I)) /), MASK=M) where M = (/ (BTEST(I,J), J=BIT_SIZE(I)-1, 0, -1), .TRUE. /). A given integer I may produce different results from LEADZ(I), depending on the number of bits in the representation of the integer (BIT_SIZE(I)). That is because LEADZ counts bits from the most significant bit. Compare with ILEN.

B.32 MAXLOC

Synopsis. MAXLOC(ARRAY, DIM, MASK)

Class. Transformational function. Intrinsic.

Optional Arguments. `DIM`, `MASK`

Description. Determine the locations of the first elements of `ARRAY` along dimension `DIM` having the maximum value of the elements identified by `MASK`.

Arguments.

`ARRAY`   must be of type integer or real. It must not be scalar.

`DIM*`   must be scalar and of type integer with a value in the range $1 \leq \text{DIM} \leq n$, where n is the rank of `ARRAY`. The corresponding actual argument must not be an optional dummy argument.

`MASK*`   must be of type logical and must be conformable with `ARRAY`.

Result Type, Type Parameter, and Shape. The result is of type default integer. If `DIM` is absent the result is an array of rank one and size equal to the rank of `ARRAY`; otherwise, the result is an array of rank $n - 1$ and shape $(d_1, \ldots, d_{DIM-1}, d_{DIM+1}, \ldots, d_n)$, where $(d_1, \ldots, d_n)$ is the shape of `ARRAY`.

Result Value.

Case (i):   The result of executing `S = MAXLOC(ARRAY) + LBOUND(ARRAY) - 1` is a rank-one array `S` of size equal to the rank n of `ARRAY`. It is such that `ARRAY(S(1), ..., S(n))` has the maximum value of all of the elements of `ARRAY`. If more than one element has the maximum value, the element whose subscripts are returned is the first such element, taken in array element order. If `ARRAY` has size zero, the result is processor dependent.

Case (ii):   The result of executing `S = MAXLOC(ARRAY,MASK)+LBOUND(ARRAY)-1` is a rank-one array `S` of size equal to the rank n of `ARRAY`. It is such that `ARRAY(S(1), ..., S(n))` corresponds to a true element of `MASK`, and has the maximum value of all such elements of `ARRAY`. If more than one element has the maximum value, the element whose subscripts are returned is the first such element, taken in array element order. If there are no such elements (that is, if `ARRAY` has size zero or every element of `MASK` has the value false), the result is processor dependent.

Case (iii): If ARRAY has rank one, the result of MAXLOC(ARRAY, DIM [,MASK]) is a scalar S such that ARRAY(S + LBOUND(ARRAY,1) - 1) corresponds to a true element of MASK (if MASK is present) and has the maximum value of all such elements (all elements if MASK is absent). It is the smallest such subscript. Otherwise, the value of element $(s_1, \ldots, s_{DIM-1}, s_{DIM+1}, \ldots, s_n)$ of MAXLOC(ARRAY, DIM [,MASK]) is equal to MAXLOC(ARRAY$(s_1, \ldots, s_{DIM-1}, :, s_{DIM+1}, \ldots, s_n)$ [,MASK = MASK$(s_1, \ldots, s_{DIM-1}, :, s_{DIM+1}, \ldots, s_n)$]).

Examples.

Case (i): The value of MAXLOC((/ 5, -9, 3 /)) is [1].

Case (ii): MAXLOC(C, MASK = C .LT. 0) finds the location of the first element of C that is the maximum of the negative elements.

Case (iii): The value of MAXLOC((/ 5, -9, 3 /), DIM=1) is 1. If B is the array $\begin{bmatrix} 1 & 3 & -9 \\ 2 & 2 & 6 \end{bmatrix}$, MAXLOC(B, DIM = 1) is [2 1 2] and MAXLOC(B, DIM = 2) is [2 3]. Note that this is true even if B has a declared lower bound other than 1.

B.33 MAXVAL_PREFIX

Synopsis. MAXVAL_PREFIX(ARRAY, DIM, MASK, SEGMENT, EXCLUSIVE)

Optional Arguments. DIM, MASK, SEGMENT, EXCLUSIVE

Description. Computes a segmented MAXVAL scan along dimension DIM of ARRAY.

Class. Transformational function.

Arguments.

ARRAY   must be of type integer or real. It must not be scalar.

DIM*   must be scalar and of type integer with a value in the range $1 \leq$ DIM $\leq n$, where n is the rank of ARRAY.

MASK*   must be of type logical and must be conformable with ARRAY.

SEGMENT*   must be of type logical and have the same shape as ARRAY.

EXCLUSIVE* must be of type logical and must be scalar.

Result Type, Type Parameter, and Shape. Same as ARRAY.

Result Value. Element r of the result has the value MAXVAL((/ $a_1, \ldots, a_m$ /)) where $(a_1, \ldots, a_m)$ is the (possibly empty) set of elements of ARRAY selected to contribute to r by the rules stated in Chapter 7.

Example. MAXVAL_PREFIX((/3,4,-5,2,5/), SEGMENT= (/F,F,F,T,T/)) is $\begin{bmatrix} 3 & 4 & 4 & 2 & 5 \end{bmatrix}$.

B.34 MAXVAL_SCATTER

Synopsis. MAXVAL_SCATTER(ARRAY, BASE, INDX1, ..., INDXn, MASK)

Optional Argument. MASK

Description. Scatters elements of ARRAY selected by MASK to positions of the result indicated by index arrays INDX1, ..., INDXn. Each element of the result is assigned the maximum value of the corresponding element of BASE and the elements of ARRAY scattered to that position.

Class. Transformational function.

Arguments.

ARRAY   must be of type integer or real. It must not be scalar.

BASE   must be of the same type and kind type parameter as ARRAY. It must not be scalar.

INDX1,...,INDXn must be of type integer and must be conformable with ARRAY. The number of INDX arguments must be equal to the rank of BASE.

MASK*   must be of type logical and must be conformable with ARRAY.

Result Type, Type Parameter, and Shape. Same as BASE.

Result Value. The element of the result corresponding to the element b of BASE has the value MAXVAL($(/a_1, a_2, \ldots, a_m, b/)$), where $(a_1, \ldots, a_m)$ are the elements of ARRAY associated with b as described in Chapter 7.

Example. MAXVAL_SCATTER((/1, 2, 3, 1/),(/4, -5, 7/),(/1, 1, 2, 2/)) is $\begin{bmatrix} 4 & 3 & 7 \end{bmatrix}$.

B.35 MAXVAL_SUFFIX

Synopsis. `MAXVAL_SUFFIX(ARRAY, DIM, MASK, SEGMENT, EXCLUSIVE)`

Optional Arguments. `DIM, MASK, SEGMENT, EXCLUSIVE`

Description. Computes a reverse, segmented `MAXVAL` scan along dimension `DIM` of `ARRAY`.

Class. Transformational function.

Arguments.

ARRAY   must be of type integer or real. It must not be scalar.

DIM*   must be scalar and of type integer with a value in the range $1 \leq$ `DIM` $\leq n$, where n is the rank of `ARRAY`.

MASK*   must be of type logical and must be conformable with `ARRAY`.

SEGMENT*   must be of type logical and have the same shape as `ARRAY`.

EXCLUSIVE* must be of type logical and must be scalar.

Result Type, Type Parameter, and Shape. Same as `ARRAY`.

Result Value. Element r of the result has the value `MAXVAL((/` $a_1, \ldots, a_m$ `/))` where $(a_1, \ldots, a_m)$ is the (possibly empty) set of elements of `ARRAY` selected to contribute to r by the rules stated in Chapter 7.

Example. `MAXVAL_SUFFIX( (/3,4,-5,2,5/), SEGMENT= (/F,F,F,T,T/) )` is $\begin{bmatrix} 4 & 4 & -5 & 5 & 5 \end{bmatrix}$.

B.36 MINLOC

Synopsis. `MINLOC(ARRAY, DIM, MASK)`

Optional Arguments. `DIM, MASK`

Description. Determine the locations of the first elements of `ARRAY` along dimension `DIM` having the minimum value of the elements identified by `MASK`.

Class. Transformational function. Intrinsic.

Arguments.

ARRAY   must be of type integer or real. It must not be scalar.

DIM*   must be scalar and of type integer with a value in the range $1 \leq$ DIM $\leq n$, where n is the rank of ARRAY. The corresponding actual argument must not be an optional dummy argument.

MASK*   must be of type logical and must be conformable with ARRAY.

Result Type, Type Parameter, and Shape. The result is of type default integer. If DIM is absent the result is an array of rank one and size equal to the rank of ARRAY; otherwise, the result is an array of rank $n - 1$ and shape $(d_1, \ldots, d_{DIM-1}, d_{DIM+1}, \ldots, d_n)$, where $(d_1, \ldots, d_n)$ is the shape of ARRAY.

Result Value.

Case (i):   The result of executing S = MINLOC(ARRAY) + LBOUND(ARRAY) - 1 is a rank-one array S of size equal to the rank n of ARRAY. It is such that ARRAY(S(1), ..., S(n)) has the minimum value of all of the elements of ARRAY. If more than one element has the minimum value, the element whose subscripts are returned is the first such element, taken in array element order. If ARRAY has size zero, the result is processor dependent.

Case (ii):   The result of executing S = MINLOC(ARRAY,MASK)+LBOUND(ARRAY)-1 is a rank-one array S of size equal to the rank n of ARRAY. It is such that ARRAY(S(1), ..., S(n)) corresponds to a true element of MASK, and has the minimum value of all such elements of ARRAY. If more than one element has the minimum value, the element whose subscripts are returned is the first such element, taken in array element order. If there are no such elements (that is, if ARRAY has size zero or every element of MASK has the value false), the result is processor dependent.

Case (iii):   If ARRAY has rank one, the result of MINLOC(ARRAY, DIM [,MASK]) is a scalar S such that ARRAY(S + LBOUND(ARRAY,1) - 1) corresponds to a true element of MASK (if MASK is present) and has the minimum value of all such elements (all elements if MASK is absent). It is the smallest such subscript. Otherwise, the value of element $(s_1, \ldots, s_{DIM-1}, s_{DIM+1}, \ldots, s_n)$ of MINLOC(ARRAY, DIM [,MASK]) is equal to MINLOC(ARRAY$((s_1, \ldots, s_{DIM-1}, :, s_{DIM+1}, \ldots, s_n))$ [,MASK = MASK$((s_1, \ldots, s_{DIM-1}, :, s_{DIM+1}, \ldots, s_n))$]).

Examples.

Case (i): The value of `MINLOC((/ 5, -9, 3 /))` is $\begin{bmatrix} 2 \end{bmatrix}$.

Case (ii): `MINLOC(C, MASK = C .GT. 0)` finds the location of the first element of `C` that is the minimum of the positive elements.

Case (iii): The value of `MINLOC((/ 5, -9, 3 /), DIM=1)` is 2. If B is the array $\begin{bmatrix} 1 & 3 & -9 \\ 2 & 2 & 6 \end{bmatrix}$, `MINLOC( B, DIM = 1 )` is $\begin{bmatrix} 1 & 2 & 1 \end{bmatrix}$ and `MINLOC( B, DIM = 2 )` is $\begin{bmatrix} 3 & 1 \end{bmatrix}$. Note that this is true even if B has a declared lower bound other than 1.

B.37 MINVAL_PREFIX

Synopsis. `MINVAL_PREFIX(ARRAY, DIM, MASK, SEGMENT, EXCLUSIVE)`

Optional Arguments. `DIM, MASK, SEGMENT, EXCLUSIVE`

Description. Computes a segmented `MINVAL` scan along dimension `DIM` of `ARRAY`.

Class. Transformational function.

Arguments.

`ARRAY`	must be of type integer or real. It must not be scalar.
`DIM*`	must be scalar and of type integer with a value in the range $1 \leq \text{DIM} \leq n$, where n is the rank of `ARRAY`.
`MASK*`	must be of type logical and must be conformable with `ARRAY`.
`SEGMENT*`	must be of type logical and have the same shape as `ARRAY`.
`EXCLUSIVE*`	must be of type logical and must be scalar.

Result Type, Type Parameter, and Shape. Same as `ARRAY`.

Result Value. Element r of the result has the value `MINVAL((/` $a_1, \ldots, a_m$ `/))` where $(a_1, \ldots, a_m)$ is the (possibly empty) set of elements of `ARRAY` selected to contribute to r by the rules stated in Chapter 7.

Example. `MINVAL_PREFIX( (/1,2,-3,4,5/), SEGMENT= (/F,F,F,T,T/) )` is $\begin{bmatrix} 1 & 1 & -3 & 4 & 4 \end{bmatrix}$.

B.38 MINVAL_SCATTER

Synopsis. MINVAL_SCATTER(ARRAY, BASE, INDX1, ..., INDXn, MASK)

Optional Argument. MASK

Description. Scatters elements of ARRAY selected by MASK to positions of the result indicated by index arrays INDX1, ..., INDXn. Each element of the result is assigned the maximum value of the corresponding element of BASE and the elements of ARRAY scattered to that position.

Class. Transformational function.

Arguments.

ARRAY   must be of type integer or real. It must not be scalar.

BASE   must be of the same type and kind type parameter as ARRAY. It must not be scalar.

INDX1,...,INDXn must be of type integer and must be conformable with ARRAY. The number of INDX arguments must be equal to the rank of BASE.

MASK*   must be of type logical and must be conformable with ARRAY.

Result Type, Type Parameter, and Shape. Same as BASE.

Result Value. The element of the result corresponding to the element b of BASE has the value MINVAL($(/a_1, a_2, \ldots, a_m, b/)$), where $(a_1, \ldots, a_m)$ are the elements of ARRAY associated with b as described in Chapter 7.

Example. MINVAL_SCATTER((/ 1,-2,-3,6 /),(/ 4,3,7 /),(/ 1,1,2,2 /)) is [-2 -3 7].

B.39 MINVAL_SUFFIX

Synopsis. MINVAL_SUFFIX(ARRAY, DIM, MASK, SEGMENT, EXCLUSIVE)

Optional Arguments. DIM, MASK, SEGMENT, EXCLUSIVE

Description. Computes a reverse, segmented MINVAL scan along dimension DIM of ARRAY.

Description of HPF Library and Intrinsic Procedures   293

Class. Transformational function.

Arguments.

ARRAY   must be of type integer or real. It must not be scalar.

DIM*   must be scalar and of type integer with a value in the range $1 \leq \text{DIM} \leq n$, where n is the rank of ARRAY.

MASK*   must be of type logical and must be conformable with ARRAY.

SEGMENT*   must be of type logical and have the same shape as ARRAY.

EXCLUSIVE* must be of type logical and must be scalar.

Result Type, Type Parameter, and Shape. Same as ARRAY.

Result Value. Element r of the result has the value MINVAL((/ $a_1, \ldots, a_m$ /)) where $(a_1, \ldots, a_m)$ is the (possibly empty) set of elements of ARRAY selected to contribute to r by the rules stated in Chapter 7.

Example. MINVAL_SUFFIX((/1,2,-3,4,5/), SEGMENT= (/F,F,F,T,T/)) is $\begin{bmatrix} -3 & -3 & -3 & 4 & 5 \end{bmatrix}$.

B.40 NUMBER_OF_PROCESSORS

Synopsis. NUMBER_OF_PROCESSORS(DIM)

Optional Argument. DIM

Description. Returns the total number of processors available to the program or the number of processors available to the program along a specified dimension of the processor array.

Class. System inquiry function. Intrinsic.

Arguments.

DIM*   must be scalar and of type integer with a value in the range $1 \leq \text{DIM} \leq n$ where n is the rank of the processor array.

Result Type, Type Parameter, and Shape. Default integer scalar.

Result Value. The result has a value equal to the extent of dimension **DIM** of the processor-dependent hardware processor array or, if **DIM** is absent, the total number of elements of the processor-dependent hardware processor array. The result is always greater than zero.

Examples. For a computer with 8192 processors arranged in a 128 by 64 rectangular grid, the value of **NUMBER_OF_PROCESSORS()** is 8192; the value of **NUMBER_OF_PROCESSORS(DIM=1)** is 128; and the value of **NUMBER_OF_PROCESSORS(DIM=2)** is 64. For a single-processor workstation, the value of **NUMBER_OF_PROCESSORS()** is 1; since the rank of a scalar processor array is zero, no **DIM** argument may be used.

B.41 PARITY

Synopsis. PARITY(MASK, DIM)

Optional Argument. DIM

Description. Determine whether an odd number of values are true in **MASK** along dimension **DIM**.

Class. Transformational function.

Arguments.

MASK   must be of type logical. It must not be scalar.

DIM*   must be scalar and of type integer with a value in the range $1 \leq$ **DIM** $\leq n$, where n is the rank of **MASK**. The corresponding actual argument must not be an optional dummy argument.

Result Type, Type Parameter, and Shape. The result is of type logical with the same kind type parameter as **MASK**. It is scalar if **DIM** is absent or if **MASK** has rank one; otherwise, the result is an array of rank $n - 1$ and shape $(d_1, d_2, \ldots, d_{DIM-1}, d_{DIM+1}, \ldots, d_n)$ where $(d_1, d_2, \ldots, d_n)$ is the shape of **MASK**.

Result Value.

Case (i):   The result of **PARITY(MASK)** is the **.NEQV.** reduction of all the elements of **MASK**. If **MASK** has size zero, the result has the value false.

Case (ii): If `MASK` is rank one, `PARITY(MASK, DIM=1)` has a value equal to that of `PARITY(MASK)`. Otherwise, the value of element $(s_1, s_2, \ldots, s_{DIM-1}, s_{DIM+1}, \ldots, s_n)$ of `PARITY(MASK, DIM=1)` is equal to `PARITY(MASK`$(s_1, s_2, \ldots, s_{DIM-1}, :, s_{DIM+1}, \ldots, s_n)$`)`

Examples.

Case (i): The value of `PARITY((/T, T, T, F/))` is true.

Case (ii): If `B` is the array $\begin{bmatrix} T & T & F \\ T & T & T \end{bmatrix}$, then `PARITY(B, DIM = 1)` is $\begin{bmatrix} F & F & T \end{bmatrix}$ and `PARITY(B, DIM = 2)` is $\begin{bmatrix} F & T \end{bmatrix}$.

B.42 PARITY_PREFIX

Synopsis. `PARITY_PREFIX(MASK, DIM, SEGMENT, EXCLUSIVE)`

Optional Arguments. `DIM, SEGMENT, EXCLUSIVE`

Description. Computes a segmented logical exclusive OR scan along dimension `DIM` of `MASK`.

Class. Transformational function.

Arguments.

`MASK` must be of type logical. It must not be scalar.

`DIM*` must be scalar and of type integer with a value in the range $1 \leq$ `DIM` $\leq n$, where n is the rank of `MASK`.

`SEGMENT*` must be of type logical and have the same shape as `MASK`.

`EXCLUSIVE*` must be of type logical and must be scalar.

Result Type, Type Parameter, and Shape. Same as `MASK`.

Result Value. Element r of the result has the value `PARITY((/` $a_1, \ldots, a_m$ `/))` where $(a_1, \ldots, a_m)$ is the (possibly empty) set of elements of `MASK` selected to contribute to r by the rules stated in Chapter 7.

Example. `PARITY_PREFIX( (/T,F,T,T,T/), SEGMENT= (/F,F,F,T,T/) )` is $\begin{bmatrix} T & T & F & T & F \end{bmatrix}$.

B.43 PARITY_SCATTER

Synopsis. PARITY_SCATTER(MASK, BASE, INDX1, ..., INDXn)

Description. Scatters elements of MASK to positions of the result indicated by index arrays INDX1, ..., INDXn. An element of the result is true if and only if the number of true values among the corresponding element of BASE and the elements of MASK scattered to that position is odd.

Class. Transformational function.

Arguments.

MASK   must be of type logical. It must not be scalar.

BASE   must be of type logical with the same kind type parameter as MASK. It must not be scalar.

INDX1,...,INDXn must be of type integer and conformable with MASK. The number of INDX arguments must be equal to the rank of BASE.

Result Type, Type Parameter, and Shape. Same as BASE.

Result Value. The element of the result corresponding to the element b of BASE has the value PARITY($(/a_1, a_2, \ldots, a_m, b/)$), where $(a_1, \ldots, a_m)$ are the elements of MASK associated with b as described in Chapter 7.

Example. PARITY_SCATTER((/ T,T,T,T /), (/ T,F,F /), (/ 1,1,1,2 /)) is [F T F].

B.44 PARITY_SUFFIX

Synopsis. PARITY_SUFFIX(MASK, DIM, SEGMENT, EXCLUSIVE)

Optional Arguments. DIM, SEGMENT, EXCLUSIVE

Description. Computes a reverse, segmented logical exclusive OR scan along dimension DIM of MASK.

Class. Transformational function.

Arguments.

Description of HPF Library and Intrinsic Procedures   297

MASK   must be of type logical. It must not be scalar.

DIM*   must be scalar and of type integer with a value in the range $1 \leq$ DIM $\leq n$, where n is the rank of MASK.

SEGMENT*   must be of type logical and have the same shape as MASK.

EXCLUSIVE* must be of type logical and must be scalar.

Result Type, Type Parameter, and Shape. Same as MASK.

Result Value. Element r of the result has the value PARITY((/ $a_1,\ldots,a_m$ /)) where $(a_1,\ldots,a_m)$ is the (possibly empty) set of elements of MASK selected to contribute to r by the rules stated in Chapter 7.

Example. PARITY_SUFFIX((/T,F,T,T,T/), SEGMENT= (/F,F,F,T,T/)) is [F T T F T].

B.45 POPCNT

Synopsis. POPCNT(I)

Description. Return the number of one bits in an integer.

Class. Elemental function.

Argument. I must be of type integer.

Result Type and Type Parameter. Same as I.

Result Value. POPCNT(I) is the number of one bits in the binary representation of the integer I. The model for the interpretation of an integer as a sequence of bits is in Section 13.5.7 of the Fortran 90 Standard.

Example. POPCNT(I) = COUNT((/ (BTEST(I,J), J=0, BIT_SIZE(I)-1) /)), for scalar I.

B.46 POPPAR

Synopsis. POPPAR(I)

Description. Return the parity of an integer.

Class. Elemental function.

Argument. I must be of type integer.

Result Type and Type Parameter. Same as I.

Result Value. POPPAR(I) is 1 if there are an odd number of one bits in I and zero if there are an even number. The model for the interpretation of an integer as a sequence of bits is in Section 13.5.7 of the Fortran 90 Standard.

Example. For scalar I, POPPAR(x) = MERGE(1,0,BTEST(POPCNT(x),0)).

B.47 PROCESSORS_SHAPE

Synopsis. PROCESSORS_SHAPE()

Description. Returns the shape of the implementation-dependent processor array.

Class. System inquiry function. Intrinsic.

Arguments. None

Result Type, Type Parameter, and Shape. The result is a default integer array of rank one whose size is equal to the rank of the implementation-dependent processor array.

Result Value. The value of the result is the shape of the implementation-dependent processor array.

Example. In a computer with 2048 processors arranged in a hypercube, the value of PROCESSORS_SHAPE() is [2,2,2,2,2,2,2,2,2,2,2]. In a computer with 8192 processors arranged in a 128 by 64 rectangular grid, the value of PROCESSORS_SHAPE() is [128,64]. For a single processor workstation, the value of PROCESSORS_SHAPE() is [] (the size-zero array of rank one).

B.48 PRODUCT_PREFIX

Synopsis. PRODUCT_PREFIX(ARRAY, DIM, MASK, SEGMENT, EXCLUSIVE)

Optional Arguments. DIM, MASK, SEGMENT, EXCLUSIVE

Description. Computes a segmented PRODUCT scan along dimension DIM of ARRAY.

Class. Transformational function.

Arguments.

ARRAY   must be of type integer, real, or complex. It must not be scalar.

DIM*   must be scalar and of type integer with a value in the range $1 \leq$ DIM $\leq n$, where n is the rank of ARRAY.

MASK*   must be of type logical and must be conformable with ARRAY.

SEGMENT*   must be of type logical and have the same shape as ARRAY.

EXCLUSIVE* must be of type logical and must be scalar.

Result Type, Type Parameter, and Shape. Same as ARRAY.

Result Value. Element r of the result has the value PRODUCT((/ $a_1, \ldots, a_m$ /)) where $(a_1, \ldots, a_m)$ is the (possibly empty) set of elements of ARRAY selected to contribute to r by the rules stated in Chapter 7.

Example. PRODUCT_PREFIX((/1,2,3,4,5/), SEGMENT= (/F,F,F,T,T/)) is $\begin{bmatrix} 1 & 2 & 6 & 4 & 20 \end{bmatrix}$.

B.49 PRODUCT_SCATTER

Synopsis. PRODUCT_SCATTER(ARRAY, BASE, INDX1, ..., INDXn, MASK)

Optional Argument. MASK

Description. Scatters elements of ARRAY selected by MASK to positions of the result indicated by index arrays INDX1, ..., INDXn. Each element of the result is equal to the product of the corresponding element of BASE and the elements of ARRAY scattered to that position.

Class. Transformational function.

Arguments.

ARRAY   must be of type integer, real, or complex. It must not be scalar.

BASE   must be of the same type and kind type parameter as ARRAY. It must not be scalar.

INDX1,...,INDXn must be of type integer and must be conformable with ARRAY. The number of INDX arguments must be equal to the rank of BASE.

MASK*   must be of type logical and must be conformable with ARRAY.

Result Type, Type Parameter, and Shape. Same as BASE.

Result Value. The element of the result corresponding to the element b of BASE has the value PRODUCT($(/a_1, a_2, \ldots, a_m, b/)$), where $(a_1, \ldots, a_m)$ are the elements of ARRAY associated with b as described in Chapter 7.

Example. PRODUCT_SCATTER((/ 1,2,3,1 /),(/ 4,-5,7 /),(/ 1,1,2,2 /)) is $\begin{bmatrix} 8 & -15 & 7 \end{bmatrix}$.

B.50 PRODUCT_SUFFIX

Synopsis. PRODUCT_SUFFIX(ARRAY, DIM, MASK, SEGMENT, EXCLUSIVE)

Optional Arguments. DIM, MASK, SEGMENT, EXCLUSIVE

Description. Computes a reverse, segmented PRODUCT scan along dimension DIM of ARRAY.

Class. Transformational function.

Arguments.

ARRAY   must be of type integer, real, or complex. It must not be scalar.

DIM*   must be scalar and of type integer with a value in the range $1 \leq$ DIM $\leq n$, where n is the rank of ARRAY.

MASK*   must be of type logical and must be conformable with ARRAY.

SEGMENT*   must be of type logical and have the same shape as ARRAY.

EXCLUSIVE* must be of type logical and must be scalar.

Result Type, Type Parameter, and Shape. Same as ARRAY.

Description of HPF Library and Intrinsic Procedures 301

Result Value. Element r of the result has the value $\texttt{PRODUCT}((/\ a_1,\ldots,a_m\ /))$ where $(a_1,\ldots,a_m)$ is the (possibly empty) set of elements of ARRAY selected to contribute to r by the rules stated in Chapter 7.

Example. PRODUCT_SUFFIX((/1,2,3,4,5/), SEGMENT= (/F,F,F,T,T/)) is $\begin{bmatrix} 6 & 6 & 3 & 20 & 5 \end{bmatrix}$.

B.51 SUM_PREFIX

Synopsis. SUM_PREFIX(ARRAY, DIM, MASK, SEGMENT, EXCLUSIVE)

Optional Arguments. DIM, MASK, SEGMENT, EXCLUSIVE

Description. Computes a segmented SUM scan along dimension DIM of ARRAY.

Class. Transformational function.

Arguments.

ARRAY must be of type integer, real, or complex. It must not be scalar.

DIM* must be scalar and of type integer with a value in the range $1 \leq \texttt{DIM} \leq n$, where n is the rank of ARRAY.

MASK* must be of type logical and must be conformable with ARRAY.

SEGMENT* must be of type logical and have the same shape as ARRAY.

EXCLUSIVE* must be of type logical and must be scalar.

Result Type, Type Parameter, and Shape. Same as ARRAY.

Result Value. Element r of the result has the value $\texttt{SUM}((/\ a_1,\ldots,a_m\ /))$ where $(a_1,\ldots,a_m)$ is the (possibly empty) set of elements of ARRAY selected to contribute to r by the rules stated in Chapter 7.

Example. SUM_PREFIX((/1,2,3,4,5/), SEGMENT= (/F,F,F,T,T/)) is $\begin{bmatrix} 1 & 3 & 6 & 4 & 9 \end{bmatrix}$.

B.52 SUM_SCATTER

Synopsis. SUM_SCATTER(ARRAY,BASE, INDX1, ..., INDXn, MASK)

Optional Argument. MASK

Description. Scatters elements of ARRAY selected by MASK to positions of the result indicated by index arrays INDX1, ..., INDXn. Each element of the result is equal to the sum of the corresponding element of BASE and the elements of ARRAY scattered to that position.

Class. Transformational function.

Arguments.

ARRAY   must be of type integer, real, or complex. It must not be scalar.

BASE   must be of the same type and kind type parameter as ARRAY. It must not be scalar.

INDX1,...,INDXn must be of type integer and must be conformable with ARRAY. The number of INDX arguments must be equal to the rank of BASE.

MASK*   must be of type logical and must be conformable with ARRAY.

Result Type, Type Parameter, and Shape. Same as BASE.

Result Value. The element of the result corresponding to the element b of BASE has the value SUM((/$a_1, a_2, \ldots, a_m, b$/)), where $(a_1, \ldots, a_m)$ are the elements of ARRAY associated with b as described in Chapter 7.

Example. SUM_SCATTER((/1, 2, 3, 1/), (/4, -5, 7/), (/1, 1, 2, 2/)) is $\begin{bmatrix} 7 & -1 & 7 \end{bmatrix}$.

B.53 SUM_SUFFIX

Synopsis. SUM_SUFFIX(ARRAY, DIM, MASK, SEGMENT, EXCLUSIVE)

Optional Arguments. DIM, MASK, SEGMENT, EXCLUSIVE

Description. Computes a reverse, segmented SUM scan along dimension DIM of ARRAY.

Class. Transformational function.

Arguments.

ARRAY   must be of type integer, real, or complex. It must not be scalar.

DIM*   must be scalar and of type integer with a value in the range $1 \leq$ DIM $\leq n$, where n is the rank of ARRAY.

MASK*   must be of type logical and must be conformable with ARRAY.

SEGMENT*   must be of type logical and have the same shape as ARRAY.

EXCLUSIVE* must be of type logical and must be scalar.

Result Type, Type Parameter, and Shape. Same as ARRAY.

Result Value. Element r of the result has the value SUM((/ $a_1, \ldots, a_m$ /)) where $(a_1, \ldots, a_m)$ is the (possibly empty) set of elements of ARRAY selected to contribute to r by the rules stated in Chapter 7.

Example. SUM_SUFFIX((/1,2,3,4,5/), SEGMENT= (/F,F,F,T,T/)) is $\begin{bmatrix} 6 & 5 & 3 & 9 & 5 \end{bmatrix}$.

C Formal Syntax Rules

This Appendix collects the formal syntax definitions from the High Performance Fortran Language Specification [14]. They use the same conventions as that document, which are in turn taken (with slight modifications) from the Fortran 90 Language Specification [17]. To summarize these conventions:

- Each rule defines the form of a single syntactic term, called a *nonterminal symbol* or simply a *nonterminal*. The nonterminal being defined appears on the first line, to the left of the **is**.
- Each rule gives one or more syntactic forms for the nonterminal that it defines. The first form appears on the first line to the right of the **is**; others appear on later lines, separated from each other by **or**.
- Each rule is numbered for identification and cross-referencing. The form of an HPF rule number is Hsnn, where s is a one-digit chapter number (from the HPF Language Specification) and nn is a one- or two-digit sequence number. A Fortran 90 rule number is of the form Rsnn, where s is a one- or two- digit chapter number (from the Fortran 90 Language Specification), and nn is a sequence number. HPF rules are reproduced below; Fortran 90 rules are cross-referenced by number, but not reproduced.
- A nonterminal name appears in *italic font*.
- A terminal (that is, literal text) appears in TYPEWRITER FONT.
- Items that are optional are enclosed in [square brackets].
- Brackets around and trailing periods after an item indicate it may be [repeated] ...
- Line breaks in a BNF rule indicate separate lines in the syntactic form.
- A name of the form *xyz-list* means a comma-separated list of *xyz* items.
- A name of the form *xyz-name* means a *name*, which must refer to an entity of class *xyz*.
- A name of the form *scalar-xyz* means an *xyz* which must evaluate to a scalar.
- A name of the form *integer-xyz* means an *xyz* which must evaluate to an integer.

References in the constraints refer to sections in the HPF Language Specification, not to this book.

C.2 High Performance Fortran Terms and Concepts

C.2.3 Syntax of Directives

H201   *hpf-directive-line*   **is**   *directive-origin hpf-directive*

H202	*directive-origin*	**is**	`!HPF$`
		or	`CHPF$`
		or	`*HPF$`
H203	*hpf-directive*	**is**	*specification-directive*
		or	*executable-directive*
H204	*specification-directive*	**is**	*processors-directive*
		or	*align-directive*
		or	*distribute-directive*
		or	*dynamic-directive*
		or	*inherit-directive*
		or	*template-directive*
		or	*combined-directive*
		or	*sequence-directive*
H205	*executable-directive*	**is**	*realign-directive*
		or	*redistribute-directive*
		or	*independent-directive*

Constraint: An *hpf-directive-line* cannot be commentary following another statement on the same line.

Constraint: A *specification-directive* may appear only where a *declaration-construct* may appear.

Constraint: An *executable-directive* may appear only where an *executable-construct* may appear.

Constraint: An *hpf-directive-line* follows the rules of either Fortran 90 free form (3.3.1.1) or fixed form (3.3.2.1) comment lines, depending on the source form of the surrounding Fortran 90 source form in that program unit. (3.3)

C.3 Data Alignment and Distribution Directives

C.3.2 Syntax of Data Alignment and Distribution Directives

H301	*combined-directive*	**is**	*combined-attribute-list* :: *entity-decl-list*

Formal Syntax Rules

H302	*combined-attribute*	**is**	`ALIGN` *align-attribute-stuff*
		or	`DISTRIBUTE` *dist-attribute-stuff*
		or	`DYNAMIC`
		or	`INHERIT`
		or	`TEMPLATE`
		or	`PROCESSORS`
		or	`DIMENSION` (*explicit-shape-spec-list*)

Constraint: The same *combined-attribute* must not appear more than once in a given *combined-directive*.

Constraint: If the `DIMENSION` attribute appears in a *combined-directive*, any entity to which it applies must be declared with the HPF `TEMPLATE` or `PROCESSORS` type specifier.

C.3.3 DISTRIBUTE and REDISTRIBUTE Directives

H303	*distribute-directive*	**is**	`DISTRIBUTE` *distributee dist-directive-stuff*
H304	*redistribute-directive*	**is**	`REDISTRIBUTE` *distributee dist-directive-stuff*
		or	`REDISTRIBUTE` *dist-attribute-stuff* :: *distributee-list*
H305	*dist-directive-stuff*	**is**	*dist-format-clause* [*dist-onto-clause*]
H306	*dist-attribute-stuff*	**is**	*dist-directive-stuff*
		or	*dist-onto-clause*
H307	*distributee*	**is**	*object-name*
		or	*template-name*
H308	*dist-format-clause*	**is**	(*dist-format-list*)
		or	* (*dist-format-list*)
		or	*
H309	*dist-format*	**is**	`BLOCK` [(*int-expr*)]
		or	`CYCLIC` [(*int-expr*)]
		or	*
H310	*dist-onto-clause*	**is**	`ONTO` *dist-target*
H311	*dist-target*	**is**	*processors-name*
		or	* *processors-name*
		or	*

Constraint: An *object-name* mentioned as a *distributee* must be a simple name and not a subobject designator.

Constraint: An *object-name* mentioned as a *distributee* may not appear as an *alignee* in an **ALIGN** or **REALIGN** directive.

Constraint: A *distributee* that appears in a **REDISTRIBUTE** directive must have the **DYNAMIC** attribute (see Section 3.5).

Constraint: If a *dist-format-list* is specified, its length must equal the rank of each *distributee*.

Constraint: If both a *dist-format-list* and a *processors-name* appear, the number of elements of the *dist-format-list* that are not "*" must equal the rank of the named processor arrangement.

Constraint: If a *processors-name* appears but not a *dist-format-list*, the rank of each *distributee* must equal the rank of the named processor arrangement.

Constraint: If either the *dist-format-clause* or the *dist-target* in a **DISTRIBUTE** directive begins with "*" then every *distributee* must be a dummy argument.

Constraint: Neither the *dist-format-clause* nor the *dist-target* in a **REDISTRIBUTE** may begin with "*".

Constraint: Any *int-expr* appearing in a *dist-format* of a **DISTRIBUTE** directive must be a *specification-expr*.

C.3.4 ALIGN and REALIGN Directives

H312	*align-directive*	is	**ALIGN** *alignee align-directive-stuff*
H313	*realign-directive*	is	**REALIGN** *alignee align-directive-stuff*
		or	**REALIGN** *align-attribute-stuff* :: *alignee-list*
H314	*align-directive-stuff*	is	(*align-source-list*) *align-with-clause*
H315	*align-attribute-stuff*	is	[(*align-source-list*)] *align-with-clause*
H316	*alignee*	is	*object-name*
H317	*align-source*	is	:
		or	*
		or	*align-dummy*
H318	*align-dummy*	is	*scalar-int-variable*

Constraint: An *object-name* mentioned as an *alignee* may not appear as a *distributee* in a `DISTRIBUTE` or `REDISTRIBUTE` directive.

Constraint: Any *alignee* that appears in a `REALIGN` directive must have the `DYNAMIC` attribute (see Section 3.5).

Constraint: The *align-source-list* (and its surrounding parentheses) must be omitted if the *alignee* is scalar. (In some cases this will preclude the use of the statement form of the directive.)

Constraint: If the *align-source-list* is present, its length must equal the rank of the alignee.

Constraint: An *align-dummy* must be a named variable.

Constraint: An object may not have both the `INHERIT` attribute and the `ALIGN` attribute. (However, an object with the `INHERIT` attribute may appear as an *alignee* in a `REALIGN` directive, provided that it does not appear as a *distributee* in a `DISTRIBUTE` or `REDISTRIBUTE` directive.)

H319	*align-with-clause*	is	`WITH` *align-spec*
H320	*align-spec*	is	*align-target* [(*align-subscript-list*)]
		or	* *align-target* [(*align-subscript-list*)]
H321	*align-target*	is	*object-name*
		or	*template-name*
H322	*align-subscript*	is	*int-expr*
		or	*align-subscript-use*
		or	*subscript-triplet*
		or	*
H323	*align-subscript-use*	is	[[*int-level-two-expr*] *add-op*] *align-add-operand*
		or	*align-subscript-use* *add-op* *int-add-operand*
H324	*align-add-operand*	is	[*int-add-operand* *] *align-primary*
		or	*align-add-operand* * *int-mult-operand*
H325	*align-primary*	is	*align-dummy*
		or	(*align-subscript-use*)
H326	*int-add-operand*	is	*add-operand*
H327	*int-mult-operand*	is	*mult-operand*
H328	*int-level-two-expr*	is	*level-2-expr*

Constraint: If the *align-spec* in an **ALIGN** directive begins with "*" then every *alignee* must be a dummy argument.

Constraint: The *align-spec* in a **REALIGN** may not begin with "*".

Constraint: Each *align-dummy* may appear at most once in an *align-subscript-list*.

Constraint: An *align-subscript-use* expression may contain at most one occurrence of an *align-dummy*.

Constraint: An *align-dummy* may not appear anywhere in the *align-spec* except where explicitly permitted to appear by virtue of the grammar shown above. Paraphrased, one may construct an *align-subscript-use* by starting with an *align-dummy* and then doing additive and multiplicative things to it with any integer expressions that contain no *align-dummy*.

Constraint: A *subscript* in an *align-subscript* may not contain occurrences of any *align-dummy*.

Constraint: An *int-add-operand*, *int-mult-operand*, or *int-level-two-expr* must be of type integer.

C.3.5 DYNAMIC Directive

H329	*dynamic-directive*	**is**	**DYNAMIC** *alignee-or-distributee-list*
H330	*alignee-or-distributee*	**is**	*alignee*
		or	*distributee*

Constraint: An object in **COMMON** may not be declared **DYNAMIC** and may not be aligned to an object (or template) that is **DYNAMIC**. (To get this kind of effect, Fortran 90 modules must be used instead of **COMMON** blocks.)

Constraint: An object with the **SAVE** attribute may not be declared **DYNAMIC** and may not be aligned to an object (or template) that is **DYNAMIC**.

C.3.7 PROCESSORS Directive

H331	*processors-directive*	**is**	**PROCESSORS** *processors-decl-list*
H332	*processors-decl*	**is**	*processors-name* [(*explicit-shape-spec-list*)]
H333	*processors-name*	**is**	*object-name*

C.3.8 TEMPLATE Directive

H334	*template-directive*	**is**	**TEMPLATE** *template-decl-list*
H335	*template-decl*	**is**	*template-name* [(*explicit-shape-spec-list*)]
H336	*template-name*	**is**	*object-name*

C.3.9 INHERIT Directive

| H337 | *inherit-directive* | **is** | **INHERIT** *dummy-argument-name-list* |

C.4 Data Parallel Statements and Directives

C.4.1 The FORALL Statement

| H401 | *forall-stmt* | **is** | **FORALL** *forall-header forall-assignment* |
| H402 | *forall-header* | **is** | (*forall-triplet-spec-list* [, *scalar-mask-expr*]) |

Constraint: Any procedure referenced in the *scalar-mask-expr* of a *forall-header* must be pure, as defined in Section 4.3.

| H403 | *forall-triplet-spec* | **is** | *index-name* = *subscript* : *subscript* [: *stride*] |

Constraint: *index-name* must be a scalar integer variable.

Constraint: A *subscript* or *stride* in a *forall-triplet-spec-list* must not contain a reference to any *index-name* in the *forall-triplet-spec-list* in which it appears.

| H404 | *forall-assignment* | **is** | *assignment-stmt* |
| | | **or** | *pointer-assignment-stmt* |

Constraint: Any procedure referenced in a *forall-assignment*, including one referenced by a defined operation or assignment, must be pure as defined in Section 4.3.

C.4.2 The FORALL Construct

H405	*forall-construct*	**is**	**FORALL** *forall-header*
			forall-body-stmt
			[*forall-body-stmt*] ...
			END FORALL

H406 *forall-body-stmt*   **is**   *forall-assignment*
                                             or   *where-stmt*
                                             or   *where-construct*
                                             or   *forall-stmt*
                                             or   *forall-construct*

Constraint: Any procedure referenced in a *forall-body-stmt*, including one referenced by a defined operation or assignment, must be pure as defined in Section 4.3.

Constraint: If a *forall-stmt* or *forall-construct* is nested in a *forall-construct*, then the inner **FORALL** may not redefine any *index-name* used in the outer *forall-construct*.

C.4.3   Pure Procedures

H407   *prefix*   **is**   *prefix-spec* [*prefix-spec*] ...

H408   *prefix-spec*   **is**   *type-spec*
                                 or   **RECURSIVE**
                                 or   **PURE**
                                 or   *extrinsic-prefix*

H409   *function-stmt*   **is**   [*prefix*] **FUNCTION** *function-name function-stuff*

H410   *function-stuff*   **is**   ([*dummy-arg-name-list*])
                                                    [**RESULT** (*result-name*)]

H411   *subroutine-stmt*   **is**   [*prefix*] **SUBROUTINE** *subroutine-name*
                                                    subroutine-stuff

H412   *subroutine-stuff*   **is**   [([*dummy-arg-list*])]

Constraint: A *prefix* must contain at most one of each variety of *prefix-spec*.

Constraint: The *prefix* of a *subroutine-stmt* must not contain a *type-spec*.

The following constraints are added to Rule R1215 in Section 12.5.2.2 of the Fortran 90 standard (defining *function-subprogram*):

Constraint: The *specification-part* of a pure function must specify that all dummy arguments have **INTENT(IN)** except procedure arguments and arguments with the **POINTER** attribute.

Constraint: A local variable declared in the *specification-part* or *internal-subprogram-part* of a pure function must not have the **SAVE** attribute.

Note local variable initialization in a *type-declaration-stmt* or a *data-stmt* implies the **SAVE** attribute; therefore, such initialization is also disallowed.

Constraint: The *execution-part* and *internal-subprogram-part* of a pure function may not use a dummy argument, a global variable, or an object that is storage associated with a global variable, or a subobject thereof, in the following contexts:

- As the assignment variable of an *assignment-stmt*;
- As a **DO** variable or implied **DO** variable, or as an *index-name* in a *forall-triplet-spec*;
- As an *input-item* in a *read-stmt*;
- As an *internal-file-unit* in a *write-stmt*;
- As an **IOSTAT=** or **SIZE=** specifier in an I/O statement.
- In an *assign-stmt*;
- As the *pointer-object* or *target* of a *pointer-assignment-stmt*;
- As the *expr* of an *assignment-stmt* whose assignment variable is of a derived type, or is a pointer to a derived type, that has a pointer component at any level of component selection;
- As an *allocate-object* or *stat-variable* in an *allocate-stmt* or *deallocate-stmt*, or as a *pointer-object* in a *nullify-stmt*; or
- As an actual argument associated with a dummy argument with **INTENT(OUT)** or **INTENT(INOUT)** or with the **POINTER** attribute.

Constraint: Any procedure referenced in a pure function, including one referenced via a defined operation or assignment, must be pure.

Constraint: A dummy argument or the dummy result of a pure function may be explicitly aligned only with another dummy argument or the dummy result, and may not be explicitly distributed or given the **INHERIT** attribute.

Constraint: In a pure function, a local variable may be explicitly aligned only with another local variable, a dummy argument, or the result variable. A local variable may not be explicitly distributed.

Constraint: In a pure function, a dummy argument, local variable, or the result variable must not have the **DYNAMIC** attribute.

Constraint: In a pure function, a global variable must not appear in a *realign-directive* or *redistribute-directive*.

Constraint: A pure function must not contain a *print-stmt*, *open-stmt*, *close-stmt*, *backspace-stmt*, *endfile-stmt*, *rewind-stmt*, *inquire-stmt*, or a *read-stmt* or *write-stmt* whose *io-unit* is an *external-file-unit* or *.

Constraint: A pure function must not contain a *pause-stmt* or *stop-stmt*.

The following constraints are added to Rule R1219 in Section 12.5.2.3 of the Fortran 90 standard (defining *subroutine-subprogram*):

Constraint: The *specification-part* of a pure subroutine must specify the intents of all dummy arguments except procedure arguments and arguments that have the **POINTER** attribute.

Constraint: A local variable declared in the *specification-part* or *internal-function-part* of a pure subroutine must not have the **SAVE** attribute.

Constraint: The *execution-part* or *internal-subprogram-part* of a pure subroutine must not use a dummy parameter with **INTENT(IN)**, a global variable, or an object that is storage associated with a global variable, or a subobject thereof, in the following contexts:

- As the assignment variable of an *assignment-stmt*;
- As a **DO** variable or implied **DO** variable, or as a *index-name* in a *forall-triplet-spec*;
- As an *input-item* in a *read-stmt*;
- As an *internal-file-unit* in a *write-stmt*;
- As an **IOSTAT=** or **SIZE=** specifier in an I/O statement.
- In an *assign-stmt*;
- As the *pointer-object* or *target* of a *pointer-assignment-stmt*;
- As the *expr* of an *assignment-stmt* whose assignment variable is of a derived type, or is a pointer to a derived type, that has a pointer component at any level of component selection;
- As an *allocate-object* or *stat-variable* in an *allocate-stmt* or *deallocate-stmt*, or as a *pointer-object* in a *nullify-stmt*;
- As an actual argument associated with a dummy argument with **INTENT(OUT)** or **INTENT(INOUT)** or with the **POINTER** attribute.

Constraint: Any procedure referenced in a pure subroutine, including one referenced via a defined operation or assignment, must be pure.

Formal Syntax Rules 315

Constraint: A dummy argument of a pure subroutine may be explicitly aligned only with another dummy argument, and may not be explicitly distributed or given the **INHERIT** attribute.

Constraint: In a pure subroutine, a local variable may be explicitly aligned only with another local variable or a dummy argument. A local variable may not be explicitly distributed.

Constraint: In a pure subroutine, a dummy argument or local variable must not have the **DYNAMIC** attribute.

Constraint: In a pure subroutine, a global variable must not appear in a *realign-directive* or *redistribute-directive*.

Constraint: A pure subroutine must not contain a *print-stmt*, *open-stmt*, *close-stmt*, *backspace-stmt*, *endfile-stmt*, *rewind-stmt*, *inquire-stmt*, or a *read-stmt* or *write-stmt* whose *io-unit* is an *external-file-unit* or *.

Constraint: A pure subroutine must not contain a *pause-stmt* or *stop-stmt*.

To define interface specifications for pure procedures, the following constraints are added to Rule R1204 in Section 12.3.2.1 of the Fortran 90 standard (defining *interface-body*):

Constraint: An *interface-body* of a pure procedure must specify the intents of all dummy arguments except **POINTER** and procedure arguments.

To define pure procedure references, the following extra constraint is added to Rules R1209 and R1210 in Section 12.4.1 of the Fortran 90 standard (defining *function-reference* and *call-stmt*):

Constraint: In a reference to a pure procedure, a *procedure-name actual-arg* must be the name of a pure procedure.

C.4.4 The INDEPENDENT Directive

H413   *independent-directive*   is   INDEPENDENT [, *new-clause*]

H414   *new-clause*   is   NEW (*variable-list*)

Constraint: The first non-comment line following an *independent-directive* must be a *do-stmt*, *forall-stmt*, or a *forall-construct*.

Constraint: If the **NEW** option is present, then the directive must apply to a **DO** loop.

Constraint: A *variable* named in the **NEW** option or any component or element thereof must not:

- Be a pointer or dummy argument; nor
- Have the **SAVE** or **TARGET** attribute.

C.6 Extrinsic Procedures

C.6.2 Definition and Invocation of Extrinsic Procedures

H601	*extrinsic-prefix*	is	**EXTRINSIC** (*extrinsic-kind-keyword*)
H602	*extrinsic-kind-keyword*	is	**HPF**
		or	**HPF_LOCAL**

C.7 Storage and Sequence Association

C.7.1 Storage Association

H701	*sequence-directive*	is	**SEQUENCE** [[::] *association-name-list*]
		or	**NO SEQUENCE** [[::] *association-name-list*]
H702	*association-name*	is	*variable-name*
		or	/ *common-block-name* /

Constraint: The result variable of an array-valued function that is not an intrinsic function is a nonsequential array. It may not appear in any HPF **SEQUENCE** directive.

Constraint: A variable or **COMMON** block name may appear at most once in a *sequence-directive* within any scoping unit.

D Formal Syntax Cross-reference

This Appendix cross-references smbols used in the formal syntax rules. Rule identifiers beginning with "H" are from the High Performance Fortran Language Specification [14]; the full rule may be found in Appendix C. Rule identifiers beginning with "R" are from the Fortran 90 Standard [17]; the full rule may be found there, or in the appendix of the Fortran 90 Handbook [1].

D.1 Nonterminal Symbols That Are Defined

Symbol	Defined	Referenced		
add-op	R710	H323		
add-operand	R706	H326		
align-add-operand	H324	H323	H324	
align-attribute-stuff	H315	H302	H313	
align-directive	H312	H204		
align-directive-stuff	H314	H312	H313	
align-dummy	H318	H317	H325	
align-primary	H325	H324		
align-source	H317	H314	H315	
align-spec	H320	H319		
align-subscript	H322	H320		
align-subscript-use	H323	H322	H323	H325
align-target	H321	H320		
align-with-clause	H319	H314	H315	
alignee	H316	H312	H313	H330
alignee-or-distributee	H330	H329		
allocate-object	R625			
allocate-stmt	R622			
array-constructor	R431			
array-spec	R512			
assign-stmt	R838			
assignment-stmt	R735	H404		
association-name	H702	H701		
call-stmt	R1210			
combined-attribute	H302	H301		
combined-directive	H301	H204		
data-stmt	R529			

deallocate-stmt	R631			
directive-origin	H202	H201		
dist-attribute-stuff	H306	H302	H304	
dist-directive-stuff	H305	H303	H304	H306
dist-format	H309	H308		
dist-format-clause	H308	H305		
dist-onto-clause	H310	H305	H306	
dist-target	H311	H310		
distribute-directive	H303	H204		
distributee	H307	H303	H304	H330
dummy-arg	R1221	H412		
dynamic-directive	H329	H204		
end-function-stmt	R1218			
end-subroutine-stmt	R1222			
entity-decl	R504	H301		
executable-construct	R215			
executable-directive	H205	H203		
execution-part	R208			
explicit-shape-spec	R513	H302	H332	H335
expr	R723			
extrinsic-kind-keyword	H602	H601		
extrinsic-prefix	H601	H408		
forall-assignment	H404	H401	H406	
forall-body-stmt	H406	H405		
forall-construct	H405	H406		
forall-header	H402	H401	H405	
forall-stmt	H401	H406		
forall-triplet-spec	H403	H402		
function-reference	R1209			
function-stmt	H409			
function-stuff	H410	H409		
function-subprogram	R1215			
hpf-directive	H203	H201		
hpf-directive-line	H201			
independent-directive	H413	H205		
inherit-directive	H337	H204		
input-item	R914			
int-add-operand	H326	H323	H324	

Formal Syntax Cross-reference

int-expr	R728	H309	H322
int-level-two-expr	H328	H323	
int-mult-operand	H327	H324	
int-variable	R607	H318	
interface-body	R1204		
internal-subprogram-part	R210		
level-2-expr	R707	H328	
mask-expr	R741	H402	
mult-operand	R705	H327	
namelist-group-object	R737		
namelist-stmt	R543		
new-clause	H414	H413	
nullify-stmt	R629		
output-item	R915		
pause-stmt	R844		
pointer-assignment-stmt	R736	H404	
pointer-object	R630		
prefix	H407	H409	H411
prefix-spec	H408	H407	
processors-decl	H332	H331	
processors-directive	H331	H204	
processors-name	H333	H311	H332
read-stmt	R737		
realign-directive	H313	H205	
redistribute-directive	H304	H205	
section-subscript	R618		
sequence-directive	H701	H204	
specification-directive	H204	H203	
specification-expr	R734		
specification-part	R204		
stat-variable	R623		
stop-stmt	R842		
stride	R620	H403	
subroutine-stmt	H411		
subroutine-stuff	H412	H411	
subscript	R617	H403	
subscript-triplet	R619	H322	
target	R737		

template-decl	H335	H334			
template-directive	H334	H204			
template-name	H336	H307	H321	H335	
type-declaration-stmt	R501				
type-spec	R502	H408			
variable	R601	H414			
where-construct	R739	H406			
where-stmt	R738	H406			
write-stmt	R737				

D.2 Nonterminal Symbols That Are Not Defined

Symbol	Referenced				
common-block-name	H702				
dummy-arg-name	H410				
dummy-argument-name	H337				
function-name	H409				
index-name	H403				
object-name	H307	H316	H321	H333	H336
result-name	H410				
subroutine-name	H411				
variable-name	H702				

D.3 Terminal Symbols

Symbol	Referenced				
!HPF$	H202				
(	H302	H308	H309	H314	H315
	H320	H325	H332	H335	H402
	H410	H412	H414	H601	
)	H302	H308	H309	H314	H315
	H320	H325	H332	H335	H402
	H410	H412	H414	H601	
*	H308	H309	H311	H317	H320
	H322	H324			

Formal Syntax Cross-reference

*HPF$	H202			
,	H402	H413		
/	H702			
:	H317	H403		
::	H301	H304	H313	H701
=	H403			
ALIGN	H302	H312		
BLOCK	H309			
CHPF$	H202			
CYCLIC	H309			
DIMENSION	H302			
DISTRIBUTE	H302	H303		
DYNAMIC	H302	H329		
END	H405			
EXTRINSIC	H601			
FORALL	H401	H405		
FUNCTION	H409			
HPF	H602			
HPF_LOCAL	H602			
INDEPENDENT	H413			
INHERIT	H302	H337		
NEW	H414			
NO	H701			
ONTO	H310			
PROCESSORS	H302	H331		
PURE	H408			
REALIGN	H313			
RECURSIVE	H408			
REDISTRIBUTE	H304			
RESULT	H410			
SEQUENCE	H701			
SUBROUTINE	H411			
TEMPLATE	H302	H334		
WITH	H319			

Bibliography

[1] J. C. Adams, W. S. Brainerd, J. T. Martin, B. T. Smith, and J. L. Wagener. *Fortran 90 Handbook*. Intertext-McGraw Hill, New York, NY, 1992.

[2] E. Albert, J. Lukas, and G. Steele, Jr. Data parallel computers and the FORALL statement. *Journal of Parallel and Distributed Computing*, 13(2):185–192, October 1991.

[3] American National Standards Institute, Inc., 1430 Broadway, New York, NY. *American National Standard Programming Language FORTRAN, ANSI X3.9-1978*, approved April 3 1978.

[4] American National Standards Institute, Inc., 1430 Broadway, New York, NY. *Reference Manual for the Ada Programming Language [ANSI/MIL-STD-1815A]*, January 1983.

[5] American National Standards Institute, Inc., 1430 Broadway, New York, NY. *Parallel Extensions for FORTRAN 77, X3H5 Language Binding, [X3H5/91-0040-C]*, 1991.

[6] American National Standards Institute, Inc., 1430 Broadway, New York, NY. *American National Standard for Information Systems Programming Language FORTRAN, S8 (X3.9-198x)*, April 1987. Revision of X3.9-1978, Draft S8, Version 104.

[7] J. W. Backus, et al. *Preliminary Report, Specifications for the IBM Mathematical FORmula TRANslating System, FORTRAN*. IBM Corp., Programming Research Group, Applied Science Division, 1954.

[8] A. J. Bernstein. Analysis of programs for parallel processing. *IEEE Transactions on Computers*, 15(5), October 1966.

[9] W. S. Brainerd, C. H. Goldberg, and J. C. Adams. *Programmer's Guide to Fortran 90*. Intertext Publications, McGraw-Hill Book Company, New York, NY, 1990.

[10] B. Chapman, P. Mehrotra, and H. Zima. Programming in Vienna Fortran. *Scientific Programming*, 1(1):31–50, Fall 1992.

[11] B. Chapman, P. Mehrotra, and H. Zima. High Performance Fortran without templates: An alternative model for distribution and alignment. In *Proceedings of the Fourth ACM SIGPLAN Symposium on Principles & Practice of Parallel Programming (PPoPP)*, San Diego, CA, May 1993.

[12] M. Chen and J. Cowie. Prototyping Fortran-90 compilers for massively parallel machines. In *Proceedings of the SIGPLAN '92 Conference on Program Language Design and Implementation*, San Francisco, CA, June 1992.

[13] G. Fox, M. Johnson, G. Lyzenga, S. Otto, J. Salmon, and D. Walker. *Solving Problems on Concurrent Processors*, volume 1. Prentice-Hall, Englewood Cliffs, NJ, 1988.

[14] High Performance Fortran Forum. High Performance Fortran language specification, version 1.0. Technical Report CRPC-TR92225, Center for Research on Parallel Computation, Rice University, Houston, TX, 1992 (revised May 1993). To appear in *Scientific Programming*, vol. 2, no. 1.

[15] High Performance Fortran Forum. High Performance Fortran journal of development. Technical Report CRPC-TR93300, Center for Research on Parallel Computation, Rice University, Houston, TX, May 3 1993. To appear in *Scientific Programming*, vol. 2, no. 1.

[16] S. Hiranandani, K. Kennedy, C. Koelbel, U. Kremer, and C. Tseng. An overview of the Fortran D programming system. In U. Banerjee, D. Gelernter, A. Nicolau, and D. Padua, editors, *Languages and Compilers for Parallel Computing, Fourth International Workshop*, Santa Clara, CA, August 1991. Springer-Verlag.

[17] International Organization for Standardization and International Electrotechnical Commission. *Fortran 90 [ISO/IEC 1539: 1991 (E)]*, May 1991. Now also ANSI X3.198-1992.

[18] K. Knobe, J. Lukas, and G. Steele, Jr. Data optimization: Allocation of arrays to reduce communication on SIMD machines. *Journal of Parallel and Distributed Computing*, 8(2):102–118, February 1990.

[19] C. Koelbel. An overview of High Performance Fortran. *Fortran Forum*, 11(4), December 1992.

[20] D. B. Loveman. High Performance Fortran. *IEEE Parallel & Distributed Technology*, 1(1), February 1993.

[21] P. Mehrotra and J. Van Rosendale. Programming distributed memory architectures using Kali. In *Advances in Languages and Compilers for Parallel Computing*, Irvine, CA, 1991. The MIT Press.

[22] J. Merlin. ADAPTing Fortran-90 array programs for distributed memory architectures. In *First International Conference of the Austrian Center for Parallel Computation*, Salzburg, Austria, September 1991.

[23] M. Metcalf and J. Reid. *Fortran 90 Explained*. Oxford Science Publications, 1990.

[24] Parallel Computing Forum. PCF: Parallel Fortran extensions. *Fortran Forum*, 10(3), September 1991.

[25] D. M. Pase, T. MacDonald, and A. Meltzer. *MPP Fortran Programming Model*. Cray Research, Inc., Eagan, MN, August 26 1992.

[26] G. L. Steele Jr. High Performance Fortra: Status report. *ACM SIGPlan Notices*, 28(1), January 1993.

[27] Thinking Machines Corporation, Cambridge, Massachusetts. *CM Fortran Reference Manual*, July 1991.

[28] United States of America Standards Institute, New York, NY. *USA Standard FORTRAN, USAS X3.9-1966*, March 1966.

[29] US Department of Defense. *Military Standard, MIL-STD-1753: FORTRAN, DoD Supplement to American National Standard X3.9-1978*, November 9 1978.

[30] M. J. Wilkes. From Fortran and Algol to object-oriented languages. *Communications of the ACM*, 36(7):21–23, July 1993.

[31] M. J. Wolfe. *Optimizing Supercompilers for Supercomputers*. The MIT Press, Cambridge, MA, 1989.

[32] M. Wu and G. Fox. A test suite approach for fortran 90d compilers on MIMD distributed memory parallel computers. In *Proceedings of the 1992 Scalable High Performance Computing Conference*, Williamsburg, VA, April 1992.

[33] H. Zima and B. Chapman. *Supercompilers for Parallel and Vector Computers*. Addison-Wesley, New York, NY, 1991.

Index

*

* notation, 54

A

abstract processors, 98, 249
ABSTRACT_TO_PHYSICAL, 239
active set, 173, 174
Ada, 73
adjustable array, 64
Advanced Research Projects Agency (ARPA), xiii
aggregate cover, 134, 249
aggregate variable group, 132, 249
alias, 67, 160
ALIGN directive, 103, 112ff, 148ff, 187, 245
align-add-operand, 115, 309
align-attribute-stuff, 113, 308
align-directive, 113, 308
align-directive-stuff, 113, 308
align-dummy, 113, 116, 308
align-primary, 115, 309
align-source, 113, 308
align-spec, 148, 309
align-subscript, 115, 309
align-subscript-use, 115, 116, 309
align-target, 115, 187, 249, 309
align-with-clause, 115, 148, 309
alignee, 113, 187, 249, 308
alignee-or-distributee, 120, 310
alignment, 100, 249
ALL_PREFIX, 255
ALL_SCATTER, 255
ALL_SUFFIX, 256
Alliant, 25
allocatable array, 55, 64
ALLOCATABLE attribute, 121ff
ALLOCATE statement, 121ff, 186, 193
American National Standards Institute (ANSI), xiii, 9
American Standards Association (ASA), 9
ANY_PREFIX, 257
ANY_SCATTER, 258
ANY_SUFFIX, 258
argument association, 71
array, 54
array assignment, 27, 56, 167, 170, 173
array combining scatter function, 208
array constructor, 61
array expression, 27
array features, 51
array intrinsic, 27
array location function, 206

array pointer, 64
array prefix function, 210
array reduction function, 207
array sequence order, 61
array sorting function, 215
array suffix function, 210
ASSIGN statement, 186, 193
assignment statement, 173, 174, 186, 187
assignment-stmt, 171
association-name, 132, 316
assumed-shape array, 64, 71, 163
assumed-size array, 64, 71, 163
atomic data object, 171, 193
atomic object, 100, 172, 249
attribute, 100
automatic array, 55, 64

B

BACKSPACE statement, 187
BBN, 25
Bell Laboratories, xiii
Bernstein conditions, 199
Bernstein's conditions, 193
bit manipulation function, 206
bit model, 76
block data program unit, 70
block distribution, 91, 103, 107
BLOCK(m) distribution, 107
block-cyclic distribution, 105

C

call-stmt, 315
Center for Research on Parallel Computation (CRPC), 11
CLOSE statement, 187
collapsed, 115, 249
collapsing alignment, 93
combined-attribute, 102, 307
combined-directive, 102, 113, 147, 306
combining scatter function,
    see array combining scatter function
comment, 17
COMMON, 70, 120, 129ff
communication, 24, 30ff, 249
COMPASS, Inc., 11
component, 134, 249
conformable, 57
control dependence, 193, 194
Convex Computer, 11
COPY_PREFIX, 259
COPY_SCATTER, 260
COPY_SUFFIX, 261
Cornell Theory Center, xiii

correspond, 107
COUNT_PREFIX, 261
COUNT_SCATTER, 262
COUNT_SUFFIX, 263
cover, 131, 134, 249
Cray pointer, 67
Cray Research, xiii, 11, 25, 67
currently allocated, 56
cyclic distribution, 91, 104, 108
CYCLIC(m) distribution, 108

D

data facilities, 51
data locality, 249
data mapping, 30, 31, 91ff, 100, 139ff, 251
  model, 98ff
  specification, 102
data object, 172
data parallel, 26, 27ff, 250
data remapping, *see dynamic mapping*
DATA statement, 186
DEALLOCATE statement, 186, 193
deferred-shape array, 64
derived type, 54, 65, 187
derived type definition, 65
descriptive mapping, 139, 144, 151ff, 245, 250
Digital Equipment Corporation, xiv, 11, 25, 54, 67
DIMENSION attribute, 103
directive, 14, 17ff, 250
directive-origin, 306
dist-attribute-stuff, 106, 147, 307
dist-directive-stuff, 106, 147, 307
dist-format, 106, 147, 307
dist-format-clause, 147, 307
dist-onto-clause, 148, 307
dist-target, 148, 307
DISTRIBUTE directive, 103ff, 147ff, 187, 245
distribute-directive, 105, 147, 307
distributee, 106, 113, 250, 307
distribution, 100, 250
distribution formats, 106
DO INDEPENDENT, 192
DO statement, 170, 186, 192, 193
dummy argument, 186, 187, 188
dummy result, 187
DYNAMIC attribute, 114, 187
DYNAMIC directive, 101, 103, 120ff, 245
dynamic mapping, 97, 140, 160, 245, 250
dynamic-directive, 120, 310

E

ease-of use improvements, 51, 52
edit descriptor, 53
element, 58
elemental intrinsic, 58, 76, 167
ENDFILE statement, 187
EQUIVALENCE, 129ff
ESPRIT, xiii
executable-directive, 306
explicit interface, 59, 70, 72, 140, 150ff, 250
explicit mapping, 134, 187, 250
explicit-shape array, 64, 71
extent, 57
external function, 70
external I/O, 187
EXTRINSIC attribute, 246
EXTRINSIC procedure, 29ff, 223ff, 250
extrinsic-kind-keyword, 227, 250, 316
extrinsic-prefix, 185, 227, 316

F

FORALL INDEPENDENT, 193
FORALL statement, 27, 167, 170, 174, 186, 188, 192
forall-assignment, 171, 311
forall-body-stmt, 171, 312
forall-construct, 170, 311
forall-header, 311
forall-stmt, 170, 311
forall-triplet-spec, 171, 311
forall-triplet-spec-list, 171
FORTRAN 77, 10, 246
Fortran 8x, 10
Fortran 90, 10, 14, 21, 27, 51ff, 241, 246ff
function, 71
function-reference, 315
function-stmt, 185, 312
function-stuff, 312
function-subprogram, 186, 312
functional parallelism, 26

G

generic procedure, 73, 76
global argument, 233
global array, 233
global code, 224
global name space, 250
global name space, 30
global variable, 186, 187, 250
GLOBAL_ALIGNMENT, 238
GLOBAL_DISTRIBUTION, 239

Index 327

GLOBAL_TEMPLATE, 239
GLOBAL_TO_LOCAL, 240
GMD-I1.T (Sankt Augustin), xiii
GOTO statement, 194
GRADE_DOWN, 263
GRADE_UP, 265
granularity, 27

H

Hewlett Packard, 25
High Performance Fortran Forum (HPFF), xiii, 11, 22
host association, 72
HPF intrinsic procedure, 203, 218, 255ff
HPF library, 15, 27, 186, 203, 218, 246, 255ff
HPF local library, 238ff
HPF-conforming, 16, 170, 171, 192, 251
hpf-directive, 306
hpf-directive-line, 305
HPF_ALIGNMENT, 266
HPF_DISTRIBUTION, 269
HPF_LOCAL, 230ff
HPF_TEMPLATE, 271

I

IALL, 274
IALL_PREFIX, 275
IALL_SCATTER, 276
IALL_SUFFIX, 277
IANY, 277
IANY_PREFIX, 279
IANY_SCATTER, 279
IANY_SUFFIX, 280
IBM, 9, 11, 25
ILEN, 245, 281
immediately aligned, 100, 251
implicit mapping, 98, 134, 251
implied DO, 61, 186, 193
inaccessible, 68
include line, 70
INDEPENDENT directive, 27, 169, 192, 245, 251
independent-directive, 192, 315
independently compiled, 70
index-name, 171
INHERIT attribute, 187
INHERIT directive, 103, 149ff, 245
inherit-directive, 149, 311
inherited template, 139, 149ff, 152, 251
initialization expression, 61
inner active set, 175
inner valid set, 174
input/output statement, 186, 187, 194

INQUIRE statement, 187, 194
inquiry function, 76
int-add-operand, 309
int-level-two-expr, 309
int-mult-operand, 309
integer number system model, 76
Intel, 24
INTENT attribute, 184, 186, 188
interconnection network, 23
interface block, 70, 188
interface-body, 187, 315
internal I/O, 186
internal procedure, 186
International Standards Organization (ISO), 10
intrinsic data type, 54
intrinsic procedure, 51, 75, 76, 185
IPARITY, 281
IPARITY_PREFIX, 283
IPARITY_SCATTER, 283
IPARITY_SUFFIX, 284

K

Kendall Square Research, 25
keyword argument, 71

L

language evolution, 51, 83
Lawrence Livermore National Laboratory, xiv
LEADZ, 285
linear function, 116
load balance, 29, 251
local argument, 233
local array, 233
local memory, 24
local name space, 251
local procedure, 224, 251
local variable, 187, 251
LOCAL_TO_GLOBAL, 240
location function, *see array location function*
loosely synchronous, 251

M

main program, 70
many-one array section, 60
mapping inquiry subroutine, 204, 252
masked array assignment, 27, 57, 62, 170, 175
MasPar, xiii, 25
master-slave parallelism, 26
MAXLOC, 206, 285
MAXVAL, 206
MAXVAL_PREFIX, 287
MAXVAL_SCATTER, 288
MAXVAL_SUFFIX, 289

Meiko, 24
memory, 23
message-passing, 24
MIL-STD-1753, 10, 246
MIMD, *see Multiple Instruction Multiple Data (MIMD)*
MINLOC, 206, 289
MINVAL, 206
MINVAL_PREFIX, 291
MINVAL_SCATTER, 292
MINVAL_SUFFIX, 292
modularization, 51, 70ff
module program unit, 70
multi-statement FORALL, 170, 173, 246
multiple entry point, 70
Multiple Instruction Multiple Data (MIMD), 24
Multiple Instruction Multiple Data (SIMD), 252

N

namelist I/O, 53
National Science Foundation (NSF), xiii
natural template, 139, 151, 252
nCUBE, 24
new-clause, 315
node program, 252
non-advancing I/O, 53
nonconforming, 252
nonsequential, 131, 134ff
nonsequential variable, 252
NOSEQUENCE directive, 131ff
NULLIFY statement, 186, 193
NUMBER_OF_PROCESSORS, 124, 203, 245, 293

O

Oak Ridge National Laboratory, xiii
obsolescent feature, 83
ONTO clause, 107, 111, 148
OPEN statement, 187
optional argument, 71
outer active set, 174

P

parallel computation, 23, 26ff
parallel computer, 23
Parallel Computing Forum (PCF), 11
Parallel Random Access Memory (PRAM), 27
PARITY, 294
PARITY_PREFIX, 295
PARITY_SCATTER, 296
PARITY_SUFFIX, 296
partial record I/O, 53
PAUSE statement, 187

PHYSICAL_TO_ABSTRACT, 239
pointer, 55, 67
POINTER attribute, 186
pointer assignment, 67, 173, 174, 186, 187
pointer associated, 67
POINTER attribute, 121ff, 186, 188
pointer-assignment-stmt, 171
POPCNT, 297
POPPAR, 297
precedence graph, 175
prefix, 185, 312
prefix function, *see array prefix function*
prefix-spec, 185, 312
prescriptive mapping, 139, 140, 245, 252
PRINT statement, 187
processor, 23
processor arrangement, 124, 252
processor-dependent, 17
PROCESSORS directive, 103, 124ff, 245
processors-decl, 124, 310
processors-directive, 124, 310
processors-name, 124, 310
PROCESSORS_SHAPE, 124, 203, 245, 298
PRODUCT_PREFIX, 298
PRODUCT_SCATTER, 299
PRODUCT_SUFFIX, 300
program unit, 70
programming model, 23
PURE attribute, 171, 172, 184, 245, 252
PURE procedure, 167

R

rank, 57, 252
READ statement, 186, 187, 193
real number system model, 76
REALIGN directive, 101, 112ff, 187, 194, 245
realign-directive, 113, 308
record, 55
RECURSIVE attribute, 184, 185
REDISTRIBUTE directive, 101, 103ff, 187, 194, 245
redistribute-directive, 105, 307
reduction function, *see array reduction function*
redundant feature, 83
remote memory, 24
removed feature, 83
replicating alignment, 96
replication, 96, 252
representational model, 76
Research Institute for Advanced Computer Science (RIACS), xiv
REWIND statement, 187
Rice University, xiii, 11

Index

rule number, 15

S

SAVE attribute, 120, 129, 186, 192
scalar processor arrangement, 125
section, 58
sequence association, 15, 85, 139, 161, 252
SEQUENCE attribute, 135
SEQUENCE directive, 131ff
sequence-directive, 131, 316
sequential, 131, 134ff
sequential common, 134, 253
sequential variable, 134, 253
shape, 57, 253
shared memory, 25
SIMD,
    see Single Instruction Multiple Data (SIMD)
Single Instruction Multiple Data (SIMD), 25, 253
Single Program Multiple Data (SPMD), 28, 223, 253
single-statement FORALL, 170, 172, 245
size, 57
sorting function, *see array sorting function*
specific procedure, 76
specification-directive, 306
SPMD,
    see Single Program Multiple Data (SPMD)
standard-conforming, 16
statement functions, 185
static mapping, 97, 245, 253
STOP statement, 187
storage association, 15, 85, 129ff, 186, 253
storage sequence, 253
stream I/O, 53
stride, 171, 253
structure, 55
structure constructor, 65
subobject, 172
subroutine, 71
subroutine-stmt, 185, 312
subroutine-stuff, 312
subroutine-subprogram, 186, 314
subscript, 171
subscript triplet notation, 58, 61
Subset HPF, 245ff
Subset-conforming, 16
suffix function, *see array suffix function*
SUM_PREFIX, 301
SUM_SCATTER, 302
SUM_SUFFIX, 302
Sun Microsystems, 67
synchronization, 24, 253
syntax rule, 15

Syracuse University, xiii, 11
system inquiry function, 203, 253

T

TARGET attribute, 68, 192
task parallel, 26, 29ff
template, 100, 253
TEMPLATE directive, 101, 103, 127ff, 245
template-decl, 127, 311
template-directive, 127, 311
template-name, 127, 311
Tera Computer, 25
Texas, xiv
Thinking Machines, xiii, 11, 24, 25
totally associated, 253
transcriptive mapping, 139, 142, 245, 254
transformational function, 76
triplet notation, *see subscript triplet notation*
type declaration statement, 65, 186
type-spec, 185

U

ultimately aligned, 100, 254
University of Vienna, 11
user-defined assignment, 65
user-defined operator, 65
user-defined type, 54

V

valid set, 172, 173
vector-valued subscript, 61

W

WHERE statement,
    see masked array assignment
where-construct, 172
where-stmt, 172
WITH clause, 115, 148

WRITE statement, 186, 187, 193